THE REGIME QUESTION

The Regime Question

FOUNDATIONS OF DEMOCRATIC GOVERNANCE IN EUROPE AND THE UNITED STATES

AMEL AHMED

PRINCETON UNIVERSITY PRESS

PRINCETON & OXFORD

Published by Princeton University Press
41 William Street, Princeton, New Jersey 08540
99 Banbury Road, Oxford OX2 6JX

press.princeton.edu

GPSR Authorized Representative: Easy Access System Europe - Mustamäe tee 50, 10621 Tallinn, Estonia, gpsr.requests@easproject.com

All Rights Reserved

ISBN 9780691269405
ISBN (pbk.) 9780691269436
ISBN (e-book) 9780691269467

British Library Cataloging-in-Publication Data is available

Editorial: Bridget Flannery-McCoy and Alena Chekanov
Production Editorial: Sara Lerner
Cover Design: Karl Spurzem
Production: Lauren Reese
Publicity: William Pagdatoon
Copyeditor: Melanie Mallon

Cover Credit © National Portrait Gallery, London

This book has been composed in Arno

10 9 8 7 6 5 4 3 2 1

For Leyla and Noor

CONTENTS

THE REGIME QUESTION

Introduction

THE REGIME QUESTION

THE REGIME question has returned to established democracies. This question, frequently boiled down to "democracy or autocracy?," contains within it multitudes of questions having to do with the status of representative government, the rules that will regulate competition between political forces, and the boundaries of the political community, among others. Long considered to have been decisively answered, today the regime question returns with great force. Challenges to existing democratic norms, practices, and institutions have emerged in various arenas of governance, with political forces consolidating on different sides of the divide. Some scholars have identified within recent political turmoil a new regime cleavage emerging in Western democracies, overtaking the old economic cleavage that has been the focal point of politics throughout the postwar period.[1] A worrying development, no doubt, but as the analysis in this book demonstrates, this occurrence is neither novel nor exceptional in the history of modern political development. Indeed, the regime question has been an enduring feature of democratic politics from the start.

In the history of Western democracy, the regime question has entailed fights not only over the extent of the franchise, which has been the focus of much of the work on democratic development in the West, but also, and crucially, over core principles of democratic governance, or the "rules of the game." Throughout the nineteenth and much of the twentieth century, these fights centered on the status of representative government vis-à-vis constitutional monarchy and other autocratic arrangements. Today, fights over the rules of the game have once again emerged as a significant vector of conflict. The return of the regime question, I argue, represents not a break with prior trajectories of political development, but a new instantiation of fights found in previous eras. These fights take place along what I term the "regime dimension," an enduring feature of democratic politics capable of dividing democracies over the very structures they are built on, as well as shaping the oppositional forces on both sides of the divide.

For much of the history of modern political development, the regime dimension has been one of the main organizing principles of democratic politics, receding only after 1945, largely in consequence of Cold War imperatives, which required the suppression of regime contention. The emergent liberal democratic capitalist world order reshaped the political landscape in many countries, creating the appearance of regime consensus and firmly establishing the economic policy dimension as the primary dimension of politics in the postwar period. In fact, what we refer to today as the Left–Right political spectrum *is* an economic policy dimension. For much of the postwar period, this economic policy dimension has been the main organizing principle of politics and party systems in Western democracies. That is to say, the fights between different political forces have centered primarily on economic management and distributive politics. Other issues have entered sporadically, but the economic dimension has dominated.

This dominance has contributed to the impression that the economic policy dimension has always been the only or most important terrain of political contestation. It also has contributed to the idea that the emergence of other dimensions of contestation represents a break from the norm. But this is far from the case. In the history of Western political development, the economic dimension has always competed with at least two other foundational dimensions: One was the national dimension, involving struggles over national unification. This was highly salient at early stages of political development but had receded in most countries by the early twentieth century. The second was the regime dimension, involving struggles over the status of representative government. This book shows that, despite receiving little attention in the scholarly literature, the regime dimension has been one of the most enduring forces in the political development of the West, and that we should not be surprised by its return to political life.

Early work on political development failed to consider the regime dimension, either collapsing it into broader considerations of national unification or assuming that once democracy had been established, or at least once consolidated, genuine regime contention would be eliminated from ordinary politics, relegated to extraordinary and episodic encounters with aspiring autocrats.[2] In this view, while struggles for inclusion may continue, fights over the democratic system of government, or the rules of the game, are settled in founding moments, and any recurrence of it signals a lack of consolidation.[3] In contrast to these views, this book proceeds from the understanding that the regime dimension represents a third foundational dimension of modern political development. Like the economic and national dimensions, the salience of the regime dimension has depended on the circumstances, but it represents a distinct axis of political organization and competition, and one that has been highly consequential for democratic politics.

The regime dimension is consequential not only because the outcomes of the struggles within it determine governing institutions and principles, but because of what regime contention does to democratic politics. Specifically, I contend that the regime dimension presents significant and underappreciated threats to democratic *governance*. During times of regime contention, democracy is imperiled not only because of the designs of aspiring autocrats, but because the nature of the conflict itself can be debilitating for effective governance, diminishing opportunities for compromise, increasing the likelihood for legislative failure and gridlock, and opening the door to executive encroachment.[4] This is because the regime dimension does not function like other policy dimensions, where, despite disagreements, entrepreneurial political actors can engage in a sort of logrolling that actually improves the likelihood of compromise. The regime question, because it relates to the very structures on which actors' political power is predicated, does not easily lend itself to compromise. Moreover, because of the existential stakes involved, once it becomes salient, the regime dimension tends to trump other policy dimensions, interrupting the formation of typical policy coalitions.

This book focuses on political development in first wave democracies, but it also aims to offer insights for contemporary democratic politics. The perspective of the *longue durée* offered here suggests that the postwar period was but a reprieve in a long history of regime contention. It was the exception rather than the rule, a midpoint rather than the end of history. It produced a stability that we may now be nostalgic for, but it was always a manufactured stability driven by Cold War imperatives, which deliberately subdued regime contention in much of Western Europe and the United States and constricted even the economic dimension to a narrow set of choices about the economic management of liberal democratic capitalist states. I return to this in the concluding chapter to place the current moment in its historical context. I offer a historical interpretation that highlights the ways in which the postwar period, often considered the "golden age" of party politics and regime consensus, was predicated on a

suppression of the regime dimension rather than a resolution of regime contention. This involved not only excluding antisystemic actors on the Right that
might threaten the democratic order, but also marginalizing regime dissenters
on the Left. In Europe, this marginalization included economic actors that dissented from the capitalist order, and in the United States, it was racial minorities
and others who challenged the prevalent system of racial exclusion.

That the postwar period has been so naturalized in our understanding of
democratic politics, so celebrated for the stability it produced, leads to a kind
of political disorientation with respect to the current moment. One of the
goals of this project is to elucidate the history of regime contention in Western
democracies such that we may better orient ourselves to the demands of the
present. This is necessary not only for scholarship, but also for politics. That
the apparent regime consensus which made possible the economic alignment
of the postwar period has begun to crumble reveals both its transient nature
and the unfinished business of regime contention it for a time concealed.

It should be stated at the outset that although the analysis in this book
speaks to the dangers of regime contention, it is *not* meant to suggest that regime contention should be avoided. Often it is necessary for democracy's
preservation and vital to the protection of particular groups within it. But the
findings of the study should alert us to the perils of regime contention, particularly its tendency to polarize in ways that make effective governance exceedingly difficult. Those who undertake regime contention today are faced with
the same dilemma that has confronted democracy's defenders from the start:
How should we fight for democracy? When the fight itself can imperil democracy, the weight of this dilemma is heavy indeed. If, as I contend, the regime
question is an enduring feature of democratic politics, so too is this dilemma.
The final chapter returns to this question with a view to elaborating how contemporary struggles are both relatable to and distinct from these earlier stages
of regime contention.

Conceptual Clarifications

The theoretical and empirical reach of this book means addressing multiple
audiences simultaneously, each of which may have a different understanding
of the concepts employed here. In offering this conceptual scheme, my goal is
not to supplant other usages but to establish, for the purposes of this study, a
common vocabulary, which, even if not perfectly applicable, is relatable to
multiple contexts and legible within various research traditions.

Several key concepts used in this study revolve around the concept of a "regime." Here I employ the understanding of a regime used in the field of democracy studies, typically a term used to characterize political systems according to their basic logic of governance. In contemporary discourse we may speak of a democratic regime or an autocratic regime. Regime categories need not be mutually exclusive or internally consistent. That is to say, democratic regimes may contain within them autocratic elements, and autocratic regimes may also contain democratic elements, but the label democratic or autocratic provides a basic, if somewhat overly simplified, understanding of the prevalent logic of governance.

The "regime question" I refer to throughout the study refers to the choice of political system, or logic of governance. This question, I contend, is foundational to the establishment of political order. But it is present not only at founding moments. Rather, it endures within political systems, pushing publics to ask repeatedly, "How shall we govern ourselves?" While the question itself is enduring, actors' understanding of the choices available in a given historical period will differ. Throughout the nineteenth and early twentieth centuries, the regime question was understood as a choice between parliamentary government via independent legislatures and constitutional monarchy with executive control over legislatures. This is, in many ways, analogous to contemporary understandings of the regime question, posed as a choice between democracy and autocracy, but it was also distinct in several respects. Perhaps most important is that for first wave democracies, mass suffrage was not seen as a distinctive marker of a regime, and indeed mass suffrage was seen as compatible with either parliamentary government or constitutional monarchy. This distinction transformed the nature of the regime question considerably. Finally, it should be stressed that, though often presented as a binary, the regime question in fact entails many questions and various possible answers within it.

From the regime question, I develop the concept of a regime dimension. The concept of a dimension aims to abstract the political space within which politics is organized. Many questions arise with the establishment and maintenance of political order. To say that any given question represents a dimension means that it has the capacity to systematically polarize politics along the lines of the choices involved. By *systematically* I mean that the question is powerful enough that most actors are forced to choose sides. Therefore, the dimension also shapes the organization of political forces on opposing sides of the divide, in this case in terms of their regime preferences.

While the regime dimension is an enduring feature of modern politics, its salience varies depending on the context. When the regime dimension becomes salient, it emerges as a primary force in the organization of politics, eclipsing the other dimensions; that is, the logic of political organization is driven by regime preferences rather than economic or national preferences. When the salience of the regime question decreases, politics becomes organized along other dimensions. Typically, this indicates that some sort of regime consensus has emerged allowing actors, even if temporarily, to redirect their attention to other policy considerations. Importantly, a reduction in the salience of the regime dimension does not mean the absence of ongoing conflicts over issues related to the regime, nor does it mean that no actors wish to disrupt the prevalent regime consensus. It means only that these forces are not strong enough to push for a reorganization of politics or a realignment of parties along the lines of regime preferences.

Times at which the regime dimension is salient I characterize as times of regime contention, that is, times when the most pressing fights among political actors are about the regime question. This represents something of a departure from the conventional usage of the term, which typically connotes fights that occur before the founding of a political order, or exceptional moments of backsliding or deconsolidation. Because one of the central themes of the work is that these questions have an enduring quality, regime contention is also taken to be an ongoing feature of democratic politics, representing both big and small fights.

Plan of the Book

The book is organized in three parts. In part 1, I develop the theoretical framework of the analysis. The first chapter unpacks the key components of the argument and the methods employed. Chapter 2 deals in greater detail with the conceptual and theoretical challenges of understanding legislative coalitions. In it, I further articulate the historical institutionalist approach employed in this study to understand change and continuity in legislative coalitions. Part 2 begins the empirical analysis of the book with a focus on European political development. Three chapters each deal in turn with one of the main case studies of the book: chapter 3 on the United Kingdom, chapter 4 on Germany, and chapter 5 on France. Part 3 aims to expand the analysis to the distinct but related context of American political development. In chapter 6, I illustrate the roots of regime contention in the United States in the antebellum period. In chapter 7, I examine the persistence of regime contention in the post–Civil War period.

The concluding chapter offers some reflections on the political development of Western democracies beyond the interwar period. In it, I relate the history of regime contention to contemporary struggles in established democracies. Though alarming, the return of the regime question, I contend, is best understood in view of the longue durée and of historical processes of development in which regime contention was central, and of which the postwar period of apparent regime consensus was the exception. In its substance, the regime contention we observe today represents both a continuation of old struggles and the appearance of new ones, reflecting the resurgence of a foundational dimension of democratic politics that has shaped political development from the start.

PART I

Theoretical Framework

1

The Regime Question and the First Wave

THE CENTRAL claim of this work is that the regime question has been a feature of democratic politics in Western democracies from the start, and that fights over the regime question were so foundational and so enduring that they came to constitute a dimension of politics with the ability to systemically polarize political forces across the regime divide. The regime dimension, I contend, emerged alongside the economic dimension and the national dimension, with important consequences for democratic governance and long-term political stability. To substantiate this claim, the core analysis of the book centers on political development during the first wave of democratization. It aims to understand (1) the emergence of the regime dimension, (2) variations in its salience over time and across different contexts, and (3) its consequences for democratic governance and political stability throughout the nineteenth and early twentieth centuries.

This chapter lays out the theoretical framework of the book. I begin in the next section with an overview of the argument. I then move to a more detailed discussion of various issues of political development to unpack the different components of the argument and the mechanisms at work. After that, I turn to a discussion of research methods and the historical institutionalist approach I take up in this study. I end with a consideration of some alternative explanations.

Overview of the Argument

I argue that institutional development at early stages of nation-state formation determined the salience of the regime dimension with important consequences for long-term democratic endurance. The central analysis of this book focuses on the politics of legislatures, which I take to be an essential site of democratic governance and an important lens through which to examine the salience of the regime dimension, historically and comparatively. While legislatures are often neglected in the study of democratic endurance and breakdown, they are a key to understanding regime stability. As one of the main vehicles through which representative government is enacted within democratic political systems, legislatures must be able to function as effective instruments of governance. When they cannot, it opens the door to encroachment of various kinds, particularly from the executive, often resulting in regime instability.

The different components of the argument are discussed at length in this chapter, but in brief, they can be understood as shown in figure 1.1.

The argument begins with the sequencing of two key institutions at early stages of democratic development: (1) *parliamentarization*, the establishment of representative legislatures with independent governing power; and (2) *mass suffrage*, the expansion of the franchise to broad sections of the population. The sequencing of these institutions and the duration of the initial period of staggered sequencing represent the key independent variables in this analysis, determining the salience of the regime dimension at early stages and shaping long-term legislative capacity, the key dependent variable, and prospects of regime stability, a contingent dependent variable.

Most accounts of the first wave focus exclusively on suffrage expansion as the measure of democratization and the most important issue actors were fighting about. Parliamentarization, or the establishment of representative legislatures, is often taken for granted or folded into narratives centering suffrage.[1] In contrast, I treat parliamentarization as a distinct stage of democratization. Moreover, I show that for historical actors at the time, the struggle over parliamentarization was at the heart of the regime question throughout the nineteenth and early twentieth centuries, and this was very much a struggle over the rules of the game.

The choice facing each country was between parliamentary government via representative legislatures and constitutional monarchy with executive control of legislative bodies.[2] Questions of suffrage expansion were secondary to parliamentarization, and in fact, mass suffrage was seen as compatible with either representative government or constitutional monarchy. Focusing on parliamentarization as a distinct act of democratization, and the sequencing of parliamentarization vis-à-vis mass suffrage, offers important leverage in understanding the dynamics of legislative politics and democratic stability in first wave democracies.

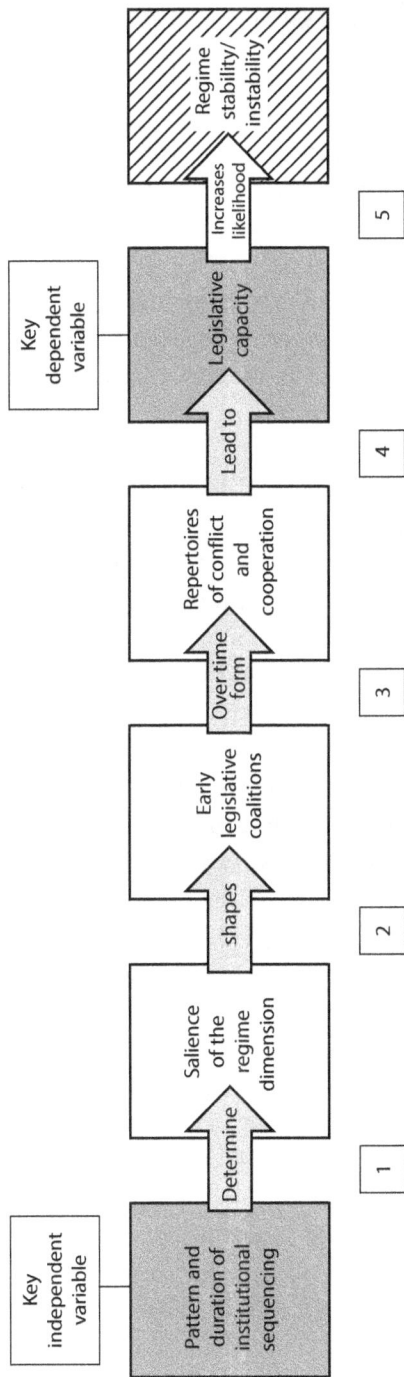

Key independent variable

| Pattern and duration of institutional sequencing |

Determine

1

Salience of the regime dimension

shapes

2

Early legislative coalitions

Over time form

3

Repertoires of conflict and cooperation

Lead to

4

Key dependent variable

Legislative capacity

Increases likelihood

5

Regime stability/instability

FIGURE 1.1. The argument

Key Links in the Argument

1. The most immediate impact of sequencing was that it determined the salience of the regime dimension in legislative politics. Because the regime question was tied to the fight for parliamentarization, early parliamentarization removed this as a vector of conflict and *decreased* the salience of the regime dimension. Early mass suffrage, on the other hand, left parliamentarization as a lingering vector of conflict and *increased* the salience of the regime dimension. Simultaneous introduction of these institutions, and other modes of sequencing considered here, often led to a more ambiguous status but one that still reveals the importance of sequencing for the salience of the regime dimension.

2. The salience of the regime dimension had a profound impact on early legislative politics and the formation of early legislative coalitions. Where the regime question decreased in salience, legislators were oriented toward substantive policy goals and legislative partners who could help them achieve those. Where the regime dimension increased in salience, legislators were oriented toward more existential regime objectives and legislative partners who could help them achieve those.

3. Early legislative coalitions and the duration of this initial period of staggered sequencing formed the basis of legislators' repertoires of conflict and cooperation. The concept of repertoires is developed throughout the analysis as a framework for understanding change and continuity in legislators' behavior, particularly the politics of legislative coalition building, which is a key feature of capacity. Repertoires represent "mental tool kits" that actors acquire based on past interactions.[3] They often guide actors to seek familiar legislative partners but can be altered through acts of political creativity undertaken by entrepreneurial legislators. Early legislative coalitions and their duration, I contend, shaped both the nature of legislators' repertoires, that is, whether it formed around regime or economic policy preferences, and their flexibility, or how easily the repertoires could be altered.

4. Legislators' repertoires had a profound effect on legislative capacity—a focal point and key dependent variable throughout the analysis. Legislative capacity is defined as the ability of legislatures to find legislative solutions to legislative problems. This includes the ability to perform core legislative tasks as well as to identify viable coalitions to support responsive policy. Legislative capacity, I maintain, is a critical if often underappreciated

feature of democratic endurance, as well as one of the things that is most imperiled when the regime dimension becomes salient.

Where rigid repertoires formed around economic policy management, legislative capacity was greatest. Where rigid repertoires formed around regime contention, legislators' ability to identify coalitions along the Left–Right economic policy spectrum was often limited, leading to low legislative capacity. Where flexible repertoires of either kind prevailed, legislative outcomes were messier but provided important opportunities for viable coalitions to form and often allowed for multiple repertoires to emerge.

5. The final link, between legislative capacity and regime stability, is a contingent but significant one. While not all legislative failure will lead to regime breakdown, repeated failures, especially in times of crisis, will increase the likelihood of regime instability. Thus, cases with low levels of legislative capacity would experience high levels of regime instability, whereas high legislative capacity would contribute to greater regime stability.

Based on this theoretical framework we can identify several paths that could be followed depending on the nature and duration of institutional sequencing (table 1.1). Within and across these modes of sequencing, modifications and combinations can have important consequences for long-term development.

Modes of Sequencing: Four Cases

To examine these dynamics, the book focuses on four cases, each representing a different mode of sequencing and corresponding path of political development. The first three cases correspond most directly to the paths identified above: the United Kingdom (1832–1939), representing the path of *early parliamentarization*; Imperial into Weimar Germany (1867–1933), representing the path of *early mass suffrage*; and the French Third Republic (1870–1939), representing the path of *simultaneous introduction*. A fourth case, the United States (1789–1939), represents a modification of the above, which I term the path of *unsettled parliamentarization*. Each path had important consequences for the efficacy of governance and long-term regime stability.

In the United Kingdom, early parliamentarization and the long duration of this initial stage of staggered sequencing had the effect of structuring politics

TABLE 1.1. Modes of Sequencing, Paths of Development

Patterns of sequencing	Duration of staggered sequence	Salience of regime dimension	Early legislative coalitions	Repertoires of conflict and cooperation	Legislative capacity	Regime stability
Early parliamentarization	Long	Low	Form around economic policy preferences	Rigid repertoires of economic management	High	High
	Short	Moderate	Form around economic policy preferences	Flexible repertoires of economic management	Moderate	Moderate
Early mass suffrage	Long	High	Form around regime preferences	Rigid repertoires of regime contention	Low	Low
	Short	Moderate	Form around regime preferences	Flexible repertoires of regime contention	Moderate	Moderate
Simultaneous introduction	NA	Moderate	Form around regime preferences	Flexible repertoires	Moderate	Moderate

and political actors around economic matters. Legislators formed rigid repertoires around economic policy management, and party alignment along the economic dimension persisted despite several regime crises that had the potential to dislodge this. Maintaining alignment along the economic dimension led to greater legislative capacity and regime stability during the interwar period, though often at the cost of an exclusionary politics along the way.

In Germany late parliamentarization, and the long duration of this initial stage of staggered sequencing, resulted in early alignment along the regime dimension and the formation of rigid repertoires of regime contention. Party alignment along the regime dimension persisted throughout the imperial period and into the Weimar Republic despite ongoing efforts within parties to move politics toward the economic dimension. The inability to balance regime considerations with economic imperatives led to low levels of legislative capacity and ultimately executive encroachment and regime instability.

In France, the simultaneous introduction of parliamentarization and mass suffrage led to a contested status for parliamentarization in the first decade of the Third Republic. The instability of these early years meant that repertoires developed along the regime dimension, but the short duration meant that these were relatively flexible repertoires. This flexibility meant that over time legislators would acquire multiple repertoires, which allowed them to move between regime and economic considerations. Perhaps the messiest of the cases, France also proves one of the most instructive: first, because the path of simultaneous introduction most closely resembles that of contemporary democracies; and second, because the ability to move between regime concerns and economic concerns and find a balance between the two, as the French for a time did, may prove the greatest hope for democracy's defense in times of regime contention.

I treat as separate, but relatable, the processes guiding American political development. While the European cases establish a theoretical model based on the context in which struggles for parliamentarization first emerged, the United States represents a modification of that model and an opportunity to evaluate it in a different context. Given the divergent conditions of nation-state formation, and especially the absence of traditional monarchical and aristocratic institutions, as well as the revolutionary nature of its founding, we would not expect to see significant regime contention in the United States, and certainly not around the question of parliamentarization or the status of representative government. Despite this, however, we see the rise of persistent regime contention very much along the lines exhibited within the European cases. I attribute this to a combination of institutional deficiencies, which left the status of representative legislatures ambiguous, and ideational transferences, which led actors to view their conflicts through the lens of European regime contention.

In this analysis the United States represents a path of early but *unsettled parliamentarization*. It was unsettled not in the sense of being vulnerable to reversals—that was true of all democracies. Rather, it was unsettled in that the founding structures left considerable room for ambiguity and varied understandings of whether parliamentarization was actually achieved. This led to ongoing regime contention throughout the antebellum period and the development of repertoires based on regime objectives, which carried into the post–Civil War period. The result was low legislative capacity, which would persist until the turn of the century, when an extraordinary period of political creativity led legislators to reform coalitions and embrace multiple repertoires, a process that would steadily increase legislative capacity and regime stability. The path specific to each of the four cases examined in this study is detailed in table 1.2.

TABLE 1.2. Modes of Sequencing: Four Cases

	Patterns and duration of sequencing	Salience of regime dimension	Early legislative coalitions	Repertoires of conflict and cooperation	Legislative capacity	Regime stability
United Kingdom (1832–1939)	Early parliamentarization, long duration (1832–1884)	Low	Form around economic policy preferences	Rigid repertoires of economic management	High	High
Germany (1871–1933)	Early mass suffrage, long duration (1871–1918)	High	Form around regime preferences	Rigid repertoires of regime contention	Low	Low
France (1870–1939)	Simultaneous introduction	Moderate	Form around regime preferences	Flexible repertoires	Moderate	Moderate
United States (1789–1939)	Unsettled parliamentarization, long duration (1789–1865)	Moderate	Form around regime preferences	Flexible repertoires	Moderate	Moderate

Periodization

The periodization employed within the case study analyses is meant to capture the impact of sequencing and the process of political development leading to the interwar period, which has been a focal point of studies of historical democratization. On the front end, the sequencing story begins as soon as either of the two key institutions are introduced: in the United Kingdom, this was during the Reform Act of 1832, which established parliamentarization with limited suffrage; in Germany, it was the unification and founding of the German imperial government in 1867, which established mass suffrage without parliamentarization; in France, it was the founding of the French Third Republic in 1870, which introduced both parliamentarization and mass suffrage; and in the United States, it was the federal Constitution of 1790, which introduced an unsettled state of parliamentarization alongside limited suffrage.

For each case study, the story culminates with a key episode during the interwar period that serves as a test of legislative capacity and democratic governance—the economic crises of the 1930s. I argue that where legislatures succeeded in finding *legislative* solutions to the economic crises of the interwar period, they would become the key to stabilizing democracy. Where they failed, it opened the door to executive encroachment that would destabilize the democratic regime. The key to their success and failure during the economic crises of the 1930s, I argue, had its roots in the initial sequencing of parliamentarization and mass suffrage and the fate of the regime dimension in legislative politics.

In the concluding chapter, I look beyond the interwar period. The Second World War, of course, did not settle the regime question for any of these polities, even those with claims to democratic triumph. Initially set aside because of the urgency of the war and later suppressed to satisfy Cold War imperatives, the regime question remained in all these polities, and it evolved and today returns once again. I offer an alternative interpretation of the postwar period, the apparent "golden age" of stable Left–Right politics and regime consensus, to elucidate its peculiarity with respect to that which came before and after, and to help situate the current moment in the history of Western political development.

Issues of Political Development

In this section I examine several issues of political development as a way of unpacking the different components of the argument and the mechanisms driving it. I begin with a general discussion of the regime dimension and then move into a more historically situated discussion of its relevance for first wave democracies. This is structured around a number of issues: What was the regime question for first wave democracies? How did it become salient? What happened when it became salient? What explains the persistence of the regime dimension? And what were the consequences for democratic governance?

The Missing Dimension

Early work on political development and party formation in Western democracies focused on two critical dimensions that took shape at the time of nation-state formation. In Seymour Lipset and Stein Rokkan's classic study, they identify a dimension related to the "national revolution." This was the process of territorial unification and centralization that created the modern European nation-state and, depending on the level of social heterogeneity within it, also produced divisions along linguistic, religious, ethnic, and cultural lines. The second dimension identified by Lipset and Rokkan resulted from the Industrial Revolution. This was the broad process of economic and structural transformation related to the rise of manufacturing industries. Depending on the nature of industrialization and commercialization within a political system, the Industrial Revolution would produce divisions along class lines as well as between urban and rural locales.[4]

As the argument goes, throughout the course of the nineteenth century, the cleavages resulting from the national revolution receded, while the dynamics of the Industrial Revolution continued to animate political actors based on their material interests within an industrializing economy.[5] This meant that even where confessional or subnational parties persisted, they too came to identify along the economic policy dimension.[6] A purported "freezing" of the party system meant that the economic dimension would remain the dominant organizing principle of party systems throughout the postwar period.[7] To be sure, *parties* changed, but party systems remained aligned along a Left–Right economic spectrum that forms the basis for modern party politics.[8]

Lipset and Rokkan's work has given rise to a substantial literature on party systems and cleavage structures in old and new democracies. Much of it has focused on applications of their model to other contexts to determine whether it captures contemporary dynamics of party systems.[9] My concern here, however, is whether their model accurately captures the historical context of first wave democracies on which it was based. One of the central claims of this book is that a third and highly consequential regime dimension is missing from their model.[10] An implicit assumption of their model is that parties competing within a democratic system at least minimally accept democracy, therefore eliminating the regime question as a major organizing force of politics. While some remnants of the predemocratic order—successor parties that continue to organize according to their opposition to the regime, or antisystemic parties that sporadically emerge—are acknowledged, these challenges are considered transient. If successful, the system reverts to autocracy. But the possibility that regime contention would endure and itself become a *dimension* of democratic politics is not seriously considered.

Following Lipset and Rokkan, much of the subsequent literature on historical cleavages has also assumed that once democratic political systems were established, and especially once they were consolidated, regime contention would subside. To the extent that scholars have recognized the significance of regime preferences to the organization of party systems, they

REGIME QUESTION AND THE FIRST WAVE   21

tend to treat such occurrences as idiosyncratic and identify regime-based parties only where they explicitly identify as such.[11] For example, the French monarchists—Orleanists, Legitimists, Bonapartists—are easily identified as parties whose primary objectives focus on the nature of the regime.[12] The problems with such an approach are twofold. First, it assumes that the regime dimension recedes once these parties are eliminated. But in fact, as I show in chapter 5, the regime dimension remained a powerful force in French politics long after the monarchists had been defeated. Second and related, the approach does not capture how the regime question shaped the entire political landscape at the time. *All* political parties, not just the declared monarchists, organized around regime preferences. Regime contention was neither idiosyncratic nor transient but a foundational dimension of politics.

Thus in lieu of the two-dimensional political landscape theorized by Lipset and Rokkan, I offer a three-dimensional understanding of the political space at the time of nation-state formation (see figure 1.2). Along with Lipset and Rokkan, I find that the national dimension had receded, though was never completely eliminated as a major cleavage, by the mid-nineteenth century.[13] But against Lipset and Rokkan's claim that this left the economic dimension as the dominant axis of competition—so much so that it has become coterminous with the Left–Right policy spectrum—I argue that the regime dimension in many countries continued to be another important axis representing a different set of priorities and an alternative logic of political organization. Indeed, in many respects the regime dimension has been the most enduring of the three.

The absence of the regime dimension from our theoretical frameworks has led us to misunderstand, or indeed to miss entirely, the long history of regime contention in first wave democracies. It has also contributed to naturalizing the Left–Right economic policy dimension as the norm and reducing the politics of established democracies to fights over distributive outcomes.

Restoring the regime dimension offers an alternative way of understanding the significance of regime contention in democracy. Typically, the regime question is considered to be something that is *outside* democratic politics. Or to think of it temporally, it is a question that is asked and answered before the establishment of a political order, and if the question is answered in favor of democracy, regime contention should subside. It may persist briefly after democracy is established, but it has no significant place within an established

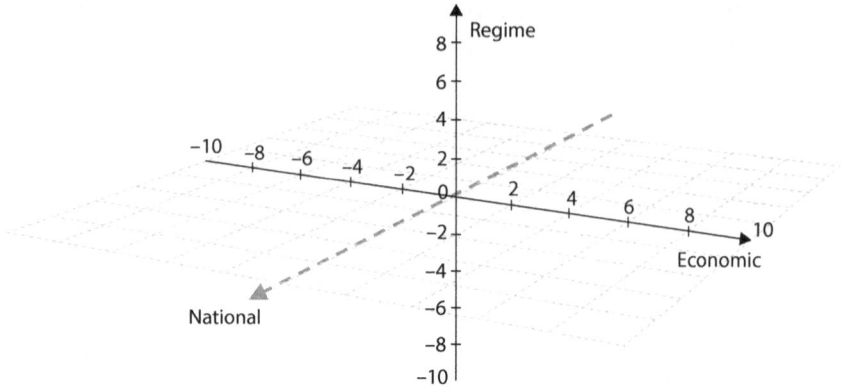

FIGURE 1.2. The regime dimension

democracy. The implication of this mistaken view is that any emergence of regime contention signals that we are outside normal democratic politics.

In contrast, the regime question understood as a dimension puts it *inside* democratic politics, dividing democracies on the very structures they are built on. That is to say, the fight for and over democracy does not end with the establishment of a democratic political order but can continue to animate political struggles between competing forces. The implication of this is that the regime dimension, like the national and economic dimensions, is never completely eliminated. It is an enduring question of democratic politics, the salience of which waxes and wanes depending on the circumstances, but it resides continuously within the political system.

The Regime Question: The Power of Representative Bodies

Because the regime question can take on many different forms, it is important to specify what precisely the content of this question was in the context of nineteenth- and twentieth-century political development. It was not simply a contest between democracy and autocracy, as neither of these was conceived as a complete political system at the time. Rather, the most salient regime fights throughout this period centered on the choice between various forms of limited constitutional monarchy and parliamentary government, broadly conceived. It was a struggle over what has been termed the *parliamentarization* of the political system. While this term originates in European struggles, I use it here in a broader sense to connote the process by which representative bodies gained independent governing power.[14]

In first wave democracies, for whom the institutional baseline for democracy was yet undetermined, the power of parliaments, or representative bodies more generally, was very much an open question. Parliaments struggled over sovereign power with the Crown and the aristocracy as well as with local authorities, and this struggle defined the regime question in early stages of political development.[15]

This represented a distinct stage in the process of historical democratization, which, as scholars have noted, did not emerge in a single watershed moment, but rather arose "asynchronically," at different times and for different purposes.[16] A growing literature on the development of European parliaments has identified many of the distinctive features of this stage. Building on an older tradition of work on the macro-foundations of parliamentarization,[17] this new research has illuminated the impact of centralization, committee structure, and procedural regularity, among other aspects of the development of parliamentary and legislative autonomy in the process of democratization.[18]

Though there was a great deal of variation among first wave democracies, parliamentarization was typically defined by the existence of popular representative bodies with four key features: (1) power over legislation; (2) power over government formation; (3) independence from the internal influence of the Crown and aristocracy; and (4) the ability to operate free from the threat of dissolution. While it was not uncommon, in parliamentarized systems, for legislative and governing powers to be shared with an executive representing the monarchy or an upper chamber representing aristocratic interests, the full achievement of parliamentarization required legislatures to be able to operate independently of these other entities.

The process of parliamentarization itself was rather circuitous. The earliest parliaments were put in place to facilitate the monarch's extraction of resources, and participation in them was considered an obligation rather than a privilege or a right.[19] The notion of representation was meant to legitimate monarchical rule and project the image of broad consultation among representatives of different interests and locales. Over time, parliaments began asserting their power and sought to establish themselves as the primary organ for the expression of popular sovereignty, with power over not only legislation but government. Of central importance in this struggle was

Parliament's autonomy from the Crown and the aristocracy, as well as its ability to exert some power over government. The expectations that prime ministers would fall without the support of Parliament or that cabinet members would be answerable to Parliament, and other such mechanisms of government accountability, all originate in this period, each the result of hard-fought battles over the control of government.

These were not fights over suffrage, though at times suffrage might be implicated in the fight for parliamentarization. The British case, for example, shows that a modest expansion of the franchise was necessary to secure the goal of parliamentarization in the Reform Act of 1832. Suffrage expansion itself, however, was not the objective. This may be surprising because today when we think of democratization, we tend to think of the successive waves of reform that extended the right of suffrage to different segments of the population. In the context of first wave democracies, however, this came much later and represented a struggle for influence within a parliamentarized system rather than a struggle for parliamentarization itself.

Nor was parliamentarization a fight for democracy. Aside from radical political movements, most rejected full democracy as untenable. Instead, parliamentarization was more frequently understood as establishing the power of representative bodies alongside other elements of government. This ideal, which came to be understood as the "mixed" or "balanced" constitution, was highly influential throughout the nineteenth century. The balanced constitution would have a lower house representing popular interests, existing alongside an upper chamber representing aristocratic interests, and an executive representing monarchical interests. Those pushing for parliamentarization may have paved the way for other democratizing reforms, but their goal was only to secure their own power and influence. This is also consistent with the "asynchronic" view of democratization, whereby institutional changes that come to be associated with democracy may not have had that as their original intent.[20]

Salience of the Regime Dimension: The Role of Institutional Sequencing

Fights over the regime question took place along what I refer to as the regime dimension. I argue that the salience of the regime dimension—that is, how strong or persistent a force it was in politics—depended on political structures

REGIME QUESTION AND THE FIRST WAVE   25

established at early stages of nation-state formation, and specifically on the sequencing of parliamentarization vis-à-vis mass suffrage. This argument builds on a significant line of scholarship that has sought to understand the importance of institutional sequencing for regime transition and stability.[21] Within this tradition, democratization is not simply a matter of amassing the requisite institutions. The process is as important as the destination in securing stable regime outcomes. Scholars have examined sequencing across a wide array of arenas, from state penetration to political participation and the development of distributive bureaucracies, in an effort to identify distinctive paths of political development.[22]

My argument builds in particular on an insight first offered by Robert Dahl in his canonical work *On Polyarchy*. Dahl posited that the introduction of contestation prior to participation gave polyarchy the greatest chance at survival.[23] According to Dahl, contestation between government and opposition via elections prior to the introduction of mass suffrage increased trust among social actors, whereas the reverse introduced competition so quickly that it left predemocratic elites wary of their prospects in the new system. Based on this, he links historical sequences to distinct development paths.

Dahl's schema has proved a useful though underspecified framework for understanding the impact of institutional sequencing because of the complexity of the institutional landscape that falls under the category of contestation.[24] Most work on this has focused on liberalization, that is, the introduction of political rights that made the mobilization of political forces possible, as the key feature of contestation.[25] The focus on liberalization has allowed scholars to broaden the argument about sequencing to later waves of democratization, but it has also led to a loss of analytical precision for first wave political development.

To be sure, liberalization was an important feature of democratic development, but it was not, in the context of nineteenth-century democratization, the key to institutional sequencing. In fact, liberalization and mass suffrage were functionally equivalent in terms of their impact on party formation and legislative politics during this period. Liberalization facilitated the rise of new parties by loosening restrictions on mobilization. Suffrage expansion did the same by introducing new waves of electors and creating constituencies for these parties.[26] Both had the effect of intensifying competition by increasing the number of competitors. Neither settled the most pressing regime question of the time, which was whether parliamentary government or constitutional monarchy would prevail.

My argument aims to refine Dahl's framework and to articulate the specific mechanisms associated with sequencing in first wave democracies. I argue that the most important dimension of contestation in these early polities was parliamentarization, and the most distinctive feature of sequencing was the order of parliamentarization relative to mass suffrage. This sequencing determined the salience of the regime dimension at early stages of political development and the dynamics of early legislative coalitions.

Key Mechanisms: Sequencing's Impact on the Salience of the Regime Dimension and Early Coalitions

Why was this sequencing so important? Why would the absence of mass suffrage not similarly increase the salience of the regime dimension? Why would alignment along the economic dimension not produce the same intensity of conflict and legislative dysfunction? In this section I unpack the mechanism behind two critical links in the argument, the impact of sequencing on the salience of the regime dimension and the impact of salience on the formation of early legislative coalitions.

The key mechanisms here are twofold: First, parliamentarization had incredible political import for the actors involved. It was parliamentarization that made the contestation for power meaningful by granting governing authority to representative legislatures. Parliamentarization was at the heart of the regime question and the central concern of actors at the time. Suffrage expansion was secondary, and in fact, mass suffrage was seen as compatible with either parliamentary government or constitutional monarchy.

Second, the timing of parliamentarization in relation to suffrage also had the important effect of structuring the political space within which legislators operated. To illustrate this, I offer here a more detailed discussion of the two extreme paths of early parliamentarization and early mass suffrage.

> *Early parliamentarization*: Where parliamentarization was introduced early, that is, introduced with limited suffrage, the parties that had access to representative bodies were typically parties of the "right" associated with upper-class interests. These parties entered legislatures in a context in which fights over the regime question had been effectively neutralized from their perspective.[27] Having secured their own inclusion, they could devote their efforts to matters of substantive policy, specifically to industrialization and economic growth.

The classic example of this was in the UK (discussed in detail in chapter 3). There, the Reform Act of 1832 introduced key features of parliamentarization while maintaining a small franchise, thereby limiting the number of parties in Parliament. A Liberal and Conservative party, both established in the 1850s, emerged in a context in which the regime question from their perspective had been settled—they had achieved parliamentarization and enough of a franchise to be competitive themselves. While suffrage continued to be a pressing regime concern for political actors outside the legislature, for those within, it was much less so. The Liberal and Conservative parties certainly had preferences on suffrage and pursued suffrage expansion for certain subsets of the population, but even that was done with a view to strengthening their economic coalitions.

This had the result of orienting the political landscape heavily toward matters of economic management, and issues such as protectionism versus free trade most clearly divided party positions. Subsequent acts of suffrage expansion introduced new actors piecemeal and, importantly, along economic lines. The new parties resulting from suffrage expansion entered the legislature in a context in which the salience of the regime dimension had been significantly diminished, and parties identified and aligned themselves primarily in terms of their economic preferences, forming enduring legislative coalitions based on shared policy objectives.

➤ *Early mass suffrage*: In contrast, where mass suffrage was introduced early, that is, introduced with limited parliamentarization, party formation and mobilization were rapid, and the regime question remained a lingering vector of conflict in politics, drawing the full range of political parties into alignment along the regime dimension and away from other issue dimensions. This is because early suffrage catalyzed party formation in a context where legislatures did not govern, making the attainment of that governing power the central focus of established parties and making regime contention a central feature of legislative politics.

This divided legislatures into pro- and antiparliamentarization camps, fighting over the very structures on which their power was predicated. Why was there a fight at all? Why wouldn't all legislators want to empower representative bodies and secure their own influence? The simple answer is that some actors benefited from an unparliamentarized system, especially those who enjoyed the patronage of, or whose interests were linked to, the Crown or aristocracy. In addition, the threat posed by the new political forces unleashed by mass suffrage, especially new socialist parties, who would have been further empowered by parliamentarization, pushed many actors to resist it. This set up a confrontation within legislatures and the formation of coalitions based on regime preferences.

A key illustration of this is found in Germany (examined at length in chapter 4). The introduction of mass suffrage at early stages of nation-state formation led to a rapid influx of new parties in the legislature. In addition to liberal and conservative parties following the British mold, there was a range of parties representing minority interests, most notably the Catholic Center Party. Soon after, they would be joined by the Social Democratic Party representing one of the strongest workers' movements in Europe. This intensified competition between actors, but more importantly, this competition often centered on regime contention. The absence of parliamentarization left the regime dimension highly salient, pushing parties increasingly to identify and align themselves in terms of their regime preferences and identify legislative partners who could help them achieve these regime objectives. Conflicts over the regime question unfolded in every corner of the Reichstag and affected legislators' positions on a wide range of policies well beyond what one might consider directly regime-related.

To be sure, both modes of sequencing involved forms of repression, and both served as tools of elite management of the process of democratization. Nevertheless, each had different consequences for long-term development.

Timing of Parliamentarization

The sequencing argument offered here hinges very much on the timing of parliamentarization in relation to mass suffrage. To identify the timing of parliamentarization, I use a variety of sources. Because parliamentarization itself developed in different stages over the course of decades, I identify an institutional cutoff based on the features most relevant to the regime question of the time—the independent governing power of representative bodies. The date of parliamentarization is understood to be the point at which several important features were achieved by representative bodies, specifically by the lower chamber of national legislatures:

1. First is power over legislation. By this I mean not only could the legislature introduce legislation, but that its approval was required for legislation. This does not mean that other bodies could not veto or reject legislation; it means only that the lower chamber had this power as well.

2. Second is the establishment of the legislature as an independent body, independent especially from the influence of the Crown and the aristocracy, which in early stages of political development often exerted considerable influence over the lower chamber. In particular, wealth and land-owning status gave these actors control over many seats in representative bodies. In some cases, the Crown could directly place representatives in the legislature. The independence of the lower chamber did not require the elimination of the Crown or aristocracy—in a parliamentarized system, usually their powers were exercised through the executive and the upper chamber as part of the idea of a "balanced constitution"—but required that their influence remain separate from the lower chamber.

3. Third is power over government formation and cabinet appointments. In parliamentary systems, this typically took the form of powers of nomination, investiture, and censure of members of government. Within presidential systems, this typically took the form of approval of cabinet nominees and powers of impeachment.

4. Finally, the last essential feature of a parliamentarized system is the ability of the legislature to operate free from the encroachment of the executive or upper chamber, and especially from the threat of dissolution. While point 2 speaks to the internal influence of outside bodies over the legislature, primarily its composition, this feature speaks to the external threat posed by these bodies to its operation. So long as the executive or other bodies could threaten to dissolve the legislature when they were not satisfied with the outcome, all the legislature's functions were compromised.

The conceptualization of parliamentarization offered here is meant to be grounded and historical, not a universal model of parliamentarization. While aspects of it may be generalized beyond this historical context, its purpose is to help us understand what actors were fighting about, and more importantly, what it would have taken for them to stop fighting about the regime question; that is, what requirements would have to be met to reduce the salience of the regime dimension.[28]

This means that parliamentarization also has a perspectival element. What constituted "power" and "independence" in a given context often hinged on actors' subjective understanding of their situations and on the broader political environment. For example, some institutional arrangements that were rejected as insufficient for parliamentarization in the United States were deemed more acceptable in the UK. Specifically, in the UK, even after the Reform Act of 1832 established the primacy of Parliament, the Lords continued to exert an aristocratic influence that could have inflamed regime contention. This can be seen, for example, with repeated meddling by the Lords in the affairs of the Commons, as well as the aggressive use of their veto. These practices were tolerated well into the late nineteenth century without igniting significant regime contention. Meanwhile, in the United States the disproportionate influence of property owners introduced by the 3/5 clause of the Constitution repeatedly inflamed regime contention. Both represented potential violations of point 2 above, and in terms of the independence of the lower chamber, one might expect the transgressions in the UK to register as more significant with actors. But in fact the reverse was true; in the United States, the influence of property owners via that 3/5 clause was seen as a significant threat to representative government and led to a regime divide capable of systematically polarizing political forces, while the influence of the Lords in the UK never rose to that level.

These different understandings can result from actors' assessment of their own strength in a given context; that is, their own sense of the practical politics surrounding the situation and the status of parliamentarization de facto. It can also result from actors' subjective construction of the situation, which may diminish some threats while exaggerating others. All of these factors played a role in actors' different reactions to the challenge of aristocratic power in the United States and in the UK, compounded by one feature peculiar to US political development—western expansion. As discussed in chapter 6, were it not for the addition of new states, there is much reason to believe that these institutions could have been accepted as the achievement of parliamentarization in the United States as they were in the UK. Each act of western expansion, however, by altering the balance of power between slave and nonslave states, also altered actors' assessment of the security of parliamentarization, and we see that these are the moments in which regime contention was highest.

Beyond these considerations, it is important to note that de facto (in practice) and de jure (in law) parliamentarization often did not coincide. In France, for example, parliamentarization was ostensibly achieved de jure with the founding of the Third Republic, but it was not until the Seize Mai crisis in 1879—in which the president was forced to submit to the wishes of the Chamber of Deputies—that we might say it was achieved de facto.[29] After that point no president would ever again challenge the principle of ministerial responsibility to the legislature. The reverse can also be seen in the UK, where the threat of dissolution was eliminated de facto in 1829, the last time the monarchy would use the threat of dissolving Parliament as a way to achieve a legislative agenda.[30] Royal prerogative remained a feature of the political system until 2011, however, when that power was formally transferred to Parliament. In this case, de facto long preceded de jure parliamentarization.

These issues all present measurement challenges, which I address in this study by triangulating several sources, including the Varieties of Democracy (V-Dem) Historical Dataset as well as a large secondary literature on the relevant dynamics of parliamentarization in different countries.[31] The V-Dem dataset is especially useful because it contains measures for both de facto and de jure achievement of the different benchmarks. The data have several limitations, however, because they do not always reflect discontinuities in practices.[32] In addition, some differences in parliamentary procedure are at times coded as different levels of parliamentarization.[33] Thus, while the data are a valuable resource, for each case I have cross-referenced the dates identified with secondary literature and archival materials to develop measures that more accurately operationalize the conceptualization of parliamentarization used in this study. Based on these resources, I identify the dates of parliamentarization for the four cases examined here as shown in figure 1.3.

The endpoint is the most significant for the present analysis as it signals the fulfillment of the four criteria of parliamentarization. As the chart in figure 1.3 shows, in no case was there a complete absence of parliamentary powers during the period examined. In most cases parliaments were established with some but not all features necessary for full parliamentarization. Yet, insofar as legislatures remained constrained in terms of their legislative function, lacked independence from other bodies, lacked power over government, or operated under the threat of dissolution, they would not be considered fully parliamentarized. For as long as these deficiencies remained, they would leave the regime question as a

Parliamentarization

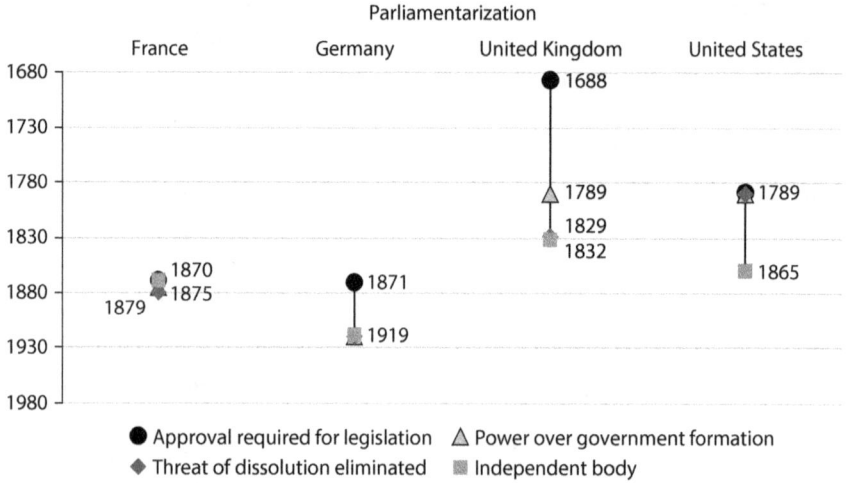

FIGURE 1.3. Parliamentarization

lingering vector of conflict and ignite regime contention within legislative bodies between those seeking to secure full parliamentarization and those seeking to block it.

In France, 1870 marked the start of the process and the point at which the Chamber of Deputies was established as an independent body with approval required for legislation. This was followed in 1875 with power over government formation and in 1879 with the threat of dissolution eliminated. In Germany, the process began in 1871 with the Reichstag's approval required for legislation. Other features evolved as de facto powers over the course of the imperial period, but none were secure until the constitution of 1919, which established the Reichstag as an independent body, with power over government formation, and the threat of dissolution eliminated. In the United Kingdom, the process began much earlier with the House of Commons' approval for legislation required in the Bill of Rights of 1688. Other important measures came later: power over government formation in 1789; the threat of dissolution eliminated in 1829; and finally, the Commons' independence established in the Reform Act of 1832 which eliminated the main vehicle by which the Crown exerted influence over Parliament, the rotten boroughs. Finally, in the United States, several of the key measures were achieved in the Constitution of 1789 with the House of Representatives granted power over government formation, its approval required for legislation, and the threat of dissolution eliminated.

The Constitution fell short in one important respect, however—the institution of "the slave representation," which was widely seen as an aristocratic arrangement undercutting the independence of the House. This institution would only be eliminated in 1865 after the Civil War.

Sequencing of Parliamentarization vis-à-vis Mass Suffrage

As with parliamentarization, mass suffrage evolved over time. For the cases examined here, I determine the timing of mass suffrage based on a minimum threshold relevant to party formation and development. This is the point at which the electorate had reached at least 50 percent of the adult male population. While this falls significantly short of contemporary standards for mass suffrage, scholars have identified this as a critical threshold for first wave democracies, especially as it pertains to the mobilization of the Left and other opposition parties.[34] Usually, this number goes directly from 0 to 100 percent, but in some cases, enfranchisement is more staggered, as in the UK, where the 50 percent threshold was not reached until the Third Reform Act in 1884. Placing the timing of mass suffrage with the timing of parliamentarization derived from figure 1.3, we find the sequences shown in figure 1.4.

Sequencing Strategies

The timing of parliamentarization relative to mass suffrage—the main explanatory factor in the present analysis—warrants some further explanation. How did these institutions become so staggered? The analysis here demonstrates that sequencing was often a deliberate choice, a strategy of political elites to manage the process of democratization. This represents a modification of some assumptions of the asynchronic view of institutional development, which typically explains the mix of institutions at any given juncture as the result of unrelated processes for which there was no road map, and actors had to navigate without much guidance. While there was certainly an experimental quality to institutional choice at the time, sequencing was not simply a matter of haphazard development. It was often a deliberate part of the process. The ability to sever the key components of democracy opened a whole "menu of manipulation" for elites, and different sequences were engineered by political leaders to produce specific outcomes.[35] This is not to say that elites had complete control of the process. In fact, they frequently miscalculated. But the sequences they initiated in pursuit of their goals were consequential

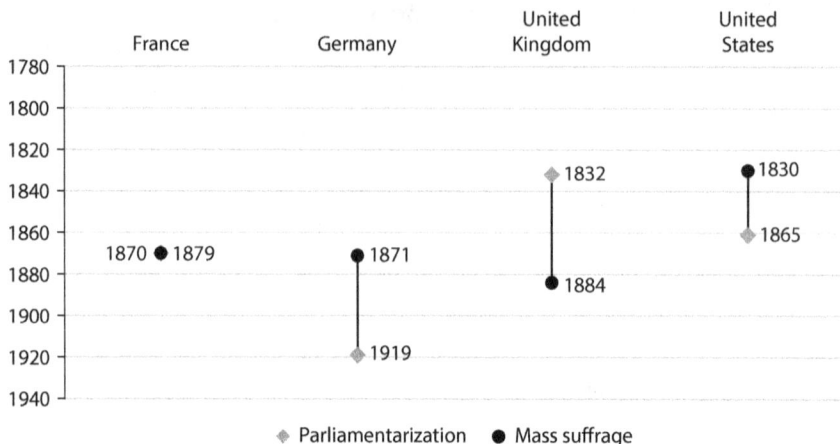

FIGURE 1.4. Historical sequences

nonetheless. The different sequencing strategies that emerged at the time are discussed in greater detail within the case study chapters, but a summary here will provide the basic logic.

For most political elites at the time, sequencing strategies were defined with respect to two specific historical events: the American Revolution and the French Revolution. These represented the two most dramatic examples of what might be considered "synchronic" political change in this period. In these models of democratization, the most significant reforms of the day, parliamentarization and mass suffrage, were brought together for the first time and designated as the key to republican government. They represented examples of revolutionary democratization, not just in their means but in their outcomes—a repudiation of both the Crown and propertied interests.[36] It was precisely the revolutionary nature of these events that made a staggered sequencing of institutions difficult, as the revolutions displaced those who would implement such countermeasures or attempt to manipulate outcomes through a specific sequencing of institutions.

Particularly jarring at the time was the French Revolution, given the structural similarities between the French ancien régime and the political systems of many European countries. It was one thing for a settler colony to reject traditional institutions, but another thing entirely for a great European power to do so. But the conservative impulse to avoid such revolutionary outcomes for many was coupled with the inescapable realization that

preventing revolution also required some concessions to the cause of reform. Piecemeal reforms, severing the main components of democratization,
particularly parliamentarization and mass suffrage, became the key to these
efforts.[37] In this context, asynchronic change became a tool of elite management, and countries learned from the experience of others what the likely
outcome of different strategies would be. This was true not only for the defenders of the old regimes of Europe, but in postrevolutionary France and
the United States as well.

The British were the first to explicitly experiment with the menu of manipulation. As discussed in chapter 3, the decision made in 1832 was to pursue parliamentarization while holding off on suffrage expansion. The aim of this move
was to strengthen Parliament in relation to the Crown, while also establishing
Parliament as the main vehicle for popular representation, meditating between
the masses and government. Universal manhood suffrage was discussed and
rejected at the time. In fact, the Reform Act was not concerned with enfranchising individuals as such. Instead, it looked to enfranchise specific counties
and boroughs to enhance the representation of interests considered to be
important for parliamentary strength. The limited suffrage expansion that
took place followed this same logic, extending suffrage only in such a way as
to equalize the franchise between counties and boroughs. The decision to prioritize parliamentarization in 1832 set up what I refer to here as the path of early
parliamentarization, which would come to be the touchstone of institutional
development for first wave democracies.

In Germany, a different lesson was learned. The experience of the French
Revolution still stood as a warning against the simultaneous introduction of
parliamentarization and mass suffrage. The experience of the British, however, suggested that parliamentarization with limited suffrage, while mitigat-
ing the revolutionary potential of reform, also had the effect of strengthening
liberal forces. At the time of Germany's unification in 1867, Chancellor Bismarck, could also look to the Prussian Parliament for evidence that early parliamentarization similarly strengthened the liberals. By this time, Bismarck
also had the benefit of another model—mass suffrage without parliamentarization as it was implemented under Napoleon, which he believed would
strengthen the conservative elements in Germany as it had in the French
Second Empire. Bismarck's decision to pursue universal manhood suffrage
without parliamentarization was made with this in mind, establishing what
in this analysis is referred to as the path of early mass suffrage. This is examined in chapter 4.

Only where the political climate would not allow elites to stagger institutions do we find simultaneous sequencing. Most notably, this was the case in Third Republic France, which found itself the beneficiary of multiple national experiments with different institutional configurations within its own history. Mass suffrage was probably the only "given" in this process. Some resisted it, but full adult male suffrage had been a feature of every French government since the revolution, whether republican or monarchical, making it untenable that the republic would be established without it. The issue of parliamentarization emerged as the main battleground. Having come out of their own experience of suffrage without parliamentarization under Napoleon, the effects of this path were well known and unequivocally rejected by Republicans who saw in it only reactionary potential. While the monarchists would have preferred this option, their inability to unite around a successor to the throne opened the door to parliamentary government. Thus, the simultaneous introduction of parliamentarization and mass suffrage reflected the inability of elites to manage the process. It resulted in a highly unstable equilibrium, however, and both mass suffrage and parliamentarization remained contested for the first decade of the republic, only to be secured in 1879.

One final path considered here represents a mix of the above. This is the path of *unsettled* parliamentarization followed in the United States and examined in chapter 6. In some respects, the United States followed the path of early parliamentarization with limited suffrage. The limitations on the franchise were achieved by devolving voting rights to the subnational level, making the right to vote for congressional representatives dependent on suffrage laws in the states. This effectively created a limited national franchise, which would not change until states began changing their laws almost three decades later. The path of early parliamentarization in this case, however, was altered by the fact that the Constitution contained certain institutional deficiencies, which left ambiguous the status of representative bodies and meant that the United States fell short of full parliamentarization. Specifically, the institution of slavery, and especially the slave representation in southern states, introduced significant distortions in the apportionment of representatives for the national legislature. By empowering wealthy landowners, it also introduced what was seen by many as an aristocratic element to the democratic body. This was exacerbated with each act of western expansion, which introduced greater disproportionality, leaving the status of parliamentarization unsettled throughout the antebellum period.

The patterns of institutional sequencing introduced during these critical junctures were all engineered to manage the process of democratization to the advantage of predemocratic elites. Of course, we now know that they all would fail at their primary objective—preventing further reform. But the choice of elites at this time would have a lasting impact on political development. The order in which institutions were introduced would set in motion a process of development that would determine the salience of the regime dimension for party formation and alignment, with significant long-term consequences for legislative capacity and regime stability.

Regime Contention and Repertoires of Conflict and Cooperation

What explains the continued salience of the regime dimension? I argue that the salience of the regime dimension, or indeed of any dimension, could remain long after the critical juncture of institutional choice through the "repertoires of conflict and cooperation" acquired by legislators in these early stages. This aspect of the argument reflects the historical institutionalist approach taken in this analysis. It posits that the impact of initial sequences may last past the point at which the specific institutional configuration in question has been eliminated. That is, the regime dimension could persist after the reason that gave rise to it—the lack of parliamentarization—had been resolved.

At its core, such an approach implies an ontological shift in our understanding of causation. In contrast to rational choice institutionalism, which sees institutions acting on actors' behavior in an immediate and direct manner, a historical institutionalist approach keeps open the possibility that an institutions' effect on behavior may be indirect and extend beyond the institution's own lifespan. The most important implication of this is that causes and consequences may not always coexist.[38] This is because the forces of history do not always act in a constant manner, and the outcomes of interest may have been set in motion by factors no longer in effect. In the context of legislative coalitions, this means that legislators' behavior in the long term may not correspond directly to the immediate institutional environment. Rather it may be derived from early stages of political development and the prevailing institutional configuration at that time. This understanding of *historical causation* is crucial in explaining outcomes among the cases examined here.[39]

Mediating between institutions and their outcomes in this analysis are what I refer to as *repertoires of conflict and cooperation*. Repertoires are understood as modes of thought derived from past interactions, which guide choices, making some options seem more desirable and others less so. Repertoires operate through a combination of psychological and cognitive processes that condition actors' willingness to pursue unfamiliar strategies, as well as political and organizational constraints imposed by previous interactions. To borrow from Ann Swidler, repertoires may be thought of as "tool kits," consisting of "habits, skills, and styles," from which people construct "strategies of action."[40] Charles Tilly similarly defined repertoires of contention as "a limited set of routines that are learned, shared, and acted out through a relatively deliberate process of choice."[41] Repertoires are constructed from past experiences, either direct or indirect. In other words, the experiences that contribute to a repertoire may be based on the actors' own interactions or the observed interactions of others; they may be based on a historical example, or even a collective memory of it. These past experiences come together to inform an actor's repertoire or their understanding of the range of actions that can be taken.

Key Mechanism: Impact of Early Coalitions on Repertoires of Conflict and Cooperation

In this analysis, repertoires represent the primary mechanism by which legislative coalitions are either reproduced or altered over time. Repertoires typically reflect past experiences with coalition partners, and the choices made will tend to favor the familiar: past partners more readily recommend themselves as future partners. This means that if early coalitions form around regime objectives, actors are likely to develop repertoires of regime contention and gravitate to regime allies in coalitional politics. Likewise, if early coalitions form around economic policy objectives, actors will likely develop repertoires of economic management, pointing them toward coalitions with economic allies.[42]

This is often the case, even if the alliance is suboptimal from a purely rationalist standpoint—that is, even if coalition partners do not serve their immediate policy interests. The reason for the stickiness of coalitions may be that other paths are unfamiliar and untested, and therefore involve greater uncertainty. In addition, coalition partners may have established channels of communication and trusted brokers that aid in bargaining among them. Taking these factors into consideration can help us understand patterns of continuity in legislative coalitions, that is, why the composition of coalitions at T^1 may influence the composition at T^{10}.

Within this approach, decisions are not made purely with a view to maximizing utility, for example, achieving an ideal policy outcome. Rather, other cognitive and psychological processes intervene to make a certain course of action seem more desirable, and they may in fact shape actors' understanding of their own self-interest. For example, there may be benefits to new coalition partners that are not fully explored because of the hurdles put in place by actors' repertoires.

Importantly, the framework of repertoires can also help us understand change. The most important feature of repertories in this respect is that the choices available to actors are not eliminated over time. In contrast to path-dependent historical institutionalist approaches, for example, where actors' choices can close off certain paths, within a repertoires framework, the choices—in this case, potential coalition partners—are always available. Repertoires may point actors in a certain direction, but they do not eliminate options, which leaves considerable room for political creativity. As we will see in the case study analyses, such creativity can lead to novel reconfigurations and alterations in legislative coalitions even in the face of powerful resistance.

The main factors that govern change or continuity have to do with the nature of the repertoire itself, or what I refer to as its *flexibility or rigidity*, qualities acquired at early stages of development.[43] In this analysis, the flexibility of repertoires, that is, how easily they can be altered, allowing actors to reform coalitions at later stages, depends on two key factors: (1) the degree of ambiguity in the initial sequencing—that is, whether it is clear to, and accepted by, actors that a given institutional pillar, either parliamentarization or mass suffrage, has been achieved; and (2) the duration of the initial period of staggered sequencing, that is, the period during which either parliamentarization or mass suffrage was secure, but not both.

The operation of repertoires of conflict and cooperation is especially important to understanding legislative capacity and regime stability in the interwar period. Following a processual, or historical institutionalist, logic, the argument advanced in this book holds that the factors leading to the observed behavior in the interwar period may not have existed in the interwar period. By this point, all four cases had achieved full parliamentarization and mass suffrage, eliminating any significant institutional variation among them. Nonetheless, the institutional context at early stages of development continued to shape party development and legislative coalitions through the operation of the repertoires inherited from earlier interactions.

Legislative Coalitions, Governance, and Stability

What were the consequences of the continued salience of the regime dimension? In the context of first wave democracies, the continued salience of the regime dimension into the interwar period would pose serious challenges to governance. At a minimum, it would strain policy coalitions established along the Left–Right economic policy spectrum. At an extreme, it would come to dominate party politics, pulling parties into alignment according to their regime preferences. In these instances, party systems came to resemble what Giovanni Sartori has described as a system of "polarized pluralism," characterized by high levels of government instability and legislative incapacity.[44] Given the intensity of economic crises during the interwar period and the demands of economic management, the continued salience of the regime dimension would put a tremendous strain on legislatures, leading to high levels of legislative failure, and in some cases, breakdown.

The emphasis on the necessity of viable economic policy coalitions is not meant to normalize the economic dimension or to suggest that this was the correct way to organize legislative coalitions; it is intended to stress that a particularity of the interwar period necessitated the kinds of center-left and center-right economic coalitions that have become so familiar to us today. Much of this was imposed by rigid economic perspectives that exacerbated the crisis and limited the range of possible responses.[45] But this situation meant that the ability to identify viable legislative coalitions to support economic policy decisions was key to stability in the interwar period. Importantly, no specific type of economic coalition was needed. As will be seen throughout these cases, both center-left and center-right coalitions proved to be highly effective. The important thing was that viable coalitions on either the Left or the Right could be identified to support economic policy, something that was only possible when legislative coalitions could form along the economic dimension.

This view departs from some canonical explanations of regime stability and instability during the interwar period, which have traditionally focused on coalitions of the Left as decisive. The canonical view originates with the work of Barrington Moore, and the importance he placed on the role of the bourgeoise.[46] In this tradition, Gregory Luebbert's study of regime outcomes in interwar Europe emphasized the importance of liberal-labor coalitions in stabilizing democracy.[47] Sheri Berman has similarly illustrated the key role of social democratic parties and the ideological variations among them in securing democratic outcomes.[48] Challenging this traditional understanding, Daniel Ziblatt has offered an alternative account, emphasizing the importance of the Right in stabilizing democracy, maintaining that the presence of a strong conservative party made the difference.[49]

Both perspectives offer important insights, but both are partial in terms of their focus, one exclusively on the Left, the other exclusively on the Right. As such, they miss key aspects of the underlying logic governing coalitional politics and political stability. In contrast, the present study seeks answers to the question of democratic endurance not in any one political force, but in the dynamics of conflict and cooperation that govern politics between political forces. In this view, the key to democratic survival is effective governance. And the key to governance is the availability of viable legislative coalitions *on the Left or the Right*. As will be seen in the case study analyes, in fact, both coalitions of the Left and coalitions of the Right at different times and in different contexts served as effective vehicles of governance and stabilizing forces in democratic politics. Therefore, this study aims to offer a systematic explanation of the dynamics within legislatures that takes into account the development of coalitions across the political spectrum.

The Politics of Budgets

To understand the importance of legislative coalitions for regime stability, each of the case studies ends with a key episode that offers an important window into the dynamics of legislative success and failure—the politics of budgets in the 1930s. Budgets offer an important test or measure of legislative capacity because they have a built-in counterfactual. Budgets represent a piece of legislation that *should* pass if legislatures are functioning properly. Passing a budget is perhaps one of the most fundamental functions of legislatures. It is not an optional piece of legislation. Whereas in other areas, legislatures may defer decisions to a later date if they cannot reach agreement, budgets must be passed. For most legislatures, this is a routine if contentious exercise. In some instances, it is an existential necessity. Thus, within this episode, we find an important test of the efficacy of legislative politics and the viability of representative government more generally: Can legislators form viable coalitions to perform necessary tasks? Can they do so under pressure? Can they fend off executive encroachment in times of crisis?

Mundane as it may sound, passing budgets in the 1930s was no small feat. The global economic crisis put tremendous pressure on national legislatures throughout the democratic world. To maintain their access to credit and satisfy the requirements of lenders, they needed to pass a balanced budget, often including strict austerity measures. Rising unemployment and inflation, however, created massive dependence on the state, and austerity measures threatened to plunge large segments of the population further into crisis, potentially bringing on political instability.[50]

For all first wave democracies, the task of passing a budget was encountered under urgently dire circumstances in the interwar period. Within the span of a few years, between 1929 and 1935, every country had to contend with the economic and political fallout of the market crash and ensuing Depression. Each was faced with similar budgetary dilemmas and a limited set of options that would satisfy both lenders and the public. And each had to resolve this dilemma under extraordinary time pressure. It was the ultimate "stress test" for legislatures. Party leaders were faced with the challenge of identifying both a set of policies that would allow the country to avoid economic collapse and a legislative coalition to support it. There were many ways to configure both ends of the legislative challenge, but no obvious formula could mechanically be applied. Nowhere was this process tidy or easy, but it was essential for the survival of democracy.

While a great deal of attention has been paid to the substance of economic policy and its role in resolving the economic crises, my interest in this episode is in the ability of legislatures to resolve the *political* crisis, identifying and carrying out legislative solutions to legislative problems. From the perspective of democratic stability, perhaps more important than whether legislatures could identify the "right" policy was whether they could identify *any* policy that could gain the confidence of a legislative majority. As I show in this book, when legislators found a solution for this and other legislative challenges, they were able to stabilize both the economy and the polity. When they could not, it opened the door to executive aggrandizement and a weakening of representative government.

The Argument

Returning to figure 1.1 and bringing together the different strands of the theoretical framework, the argument advanced in this work, and the mechanisms within it, can be summarized as shown in figure 1.5.

In sum, patterns of institutional sequencing at early stages of political development determined the salience of the regime dimension relative to others. This shaped early legislative coalitions and formed the bases of legislators' repertoires of conflict and cooperation, with some forming along the lines of regime contention and others along the lines of economic management. The repertoires actors inherited from previous interactions in turn determined legislative capacity. Finally, legislators' ability to form viable coalitions to respond to the demands placed on legislatures, especially in times of crisis, affected regime stability. This is because the inability to respond opened the door to executive encroachment, while effective responses helped to secure the power of representative bodies. At the center of figure 1.5, and at the heart of the argument, we find legislative coalitions and the repertoires of conflict and cooperation they adopt. Legislative coalitions, as a critical vehicle of democratic governance, and repertoires as the primary mechanism through which they are reproduced or altered represent key steps in the argument. Both are discussed in greater detail in chapter 2.

Research Methods

Several methodological choices shape the analysis in the book and the types of inferences that can be drawn. These include cross-case comparison, within-case critical juncture analysis, methodologies of historical interpretation, and the choice of materials. Here I discuss each component and how they combine to offer a rigorous assessment of the argument.

Cross-Case Comparison

The analysis here is built around the examination of four cases that have been foundational to the study of political development: the United Kingdom, Germany, France, and the United States. The case selection combines a most-similar case design for the first three cases, with an evaluation of ideal types for the fourth. The first three cases can be considered most similar in terms of

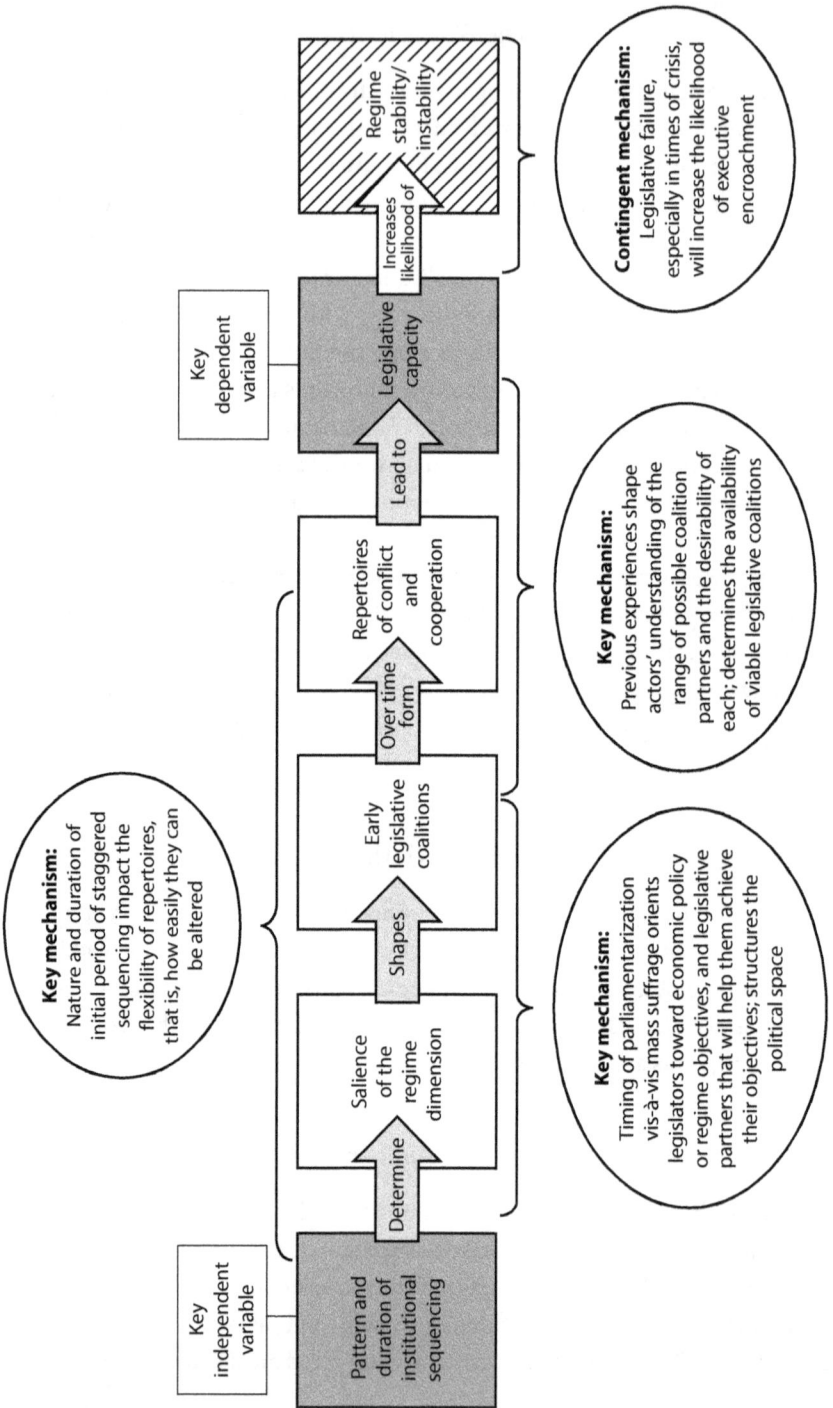

Key mechanism:
Nature and duration of initial period of staggered sequencing impact the flexibility of repertoires, that is, how easily they can be altered

Key independent variable

Pattern and duration of institutional sequencing

Determine →

Salience of the regime dimension

Shapes →

Early legislative coalitions

Over time form →

Repertoires of conflict and cooperation

Lead to →

Key dependent variable

Legislative capacity

Increases likelihood of →

Regime stability/instability

Key mechanism:
Timing of parliamentarization vis-à-vis mass suffrage orients legislators toward economic policy or regime objectives, and legislative partners that will help them achieve their objectives; structures the political space

Key mechanism:
Previous experiences shape actors' understanding of the range of possible coalition partners and the desirability of each; determines the availability of viable legislative coalitions

Contingent mechanism:
Legislative failure, especially in times of crisis, will increase the likelihood of executive encroachment

FIGURE 1.5. Argument and mechanisms

their common experiences with the feudal structures that set in motion the fight over the regime question at the heart of this analysis. These similarities allow us to assess the impact of institutional sequencing, which varied systematically across cases: the United Kingdom, where parliamentarization was introduced prior to mass suffrage; Germany, where mass suffrage preceded parliamentarization; and France, where parliamentarization and mass suffrage were introduced simultaneously. Each case illustrates a distinctive path of development and corresponding outcomes for legislative capacity and regime stability in the interwar period.

The analysis of the United States moves to a different mode of inquiry and a different method of comparative analysis, employing an evaluation of ideal types rather than case-based comparison. The different structural foundation in the United States, and particularly the break with monarchical institutions, makes wholesale incorporation of the United States into a most-similar case design difficult. With an evaluation of ideal types, however, we can "translate" some of the conceptual categories derived from the European cases to assess the utility of the theoretical model in explaining the observed social action in the United States.[51] The approach proves quite fruitful in uncovering aspects of US political development that have gone largely unappreciated. Given the revolutionary nature of its founding and the break with the traditional European institutions of monarchy and aristocracy, we would not expect to see in the United States any of the regime contention found in the other cases. Nonetheless, we find that, even absent deep monarchical and feudal structures, certain institutional deficiencies with respect to parliamentarization, along with ideational transferences from the experience of European political development, led to analogous fights in the United States. This was enough to ignite regime contention throughout much of the nineteenth century and illustrates that even slight alterations in institutional configurations can influence the salience of the regime dimension with long-term consequences for legislative capacity and regime stability.

The comparative approaches taken in this study put it within the tradition of comparative historical analysis, and the inclusion of the United States also adds a comparative area studies dimension to the work.[52] Such an approach holds that comparison across traditional geographic areas is a mode of "triangulation" that can increase confidence in inferences.[53] For historical research it is especially valuable as it can reveal historical connections that challenge contemporary understandings of what constitutes the relevant area. This critical and grounded approach to political geography is important for the study of European and American political development, given the inter-connectedness of these areas across the political space of the nineteenth and early twentieth centuries.[54]

Within-Case Analysis: Critical Junctures + Repertoires

To analyze processes of political development over time within each case, I rely on critical juncture analysis. Critical juncture analysis is a powerful tool in the historical institutionalist toolkit and is especially suited to examining institutional origins and their impacts.[55] Within this approach, a critical juncture is understood to be a period of relative openness, usually brought on by an exogenous shock to the system, which loosens constraints on actors, allow-ing them to pursue new strategies. The institutions established within a critical juncture are understood to have a self-reinforcing mechanism, which means that the institutions can live on past the reasons that gave rise to them and past the point at which they might be considered "rational choices."[56] In this analy-sis, I take the initial stage of institutional choice as the critical juncture that set in motion processes of political development and determined the salience of the regime dimension relative to others in shaping early legislative coalitions. In each case, the critical juncture is examined in detail to illustrate that it was indeed a distinct period of relative openness in which many paths were possi-ble and to demonstrate the highly contingent nature of the outcomes.

In addition to the critical juncture of institutional choice, the analysis is built around three subsequent episodes in each case that offered significant opportunities for actors to reform legislative coalitions. Importantly, these episodes are found across all four cases, adding considerable analytical lever-age in the comparison of outcomes:

1. The first episode came at the turn of the century with the rise of labor, both as independent parties and as strong currents within parties. This was facilitated in each case by the international mobilization of workers' organizations and the domestic liberalization of laws regulat-ing associations. Whether economic or regime consideration had influenced prior coalitions, the entrance of this new potential eco-nomic foe or ally could have provided incentive for parties to alter alliances.

2. The second episode came after the First World War and also offered opportunities to reform coalitions in either direction. This period saw

increased radicalization within the labor movement and the rise of Communist challengers after the Bolshevik Revolution. As such it heightened regime anxieties and could have pushed legislators toward regime coalitions. At the same time, within all four cases this period also marked the point at which mass suffrage and parliamentarization had been achieved. Having satisfied these regime demands, this moment of democratization held important opportunities to reform coalitions away from regime and toward economic alliances.

3. The third episode came after the market crash of 1929 and centered on legislators' response to the economic crises, specifically around the challenge of passing budgets. This final episode offers an anatomy of legislative success and failure. In each case, the economic crisis put tremendous pressure on legislatures to identify viable economic coalitions and alter existing coalitions if necessary to do so.

These episodes provide important opportunities for counterfactual analysis.[57] In each episode, conditions changed such that we would expect coalitions to change. But as we will see in the case study analyses, success in reforming coalitions varied from episode to episode and from case to case.

This variation is difficult to accommodate within existing approaches to critical juncture analysis, which tend toward the expectation of continuity beyond the critical juncture, as a result of either actors reaching an equilibrium point or increasing returns from path-dependent processes.[58] While the explanation of long-term continuities is a signal strength of critical juncture analysis, it can lead to a "stability bias," which hinders our ability to explain change.[59]

To address these challenges, in this analysis I develop a distinct approach to critical juncture analysis that centers repertoires as the vehicle through which actors' decisions are made. Discussed at length in chapter 2, this approach offers a robust theory of both change and continuity within a critical juncture framework. In brief, I understand the choice to reform legislative coalitions or not as a function of the repertoires that actors developed in previous interactions. The most distinctive feature of this approach compared to equilibrium and path-dependent approaches is that it does not stipulate that paths are closed off over time, nor does it assume that actors are satisfied with the status quo. Like equilibrium and path-dependent approaches, repertoires have a self-reinforcing aspect, as actors will tend toward the familiar. Unlike other approaches, however, within a repertoires framework, the full range of choices—in this case, coalition partners—remains available to actors, and there are always actors who might seek to alter repertoires. Their ability to do so will depend on the relative flexibility of the repertoire itself, a quality acquired at early stages of development based on the nature and duration of the initial stage of sequencing.

These tools structure the within-case analysis throughout the book. Each case study begins with an examination of the critical juncture of institutional choice that sets in motion the sequencing process, shaping early legislative coalitions and the repertoires of conflict and cooperation they adopt. In addition, I examine three subsequent episodes in which the legislative coalitions that were established during the critical juncture and the repertoires of conflict and cooperation they came to engender could have been altered. The final episode also serves as a test and measure of legislative capacity based on the repertoires acquired over time and the ability of legislatures to fend off legislative encroachment and stabilize democratic governance.

Methods of Historical Interpretation

Historical analysis always presents challenges to understanding, given the distance of the subject matter from our own context and the fact that typically we can learn about it only through documents and artifacts rather than direct experience or observation. Without the proper orientation toward this distance, there is a temptation to impose contemporary categories and concepts onto historical contexts in ways that may hinder understanding.[60] The approach employed in this analysis aims to address these challenges of historical interpretation through a contextualist methodology.[61] This approach aims for a "forward reading" of history that seeks to place events and words in context and understand fights as the actors understood them.[62] It is especially suited for the examination of actors' motivations and a processual understanding of development. Rather than inferring motivations from outcomes, it seeks a grounded understanding of how actors understood their own situation and the choices before them. It alerts us to the fact that the choices made may not make sense from the perspective of the "finish line" or in terms of universalist rationalist expectations, but may be best understood in terms of the historical particularity of contexts and actors' motivations.

In addition to the contextualist approach, the evaluation of ideal types in the analysis of the United States introduces a reflexive orientation.[63] With an evaluation of ideal types, the presumption is that we go into the investigation not with a blank slate, but rather with certain theoretical models that are formalized to compare to the observed patterns of social action.[64] This approach is consistent with a comparative area studies framework, where the insights developed in one region of the world are assessed in another.[65] In this respect it represents a "sideways reading" of history that seeks not only to develop a grounded understanding of that particular context, but to relate it to others. The goal of this evaluative exercise is not generalization but explanation. It is an approach geared toward open-ended historical exploration and helps to accommodate cases that do not fit neatly into variable-based comparison but would nonetheless contribute to historical understanding of the subject matter.

Choice of Materials

These methodologies drive the choice of evidence used in the study. In addition to traditional historical narratives about the period, evidence from party platforms, minutes of party meetings, the text of legislative debates, cabinet meetings, personal correspondence of party leaders, and newspaper records are used to understand how actors understood their context, what they were fighting about, and their motivations for action. These sources help to elucidate the factors contributing to both continuity and discontinuity, specifically to uncover the role of regime relative to economic preferences in the formation of legislative coalitions. The combination of historical sources is intended to triangulate different interpretations of historical events.[66]

The balance of evidence between primary and secondary sources varies depending on the specific analytical and interpretive challenge. Much of the analysis uses secondary sources to piece together the complex processes of development examined here. Yet, where my reading challenges the received understanding of political development or offers a revisionist historical interpretation, I move to primary sources to gain insight into actors' subjective understanding. This is the case for much of the analysis of the United States, which offers an alternative interpretation of the impact of regime contention on political development. The balance is also tilted toward primary sources in the United Kingdom, where the interpretation of the Reform Act of 1832 differs in important respects from much of the received wisdom. In France, around the period of the Dreyfus affair, when multiple repertoires come into play, and in Germany during critical periods of regime contention in the

Imperial Reichstag, the analysis also relies heavily on primary sources to substantiate the claims. Nonetheless, neither primary nor secondary sources are free of bias or offer a more authentic reading of historical contexts. In this analysis both are approached with a critical lens toward the particularity of the viewpoints they impart.

Alternative Explanations

I devote the last section of this chapter to a discussion of some alternative explanations for regime outcomes in the interwar period. In terrain as well trodden as that of historical political development, and in cases as well studied as the four examined in this book, the number of alternative explanations is too great to thoroughly review here. Some have already been encountered in the discussion above, and several others emerge in the case study analysis. In this section, however, I address three explanations of regime outcomes in the interwar period that are frequently cited in the literature and are especially relevant to the present analysis because they speak to the dynamics of legislative success and failure and could be potential confounders to the argument advanced in this study. This is not meant to be an exhaustive examination or refutation of these explanations. Indeed, each offers important insights into the dynamics of the interwar period. What I aim to demonstrate here is that none offers a systematic explanation of legislative capacity or regime outcomes across the cases examined in this study.

Ideology of Socialist Parties

An argument that has been advanced to explain divergent outcomes in the interwar period has to do with the nature of socialist parties, specifically their ideological orientation toward electoral competition and parliamentary responsibility. The attention to socialist parties makes sense. As big players throughout Europe during the interwar period, their participation could make or break any coalition. Moreover, whether they adopted reformist or revolutionary ideologies would affect both their willingness to participate in coalitions and other parties' receptivity to such participation. Therefore, in cases such as in the UK, where the Labour Party was reformist, socialists could more easily sustain cooperation with liberals.[67] For more radical socialist parties, such as the German Social Democratic Party (SPD), the barriers to cooperation were political and ideological. Politically, their revolutionary agenda, especially on economic matters, would put them at a greater distance from the German Liberals. And ideologically, the relative radicalization of the German Socialists meant that they were slower to embrace parliamentary politics and in fact were somewhat ambivalent toward electoral competition for the first decades of the Imperial Reichstag.[68] They also maintained in their platform a prohibition against cooperation with bourgeoise governments.

These variations among socialist parties are certainly important to the present analysis, but they fall short of explaining outcomes for several reasons. First, at least in part, the ideological orientation of socialist parties is endogenous to the developmental story of this study. The repertoires of conflict and cooperation they developed as a result of early or late participation shaped each party's ideology and composition. As has been noted by numerous scholars, the suppression of labor mobilization and the cooptation of labor organizations by the Liberal Party in the UK contributed significantly to the reformist posture ultimately adopted by the British Labour Party. The German SPD, on the other hand, developed in a context where it had to fight not only for its own inclusion but for parliamentary government, leading to greater radicalization and a more antagonistic position toward parties of the Right (Conservatives and Liberals). In other words, this radicalization was intertwined with the repertoires of regime contention they adopted.

Importantly, while these repertoires led the German SPD to reject cooperation with parties of the Right, it strengthened its ties to both the Catholic Center Party and the Left Liberals, its allies in the struggle for parliamentarization. While it maintained a prohibition on participation in bourgeois government, even that was eased on the eve of the First World War. During the war, it participated with its regime allies in the Interfraktioneller Ausschuss, or IFA, a Reichstag coordinating committee that functioned as a shadow government during the war.[69] After the war this same assemblage of parties, including the SPD, formed the Weimar Coalition, the founding coalition that ushered in the new republic. Thus, much like the British Labour Party, the German SPD did in fact cooperate with bourgeois parties, but its choice of partners was driven by regime preferences.

Perhaps an even more important factor to consider in understanding the impact of Socialist Party ideology is the distinction between governing coalitions and legislative coalitions. Even among the more radicalized of the socialist parties, the prohibition against cooperation with bourgeois parties was a prohibition against entering into governing coalitions and especially against accepting ministerial responsibility within such governments. It was not, however, a prohibition against participation in legislative coalitions, which is the focus of the present analysis. As discussed in the next chapter, legislative coalitions often operated independently from government coalitions. And most socialist parties that rejected participation in government coalitions had no hesitation about entering into legislative coalitions. This will be seen most clearly in the case of the French SFIO and the German SPD, two parties that often declined government responsibility but were major partners in legislative coalitions.

It is instructive to compare here legislative coalition patterns in the British case, where we find one of the most reform-minded socialist parties of Europe, with the German case where we find one of the most radical. Figures 1.6 and 1.7 are based on roll call analysis of legislative voting behavior using a networks approach to identify coalitions.[70] It groups legislators into the same coalitions if they vote more consistently together than they do with those outside the coalition. As we can see, though the coalition partners are different, the socialist party in the UK (Labour) is just as likely to be placed in a legislative coalition as that in Germany (SPD). For both cases, there is one legislative period in which socialist parties form their own coalition, which means that they display voting patterns distinctive enough that they cannot be placed in any other coalition. In all other legislative sessions, however, they are placed squarely within coalitions with other dominant parties. In terms of how frequently they are identified within an interparty legislative coalition and how frequently they are not, there is no difference between the two socialist parties. Thus, their ideological disposition did not determine their willingness to participate in legislative coalitions, even if, in Germany, it did at times lead them to decline participation in governing coalitions.

Finally, during the interwar period, the SPD did in fact join government on several occasions—in 1921 under Center Party Chancellor Joseph Wirth, in 1923 under Liberal Party Chancellor Gustav Stresemann, and in 1928 under SPD Party Chancellor Hermann Müller. But for both the German SPD and the British Labour Party, participation in the government coalition was not a predictor of their position within legislative coalitions. In the end, the main differences we find in patterns of coalition formation is not *whether* the

UK legislative session 31: 1918–1922

250
200
150
100
50
0

Coalition 1   Coalition 2   Coalition 3

Labour

■ Coalition conservative   ■ Labour   ▨ Coalition liberal
▨ Irish unionist   ■ Irish nationalist

UK legislative session 32: 1922–1923

400
350
300
250
200
150
100
50
0

Coalition 1   Coalition 2

Labour

■ Conservative   ▨ Labour   ▨ Liberal   ▨ National liberal

UK legislative session 33: 1923–1924

350
300
250
200
150
100
50
0

Coalition 1   Coalition 2

Labour

■ Conservative   ▨ Labour   ▨ Liberal   ▨ Ulster unionist

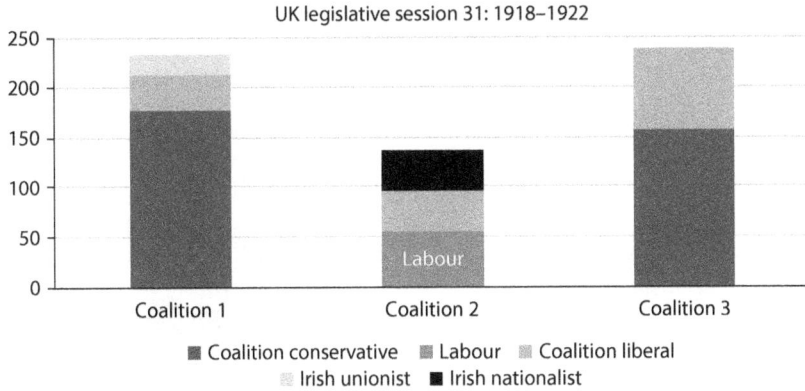

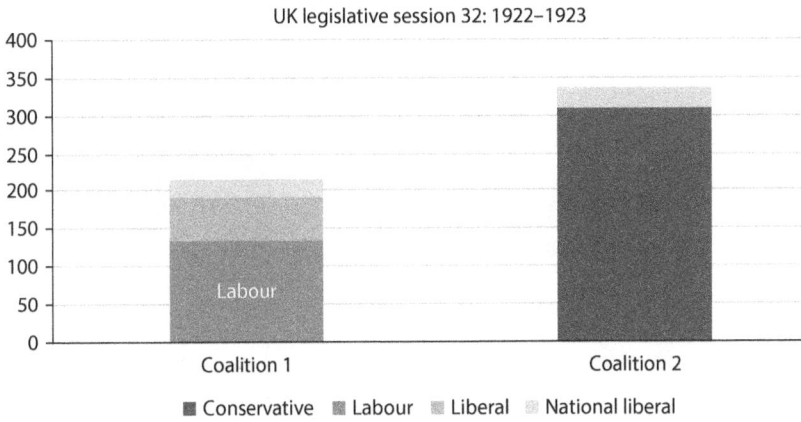

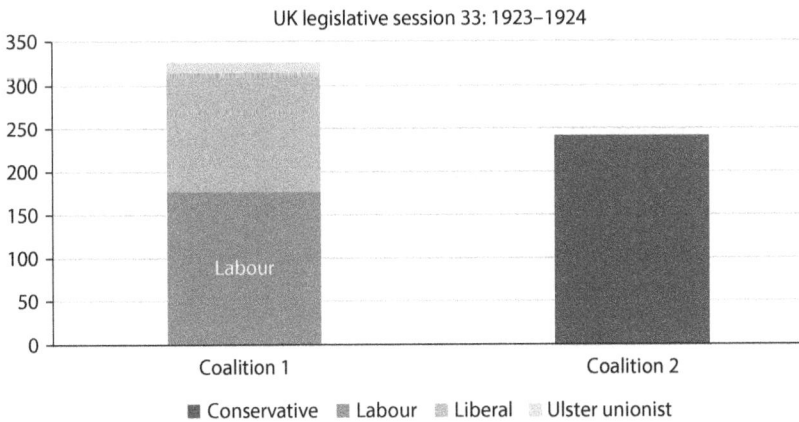

FIGURE 1.6. UK interwar legislative coalitions

UK legislative session 34: 1924–1929

■ Unionist   ■ Labour   ■ Liberal

UK legislative session 35: 1929–1931

■ Conservative   ■ Labour   ■ Liberal

UK legislative session 36: 1931–1935

■ Conservative   ■ Labour   ■ Liberal   ■ Liberal national

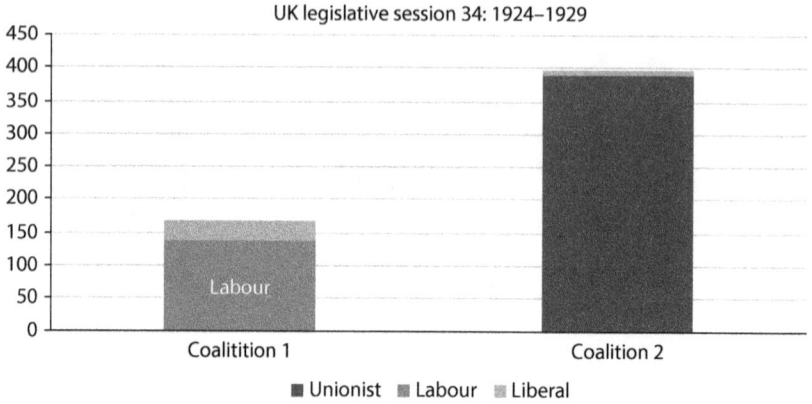

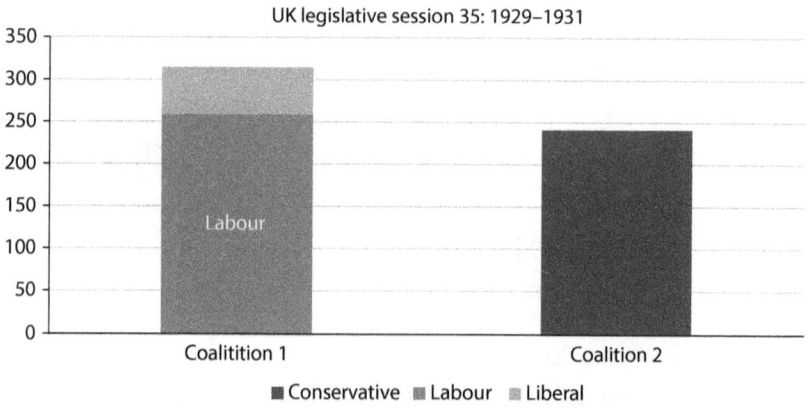

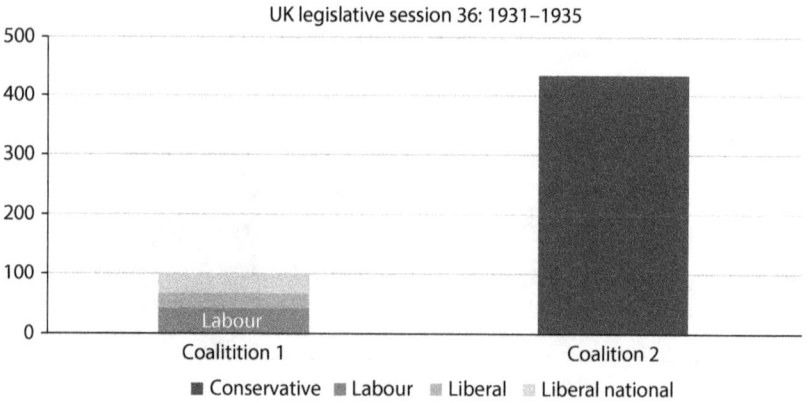

FIGURE 1.6. (*continued*)

Weimar legislative session 1: 1920–1924

■ Conservative ▨ Socialist ■ Left liberal ░ Liberal ▨ Zentrum

Weimar legislative session 2: 1924

■ Conservative ▨ Socialist ■ Left liberal ░ Liberal ▨ Zentrum

Weimar legislative session 3: 1924–1928

■ Conservative ▨ Socialist ■ Left liberal ░ Liberal ▨ Zentrum

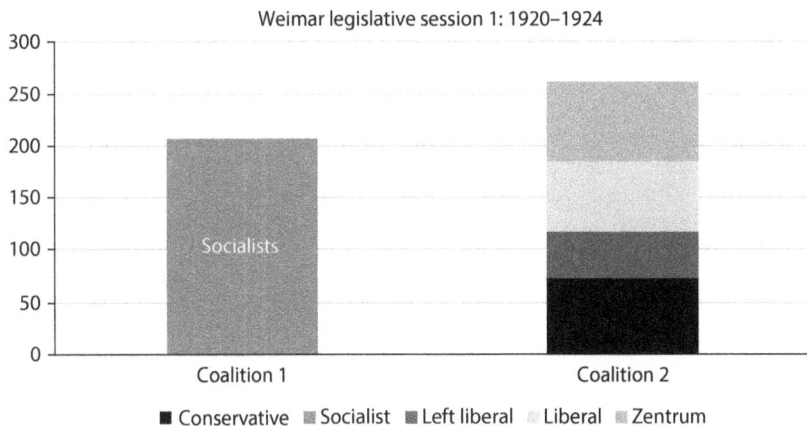

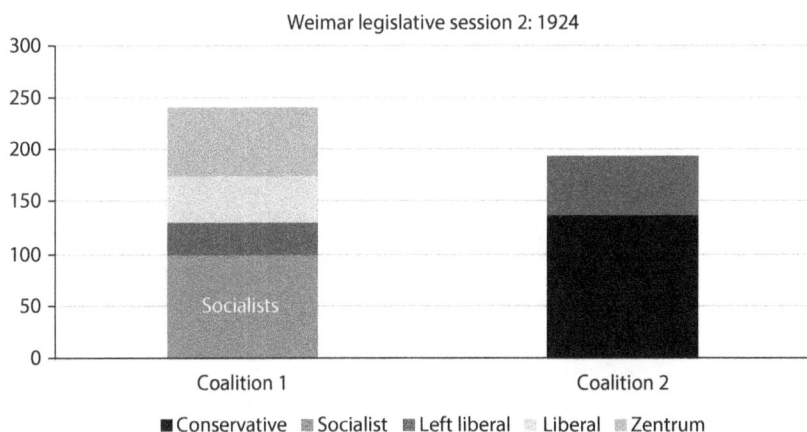

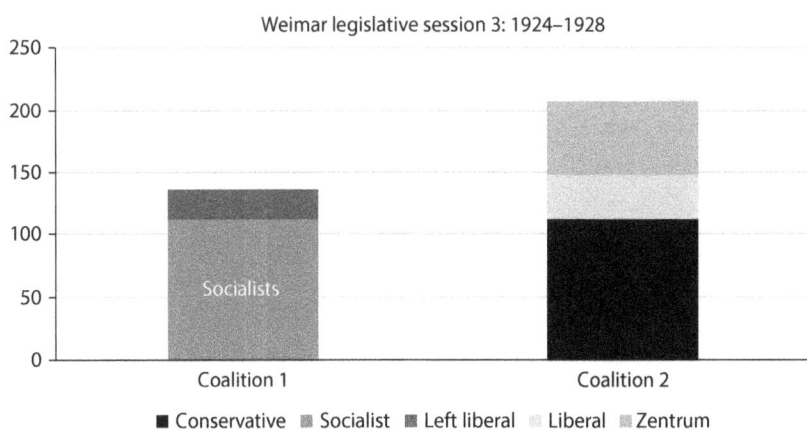

FIGURE 1.7. Germany interwar legislative coalitions

Weimar legislative session 4: 1928–1930

Weimar legislative session 5: 1930–1932

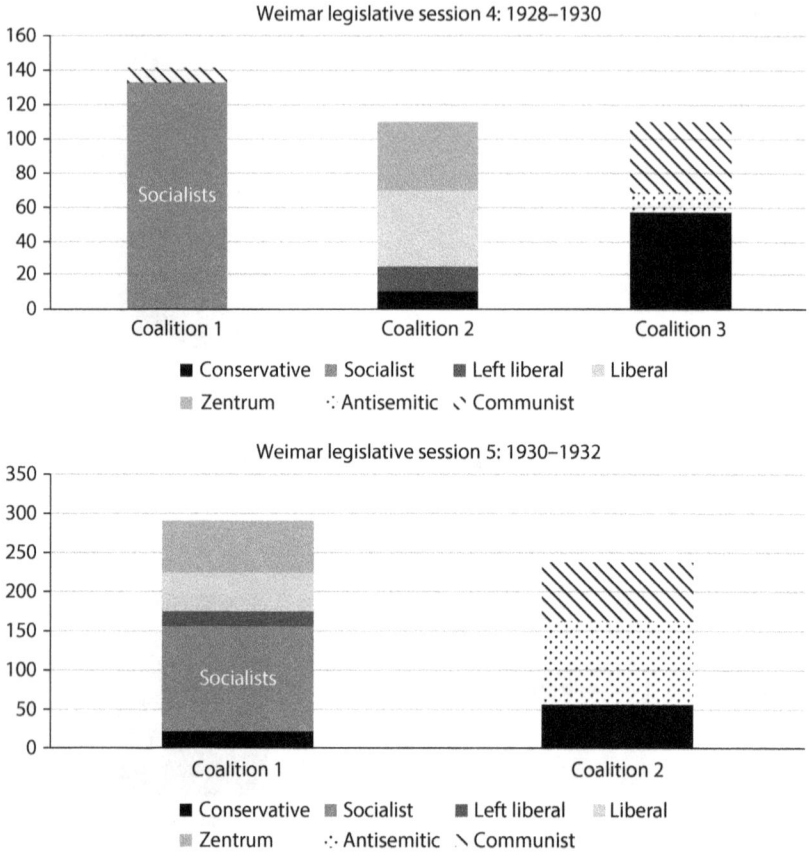

FIGURE 1.7. (*continued*)

socialists joined legislative coalitions but the kinds of coalitions they joined, which in the UK formed around economic policy preferences and in Germany around regime preference.

Political Structures

Another common explanation of legislative success or failure in the interwar period has to do with political structures, including the electoral system and related phenomenon of the party system. Of particular concern here has been the extent of party system fragmentation, which was especially significant in the German case. By the end of the Weimar Republic, more than twenty parties held seats in the Reichstag. This fragmentation of the party system has been used by numerous scholars to explain the legislative dysfunction of the German Reichstag and its consequences for regime instability.[71]

Party systems, however, are a weak predictor of legislative coalitions for at least two reasons. The first is that the German party system was not exceptional. In fact, among the cases examined here, the French party system looks very much like the German. If we considered the effective number of parties throughout this period, we would find that the French system does not differ in terms of its fragmentation—the average effective number of parties in Germany was 5.9, and in France, it was 5.2 (table 1.3). Even if we look at the composition of the party system—that is, the kinds of parties within it—there is no systematic difference between France and Germany, both of which during this period had some combination of the traditional conservative and liberal parties, along with a socialist party, a communist party, and various fascist party currents that manifested at different times.[72] The party system of the United Kingdom is distinct from the French and the German and more closely resembles the typical two-party system, but it also displays some fragmentation, with the average effective number of parties at 2.4. Moreover, one of its two dominant parties in the interwar period was the Labour Party, not the centrist catchall party often associated with two-party systems.[73] Only the United States maintained a stable two-party system with centrist catchall parties throughout this period. This is not to say that party fragmentation and cohesion do not matter for legislative politics, but they cannot systematically explain either legislative coalitions or regime outcomes across cases.

Another reason that party systems are a weak predictor of legislative capacity is that forging coalitions *within* parties may be just as challenging as forging them between parties. This means that even within a two-party system, the ability to identify viable legislative coalitions is not a given. In the United States, though a stable two-party system has prevailed for much of the post–Civil War period, the assemblage of actors combined within these parties made coalition building exceedingly difficult. The period after the Civil War, especially until the realignment of 1896, is known for endemic legislative incapacity resulting from dysfunctional party coalitions.[74] This shows that parties cannot be considered proxies for legislative coalitions, and even stable two-party systems where one party has a clear majority cannot be assumed to have stable and easily identifiable legislative coalitions to support policy agendas.

TABLE 1.3. Effective Number of Parties in the Interwar Period

Country	Year	Value	Country	Year	Value	Country	Year	Value	Country	Year	Value
France	1919	5	Germany	1924 M	7.1	United Kingdom	1918	2.7	United States	1918	2
France	1924	4	Germany	1924 D	6.2	United Kingdom	1922	2.6	United States	1920	2
France	1928	5.6	Germany	1928	6.1	United Kingdom	1923	2.9	United States	1922	2
France	1932	6.3	Germany	1930	7.1	United Kingdom	1924	1.9	United States	1924	2
			Germany	1932 J	4.3	United Kingdom	1929	2.4	United States	1926	2
			Germany	1932 N	4.8	United Kingdom	1931	1.7	United States	1928	2
									United States	1930	2
									United States	1932	2
									United States	1934	2
Average		5.2	Average		5.9	Average		2.4	Average		2

Effective number of parties calculated based on the method developed by Markku Laakso and Rein Taagepera, "'Effective' Number of Parties: A Measure with Application to West Europe," *Comparative Political Studies* 12, no. 1 (1979): 3–27.

Economic Crises

Another argument that has been offered to explain interwar regime outcomes has centered on the impact of economic crises in the interwar period. This argument focuses on both general economic conditions and the impact of the market crash of 1929, the severity of which varied across cases.[75] Many scholars have focused especially on the German case, arguing that it faced exceptional challenges, operating under the crushing weight of reparations and hyperinflation, with the market crash being the final blow. This received wisdom has been transmitted without always being thoroughly interrogated, however. The first questions that arise have to do with the accuracy of the empirical claims. While the terms of the Versailles Treaty were indeed exceedingly harsh and put tremendous pressure on the German economy in the years immediately after the First World War, these terms were quickly modified, first by the Dawes Plan, negotiated in 1924, which corrected for some excesses in the earlier peace terms and linked reparations to the performance of the German economy.[76] This was replaced in 1929 by the Young Plan, which introduced additional modifications and further eased the terms of reparations. In fact, by the end of the interwar period, reparations were not a significant factor in the German economy.[77] Ironically, France, as the main beneficiary of reparations, ended up worse off as a result of these changes.

A second point has to do with effects of the economic crisis following the market crash of 1929. While this was undoubtedly a major destabilizing factor throughout Europe, the impact of economic crisis on legislative capacity is unclear. Crisis does not necessarily lead to gridlock and inaction. A sense of emergency may in fact produce the opposite. The economic difficulties faced by the Weimar regime were serious indeed. As serious as these challenges were, however, they do not explain the inability of the Reichstag to respond. Here it is necessary to separate out the economic crisis from the political crisis, specifically that, for critical pieces of legislation such as the Budget Act of 1930, on which the country's financial solvency hinged, there were *no* viable legislative coalitions to support *any* budget. The problem was not that the Reichstag produced the wrong response; it was that it produced no response. Faced with the impending collapse of the economy, legislators were unable to act. The point here is not to question whether crisis leads to instability, but to stress that crisis is not determinative of legislative capacity. Moreover, legislative incapacity can be seen as itself contributing to the severity of the crisis, as has been noted by scholars of the period.[78]

All three alternative explanations examined here offer important insights into the dynamics of the interwar period. None offers an adequate explanation because, as I argue in this study, the roots of legislative capacity and regime stability in the interwar period are not to be found in that period. They originate in an earlier stage of political development, the impact of which can only be understood as a function of *historical* causation. In the next chapter I aim to develop this further by elucidating the significance of legislative coalitions for democratic governance and stability, and by developing a historical institutionalist approach to legislative coalitions that offers a robust framework for examining legislative behavior over time.

2

A Historical Institutionalist
Approach to Legislative Coalitions

THE ARGUMENT offered in this work places legislative coalitions at the center of democratic politics and regime stability. The ability to identify viable legislative coalitions to support responsive policy, especially in times of crisis, I contend was key to democratic stability in the first wave. Much of the book is focused on understanding the origins and evolution of legislative coalitions in the four cases examined. In this chapter I seek to develop a robust conceptualization of legislative coalitions to support this analysis and to highlight the importance of this often-neglected feature of democratic governance. I also offer a novel historical institutionalist approach to understanding change and continuity in legislative coalitions over time.

By legislative coalitions, I mean groups of legislators who explicitly or implicitly assent to passing a policy agenda. I consider legislative coalitions to be important phenomena, embodying the kind of coordination and cooperation necessary for a functioning democratic politics. In some cases, as in France, these structures become formalized, but often they remain informal, persisting through large and small acts of political creativity in which legislators must continually define and redefine priorities, assess and reassess possibilities. They are connected to parties but independent of them. They are connected to governments but also independent of them. They have histories that enable continuity, but they also respond to acts of political entrepreneurship aimed at change. They are often discernable only from the perspective of the longue durée.

Legislative coalitions are certainly not the only way to study party politics or legislative behavior. But they are an important measure of the strength of legislatures and the viability of representative government. They are, in a very specific sense, the vehicle through which self-governance is enacted. Unless one party holds an absolute majority, and even then, since absolute party discipline is difficult to achieve, parties must forge alliances to pass legislation.[1] Successful legislative coalitions embody the kinds of political compromise that make democratic politics possible. Parties' ability to forge compromise is essential not only for the substantive policy outcomes that result but to forestall executive encroachment, which is ever ready to supplant the legislative process.

But how do we understand the development of legislative coalitions? How do they form, and what might explain variations in the nature and composition of coalitions? In this chapter I develop a historical institutionalist approach to understanding legislative coalitions. It draws on the study of legislative behavior as it has developed in two distinct areas of inquiry, one geared toward the study of parliamentary systems and focusing heavily on European parliaments, and another geared toward the context of presidential systems, which has been dominated by the study of the United States Congress. Both have led to important insights, but neither has offered a view of the development of legislatures or legislative coalitions that can help us understand how they may affect regime stability. For one—the parliamentary context—legislative coalitions are often seen as inconsequential. Instead, this literature typically focuses on governing coalitions, assuming the dependence of legislative delegations on parties in government. For the other—the presidential context—legislative coalitions are highly consequential but transient. Dominated by a rationalist view of legislative behavior, this body of literature treats legislative coalitions as a function of individual legislators' or parties' self-interest, easily reformed when expected utilities shift.

These blind spots have made it difficult to appreciate patterns in legislative coalition formation over time and how they may influence regime stability. This is particularly important in the context of new and transitioning democracies, including all four cases examined in this study. Particularly where governments are weak or formal institutions are not stable enough to structure politics, legislatures often develop their own logic of governance. In this context especially, legislative coalitions can play an important role in either stabilizing or destabilizing politics. To understand this, however, it is necessary to apply a developmental perspective to the study of legislative coalitions, one that places legislative behavior "in time."[2]

The approach I offer here addresses this blind spot. It is a historical institutionalist approach that centers repertoires of conflict and cooperation as the framework for understanding change and continuity of legislative coalitions over time. Rather than view alliances as transient, as does much of the literature oriented toward rationalist explanations, this approach seeks to understand patterns that develop over time and make some kinds of alliances possible and others more difficult. Coalitional patterns, I contend, follow not only from ideology or self-interest, but also from history, specifically the history of interactions with coalition partners over time.

I begin by examining the literature on legislative behavior with a view to both identifying its limitations and exploring how it may inform a developmental approach to understanding coalitions.

Legislative Coalitions in Parliamentary Settings

An extensive body of scholarship has examined legislative politics within parliamentary systems. Because this line of scholarship focuses on parliamentary systems where the executive and legislative branches are fused and parties are thought to be strong, this work tends not to deal directly with legislative coalitions, focusing instead on governing coalitions as the key to understanding legislative politics. Though these are typically multiparty systems that require coalitions to function, it is often assumed that these coalitions will reflect the official governing coalition, and therefore attention is focused on the executive.[3] With few exceptions, these studies tend to treat legislative politics as a residual category and legislative coalitions as a byproduct of cabinet coalitions.[4] Rather than stressing legislative voting behavior through an examination of roll call voting, many of these studies focus on bills as manifestations of coalitions and tend to look at either bill sponsorship or the substance of the bill as a reflection of the ideological compositions of coalition parties. Legislative party delegations are thought to be mere extensions of governing parties. Thus, if party discipline holds, the activities of the governing party are assumed to offer a better indication of the prevalent political dynamics. When legislative delegations depart from their parties' formal position, either with or against the government, it is interpreted as a form of party weakness that is inherently destabilizing for democracy.

While the importance of cabinets in parliamentary systems cannot be disputed, the excessive focus on governing coalitions has meant that the politics of legislative coalitions has received little attention in its own right. This has led to the neglect of important dynamics of legislative politics. For example, it has been shown that even in established and highly institutionalized parliamentary systems, legislative delegations regularly challenge their party's official positions.[5] This is true both for parties in the opposition and for those in government.[6] In addition, the instrument of legislative review has been noted to highlight the independent politics of legislative delegations.[7] Because their work is more concealed from the public eye, legislative delegations develop their own patterns of conflict and cooperation that cannot be reduced to the politics of the executive.

Moreover, even if the focus on governing coalitions were justified in established democracies, it offers little guidance in understanding the more fluid dynamics of legislatures in new or transitional democracies, where the political space is less structured and the connection to government less firmly established. In these contexts, legislative coalitions often follow a different logic than executive coalitions. This is especially salient for first wave democracies given the pivotal role of socialist parties throughout this period, as well as the conflicted nature of these parties regarding governing coalitions. Many socialist parties maintained in their party platforms explicit prohibitions against participation in bourgeois governments.[8] This, however, did not usually translate to the legislative arena, where socialist parties often formed coalitions with bourgeois parties to advance a policy or regime agenda. Ministerial abstention combined with legislative cooperation was in fact a common feature of socialist party politics throughout the early decades of the twentieth century. These dynamics played a decisive role in several of the cases under consideration here.

Finally, it must be stressed that focusing only on the politics of governing coalitions does not offer much insight into the dynamics of governance and legislative capacity. Indeed, for the cases examined here, we find high levels of government and ministerial instability across the board, with frequent changes in cabinet members, coalition parties, and government leadership. Along with this, we also see a high frequency of minority governments. This means that looking at governing coalitions does not give us sufficient insight into how legislatures were able to form viable coalitions and actually pass legislation, since they would have needed to exceed the governing coalition to do so.

Of course, this type of instability has long been associated with the Weimar Republic, which saw eighteen governments in fourteen years, most of which were minority governments (see appendix, table A.1). Many have attributed the fall of the republic to this inability to maintain stable governments. Yet, similar levels of instability characterized many of Europe's emerging democracies at the time. Even in the United Kingdom, where a strong tradition of majoritarianism and a stable two-party system has characterized much of the modern era, we find very high levels of government instability. Between 1832 and

1932 the UK saw thirty-nine different governments, with each lasting an average of eighteen months.[9] Of those, sixteen were minority governments, and another six were coalition governments resting on very loose affiliations among parties.[10] If we were to look at just the interwar period, the UK does look relatively more stable, though that period was also plagued with minority governments. If we look at the broader history of development in the UK, however, we see frequent changes of leadership and many governments that existed without a stable majority in Parliament (see appendix, table A.2).

This of course pales in comparison to France, which between 1870 and 1931 saw eighty-seven governments and over three hundred cabinet ministers (see appendix, table A.3).[11] Notoriously unstable, French governments were a revolving door for political leaders, currents, and ideologies. While such instability far surpasses that of most countries at the time, and could have undermined the regime on several occasions, in France it led to an important innovation—the formalization of a legislative coalition independent of the governing coalition. The Délégation des Gauches, which helped the country navigate a tumultuous period of ministerial uncertainty, emerged in response to a vacuum in executive leadership and existed explicitly as a legislative alliance.[12]

This all points to the fact that even in parliamentary systems, to understand regime stability as well as the function of legislatures, we need to look beyond governing coalitions to a framework that takes seriously legislative coalitions as structures that often function independently of their parties in government. Moreover, the independence of legislative coalitions from governing coalitions did not work systematically in favor of one outcome or another, but rather depended on the specific dynamics of conflict and cooperation that had developed within legislative bodies. In some cases, this yielded more cooperation on policy, and in some cases less.[13] This is all the more reason that legislative coalitions must be considered as an independent force in democratic politics and studied systematically to understand the kinds of politics they produce.

Legislative Coalitions in Presidential Settings

Within presidential systems, the independence of the legislative branch from the executive has made it necessary to study legislative coalitions as a separate force in politics and has led to a significant body of scholarship examining the dynamics of coalition formation. Much of this literature has emerged from the study of the US Congress, and in contrast to work focused on parliamentary politics, this body of scholarship sees legislative coalitions as highly consequential in defining and carrying out policy agendas, but also as transient formations reflecting only the immediate institutional and policy context.

One current of this literature adopts a rationalist orientation toward legislative behavior and tends to be very candidate centered. This approach is characterized by a methodological individualism, focusing on legislators' expected utility from conflict and cooperation. Parties play a secondary role, operating as stand-ins for groups of legislators when convenient and receding into the background when not.[14] Against an older tradition of scholarship that assumed, without always demonstrating, the influence of parties, this vein of scholarship has treated the push and pull of party politics as secondary to individual legislators' self-interest in securing reelection, something best achieved by pursuing desirable policy. In this view, any appearance of party voting would reflect shared ideology rather than a function of the influence of parties per se.

Much of this builds, implicitly or explicitly, on William Riker's foundational works on the logic of coalition formation.[15] In these works, Riker developed a theory of minimum winning coalitions, challenging the work of Anthony Downs, who had argued that parties had an interest in forming the largest coalitions possible. Riker posited three guiding principles that determine coalition formation: the *size principle*, which holds that winning coalitions will be made up of as few people as possible; the *strategic principle*, which holds that players will keep changing their strategies and coalition partners until they can get the best possible payoffs; and the *disequilibrium principle*, which posits that coalition politics is inherently unstable and subject to constant reform. Riker developed this as a general theory of coalitions, meant to apply to coalition formation in many contexts. Indeed, it has been fruitfully deployed to understand governing coalitions in parliamentary settings as well.[16]

Of the various propositions in the theory, the size principle has received by far the most attention, in part because it directly measures a legislature's ability to legislate, and in part because the other principles are thought to follow from size. Its predictions, however, have encountered many problems and weak empirical support. Although Riker maintained that "in social situations similar to n-person, zero-sum games with side payments, participants create coalitions just as large as they believe will ensure winning and no larger," scholars have found that in fact winning coalitions often far exceed the minimum.[17]

Attempts to understand the logic of oversized coalitions have led to numerous challenges, refinements, and modifications of the size principle. Some have challenged the assumptions of symmetry in Riker's game.[18] Others have pointed to the role of uncertainty, particularly in large legislative bodies, as a factor driving up coalition size.[19] Others still have modified it based on the expectation of iterative games rather than single interactions, and many have argued that larger coalitions can have important political effects beyond the immediate objectives.[20] A contrasting theory of "universalism" holds that oversized coalitions may be desirable even if the rewards are not exclusive.[21]

In the context of the US Congress, perhaps the most influential of these modifications has come from scholarship emphasizing the effects of institutional rules on legislative behavior. This approach, which is best understood as a kind of a rational choice institutionalism, holds that because legislative success depends on institutionally defined rules, the structure and size of coalitions will depend on prevalent rules.[22] In *Pivotal Politics*, Keith Krehbiel argues that the size of coalitions will depend on institutionally defined veto players who act as pivots, signaling to fellow legislators when joining a coalition is advantageous. This means that in Congress, supermajoritarian features such as the veto override and filibuster will therefore increase the size of winning legislative coalitions beyond simple majorities.[23] The pivotal politics model has been highly influential and garnered much confirming evidence. It has also helped explain factors that may lend stability to legislative bodies despite the appearance of disequilibrium.

The main challenge to the pivotal politics model has come from scholars who have sought to bring parties back in through different routes. Some have argued that pivotal politics does not negate the role of parties but that it rests alongside party influence. For those espousing a theory of conditional party influence, the power of parties is thought to ebb and flow with the level of internal cohesion within parties.[24] Thus we would expect to see variation over time in how much influence parties have and how much legislative behavior is driven by individual legislator preferences. The most powerful challenge to the pivotal politics model, however, has come from the bolder claim that parties exert influence over policy by way of agenda-setting power. This argument has been offered most forcefully by Gary Cox and Mathew McCubbins, who have argued that since many of the most important institutional rules that influence legislative behavior are controlled by the majority party, institutional influence is in fact endogenous to party influence.[25] Majority parties use their control of the legislative process to limit the range of policy outcomes. In this way, parties act as legislative cartels or procedural coalitions who have an indirect but powerful influence on policy.

The range of approaches to the study of legislative coalitions has offered important insights that get us part of the way to understanding the dynamics of conflict and cooperation in legislatures. Yet, their utility in understanding the *development* of legislative coalitions and how that may affect regime stability is limited by two main factors. First, these approaches are heavily biased toward successful legislation; that is, they have much more to say about cooperation than conflict. In general, approaches relying on an analysis of roll call votes, as many of these studies do, can typically measure only successes. They cannot identify failures, much less near misses. This poses not just methodological but theoretical problems in understanding legislative failure. A piece of legislation that does not garner a winning coalition is relegated to an analytical oblivion. While it might be adequate in many instances to treat the absence of legislative success as a nonevent, there are important occasions in which nonlegislation is in fact a legislative failure. The example of budgets discussed throughout this work is one such occasion. Yet, neither candidate-centered approaches nor party-centered approaches have much to say about what accounts for legislative failure.

Related to this is a second limitation of these approaches, which in various ways adopt a rationalist orientation toward legislative behavior: they lack a sensibility toward time and temporality. In this vein of scholarship, coalitions form through the play of self-interest and are easily reformed once expected utilities shift. Any observed regularity in behavior is the outcome of forces that act constantly on individuals, whether self-interest, party influence, or institutional incentives. In this view, all time is the same; the only things that vary are calculations of gain. Moreover, all votes are independent. How one votes at T1 has no bearing on how they vote at T2. Each vote represents a snapshot—a moment in undifferentiated time. This can be seen most clearly within candidate-centered game theoretical analyses, but it is also a factor within institutional approaches that adhere to a rational choice institutionalism, as they tend to treat institutions as coordinating mechanisms for actors to advance their individual goals.[26] When the institution changes, the behavior is expected to change. The institution itself is epiphenomenal, merely providing a conduit for other forces, which are the true movers. This approach can measure change over time, but time itself is not a factor; the history of legislative behavior does not affect the present or the future.

Party-centered approaches do not escape this kind of ahistoricity. This body of work shifts the unit of analysis but still sees coalitions as a function of parties' strategic calculations, with coalitions easily reformed when party objectives shift. Within this view, parties and intraparty organizations play a big role in driving outcomes, but they too are not constrained by previous rounds of interactions.[27] While parties contain and direct the behavior of individual members, they may shift course at their discretion. Again, in these works, institutions merely define the equilibrium, but their influence is transient. When the institution changes, the behavior is expected to change.

But what if the behavior does not change with the institution? What do we make of that? Patterns of legislative coalitions established in early stages of development are surprisingly sticky, sometimes resisting reform even when the circumstances are most opportune. They can and do change in some instances, but this too does not always correspond to institutional change. To understand both change and continuity, we need a different approach, one that goes beyond analysis of roll call votes and snapshots of legislative successes. Below I articulate a historical institutionalist approach to legislative behavior that is better suited to this task. It builds on an extensive body of literature, which has demonstrated the utility of a historical institutionalist framework in many realms but has been surprisingly absent from the study of legislative behavior. This is meant not to supplant the approaches discussed above, but to open avenues for examining a different set of questions.

A Historical Institutionalist Approach to Legislative Coalitions

A robust and growing body of scholarship has articulated a distinctive historical institutionalist approach to the study of politics. This work shares with other institutionalisms a deep appreciation for the role of institutions in shaping political outcomes.[28] By establishing the rules for strategic interaction and as vehicles for the pursuit of policy agendas, institutions are thought to structure political interactions in consequential ways. In the words of Kathleen Thelen and Sven Steinmo, "Institutions provide the context in which political actors define their strategies and pursue their interests."[29] In this view, institutions are not thought to be determinative of outcomes, but they do define actors' opportunities and constraints, thus delimiting the range of possible outcomes and potentially making some more likely.

Unlike other institutionalisms, the explanatory force of historical institutionalism comes from its use of history and understanding of processes in time.[30] In contrast to rational choice institutionalism, for example, which tends to see institutions as coordinating mechanisms used to generate and maintain equilibria among actors pursuing their individual self-interest, historical institutionalists tend to focus on "how institutions emerge from and are embedded in concrete temporal processes."[31] Self-interest of course plays a role for historical institutionalists, but rather than viewing political actors as rationalist maximizers, they tend to see them as satisfiers whose self-advancement is constrained by rules not entirely of their own making. The options available to actors at any given moment will be defined by the institutional context.

In addition to seeing actions as constrained by institutions, historical institutionalists see them as also constrained by their temporal placement in unfolding processes. Indeed, the signal strength of such approaches, and that which most readily distinguishes them from others, is their treatment of time.[32] In contrast to other approaches, which tend to adopt an undifferentiated view of time, historical institutionalist approaches are especially attentive to the way in which time operates differently depending on the context. This includes attention to tempo and the idea that time can move fast or slowly depending on actors' perceptions.[33] It also places great emphasis on timing, positing that *when* an event happens, and not just the *what* or *how* of its happening, can affect the outcomes.[34] From historical institutionalism we get the analytical perspective that time can be continuous and discontinuous. And we learn about the importance of the "event" in altering structures and influencing subsequent paths of development.[35]

Perhaps most importantly, we get from historical institutionalism a distinctive logic of *historical causation*, which entails many things, but most important for the current investigation is the idea that the causes of the things we wish to understand may not coexist with or move linearly toward the outcomes. Against the rationalist assumption of universal forces acting uniformly at all times, or in other words, that institution X leads to behavior Y in an immediate sense, historical institutionalists maintain that Y may persist long after X has vanished.[36] It is for this reason that institutions established at critical junctures may affect political development so profoundly that changing the institution does not alter actors' behavior.[37] As Paul Pierson explains, "Actors do not inherit a blank slate that they can remake at will when their preferences shift or unintended consequences become visible."[38] This idea has been a central component of historical institutionalist approaches, bringing fresh insight to a great many areas of study.

Given how extensively this approach has influenced scholarship on political development, it is surprising that it has been absent from the study of legislative coalitions. Certainly, important contributions to the study of legislative politics fall within the historical institutionalist paradigm. Most have focused on the development of legislative institutions and specifically on the dynamics of institutional change.[39] But the study of legislative coalitions has been dominated by rationalist approaches of various kinds, leaving us without robust accounts of the development of legislative coalitions over time.[40]

I develop a historical institutionalist approach that aims to explain both change and continuity over time. This begins with recognizing that legislators do not come to the table with a blank slate. For every vote and every decision, they bring with them a history of interactions, both successful and failed, that shape their preferences and condition their expectations of the future. The specific historical institutionalist tools I take up fall within the framework of critical juncture analysis, but with an important modification that makes such analysis more attuned to the dynamics of legislative coalitions. Specifically, I offer *repertoires* as the main vehicle through which legislative coalitions are reproduced or altered, an alternative to both equilibrium and path-dependent models of political development, that can provide a robust theory of change and continuity within a critical juncture framework.

Critical Juncture Analysis: From Equilibrium to Path Dependence to Repertoires

Critical juncture analysis has been central to historical institutionalist studies and is especially helpful in examining institutional origins and their effects. Within this framework, a critical juncture is understood to be a period of relative openness, usually brought on by an exogenous shock to the system, which loosens constraints on actors, allowing them to pursue new strategies. The institutions established within a critical juncture are understood to have self-reinforcing qualities, which means that the institutions themselves can live on past the reasons that gave rise to them and past the point in which they might be considered "rational choices." Critical juncture analysis is a powerful tool in the historical institutionalist toolkit and is employed here to explain why legislative coalitions established at early stages of party formation and political development may have long-lasting effects on coalitional politics and under what conditions they may be altered.

Critical juncture analysis has seen considerable innovation from early articulations, which followed a model of punctuated equilibrium, to later theories, which relied on path-dependent processes and stressed "increasing returns" as the mechanism by which institutions become self-reinforcing after the initial critical juncture. Each in different ways has been vulnerable to what critics have called the "stability bias," that is, the expectation of institutional continuity and lock-in beyond the rapid and potentially radical changes experienced during the critical juncture. Even if not inherently biased toward continuity, such approaches tend not to have a robust theory of institutional change.

The charge of stability bias is most forcefully wielded against early articulations of critical juncture analysis rooted in economic models of punctuated equilibrium, whereby a brief period of radical change, usually brought about by exogenous factors, establishes structures that continue largely unaltered until the next critical juncture. In this view, institutional development is understood as a process of rapid change followed by stasis, which represents an equilibrium point for actors. Equilibrium—that is, the notion that no actors have strong incentives to alter the status quo—is the primary mechanism by which institutions become self-reinforcing. This approach tends to view structures as highly deterministic of actors' choices and the maintenance of institutions as an expression of rational utility-maximizing behavior.[41]

Subsequent work on critical junctures has sought to soften these assumptions, maintaining the importance of critical junctures without overstating the expectation of continuity. They have done so in particular through the framework of path-dependent development. Path dependency offers an alternative mechanism to understand the self-reinforcing nature of institutional development. In contrast to the equilibrium model of earlier approaches, path-dependent critical juncture analysis emphasizes increasing returns, positive feedback loops, and institutional lock-in to understand how institutions become sticky over time.[42] These mechanisms stipulate that once actors choose to go down a certain path, they accrue benefits as a result of continuing down this path (increasing returns); those benefits are reinforced when other actors make similar choices (positive feedback); and once enough actors make such a choice, it is difficult to go back (lock-in).

In this view, critical junctures are understood to be periods of relative openness in which many paths are available to actors, followed by a progressive narrowing of options as a result of actors' choices. According to Pierson, some historical junctures are understood to be "critical" because "they place institutional arrangements on paths or trajectories, which are then very difficult to alter."[43] Similarly, Giovanni Capoccia and R. Daniel Kelemen maintain that critical junctures involve choices that "close off alternative options and lead to the establishment of institutions that generate self-reinforcing path-dependent processes."[44] Others have similarly described such junctures as "choice points" that produce lasting legacies.[45]

The move to path-dependent development represents an important step in the evolution of critical juncture analysis. In contrast to the idea of equilibrium, the self-reinforcing mechanism within path-dependent critical juncture analysis is processual and dynamic. Increasing returns, positive feedback loops, and institutional lock-in develop as processes unfold. Moreover, while early articulations of critical juncture analysis associated with the punctuated equilibrium model tended to view critical junctures as highly determinative of actions, subsequent work has tended to emphasize contingency. Events in a critical juncture are thought not to determine the outcome, but rather to set actors on certain paths that can be altered at later stages, though it becomes increasingly difficult to do so. Importantly, though paths may narrow at every stage, actors have options and continue to make meaningful and consequential choices.

Even with these important innovations, however, critical juncture analysis has been vulnerable to the charge of stability bias; that is, it still tends to lean toward the expectation of continuity. This, in fact, is the source of its greatest strength—that it can show historical or distal causes of outcomes that may not easily be explained by present conditions. The ability to demonstrate continuity, or the legacies of antecedent conditions, has made this a powerful tool of historical institutionalist analysis. Yet, it leaves critical juncture analysis without a robust theory of change. While the emphasis on contingency is helpful and important in breaking away from highly deterministic models of political development, it can amount to a kind of theoretical hand waving that does not provide adequate tools for explaining change. As Capoccia has noted, one of the key strengths of critical juncture analysis—path dependence—is also one of its key limitations.[46]

In particular, the principle of increasing returns, which has been used to explain the stickiness of institutions within a path-dependent process, has been challenged by theories of gradual institutional change. One of the key challenges is that increasing returns do not accrue evenly to all actors, and that, given the differential distributional benefits of any given status quo, there will always be endogenous sources of change. As James Mahoney and Kathleen Thelen have stressed, institutions are "distributional instruments laden with power."[47] This means that institutions will produce winners and losers, and the latter will always have incentives to pursue change.[48]

While many aspects of the gradual institutional change model prevent wholesale combination with a critical juncture approach, its view of the endogenous sources of change is especially helpful for the present study. As will be apparent in the empirical analysis, at no point did efforts to reform coalitions stop in any of the cases examined here. At no point did actors cease to imagine new and unorthodox alliances. While the likelihood of success may have changed with the circumstances, efforts to alter the status quo never stopped. In fact, one of the most striking aspects of the struggle over legislative coalitions is that in each case and in each episode, agents of change emerged with radical challenges to the status quo. This was true not only in cases where the change was successful, but also in the unsuccessful cases. And it was not marginal actors who pursued change but formidable political forces. Whether we look at Joseph Chamberlain's efforts to unite the Conservatives with the Liberal Unionists in a regime coalition in the United Kingdom or Gustav Stresemann's efforts to move the German Liberals toward an alliance with the Left, agents of change were never far from view. Their ambitions were not diminished by antecedent conditions, though their success depended on the broader political context and, specifically, on the repertoires they inherited.

Moreover, the paths available to actors did not consistently narrow. Specifically, the types of coalitions envisioned and attempted remained highly heterogeneous and surprisingly bold. For example, even after the German Liberal Party had come to be dominated by right-wing industrialists, a development that should have foreclosed paths of cooperation with the Left, powerful forces within the party continued to push for a center-left coalition with the Socialists. As late as 1929, this was on the table as a viable option.[49] In another powerful example, even after the French Communist Party had repeatedly denounced the center-left politics of Léon Blum's SFIO (French Section of the Workers' International), another development that might have foreclosed future cooperation, they ultimately found a way to join Blum's National Unity Coalition in 1936.[50] Such occurrences defy the expectations of increasing returns found within path-dependent critical juncture analysis, and especially the notion that certain paths become closed off. The extravagant ambitions of coalitional entrepreneurs should not be so common outside critical junctures. But, in fact, we find that efforts to reform coalitions, often in radical ways, never stop.

These dynamics alert us to the fact that legislative coalitions may be resistant to the mechanism of increasing returns. They typically operate as informal agreements, and even when they are formalized, they do not generally acquire the same level of bureaucratic entrenchment or resource allocation as other institutions, thus eliminating key elements of increasing returns. Moreover, the politics of coalition making is the realm of creativity and entrepreneurship, and we should expect agents of change to emerge regularly. Yet at the same time, empirical analysis reveals a stickiness to legislative coalitions that suggests a stronger role for historical legacies than theories of gradual change might anticipate.

To help navigate the dynamics of change and continuity within legislative coalitions, I turn to the framework of repertoires, which offers an alternative to the principle of increasing returns found within path-dependent processes and potentially a means of moderating the expectation of continuity. I understand repertoires to be modes of thought based on past interactions, which guide choices, making some options seem more desirable and others less so. Repertoires operate through a combination of psychological and cognitive processes that condition actors' willingness to pursue unfamiliar strategies, as well as political and organizational constraints imposed by previous interactions. To borrow from Ann Swidler, repertoires may be thought of as "tool kits," consisting of "habits, skills, and styles," from which people construct "strategies of action."[51] They are constructed from past experiences, either direct or indirect, and inform actors' understanding of the universe of possible actions.[52]

The most significant feature of repertoires for path-dependent theories of change is that they do not close off paths. That is, the choices available to actors are not eliminated as processes unfold. Within the framework of repertoires, all choices are available within even the most restrictive repertoires, making it possible for actors to engage in acts of political creativity, opening paths that may have seemed closed off in earlier interactions. Their likelihood of success, however, is not simply a matter of agency. The dynamics of change and continuity depend on the *flexibility* of the repertoires inherited, a characteristic that emerges from initial conditions of development. The more flexible the repertoire, the more likely are agents of change to succeed in altering the status quo. The flexibility of a repertoire itself can change; that is, a flexible repertoire can become rigid or transformed in other ways over time, but it is this quality of the repertoire, and not the principle of increasing returns, that determines the likelihood of change at any given point.

This view of repertoires helps us understand patterned behavior over time without the determinism of earlier approaches. It also offers an important alternative to equilibrium models of critical juncture analysis as well as path-dependent models, both of which tend toward the expectation of continuity after the critical juncture, as a result of either an equilibrium among actors who are satisfied with the status quo or increasing returns to actors for continuing along a certain path.

I offer a comparison of how actors' choices would be theorized within these different approaches to critical juncture analysis in figure 2.1. A, B, C, and D represent the choices available to actors during the critical juncture. Each approach offers a different theory of change and a different understanding of the choices available at later stages (T1, T2, and T3). With the equilibrium model, the multiplicity of choices during the critical juncture quickly narrows into an institutional equilibrium (C), eliminating all but the prevailing institutional preference. Within the path-dependent approach, the choices gradually narrow based on actors' choices, until they ultimately reach a point of institutional lock-in (BDC, then BC, then C). Within a repertoire framework, all choices remain on the table, but some will seem more desirable (in bold in figure 2.1), and others less so, depending on the nature of the repertoire. And the desirability of different choices may change depending on the flexibility of the repertoire. For example, within a flexible repertoire, the preferred options move from BC to ABC and then to AB, and they may move back over time.

The framework of repertoires is especially helpful in understanding the main empirical puzzle of the book—change and continuity of legislative coalitions—as actors never cease to imagine new and unorthodox alliances, but their success in altering existing coalitions varies across contexts.

Change and Continuity within a Repertoires Framework

To evaluate this model of change and continuity, the empirical analysis of each case is structured as follows: Each case study begins with an examination of the critical juncture of institutional choice that sets in motion the sequencing process, shaping early legislative coalitions and the repertoires of conflict and cooperation they adopt. Within this framework, repertoires could form around either economic management or regime contention, and they could be rigid or flexible. In addition, I examine three subsequent episodes in which the legislative coalitions established during the critical juncture and the repertoires of conflict and cooperation they came to engender could have been altered. The first came at the turn of the century with the rise of labor, via independent parties and as strong currents within parties. The second came after the First World War, which ushered in a period of radicalization within the labor movement and the rise of Communist challengers after the Bolshevik Revolution. The third episode came after the market crash of 1929 and centered on legislators' response to the economic crises and specifically to the challenge of passing budgets. These episodes involve a kind of counterfactual

Equilibrium			
Critical juncture	T1	T2	T3
A			
B			
C	C	C	C
D			

Path dependent			
Critical juncture	T1	T2	T3
A			
B	B	B	
C	C	C	C
D	D		

Repertoires (Rigid)			
Critical juncture	T1	T2	T3
A	A	A	A
B	**B**	**B**	**B**
C	**C**	**C**	**C**
D	D	D	D

Repertoires (Flexible)			
Critical juncture	T1	T2	T3
A	A	**A**	**A**
B	**B**	**B**	**B**
C	**C**	**C**	C
D	D	D	D

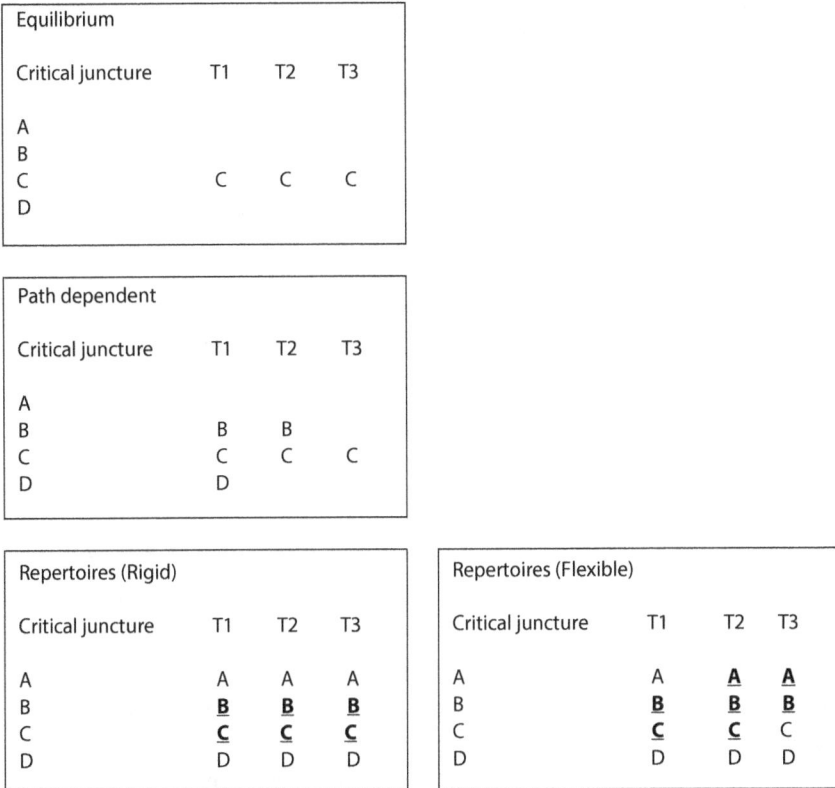

FIGURE 2.1. Theorizing choices within critical juncture analysis

analysis, as all three periods introduced significant opportunities to reform the coalitions inherited from previous stages of political development. As such, they help us assess change and continuity in repertoires of conflict and cooperation beyond the initial critical juncture of institutional choice. Mapping this understanding onto the cases examined here helps account for why we see change in some instances but not in others (table 2.1).

Note that some critical juncture analysis might take each of these episodes as another critical juncture. Such an approach, however, would be unsatisfying both empirically and theoretically. Empirically, while all these episodes involve an element of exogenous change that serves as the basis of the counterfactual analysis, insofar as legislative coalitions are concerned, they do not rise to the level of a critical juncture because most of the actors remain unchanged, and they bring to the table already established repertoires. These were

TABLE 2.1. Change and Continuity in Repertoires

	Critical juncture	Episode 1	Episode 2	Episode 3
United Kingdom	Rigid repertoires form around economic management	No change	No change	No change
Germany	Rigid repertoires form around regime contention	No change	No change	No change
France	Flexible repertoires form around regime contention	Change → mixed repertoires	No change	No change
United States	Flexible repertoires form around regime contention	Change → mixed repertoires	No change	Change → economic repertoires dominate

openings, no doubt, but they did not represent the same open-ended possibilities that existed before repertoires were in place. In addition, treating all episodes as critical junctures leads to a kind of theoretical circularity that can render such analysis unfalsifiable: critical junctures are defined as events that produce continuity and if change happens the juncture is determined to have been not so "critical."

The approach identified here aims to avoid this circularity by identifying a single critical juncture that puts in place repertoires of conflict and cooperation and explains variations in outcomes based on the flexibility of the repertoires. The repertoires identified here are labeled as either flexible or rigid, reflecting the ease with which they can be altered. As a critical juncture approach might anticipate, overall, the development of repertoires tends toward continuity. But crucially, there were also significant and highly consequential instances of change—France in 1903 and the United States in 1896 and 1932. In each case and in each episode, outcomes are a function of the flexibility of repertoires that prevailed in those contexts.

PART II

European Political Development

Part II Introduction

THE REGIME QUESTION AND EUROPEAN POLITICAL DEVELOPMENT

EUROPE IS a useful starting point for the present analysis given its centrality to the emergence of a specific constellation of democratic institutions throughout the nineteenth and early twentieth centuries. The regime question, as it was understood at the time, originated in European struggles to overcome feudal institutions and assert the power of representative legislatures. To be sure, Europe is not the only important or useful site where one can examine nineteenth-century political development, and claims of the centrality of Europe here are not normative but empirical and historically situated. Through both its direct and indirect influence, Europe defined the terms of regime contention for much of the Western world. These terms were translated and reinterpreted for different contexts, but similar dynamics were found even in places such as the United States, with highly divergent conditions of nation-state formation. Thus, in establishing a baseline model for understanding the nature and impact of these struggles, Europe offers an important point of entry.

I pursue the analysis through a comparison of three foundational cases in the study of European political development: the United Kingdom (1832–1939), Imperial into Weimar Germany (1867–1933), and the French Third Republic (1870–1939). The analysis rests on a most-similar case design, which aims to hold constant certain factors that may account for variations in outcomes across cases to assess the impact of the factors being examined—in this instance, institutional sequencing.[1] The temporal and geographic proximity of these cases allows us to locate them in a common historical context. While temporal and geographic proximity should not be taken as themselves controls, they do provide us with key similarities in terms of the originary political, social, and economic structures: all three cases share in common the feudal structures that set in motion the fight over the regime question at the heart of this analysis.

Certainly, these cases display important differences as well, differences that have been the subject of scores of books and articles seeking to explain the fate of democracy in interwar Europe. These differences, however, fall within the category of alternative explanations, some of which are addressed in the introduction, and others within the case study analysis. They do not represent the kind of dissimilarity that would inhibit a most-similar case comparison. Indeed, most of the analyses offering alternative explanations are based on a most-similar case comparison but offer different explanations to account for divergence.[2] And many of the divergences they note emerged over the course of the nineteenth century. At the start of this period, however, most would identify these cases as similar enough that a theoretical intervention is required to explain their divergent paths.

The key intervention in this analysis centers on institutional sequencing at early stages of political development. These cases offer significant analytical leverage as each represents a different mode of sequencing with respect to two key institutions, parliamentarization and mass suffrage: the United Kingdom representing the path of *early parliamentarization;* Germany, the path of *early mass suffrage;* and France, the path of *simultaneous introduction.* The analysis in the following chapters aims to show that each path had important consequences for legislative politics, the efficacy of governance, and regime stability during the interwar period.

Note that the source of inference in this analysis is not only the cross-case comparison, but also, and perhaps more importantly, the within-case analysis, which offers systematic examination of processes over time.[3] This processual analysis is guided by a critical juncture framework, allowing for greater leverage in understanding the impact of initial conditions on subsequent political development. In other words, these cases do not just vary systematically along the lines of the independent and dependent variable; most would agree that with just three cases, this would be a weak source of inference. In addition to the cross-case variation, much of the explanatory force of the argument is derived from within-case processual analysis demonstrating the impact of institutional choice at a critical juncture on subsequent patterns of political development.

3

Early Parliamentarization in the United Kingdom

THE DOMINANCE OF REPERTOIRES OF ECONOMIC MANAGEMENT

ON SEPTEMBER 8, 1931, the British Parliament led by Ramsay MacDonald, the Labour Party's first prime minister, passed a budget incorporating several austerity measures needed to secure the country's credit line and stabilize the economy in the face of a global economic crisis. Among the more controversial measures were plans for reducing unemployment benefits, which were fiercely opposed by a significant faction of MacDonald's Labour Party. In the months prior, he had rejected calls from Labour MPs (Members of Parliament) to invoke an Enabling Act to allow the party to pass legislation and bypass a gridlocked Parliament, in which both Liberals and Conservatives had insisted on reductions to unemployment benefits. In lieu of such extra-parliamentary measures, MacDonald instead agreed to lead a National Unity government, comprising predominantly Conservatives and a few Liberal and Labour MPs whom he convinced to join him. The leader of the Labour Party, unable to identify a coalition on the Left, instead agreed to lead a center-right coalition to pass the necessary measures.

The part of this story that has received the most attention is the fact that MacDonald was willing to go against his own party to join the National Unity government—a move that would get him expelled from the party. What often gets overlooked in this story, however, is the fact that there was a viable coalition available to pass the necessary policies. MacDonald's extraordinary decision to preside over a center-right coalition, viewed by some as a betrayal and by others as heroic, was a singular act of political creativity. But what emboldened him in this move is that he saw an opportunity to get out of the crisis without resorting to extra-parliamentary means. This is a sharp contrast to the position German Chancellor Heinrich Brüning faced in that same year, as he struggled to identify a coalition to pass a budget under similarly dire circumstances. The struggles in the German case are discussed in the next chapter, but what is important to note here is that MacDonald's success and Brüning's failure are not simply matters of political skill. The political development of both countries set them on paths that would strengthen the possibility of legislative success in one case while making legislative failure more likely in the other. In both cases, the key to success or failure hinged on the ability of legislators to form viable interparty legislative coalitions to pass necessary economic policy.

One of the central themes of this book is that the nature and stability of legislative coalitions has its roots in the dynamics of institutional sequencing and party formation at early stages of political development. Nowhere is this more evident than in the case of the United Kingdom. There, the critical juncture of institutional choice, the Reform Act of 1832, saw the introduction of parliamentarization without mass suffrage. This act of early parliamentarization meant that parties emerged in the mid-nineteenth century in a context in which the regime question had been effectively neutralized from their perspective, and substantive policy considerations—specifically regarding management of the economy—were paramount. The nature of initial sequencing and the duration of the institutional configuration of early parliamentarization (1832–1884) meant that repertoires of conflict and cooperation in this case emerged around economic management, and they emerged as relatively rigid repertoires.

These repertoires would be tested in subsequent episodes during which both dominant parties, the Liberal Party on the Left and the Conservative Party on the right, faced existential threats from internal and external challengers, which ignited regime contention. These episodes afforded opportunities to significantly reform legislative coalitions, away from the economic coalitions that had been established midcentury and toward regime coalitions. The first came in the early 1900s when the Liberal Unionist challenge on the Right and the Labour challenge on the Left threatened to move the system to alignment along the regime dimension. The first episode ends with the Home Rule Crisis, which on the eve of the First World War posed one of the most intense regime threats the country had seen. The second episode came after the First World War, when the radicalization of labor and the prospect of the first ever Labour government once again brought back the specter of regime contention. The third episode centers on the budget crisis of 1930 and the challenges of coalition formation during this period. This periodization is illustrated in figure 3.1.

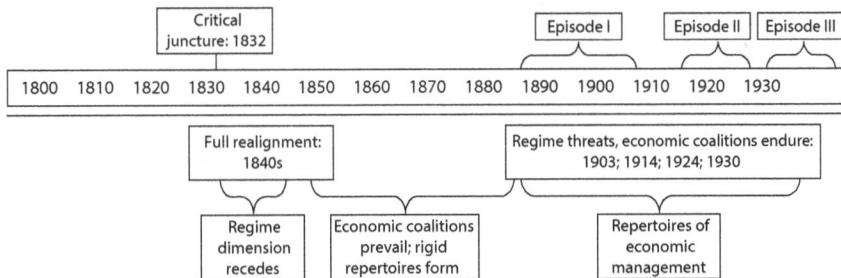

FIGURE 3.1. UK timeline

In the UK, the emergence of rigid repertoires of conflict and cooperation meant that the economic coalitions that took hold in the 1840s endured throughout the nineteenth and early twentieth centuries. In this case, the extended period of alignment along the economic dimension after the introduction of early parliamentarization led to repertoires of conflict and cooperation based in economic management. Despite the pull of regime contention during all three subsequent episodes, the repertoires inherited from earlier periods of party development brought the system back to alignment along the economic dimension, even as realignment *within* the economic dimension introduced entirely new parties, displacing the predemocratic hegemony of Liberals and Conservatives. This was true even of MacDonald's National Unity government, which, despite MacDonald's efforts, did not successfully reform coalitions or significantly alter repertoires, but instead utilized existing coalitions. MacDonald's extraordinary creativity notwithstanding, his was a center-right economic coalition reflecting decades of political development and party alignment along the economic dimension. In the end, democratic stability hinged on the availability of legislative coalitions that could effectively respond to the economic crisis, coalitions that reflected the distinctive nature of institutional sequencing and political development in the UK.

Critical Juncture: Parliamentarization and the Reform Act of 1832

The typical image of political development in the United Kingdom was of a country blindly feeling its way in the dark, charting a path of incremental change that somehow managed to strike the exact right balance to sustain stable and progressive democratic development. It has been noted that in first wave democracies, institutions developed asynchronically at different times and for different purposes.[1] This is certainly true for the United Kingdom. Yet, the assumption has always been that this was part of an organic process of development, in which there was no road map, and actors had to navigate without much guidance. One important fact puts a dent in this image: by the time of the first Reform Act of 1832, there were, in fact, not one but two examples of democratization, the first ushered in by the American Revolution, and not a few years later, another found in the French Revolution. While these models inspired many reformers, for the old guard, they served as a warning of the potential of such movements to uproot the traditional political order, even one as deeply embedded as the British.[2]

In these models of democratization, the two most significant reforms of the day, parliamentarization and suffrage expansion, were brought together for the first time and designated as the key to republican government. They represented examples of revolutionary democratization, not just in their means but in their outcomes—a revolutionary repudiation of the Crown and propertied interests. Particularly impactful was the French example, given the structural similarities of the ancien régime and the British system. It was one thing for a settler colony to reject traditional institutions, but another thing entirely for a great European power to do so. And as revolution gave way to the Reign of Terror, anxiety over the potential ramifications of this mode of democratization grew, as did the conservative backlash.[3]

What the Reform Act of 1832 was intended to do primarily was to temper the revolutionary fervor that had spilled over into England. And it was meant to do this by severing the features of democratization that had been fused in these revolutionary acts, establishing parliamentary sovereignty but holding back the popular franchise. In this way, the asynchronicity of political development in the United Kingdom was not a function of unmanaged development, nor was the resulting institutional configuration a concession to popular demands. In 1832 asynchronic change became a tool of elite management.[4]

This aspect of the Reform Act of 1832 has not been fully appreciated by scholars of democratization because so often it is viewed through the lens of suffrage. We read backward onto 1832 the subsequent events of 1867, 1884, and 1918, casting it as the first step in the country's gradual move toward universal suffrage.[5] Indeed, only by constructing 1832 as part of this trajectory of suffrage expansion can it be viewed as a watershed, since the actual franchise expansion that took place at this stage was rather disappointing, adding a meager 200,000 electors in a country of 23 million.[6] While usefully shedding light on some aspects of democratization, this retrospective reading has also made it hard to understand the events of 1832 on their own terms. It introduces a kind of teleology whereby events in the past are explained by events in the future, suggesting that the same forces that produced the later Reform Acts also prevailed for the former.[7]

As the historical record reveals, however, suffrage reform was not the primary objective of the 1832 Reform Act. To be sure, this was the goal of reformers, and popular mobilization, which at points seemed to have revolutionary potential, surely demanded it. And just as surely, those involved in crafting the reform bill intended it as a means of averting revolution. The years immediately preceding the passing of the Reform Act saw the July Revolution in France and political upheaval later in Belgium, Poland, Prussia, Italy, and Portugal. The threat was a credible one, and it no doubt figured prominently in the minds of political actors. But to say that the Reform Act was intended to diminish the threat of revolution is not to say that it was a concession to reformers' demands for suffrage expansion.[8]

In fact, suffrage expansion in the conventional sense was explicitly weighed and rejected.[9] Instead, the focus was on enfranchising and disenfranchising boroughs and counties, and the only suffrage expansion seriously discussed was that which would be required to equalize the franchise across those units. The difference is subtle but significant. The franchise of individuals would serve the goal of popular sovereignty; the franchise of political units would secure parliamentary sovereignty, and it was the latter that politicians aimed to achieve with the Reform Act. Their goal was to establish Parliament as the foremost representative body of the nation, ensuring that it remained the main intermediary between public opinion and the executive. Thus conceived, parliamentary sovereignty was meant to guard against royal encroachment and aristocratic power on the one hand and to preempt full democratic governance on the other.[10]

To understand better how the borough and county franchise fit into this, consider the broader context of parliamentary government in the UK. At the time of the Reform Act, the relationship between Parliament and the Crown was ambiguous. Over the preceding decades, the strength of Parliament versus the Crown had grown significantly, and Parliament had emerged as the main venue for popular contention.[11] The Crown, however, still retained significant influence over Parliament. The most direct was in the requirement that the Crown assent to all legislation. Though the last instance of a monarch actually denying assent to legislation was in 1708, royal prerogative remained a feature of the English constitution.[12] Its impact has been felt not only in the denial of assent but in the *threat* to deny assent, which the Crown used to block legislation well into the nineteenth century. The mere threat was sufficient to turn back Parliament in matters as critical as Catholic emancipation in 1807 and again in 1829.[13]

Another area where the Crown vied with Parliament was in control of the cabinet. In this respect, a set of reforms introduced in 1780 signaled an important shift from what was considered a nominal cabinet to an effective one, with a more formal role for ministers. Yet, there was no expectation that ministers would be accountable to Parliament, and no means of bringing the government under the control of a representative body. This was an especially pressing matter when it came to the prime minister. Though by 1780 there was already the expectation that the prime minister would fall without the support of Parliament, it was the monarch who appointed and dismissed, and as late as 1834, the Crown attempted to replace a prime minister against the wishes of Parliament.[14]

Perhaps the most powerful and long-lasting feature of the Crown's influence came in the form of patronage for members of Parliament, both direct and indirect. This more than anything was the target of the Reform Act. It had been mitigated somewhat by the reforms introduced in 1780, which limited the funds available to the monarch.[15] This curtailed the Crown's ability to offer patronage for parliamentary "placemen," MPs who were understood to be in government service. These reforms, according to historian Ian Christie, "aimed against the aggregate distribution of government money in all the ways that might directly or indirectly affect the composition of the House or the voting of members." And in terms of direct influence, these reforms were effective. Christie estimates the number of placemen who served at pleasure in 1780 to be 200 out of 585.[16] In 1822 a select committee report put that number at 89.[17]

While the direct influence of the Crown was diminished in this way, indirect influence remained and even grew in this period through the control of nomination and pocket boroughs, where the monarch's support of a few key electors could easily confer electoral victories.[18] These districts typically had very few qualified electors. In some of the more notorious examples, such as Old Sarum and Gatton, there was an electorate of 1.[19] Out of the 514 members representing England and Wales, an estimated 370 were selected by only 180 property-owning patrons.[20] Though the MPs elected in these districts were not placemen in the direct hire of the government, their political fortunes hinged very much on the monarch's approval. In these "nomination boroughs," or "rotten boroughs," as they came to be called, the influence of the Crown could be most directly felt. Well into the nineteenth century, the influence of the Crown was such that the monarch could deliver and take away majorities to any minister.[21] So long as the Crown could control parliamentary majorities in this way, the independence of Parliament was significantly curtailed, and all other powers were of little value.

This feature of the Crown's remaining powers was the main target of the Reform Act of 1832. For decades, the Whig Party had decried this form of influence, which Lord John Russell argued had created for the Crown a system "more completely organized and adapted . . . to the purpose of parliamentary influence" than ever before.[22] Others made similar points that "though it may be true that there were fewer placemen in the house now than formerly, that would not shew that the influence of the Crown had undergone any diminution. The unobserved influence of the Crown out of doors, growing out of the appointment to the various numberless offices under the patronage of the government, was alarmingly progressive."[23]

The public pressure for reform that emerged in the 1830s provided an ideal opening for political forces wishing to pursue a reform agenda. Inspired by revolutions across Europe, protesters called for sweeping parliamentary reforms and significant expansion of the franchise. Parliament took up the issue under duress. But far from envisioning what they were doing as a move toward democratization, the express goal of their efforts was to introduce a reform package that would allow for the preservation of existing institutions. To this end, discussions of the franchise were shifted from the enfranchisement of individuals, which was reformers' intent, to the enfranchisement and disenfranchisement of counties and boroughs according to an elaborate schedule developed by the prime minister in consultation with King William.[24] The only suffrage expansion that resulted was an extension of this scheme and included only that which was necessary to standardize the franchise between counties and boroughs, which until that point had developed in a haphazard manner.

The details of the schedule developed for boroughs and counties reveal a great deal about the goals. It did disenfranchise several nomination boroughs, as had been expected. But that left open multiple seats to be distributed, and the choice of which boroughs and counties would be enfranchised in their stead did not follow uniform logic. Certainly, the largest and most underrepresented boroughs, such as Birmingham, Manchester, and Leeds, received additional representation. But alongside these larger districts one finds towns such as Frome also enfranchised, despite its relatively small population of

12,000, because of the importance of its wool industry. This was the case for Walsall, with a population of 15,000, due to its investment in iron and leather industries. It is estimated that nearly 100 seats were distributed in this manner according to the schedule presented to Parliament.[25]

In fact, uniformity in apportionment was never the goal. This much was made clear by Russell in his defense of the schedule that was developed: "A regular distribution of an equal proportion of members to equal population might be a wise and great scheme, but the proposers of this measure had not thought fit to bring such a plan before parliament."[26] This is because the Reform Act was intended to enhance the representation not of persons but of interests. In doing so, its advocates sought to establish Parliament as the true representative of all interests in the country. Those who spoke in its defense emphasized that the desired reform would make the Commons a true vehicle of national representation, by which they meant not one representing a broad franchise but a multiplicity of interests (particularly manufacturing, which was severely underrepresented). While there was surely a class dimension to this, it also reveals that the goal of the Reform Act was to strengthen Parliament in relation to other bodies that might claim to represent the nation as a whole, particularly the Crown.

The Reform Act of 1832 is widely considered a critical juncture and a turning point in the political development of the United Kingdom. If 1832 is to be considered a critical juncture, however, it is not for the suffrage expansion that was introduced but rather the extent to which it advanced the process of parliamentarization.[27] According to Karl Polanyi, the "parliamentary reform bill of 1832 put an end to the ancient regime."[28] It did so by asserting the power of the Commons over the peers and establishing its independence from the Crown. Beyond this point, never again would a monarch threaten Parliament with dissolution or withhold assent to legislation. The 1830s would see many practices end as power gradually shifted to Parliament. How could such a simple set of changes yield such massive shifts in the practice of governance? The key was always the nomination boroughs. Their elimination stripped the Crown of what it most needed—parliamentary majorities. Without the ability to manufacture them, the monarch had only the ability to override them, and risk losing legitimacy and constitutional standing as a result. The elimination of these nomination boroughs and their replacement with centers of manufacturing power throughout the country gave Parliament political leverage it never had before. To be sure, even after 1832, the Commons still governed along with two unelected bodies under the banner of the "balanced constitution," but in view of the foremost regime question of the day, it had succeeded in achieving parliamentarization. As Parliament increased in power over the next decade, the regime contention ignited by the fight over the Reform Act would subside, giving way to robust competition along the economic dimension. New parties would enter Parliament in a context in which the regime question had effectively been neutralized.

Party Formation and Realignment, 1832–1868

Perhaps the most important aspect of the timing of parliamentarization in the United Kingdom is that it took place not only before suffrage expansion, but also before modern party formation. In fact, parliamentarization helped to catalyze the formation of modern parties at this time. Though parties existed in name prior to this period, they lacked the organizational structure and programmatic features of modern parties.[29] The Tory and Whig label indicated loose affiliations of legislators who identified with a certain ethos, but they valued independence above cohesion. Legislators' political sympathies fluctuated from one topic to the next.[30] Certainly there was a government and opposition as early as 1807, when the Ministry of Talents formed as the first grand coalition in the history of Parliament, signaling a recognition of the opposition. These divisions, however, did not revolve along party lines but rather represented MPs' dispositions with respect to supporting the executive. These dynamics reflected the prevalent influences over parliamentary affairs in early stages of development, specifically the fact that, until this point, the Crown had more power over the electoral fate of MPs than did parties.[31]

The Reform Act of 1832 changed this considerably. By diminishing the monarch's capacity for patronage and disenfranchising most of the pocket boroughs, the act significantly hindered the influence of the Crown. Moreover, parliamentarization increased the significance of parties by enhancing the competitiveness of constituencies and making MPs more reliant on the party. As MPs increasingly had to appeal to electors with whom they had no relationship of patronage, party organization became an important resource, and the role of the independent MP less appealing strategically, even if many held onto the idea of it nostalgically.[32]

The advent of parliamentarization also diminished a major axis of conflict related to the regime question that had defined the previous era. This of course did not happen overnight. In fact, in the initial stages of party formation,

legislative coalitions typically broke down along the lines of regime preferences.[33] The next section examines the immediate postreform period and the
transformations that ultimately resulted in realignment in the 1840s.

Breaking the Hold of Regime Contention: Repeal of the Corn Laws

For over a decade after the Reform Act, the main axis of alignment in Parliament remained along the lines of regime contention.[34] This alignment, inherited from the struggle over the Reform Act, actually gave Parliament a certain
stability and gave political groupings some cohesion, inaugurating what is
typically considered to be the beginning of the two-party system in British
politics.[35] On one side, Tories, Ultra-Tories, and Conservatives cohered
around the need to preserve the traditional constitutional order, specifically
"the defense of the church, of the monarchical constitution, and of the House
of Lords."[36] Opposite this group was a varied assemblage of Liberals, Whigs,
and Radicals, who staked out a political identity in the quest to strengthen the
power of Parliament.[37]

   Economic matters did not at the time represent a major axis of conflict
between government and opposition. This is not to say there were not fierce
disagreements between groups, but the major dividing line that would come
to link conservatism with protectionism and liberalism with free trade later in
the Victorian period had not yet taken shape. According to historian Norman
Gash, up until 1842, these divisions could not yet be detected. Rather, if the
parties offered alternatives on economic matters, according to Gash, "it was
not between Free Trade and Protection, but between two systems of Protection, or it might equally well be said, two modified versions of Free Trade."[38]

   This economic consensus was rapidly and radically disrupted by the sudden
shift of Conservative leader Robert Peel on one of the most controversial
matters of the day—Repeal of the Corn Laws. The Corn Laws and Peel's role
in their repeal reveals the complexity of regime and economic considerations
during this transformative moment. The Corn Laws were protectionist tariffs
imposed on the import of corn and other grains. They allowed for the duty-free
import of grains only when the domestic price reached 80 shillings per unit. In
place since 1815, these laws had protected domestic agriculture from competition, but they also drove up the cost of living throughout the country. This had
the greatest impact on the poor, for whom any increase in the cost of bread—
the benchmark on which subsistence was measured—could be devastating.

Almost as soon as the Corn Laws had been put in place, reformers sought their repeal. The Anti-Corn Law League, formed in the 1820s, aggressively mobilized against the laws, linking them to the hardships of the working classes. A rapid economic downturn in the 1840s heightened scrutiny of the Corn Laws and added fuel to the appeals of repealers. This was compounded by a famine in Ireland, which led to further unrest along both class and nationalist lines.

Under these circumstances, Peel, a longtime opponent of reform, was converted to the cause of the repealers. Historians have contested that this was purely a concession to pressures from below and indeed have questioned whether economic motivations were even at work in the decision. Rather, the historical record strongly suggests that this move, which would ultimately end with a party realignment along the economic dimension, ironically was motivated by a regime logic. Specifically, Peel was trying to head off an agenda of political reform. As the economic demands of repealers went unheeded, they progressed to demands for political reforms. Leaguers converged with Chartists to argue that the only way to secure the protection of workers from economic hardship was direct representation.[39] As mobilization escalated to popular unrest, Peel feared that the lack of concessions on economic reform could lead to political reforms that would undermine the traditional order he had worked his entire career to preserve and what he saw as the raison d'être of the Conservative Party.[40]

Peel moved to repeal against the strong opposition of his copartisans who saw in it an attack on landed interests that would pose a danger to the traditional order. Nonetheless, Peel rejected the appeals to what he saw as narrow economic interests, insisting that the first priority had to be the preservation of the balanced constitution, securing the place of the Lords, the Crown, and the church, along with the Commons.

For Peel, an old Tory who was still steeped in the regime contention of the previous era, the purpose of a conservative party was precisely that—to conserve the established order. It was not to pursue a policy agenda, much less one based on a narrow view of economic interests.[41] Much has been made of Peel's abrupt conversion and his role in the breakup of the party he had helped build. But as historians have noted, Peel's attitude toward parties was highly instrumental.[42] The preservation of the party or even its electoral success was not a goal in itself. Rather the purpose of parties and electoral competition for Peel was to form government and to provide a majority to the executive. And the purpose of a conservative party even more so was to deliver majorities that helped to conserve the established order.[43] This logic, Peel would soon discover, was by the 1840s already obsolete. Many within his party were no longer interested in the old issues of regime contention, and Peel's aggressive reduction of protectionist tariffs would produce a strong backlash that, in the following decade, would lead to a complete realignment toward the economic dimension.

Economic Coalitions and the New Party System

The repeal of the Corn Laws opened the door to a massive party realignment, which would see legislative coalitions increasingly cohere along the economic dimension. Specifically, the rejection of Peel's regime-based logic led to a realignment and the formation of new coalitions that could protect economic interests. The most significant factor in this process was the breakup of the old Tory Party, which created two groups: Peelites, who supported the end of protectionism, and independent Conservatives, who sought to restore protectionist policies. Both groups would remain in limbo for some time in search of a new coalitional politics in Parliament.[44] The Peelites, who ran under their own party label in 1852, would ultimately break off entirely in 1858 to join the Whigs and Radicals in forming the Liberal Party, a coalition that made possible a coherent free trade economic agenda.[45] And independent Conservatives would form the basis of a reinvented Conservative Party, organized around a strongly protectionist economic agenda.

The breakup of the Tory Party would not only reshape the party system but provide it with new leaders. The two giants of Victorian party politics—Benjamin Disraeli and William Gladstone—both emerged from the ranks of the Tory Party. Rising in prominence as they repeatedly clashed over matters of fiscal policy, each brought a distinctive vision of economic management that would become the basis of the Conservative and Liberal Parties. And both were major forces in the emerging economic alignment of the 1840s and 1850s.

Very often clashes between the two came in the context of the annual budget. Peel's repeal of the Corn Laws had begun to define the contours of the economic division with the removal of many (though not all) protectionist tariffs. An equally important matter at the time, however, was the issue of the income tax, which Peel had put in place for the first time in 1842 as a stopgap to supplement government revenues, and which was continued after 1846 to help make up the shortfall from the reduction in tariffs. Within these two forms of revenue— tariffs and taxes—was a more fundamental clash over who should bear the burden of funding the state. Finding a socially acceptable balance had always been a central challenge of legislatures, and this was no less true in this case.

The Peelites—those who supported Peel's repeal of the Corn Laws and would later form the basis of the Liberal Party—prided themselves on being the champions of a balanced society, and fiscal questions figured centrally in that. Since direct taxes tended to fall mostly on the propertied classes and indirect taxes (in the form of tariffs) disproportionately on the working classes, finding a balance between the two was important to their vision. For them, the income tax became a useful tool of fiscal management as it provided another way of finessing that balance through different distributive schemes.[46]

Though by the 1850s Conservatives had accepted the need for an income tax, the way in which it would be implemented was a matter of great contention. The issue blew up in debate over the budget in 1852. A budget resolution introduced by Disraeli, at the time chancellor of the exchequer, proposed a graduated and differentiated income tax, which would establish different income brackets and assign a tax level accordingly. This fairly progressive reform was a surprise coming from the Conservatives. It was a populist gesture aimed to demonstrate the sympathies of Conservatives with the laboring classes, offered by Disraeli in an attempt to co-opt Radical MPs in Parliament.

The measure was strongly opposed by Peelites, who saw in it a dangerous precedent. Specifically, the principle of differentiation, it was feared, would fuel class antagonisms. This was most forcefully put by Gladstone, who delivered an impassioned speech in the Commons. Gladstone's objection was that by codifying income brackets, they would effectively be recognizing classes as the basis for government decisions. In private correspondence he would refer to Disraeli's budget as the "least Conservative in a century."[47] In proposing his own alternatives, he would later maintain that "a consistently developed graduation" had a "direct tendency to communism" by setting "class against class simply as they are high or low."[48] In the final vote, Peelites joined the Whigs to defeat the resolution.[49]

Defeat of the budget in 1852 brought down the government. In its place, a new government would form, for the first time joining the Peelites with the Whigs and Radicals. Gladstone endorsed the idea of forming a "mixed government," a coalition to defend the income tax, but he vehemently denied that there would be any merger of parties and reassured his colleagues that "political questions" would be left open.[50] In other words, the alliance would be forged along economic lines without committing them to the political reform agenda of the Radicals. He stressed that each member would retain their independence on political matters: "By a mixed government, I mean something different from a fusion of parties. A mixed government may honorably be formed, but a fusion of parties could not, with a reserve upon political questions more remotely impending, such as Parliamentary Reform; a reserve to this extent that upon all the particulars and details of such a measure . . . every man will retain an entire freedom."[51] Peelites, who were still fairly conservative in their political outlook, might not have supported the coalition otherwise.

At the head of the new government would be Lord Aberdeen, a Peelite and close ally of Gladstone. Gladstone would be offered the position of chancellor of the exchequer, replacing Disraeli. For Gladstone, the opportunity to intervene in the income tax matter was enough inducement to join the Aberdeen cabinet. The fact that he would be replacing Disraeli as chancellor of the exchequer made the role all the more appealing.[52] Over the course of the following parliamentary session, the line dividing the economic agendas of the Aberdeen Coalition and the Conservatives would become more entrenched.

When the Aberdeen Coalition fell in 1858, it was all but a foregone conclusion that the union between the Peelites and Liberals would become formalized. An electoral pact forged in the following election would result in the official formation of the Liberal Party. In contrast to the Peelites' position in 1852, on this occasion they accepted political reform as part of the coalition's agenda, an important shift that would help put lingering regime contention to rest. This was the final step in the realignment that would unite the advocates of free trade in the Liberal Party against the champions of protectionism in the Conservative Party, thereby establishing the economic dimension as the main axis of party alignment that would define the modern party system.

Alongside the deepening economic cleavage was an equally consequential emerging regime consensus. This was signaled not only by the Peelites' conversion to a reformist agenda, but also, and perhaps even more consequentially, by the Conservatives' embrace of parliamentary reform the very next year. This included, among other things, significant expansions of the franchise. In fact, the first major reform bill focusing on suffrage expansion was offered by the Conservatives in 1859. Rather than fighting suffrage expansion, Conservatives chose to mobilize it in their parliamentary efforts. Though the 1859 reform bill was ultimately defeated, it ushered in a new period in Parliament in which both parties competed over suffrage expansion, looking to recruit growing segments of the population to their party base. Importantly, the enfranchisement of new voters took place along economic and class lines, with Conservatives focused on agrarian labor and Liberals on industrial workers. By the time of the Reform Act of 1867, or Second Reform Act, party alignment along the economic dimension was well established and repertoires of economic management had begun to take hold.[53] The subsequent Reform Acts served to reinforce this, progressively enfranchising voters along economic lines and reinforcing the Left–Right economic alignment within a two-party system.[54]

This economic alignment would be tested in subsequent episodes, as both Liberals and Conservatives faced existential threats from internal and external challengers. These represented moments of regime contention that provided opportunities to reform coalitions away from the economic dimension and toward the regime dimension. The repertoires of conflict and cooperation inherited in earlier periods of party development, however, brought the system back to center-left and center-right coalitions, even as entirely new parties emerged, displacing the predemocratic hegemony of Liberals and Conservatives.

Episode 1: Coalitional Realignment
within the Economic Dimension, 1884–1914

The previous period introduced a party alignment dominated by economic considerations. The first test of this came at the turn of the century and was brought on by two events that presented existential challenges to the existing parties and offered opportunities for realignment—the first was the rise of the Liberal Unionist Party over the question of Irish Home Rule, and the second was the rise of the Labour Party.[55] This episode saw a period of regime contention and possible realignment toward the regime dimension. Yet, the terms of economic contestation established in earlier periods of party development pulled parties back to alignment along the economic dimension, with protectionism and free trade serving as the critical divide. In the end, a form of realignment does take place, but instead of turning to the regime dimension, we see in 1906 a coalitional realignment *within* the economic dimension and parties forming alliances with ideologically adjacent parties along those lines.[56]

The Liberal Unionist Challenge

The question of Irish Home Rule, which had always been in the background of British politics, moved to center stage in 1886 when William Gladstone, head of the Liberals and then prime minister, declared his support for Irish Home Rule, introducing a bill that would partially devolve power to the

Irish Assembly.[57] This move not only was a radical departure for Gladstone, who had long opposed any changes to the Act of Union, but was also a significant disruption of the consensus that had been forged on a matter of significant regime contention. Its resolution had for some time allowed the regime dimension to fade into the background. Gladstone's move to alter this status quo reignited a decades-old controversy over Irish Union, and with it, the place of the church, which was seen as a cornerstone of the English constitution.

Since the 1870s Irish separatists had campaigned for home rule under the banner of the Irish Parliamentary Party. The 1886 bill, devised by Gladstone with little consultation with either members of his own party or the Irish separatists, was offered as a means of preempting a more radical movement for separation. The bill sparked intense divisions in the Liberal Party, with 93 Liberal MPs joining Conservatives to defeat it in a vote of 341 to 311. With the defeat of the bill, Parliament was dissolved. New elections called for June of that year saw the dissident Liberal MPs run independently under the banner of the Liberal Unionist Party.[58] More than seventy Liberal Unionists were elected in that year, a number that would hold steady for the next several electoral cycles, ushering in a period of three-party competition. The fragmentation meant that the period also saw the rise of minority and coalition governments, placing even greater pressure on legislative coalitions to stabilize politics.[59]

The Liberal Unionist Party offers a useful lens through which to examine the strength of party alignment at the time, as it was a party formed along the old lines of regime contention, foregrounding MPs' preferences on the constitutional order and bringing together a group with heterogeneous economic preferences.[60] In many ways it hearkened back to, and was often understood in terms of, the old Whig Party.[61] The electoral success of the party made it pivotal in Parliament and effectively blocked any movement on Irish Home Rule for the two decades of its existence. The informal ties with the Conservatives were formalized in 1895 when the Liberal Unionists joined the Salisbury government to form the first Conservative–Liberal Unionist government, a coalition with conflicting economic interests but common outlooks on the question of Irish Home Rule.

The defection of Liberal Unionists left the Liberal Party quite vulnerable. After decades of Liberal dominance in Parliament, the party suffered successive losses in 1886, 1892, 1895, and 1900, all at the hands of the Conservative–Liberal Unionist alliance.[62] In Parliament, the Liberals could look only to the Irish Nationalists for support, but they were too few to offer any serious reinforcement.

With the Conservative–Liberal Unionist alliance and the Liberal–Irish Nationalist alliance, parties began to increasingly look like they might revert to alignment along the regime dimension. The viability of the Liberal Unionist Party and the potential realignment it represented, however, was put to the test beginning in 1903. A tariff reform bill introduced by Joseph Chamberlain, the Liberal Unionist leader who at the time was serving as colonial secretary, was the pivotal moment. The bill would have restored some protectionist policies, giving preferential terms to the colonies and empowering the UK to retaliate against the tariffs of other countries. A dramatic shift for Chamberlain, a Radical and longtime defender of free trade, the move introduced immediate divisions among the Liberal Unionists and placed pressure on the Conservative–Liberal Unionist coalition government. Chamberlain had gradually been won over to the cause of limited protectionism, seeing in it the only path of economic viability given the increasing German and American encroachment on traditional British export markets and the increasingly protectionist nature of international trade at the turn of the century.[63] He insisted that tariff reform was "the great question of the future, and the one on which party divisions will ultimately settle themselves."[64]

Free trade Liberal Unionists pushed back, forcing Chamberlain to step down. Prime Minister Arthur Balfour managed to keep the Conservative–Liberal Unionist coalition together by adopting a doctrine of "fiscal neutrality," which amounted to inaction and disappointed both sides.[65] In practice, neutrality left free trade Liberal Unionists vulnerable in liberal-leaning constituencies, which expected a firmer commitment to free trade.[66] This combined with a resurgence of protectionist sentiment among Conservatives after 1906 pushed most free trade Unionists back to the Liberal Party. Those embracing protectionism remained independent in the following years but were ultimately absorbed by Conservatives in 1912 when the Liberal Unionist Party disbanded.

The regime logic behind the Liberal Unionist challenge and the economic logic behind its ultimate defeat demonstrate two important features of this episode: first, that there were significant opportunities to reform coalitions and even an attempted realignment; and second, that actors made meaningful choices that kept the existing economic alignment intact. Some of this has been obscured by the fact that those who ultimately broke off were divided along class lines, leading many to interpret Liberal Unionism primarily as a rebellion of aristocratic old Whigs pursuing economic interests.[67] Certainly, there had been long-standing divisions within the Liberal Party between the old Whig faction of landed aristocracy and the Radical faction with its working-class orientation. Yet, these divisions were replicated within the Liberal Unionist Party itself, and as the makeup of the original defectors reveals, this was anything but a class-based party.[68] Rather, it brought together a heterogeneous group united primarily by their orientation toward the Irish question, with its various implications for the political regime. That this group broke off in the first place shows the potential for regime contention to interrupt existing coalitions well into the 1900s. That MPs reverted to their old alignment when economic matters were on the line shows that the economic dimension still dominated legislative politics, and that regime preferences would be subverted to substantive policy preferences when the two collided.

The Labour Challenge

Alongside these events, a separate storyline emerged, one that would reshape the face of modern British politics—the rise of the British Labour Party. This event had the potential to further ignite regime contention, and reactions to the Labour Party at first had much of the acrimony found in other countries at the time. Unlike other countries, however, the alliances that had been forged between the Liberal Party and labor organizations, as well as the relative ideological moderation of labor in the UK, helped to ease the transition from labor as an intraparty organization to Labour as an independent party. The vulnerabilities of the Liberals relative to the Right, at this time reinforced by the Conservative–Liberal Unionist coalition, further motivated them to embrace an alliance with their economic allies on the Left. In the end, this episode too finds parties returning to their economic alignments, with the rise of the Labour Party in fact helping to consolidate politics along the economic dimension. While a kind of coalitional realignment does take place, it merely shifts parties along the economic dimension, rather than reorienting them toward the regime dimension.

The rise of the Independent Labour Party (ILP) was not entirely unanticipated. In fact, it was with this looming threat in mind that the engineers of the Third Reform Act of 1884 approached the design of the new electoral system.[69] While enfranchising a significant portion of the adult male population, the Reform Act also was accompanied by the introduction for the first time of a system of uniform single-member districts, devised by the boundary commission to protect the Liberal and Conservative hold on the electorate.[70] In addition to that, plural voting was retained, weighting the preferences of wealthier electors over the newly enfranchised working classes. It was hoped that this combination of safeguards would be enough to hold off labor mobilization even with the enfranchisement of a sizable working-class electorate.

Certainly, these safeguards made winning elections more difficult for Labour candidates, and in the election of 1895, this was very apparent. More than forty candidates supported by several nascent labor organizations all failed to win election. The experience convinced them of the need to band together for a more coordinated approach to parliamentary elections. In 1899, the Trade Union Congress, long the main organizing vehicle for labor in Parliament and beyond, convened a conference bringing together representatives of the three main parliamentary groups: the Independent Labour Party (ILP), the Social Democratic Federation (SDF), and the Fabian Society (FS).[71] At the conference, representatives of the three organizations passed a motion introduced by Keir Hardie, chair of the ILP, to establish "a distinct Labour group in Parliament, who shall have their own whips, and agree upon their policy, which must embrace a readiness to cooperate with any party which for the time being may be engaged in promoting legislation in the direct interests of labour."[72] This came to be known as the Labour Representation Committee (LRC) and served as a coordinating body for labor's activity in Parliament and electoral mobilization outside.

By 1900 there were already signs that Labour would break through the electoral barriers. The Independent Labour Party, established in 1895, succeeded in the 1900 general election in electing its first two representatives—Keir Hardie, party chair, and Richard Bell. In by-elections in 1902, they added three more to their ranks.[73] Even looking at the seats they contested and lost, their vote share dramatically improved from the previous election, and in several three-way competitions, they placed ahead of the Liberal candidate.[74] In addition to the vote splitting, which worked in favor of Conservatives, the fact that Labour candidates were polling ahead of Liberals presented a significant electoral challenge.

These were not good signs for the Liberals and could have ignited regime contention, as the socialist threat had in many other democratizing countries at the time. Indeed, many Liberals saw the socialist threat as a regime challenge and moved to repair relations with the Liberal Unionists to hold off Labour.[75] Two things helped to contain these anxieties: First, there were already strong ties between the Liberals and Labour. This was aided by the fact that the British labor movement was relatively moderate in its ideological orientation, allowing for such early ties to achieve policy objectives. This feature of the British labor movement and the special status of Lib-Labism in the UK have been well documented and need not be repeated here.[76] What is important to note is that from the very early stages of political mobilization, Labour had established ties with existing parties. Within the framework of this analysis, this means that for both Liberals and Labour representatives, cooperation was very much a part of the repertoires acquired from earlier interactions, repertoires formed around economic objectives. In early stages, many Labour MPs in fact originated in the Liberal Party. Thus, forging closer ties with them would not have significantly altered the status quo.[77] In fact, for some time, there had been electoral coordination within the Liberal Party in the form of local primaries that would allow electors to choose between a workers' representative and a "Liberal-Whig."[78] These cooperative relations, which Liberals had long dominated, gave them confidence that they could endure the rise of the new challengers and benefit from continued electoral cooperation. While until this point the ties were with an intraparty organization, they were not hard to translate to interparty cooperation.

The second factor influencing the Liberal Party's receptivity to Labour was the affinity of their views on free trade and the opportunity to build a stronger legislative coalition along these lines. The defection of the Liberal Unionists in the previous years played an important role in these calculations. Having lost its right wing, the Liberal Party found itself both more electorally vulnerable and freed up to pursue an alliance with the Left. The divisions emerging within the Liberal Unionists in 1903 over trade policy opened the door for the Liberal Party to further exploit the cleavage, taking advantage of the popularity of free trade among the public. The Liberals set out to make trade the central issue of the coming election, and in that effort, they found a natural ally in Labour.

In 1903, Liberal leaders decided to engage Labour in an electoral pact that would allow them to coordinate candidates for their mutual benefit. The pact was negotiated by Ramsay MacDonald, chair of the LRC, and Herbert Gladstone, chief whip of the Liberal Party. Negotiated in secret, the pact would no doubt have caused divisions in both parties. But a landslide victory for the Liberal-Labour coalition in the election of 1906 provided all the justification needed for the alliance. The success of the pact confirmed for both parties the compatibility of their constituencies and the viability of continued cooperation to advance industrial and manufacturing interests. Gladstone maintained that he could find "no material point of difference" between the parties on points of economic policy.[79] In 1906, the LRC would officially take on the label of Labour Party, a shift that had no impact on its openness to cooperation with the Liberal Party. Such cooperation would come to form the basis of Lib-Labism in the UK and, until the Labour Party eclipsed the Liberals in 1923, would serve as the basis of Liberal dominance in Parliament.[80]

As a test of the endurance of repertoires of conflict and cooperation established at the critical juncture, this episode is very revealing. A period that begins with Irish Home Rule as the dominant axis of contention ends with a return to protectionism and free trade taking center stage once again. And what looked like a potential realignment along the regime dimension ended in 1906 with a coalitional realignment *within* the economic dimension. Resisting the pull of regime contention, MPs sorted along economic lines, with protectionist Unionists joining with Conservatives and free trade Unionists coalescing with Liberals, now joined by Labour, to form a coalition, quite diverse in its political ideologies but united by their shared economic interests. The pursuit of substantive policy alliances to serve electoral goals was the essential choice made possible by the path of early parliamentarization. By pushing regime contention to the background, early parliamentarization allowed for legislative coalitions to coalesce around economic policy.

Regime Challenges, Rigid Repertoires: The Parliament Act and the Third Irish Home Rule Bill

The coalitional realignment of 1906 helped consolidate legislative coalitions along the economic policy dimension. Importantly, this did not mean that regime threats were eliminated or that regime contention would disappear. But it did mean that the salience of the regime dimension for the organization of political competition was reduced such that even when regime challenges emerged, legislative coalitions based on the logic of economic management endured. In fact, this period is ripe with regime challenges that could have dislodged existing coalitions.

The first challenge came only a few years after the realignment of 1906, when the House of Lords vetoed the "People's Budget," contending that it excessively taxed property and labeling it a "socialist revolution" intended to undercut the power of the landed aristocracy.[81] The exercise of the veto by this unelected body violated the norm of deference to the House of Commons and demonstrated that existing law provided no means of adjudicating disputes between the two bodies.

This regime challenge was met with solidarity in the House of Commons, with all major parties rejecting the encroachment of the Lords. This solidarity was hard won, as many Conservatives initially expressed support for the Lords and the principle of the protection of property. Had the regime dimension been more salient, legislators might have split on the matter, which touched on a key feature of parliamentarization. Indeed, in other countries, such challenges did lead some legislators to support curtailments on the power of Parliament (and by extension their own power) out of fear that Parliament would become captured by radical interests with the introduction of suffrage. Conservatives who typically enjoyed the patronage of, or whose interests were linked to, the Crown or aristocracy could easily conclude that their interests were better served by these bodies. This can clearly be seen in the German case discussed in the next chapter.

In the UK, however, this potential regime cleavage was held off. Extended negotiations among party leaders led to the Parliament Act of 1911, which affirmed the power of the Commons in various areas of legislation. Importantly, it stripped the Lords of the power to veto "money bills," and replaced the Lords' veto over other public bills with a power of delay. The resolutions represented a skilled balancing of economic interests in the Commons, and perhaps most remarkable in this flareup is that the regime challenge presented by the Lords did not manage to dislodge existing coalitions. Had the regime dimension been more salient, we might have expected to see defections among Conservatives in the Commons, for example. Yet, they too wanted to curtail the Lords' power over money bills and voted overwhelmingly in favor of the act.[82]

Even as this regime challenge was resolved, an even greater threat was on the horizon with the return of the question of Irish Home Rule. There is perhaps no greater example of the rigidity of repertoires of economic management and the resistance of legislative coalitions to change than is found in this episode. Ignited by the Third Home Rule Bill, introduced by the Liberal government in 1912, this crisis, which extended to the eve of World War I in 1914, represented one of the most intense regime-threatening events in the country's history. While the question of Irish Home Rule had always been laced with regime contention due to its implications for the status of the church and, by extension, the Crown, on this occasion what made it especially explosive was the mobilization of Ulster Unionists resisting home rule on the grounds that the Protestant majority would come to be dominated by the Catholics in Ireland. Home Rule in Ireland, they maintained, would be "Rome rule."[83] Ulster Unionists demanded the exclusion of Ulster from the Home Rule Bill and became increasingly militant in their tactics, mobilizing approximately 100,000 local militia members under the banner of the Loyal Orange Order.[84]

It was not the challenge from Irish Unionists that presented the greatest regime threat, however, but rather their influence over British Conservatives and other sympathizers. The crisis came to a head in 1913 when British army officers defied orders and refused to enforce home rule in Ulster. Perhaps most alarming is that Conservative Party leadership did not denounce but appeared to countenance this break with the rule of law. In an infamous speech, Andrew Bonar Law, the leader of the Conservative Party, maintained, "The government are trying to carry through the measure in an entirely unconstitutional way and they cannot be prevented from succeeding unless action is taken by us which goes much beyond ordinary Parliamentary opposition."[85] Elsewhere he had given a blustering speech, arguing that "we shall not be restrained by the bonds which would influence us in ordinary political struggle . . . [there is] no length of resistance to which Ulster can go in which I would not be prepared to support them,"[86] signaling that Conservatives were prepared to operate outside the rules of the democratic game. The regime stakes were stressed in the Liberal camp as well, as one Liberal MP put it: "For the first time in modern English history a military cabal seeks to dictate to government the bills it should carry or not carry into law. . . . This move by a few aristocratic officers is the last throw in the game."[87] Lloyd George put a finer point on it: "We are confronted with the greatest issue raised in this country since the days of the Stuarts. . . . We are not fighting about Ulster. We are not fighting about Home Rule. We are fighting for all that is essential to civil liberty in this land."[88]

Historians have maintained that the Conservative leadership's public position was mostly bluster, pointing to internal correspondence that suggested a more moderate view of the conflict as well as Bonar Law's ultimate acceptance of a compromise that all but ceded the question of home rule. Whether sincere or strategic, the rhetoric surely had the potential to pull actors toward the regime dimension. Remarkably, however, it did not affect legislative coalitions. When the Conservative party appeared to back the regime challenge, and later when Bonar Law capitulated on the question of home rule, had the regime dimension been salient, we might have expected to see disruptions to existing legislative coalitions. In fact, this is precisely what we saw in earlier iterations of the Home Rule Crisis. On this occasion, however, coalitions were unaltered. Legislative coalitions after the introduction of the Second Home Rule Bill and those after the Third Home Rule Bill are compared in figures 3.2 and 3.3.

UK legislative session 23: 1886–1892

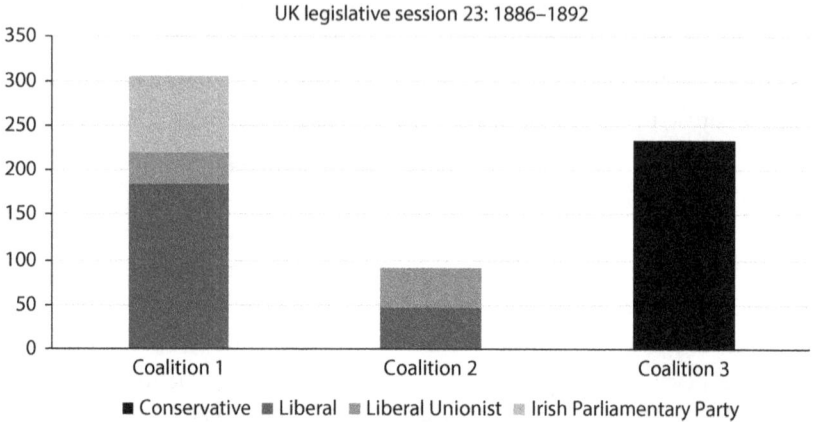

FIGURE 3.2. UK Parliament 23rd session (1886–1892) party coalitions

UK legislative session 30: 1910–1918

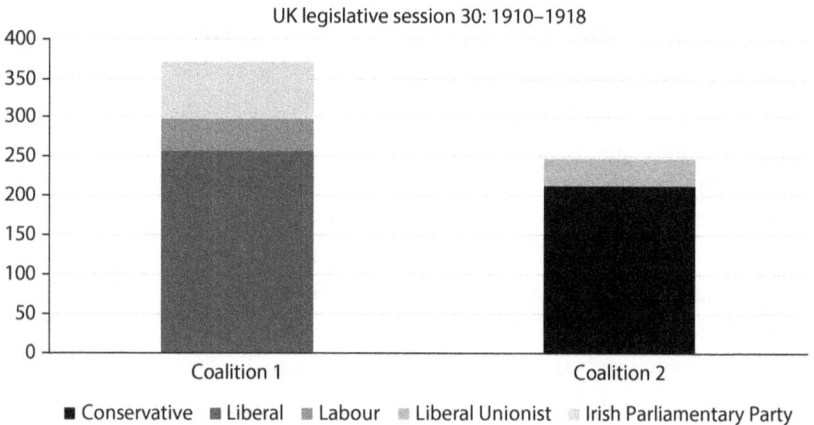

FIGURE 3.3. UK Parliament 30th session (1910–1918) party coalitions

After the Second Home Rule Bill in 1886, we see a notable fragmentation of coalitions that is not resolved until the realignment of 1906 (fragmentation is indicated here by the presence of three coalitions within a two-party system). After the Third Home Rule Bill, there is no such fragmentation, suggesting that coalitions based in legislators' policy preferences had become so entrenched and repertoires so rigid that even intense regime contention could not dislodge them. These rigid repertoires, affirmed on the eve of the First World War, would be critical in navigating the numerous crises of the interwar period.

Episode 2: Interwar Politics and the Rise of Labour

The next big test of party alignment came in the aftermath of WWI. The war had dramatically transformed the political landscape in the UK as it had in so many European countries. The need to acknowledge the contribution of workers and soldiers to the war effort brought a final push for suffrage expansion, which led to the enfranchisement in 1918 of the remainder of the adult male population not enfranchised under the previous Reform Acts, as well as establishing a qualified franchise for propertied women above the age of thirty. This introduced approximately 4 million new voters, many of whom would have gravitated toward Labour.[89] This expansion of the franchise was accompanied by a general radicalization of workers in the aftermath of the Russian Revolution. The rise of Bolshevism fueled fears that the kind of moderation that had long been the hallmark of British Labour would be swept aside in the revolutionary fervor.

These events threatened the regime consensus that had prevailed in previous periods, as well as the alliance forged between the Liberal and Labour Parties. The focal point of this episode would be the rise of the first Labour government in 1924, which greatly strained the economic alliance in Parliament. The endurance of economic coalitions, owing largely to the inherited repertoires of economic management, aided in Parliament's ability to navigate the numerous economic challenges of the interwar period.

The First Labour Government

Against the backdrop of labor radicalization, the election of 1923, in which Labour eclipsed the Liberal Party and emerged for the first time as the second largest party, threatened to ignite regime contention in ways that earlier episodes had not. Complicating this was the fact that the election returned a hung Parliament, in which no party held a majority. In fact, it was the most even three-way split in British electoral history, with the Conservatives receiving 258 seats, Labour 191, and the Liberals 151. With no party holding a majority, a process of negotiation began as to who would form the government. While the choice was between the Conservatives and Labour as the two highest vote-getting parties, it was the Liberals who were the pivotal players since without their support, neither government would be viable.

The decision was not a straightforward one. On the one hand, with two decades of cooperation under their belt, the Liberal and Labour Parties had established important policy linkages. On the other hand, supporting a Labour government for the first time would have meant putting aside lingering fears that socialism, now emboldened by Bolshevism, could have severe material and political consequences. If Soviet Russia was any indication of what such a government might mean, the entire constitutional order was at stake. The Liberal leader H. H. Asquith remarked at the time that his mailbox had been flooded with frantic appeals to "save the country from Socialism and from Confiscation."[90]

Contributing to these anxieties, Labour did not disavow links to Bolshevism and openly displayed signs of radicalization. Labour leader Ramsey MacDonald had written in the wake of the Russian Revolution that "Labour is drawn to Lenin, not because it associates itself with all that Lenin does or stands for, but because he is fighting its battle, and because it is not deeply influenced by accusations of tyranny.... The Russian Revolution has been one of the greatest events in the history of the world, and the attacks that have been made upon it should rally to its defense everyone who cares for political liberty and freedom of thought."[91] Such rhetoric heightened the stakes of a potential Labour government and could have brought with it a realignment along regime lines with the Liberals joining the Conservatives to defeat Labour's chances of forming its first government.

What prevented such a realignment at the time was once again the shared policy objectives of the Liberal and Labour Parties. Specifically, the question of protectionism versus free trade loomed large, and Soviet relations played a central role. The issue of trade with the Soviet Union had been one of the major vectors of conflict since the end of the war. At first, the United Kingdom had joined with the Allies in a blockade of Soviet goods. This had taken a considerable toll, not only because the Soviet Union had been a major market for British manufactured goods, but also because it was the primary exporter of wheat and flax to the United Kingdom. By 1920, the blockade had resulted in skyrocketing food prices and increased unemployment, all while yielding no perceivable political gains.

In 1920, the Liberal government, led by Lloyd George, had resolved to end the blockade and restore diplomatic relations.[92] In defending this move, George stressed its economic importance: "Russia is one of the greatest re-sources for the supply of food and raw materials. The present condition of Russia is one of the contributing causes to the prevailing high prices."[93] Though ending the blockade would remove one of the main instruments avail-able to the Allies to fight Bolshevism, he maintained that "high prices are un-doubtedly in all lands the most dangerous form of Bolshevik propaganda."[94]

In May 1920 the Liberal government embarked on negotiations for the first Anglo-Soviet Trade Agreement, which it concluded and signed in March the following year.[95] It was in fact the first European nation to sign such a treaty with the Soviets.

Almost as soon as the agreement was ratified, Conservatives set out to undo it. Led by the anti-Bolshevik die-hard Bonar Law, a Conservative government took office the following year with the goal of reorienting foreign policy. Under Law's administration, relations between the two nations were characterized by a "frost-bitten diplomacy," with Law going so far as to threaten to cease all relations over Soviet involvement in Asia.[96] Law was replaced by Stanley Baldwin before he could make good on the ultimatum, but the chilly atmosphere remained, and the economic effects were quickly felt, in terms of rising food prices and unemployment. This played a significant role in the Conservatives' loss of seats in the election of 1923. Though still holding a plurality of seats, they lost their majority, setting up the hung Parliament in which Labour was the second largest party and the Liberals held the balance.

Promising to restore and deepen trade relations through a series of commercial treaties, Labour found its popularity surging. Surpassing the Liberals, who had been on a steady decline since their landslide victory in 1906, Labour used their free trade stance to position themselves as a party of government in 1923. At the Labour victory rally after the elections, MacDonald declared: "The pompous folly of standing aloof from the Russian Government will be ended. Ended, not because we agree with what the Russian Government has done— that is not our business. . . . I want trade; I want negotiations; I want a settlement from the coasts of Japan to the coasts of Ireland."[97]

This is precisely what lay in the balance with a Labour government— questions of economic management in which Liberals had a significant stake. And this is what helped retain the traditional party alignment along the economic dimension and resist the pull of regime contention. The promise of a continuation of free trade, which the Liberals saw as essential for economic prosperity and electoral success, was enough to convince them to take the unprecedented step of supporting the first ever Labour government. Liberal support was not without hesitation, but Asquith agreed to support a Labour government "for a few months at any rate, because there was no practical alternative at the moment."[98] They could not have known that Labour would permanently displace them as the party of the Left, but it is significant that Liberals were willing to take the chance to fend off protectionism once again.[99]

Episode 3: The Budget Crisis of 1931

The final test of legislative coalitions came, as it did in many countries, in the wake of the economic crisis of 1929 and over the budget. The election of 1929 gave the Labour Party its first victory, though still not a majority. Labour won 287 seats to the Conservative's 260, with the Liberals again holding the balance with a small but significant delegation of 59 MPs. Labour formed a minority government, which would have been a challenge under any circumstance but was even more so given the magnitude of the crisis it faced and the complex nature of economic management after the market crash and onset of the Great Depression. For the first year of its existence, the cabinet deftly navigated one crisis after another. For most matters it could count on the support of the Liberal Party, though they were not formally part of the government.

As the crisis deepened, however, it became more challenging to identify viable coalitions to support economic policy. By 1931 the situation was dire. The pound had fallen dramatically, and the country was perilously close to exhausting its gold reserves. The government needed an infusion of capital to avoid an economic collapse. The challenge was similar to that which many other countries faced at the time: to keep credit open and satisfy the requirements of American lenders, strict budgets had to be kept, and this required high levels of fiscal austerity. Rising unemployment and high food prices, however, made the austerity measures promoted by the banks difficult to implement without significant backlash and, potentially, political instability.

The government commission tasked with identifying ways to balance the budget issued a report in summer 1931 stating that it anticipated a deficit of 120 million pounds. To raise revenue, it recommended new taxation totaling 24 million pounds. It further recommended a reduction in expenditure of 96 million, which would include a 20 percent reduction of unemployment benefits.[100] The last point would prove the most controversial, as it stirred up clashes over who should bear the burden of the economic crisis. Labour MPs rejected any proposal that would reduce benefits, while Liberals and Conservatives insisted that all should be expected to make a sacrifice for the national good.

MacDonald's minority government required some level of support from either the Liberals or the Conservatives to pass a budget. Several rounds of negotiations, shuffling back and forth between the Labour cabinet and opposition leaders, left the two still far apart. Labour leaders were willing to make concessions on austerity measures amounting to 56 million pounds with no reduction to unemployment benefits. Liberal and Conservative leaders insisted on cuts amounting to 78 million pounds as the minimum necessary to satisfy the bankers and restore confidence. The impasse lasted through much of August that year, with pressure mounting and the press declaring that an economic collapse was imminent.[101] What divided the two groups was essentially 22 million pounds in cuts to unemployment benefits. In one last push to find a compromise, MacDonald proposed a cut of 12 million to unemployment benefits. He took it to the opposition leaders first. They agreed reluctantly, provided that the Bank of England approve the amount as sufficient to restore confidence. MacDonald sought and received this approval and brought it back to the Labour cabinet. The cabinet split down the middle, with eleven supporting the proposal and ten opposed, making it impossible for MacDonald to proceed.[102]

The startling similarity of the contours of the budget fight in the UK to those in France and Germany reinforces both the importance of this moment and the challenge it presented to all governments. And much like those cases, the impasse placed a great strain on legislative politics and confidence in parliamentary government. A final and highly significant point of similarity is that in the UK as well, an Enabling Act was proposed to deal with the crisis.[103] This would have given the Labour government emergency powers, allowing it to bypass Parliament and pass legislation without the support of the opposition. It was argued that this was a necessity for any socialist government given the anticipated hostility of the bourgeois parties to Labour's social and economic agenda.[104]

The viability of such an approach, however, was not clear. There were doubts among cabinet members about whether they could get such emergency powers, as these would still have to be approved by Parliament. As George Lansbury, cabinet minister and one of the chief architects of the Labour budget, remarked on this episode, "[W]e ourselves were only a minority and could not, even if we wished, get emergency power to take over the banks and control credit."[105] In addition, MacDonald could not be convinced to take such a radical approach while other parliamentary options remained. He recognized that while he could not form a majority in support of his budget through the Labour government, a majority could be found among the opposition in support of a budget not so different that would respond effectively to the economic crisis. On August 21, rather than delaying matters further to debate the possibility of extra-parliamentary measures, MacDonald asked the cabinet to resign and called for new elections.

Fear that a center-right coalition passing austerity measures would lead to political unrest, the king contacted MacDonald within days asking him to form a National Unity government, not based in parties but drawing on talents from across the political spectrum. MacDonald accepted this highly controversial proposal and agreed to lead the Unity government—a move that would get him and the handful of Labour MPs who followed him expelled from the party. The Liberal Party too split, with a faction joining the Unity government and the rest remaining independent. In the end, the Unity government was essentially a center-right coalition with MacDonald at the helm. After new elections were held, the character of the coalition was even more clear. The Unity slate swept to a landslide victory with 554 seats total. Of that, Conservatives accounted for the bulk of the coalition, with 470 seats; the Liberals, 35; and dissident Labour, only 13. The National Unity government proceeded to implement its economic program over the ongoing protests of the Labour and Independent Liberal Party.[106]

Even under the National Unity government, some level of emergency power was sought to hasten the process. MacDonald opted for a rather esoteric constitutional feature known as "orders in council."[107] This was different from an Enabling Act in that it would establish councils to make cuts in different services, including education, health insurance, unemployment insurance, and roads. These decisions would have the force of an act of Parliament and would allow the executive to take on legislative functions. In this respect, the British example also represents some aggrandizement of executive power. It was, however, quite different from the use of emergency powers in Germany in that its main purpose was to streamline the legislative process rather than contradict the will of the legislature. Moreover, the move to orders in council had the backing of a National Unity government, comprising nearly 90 percent of the MPs in the Commons. It essentially delegated rather than displaced parliamentary power.

The difficulties encountered in the United Kingdom, France, and Germany at this time bear stunning similarities. But in the United Kingdom, as in France, the ability to identify a legislative coalition to pass a budget—an essential function of the legislature—meant that they could withstand the crisis without endangering parliamentary government. And in the United Kingdom, as in France, the coalitions formed were somewhat unconventional, reflecting the pressure that all governments were under and the need for extraordinary acts of political creativity to identify both a coalition and a set of policies it could support. In this way the crisis served as a stress test for parliamentary government, revealing either the weakness or resilience of legislatures. It is also noteworthy that in all three countries, the UK, France, and Germany, emergency powers were considered, but only in Germany were they fully employed. In the UK, resilience came not only from the short-term strategies of legislators and party leaders, but also from the repertoires of conflict and cooperation inherited from early stages of development that oriented them time and again toward substantive policy coalitions. This meant that there were viable legislative coalitions available to perform a task as simple as passing a budget and one as grand as preserving the integrity of parliamentary government.

In this foundational case of political development, we see the logic of early parliamentarization on display in purer form than in any other. This chapter examines the original critical juncture introducing parliamentarization without suffrage expansion and tests the impact of this sequencing in three subsequent episodes that offered significant opportunities for realignment. I show that early parliamentarization oriented legislative politics toward substantive policy considerations, shaping both the nature of party formation and the dynamics of legislative coalitions. Analysis of legislative politics reveals that within decades of the critical juncture, parties coalesced along the economic policy dimension, forging alliances around the question of protectionism versus free trade. The period in which parliamentarization was established without mass suffrage lasted for over five decades, leading to entrenched repertoires of conflict and cooperation rooted in economic objectives. This did not eliminate regime challenges, but it meant that even intense challenges could not dislodge coalitions established along the economic policy dimension.

On several occasions throughout the nineteenth and early twentieth centuries, regime challenges emerged, threatening to move the party system toward the regime dimension. The most significant were around the issue of Irish Home Rule, which in 1886 and again in 1912 produced intense regime contention. Importantly, however, these periods did not increase the salience of the regime dimension in legislative politics; that is, parties did not move toward alignment along the regime dimension. In 1886 the issue led to a period of fragmentation and then realignment within the economic dimension, and in 1912, despite the severity of the regime threat, there was no significant change in legislative coalitions.

The rigidity of repertoires of conflict and cooperation can also be seen in the interwar period. Two episodes illustrate that despite significant opportunities to reform coalitions toward the regime dimension—first in response to labor radicalization and the formation of the first Labour government, and later in response to the economic crises of the 1930s—established coalitions endured. The path of early parliamentarization in the UK illustrates that regime contention is never eliminated, nor do actors cease to attempt to alter existing repertoires of conflict and cooperation. Yet, the rigidity of the repertoires established in early stages of party system formation meant that these coalition patterns were highly resistant to change. Importantly, this facilitated effective governance even as intense threats to the regime continued to emerge.

4

Early Mass Suffrage in Germany

THE DOMINANCE OF REPERTOIRES
OF REGIME CONTENTION

ON JULY 16, 1930, Heinrich Brüning, chancellor of the Weimar Republic, invoked Article 48 of the German constitution, a measure that would grant
emergency powers, allowing him to rule by presidential decree. This feature
of the Weimar constitution, which would notoriously be used just a few years
later by Adolph Hitler to bring an end to parliamentary government and the
democratic republic, was employed in this instance to overcome a legislative
impasse over something that daunted many legislatures at the time—passing
a budget. It came after numerous attempts to build a legislative coalition to
pass a budget that would allow the country to remain financially solvent after
the market crash of 1929.

The Reichstag at the time faced a crisis similar to that of other democratic
legislatures. To maintain their access to credit and satisfy the requirements of
American lenders, they needed to pass a balanced budget, often including
strict austerity measures. Rising unemployment and inflation, however, created massive dependence on the state, and austerity measures threatened to
plunge large segments of the population into crisis and potentially bring on
political instability. The impasse emerging from this dilemma proved insur-
mountable. After several budget proposals with various permutations offering
concessions in turn to each party and parliamentary group, Brüning moved to
pass the budget through presidential decree. Having failed to identify a legislative coalition on either the Left or the Right, the executive took the matter out
of the hands of parliament in a move that none could have known at the time
would open the door to successive acts of executive aggrandizement, ultimately ending with the permanent dismissal of parliament. This episode was

hardly the exception, however. Such impasses were the norm of Reichstag politics, which Giovanni Sartori described as a system of "polarized pluralism," characterized by high levels of government instability and legislative incapacity.[1]

The analysis in this chapter aims to show that the legislative dysfunction found in this pivotal episode had to do with the repertoires of conflict and cooperation inherited from decades of regime contention in the Reichstag, which pulled parties out of alignment on economic policy and made the formation of viable economic policy coalitions exceedingly difficult. The rigidity of these repertoires meant that, well past the point at which the question of parliamentarization had been ostensibly settled, the regime dimension remained highly salient in German politics. The persistence of the regime dimension had its roots in early stages of nation-state formation, specifically the choice of institutions during the critical juncture of unification and the founding of the German imperial government. In contrast to the British case, where the choice was to introduce parliamentarization with limited suffrage, in Germany, the choice was the opposite, to introduce full manhood suffrage while restricting the power of parliament. As discussed below, this was a deliberate choice of Chancellor Otto von Bismarck, who saw in this institutional configuration a strategy of consolidating conservative power.

The consequence of late parliamentarization was that regime contention would become a central axis of party politics within the Imperial Reichstag, which, owing to mass suffrage, saw an explosion of parties within the first decades of the Reich. The salience of the regime dimension would lead to the formation of legislative coalitions around regime preferences. This was especially consequential for the two pivotal parties of the center: the National Liberal Party (NLP), which moved to the right to join the conservative government coalition, and the Catholic Center Party (Zentrum), which moved left to join the progressive opposition. This period of primary regime contention lasted almost five decades, leading parties to adopt rigid repertoires of regime contention that would carry over to the Weimar period, undermining both legislative capacity and regime stability.

The critical juncture of institutional choice is examined below along with three subsequent episodes that tested the endurance of early legislative coalitions. The first was during the Wilhelmine period (1890–1919), which saw the liberalization of political competition and the rise of the Social Democratic Party (SPD). The second came at the start of the Weimar Republic in 1919, which marked the success of parliamentarization and offered the potential to set aside the regime question to pursue policy-based legislative coalitions. The

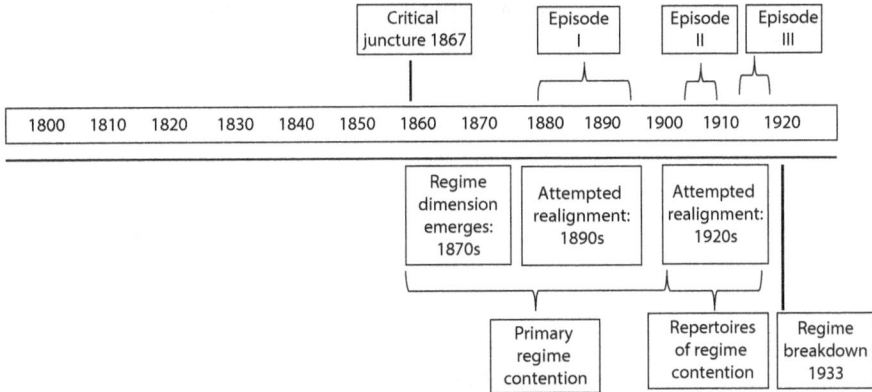

FIGURE 4.1. Germany timeline

final episode came following the market crash of 1929 and centers on the economic crisis of 1930, which demanded an effective legislative response on the
budget. All three episodes introduced significant opportunities to reform legislative coalitions and alter or augment the repertoires of regime contention
inherited from previous stages of political development. And during each period, there were concerted efforts within the pivotal parties, the NLP and the
Zentrum, to bring about a realignment. These efforts ultimately met with
defeat as the regime question resurfaced, returning each party to a state of
misalignment on their economic policy objectives. The pattern illustrates,
however, the highly contingent nature of political development, revealing
both the intraparty struggles that kept open the path to possible realignment
and the stickiness of coalition patterns that pulled parties back to the regime
dimension. The periodization is visualized in figure 4.1.

The *Sonderweg* and German Political Development

The analysis in this chapter presents a challenge to notions of exceptionalism
that have been a common feature of scholarship on German political development. Indeed, Germany represents one of the great purported exceptions
within the study of political development, the other, of course, being the
United States. A long line of scholarship has maintained that German political
development represented a *Sonderweg*, or "special path," in which a distinctly
antidemocratic political culture, rooted in the imperial period and even earlier,
stunted political development and set Germany off on an autocratic path.[2] The

lack of parliamentarization was a central feature of this exceptional path, with suffrage expansion simply providing cover for "pseudo-constitutionalism" and "sham democracy,"[3] but not the basis for meaningful political change.[4] Such accounts see the failure of democracy as a result of these latent antidemocratic attitudes, which finally prevailed in 1933.

Many have challenged this notion of German exceptionalism and the idea that a consistently antidemocratic impulse shaped political development. Some have pointed to the complexity of the democratic landscape across nineteenth-century Europe to show that, given variations in institutional configurations, the German system was not such a great outlier.[5] Others have argued that the lack of parliamentarization did not completely negate democratic politics but altered the dynamics.[6] Going even further, some have maintained that an incremental parliamentarization was in fact taking place, pointing to the numerous challenges to executive power within the Imperial Reichstag, especially in the decade preceding the First World War.[7] Important as these critiques of the Sonderweg have been as correctives, they have also been criticized for obscuring important continuities in German history.[8]

This analysis falls in line with the challenges to the Sonderweg thesis but takes a historical institutionalist approach that seeks to understand both continuities and discontinuities as part of a complex process of development. I take the view that the German path, while distinctive, was not exceptional. The explanation offered here explains outcomes as a function of meaningful choices made by actors at pivotal points, rather than a constant immutable undemocratic impulse. At each point, antecedent conditions structured the options via the formation of repertoires of conflict and cooperation but did not determine the choices of actors. Indeed, the initial sequencing of institutions came about through the decisions of key actors during a critical juncture in which many other choices were possible. Further, while I make no claims about whether political development in the imperial period was in fact leading to further parliamentarization or full democratization, I identify significant moments of regime contention across and within parties, indicating that regime preferences were far from settled. The implication of this perspective is that Weimar fell not simply because forces opposed to democracy prevailed, but because the choice of institutions at a critical juncture structured politics in ways that would lead to repeated legislative failure and undermine governance, opening the door to those undemocratic forces. I begin with an examination of the critical juncture of institutional choice to show both the open-ended possibilities offered within this period and the contingency of outcomes.

Critical Juncture: Bismarck
and the Misalignment of Politics

The path of early mass suffrage in German political development originates with the decision to establish full adult male suffrage in 1867 as part of the constitution of the North German Confederation, well before parliamentarization. This period bears all the markings of a critical juncture, with high levels of contingency and uncertainty. The political upheaval brought about by state formation and unification unsettled established patterns of political interaction and ushered in a period of brief but radical openness in which actors' decisions were less constrained. Only in this context could such an expansive measure of suffrage expansion have been contemplated. Going into this period, the idea of universal male suffrage was rejected by the entire political class. Its ultimate inclusion came down to a magnificent gamble on the part of Chancellor Bismarck, who saw in suffrage expansion a strategy of political dominance.

How Bismarck came to be won over to the side of universal manhood suffrage is not a straightforward matter. The measure introduced in the constitution in 1867 was more extensive a franchise than that which existed in any of the German states prior to unification. It was the suffrage of 1848, which was quickly rolled back, and which Bismarck had previously referred to as "anarchy."[9] The change in his views came about from a combination of external and internal influences.

External influences included three historical cases that served as laboratories of institutional choice, each offering a different pattern of sequencing. The first was the model found in the French Revolution, in which parliamentarization and full adult male suffrage were introduced simultaneously. Indeed, this was the implicit model for most at the time, either as something to guard against or to aspire to. For Bismarck and other conservative forces, it was certainly something to guard against given the radical transformations it ushered in.

Another model available at the time was that of the British, who introduced parliamentarization prior to suffrage expansion. While this institutional configuration moderated the outcome of suffrage expansion, it also consolidated liberal dominance in the political order—an outcome that Bismarck also wished to avoid. In observing the operation of limited suffrage in Prussia, Bismarck came to believe that limited suffrage bolstered middle-class interests and liberal dominance.[10] He was emboldened in this belief by a most unlikely influence— that of Ferdinand Lassalle, leader of the Social Democratic Party. Lassalle had long advocated for universal suffrage and removal of the three-tier voting system for the Prussian Diet. According to Lassalle's analysis, this institutional configuration had not only hindered the rise of the Social Democratic Party, it had propped up the Progressive Party, which according to Lassalle was the main enemy of social democracy. There he found an unlikely ally in Bismarck, who also saw the Progressive Party as a threat.

Lassalle and Bismarck met secretly on many occasions and exchanged several letters between 1863 and 1864.[11] Lassalle convinced Bismarck that limited suffrage was the salvation of the Liberals and that its eradication would be their downfall. These unlikely bedfellows would soon part ways, as it was clear that Bismarck had no interest in extending the liberties Lassalle thought essential for socialism to thrive (freedom of assembly, freedom of the press, and other liberalizing measures), but Lassalle's analysis of the situation in Prussia remained a powerful influence on Bismarck's thinking.

This led Bismarck to adopt a different strategy: embracing full manhood suffrage while curtailing the power of parliament. A model for this institutional configuration was also available for Bismarck's benefit—that of Napoleon III, who had successfully used universal suffrage in France to win over the public to the side of monarchical rule and to overcome the liberalizing forces of the Second Republic. Bismarck expected this configuration to similarly lead to an advantage for conservative forces in Germany. He told the Prussian House of Commons, "Universal Suffrage, doing away as it does with the influence of the Liberal bourgeoise, leads to monarchical elections."[12] He believed that the rural population would support the conservative parties, and since nearly 70 percent of the population at the time still resided in the countryside, this would further consolidate his domination of the political scene.[13]

The relationship between Lassalle and Bismarck is not only a historical peculiarity, but evidence of the open-ended possibilities contained within this critical juncture. Several options were available to actors at the time. And far from a structurally determined byproduct of an undemocratic predisposition, the choice was a highly contingent one in which both prodemocratic actors and antidemocratic actors played decisive roles. The outcome coming out of this critical juncture could not have been anticipated going in. And when Bismarck proposed it to the Constituent Assembly, they were indeed caught off guard. This was especially true of the Liberals, who had preferred a more modest franchise along with full parliamentarization.[14]

It has been argued that the German Liberals' reluctance to accept suffrage reform was a function of the structural weakness of the middle classes.[15] Note, however, that their resistance to suffrage was no different from the position of the British Liberals at the time of the First Reform Act. In fact, the British model was precisely the precedent German Liberals had in mind. Prominent Liberals such as Benedikt Waldeck warned that the masses were not yet ready for suffrage, arguing that a system of national public education needed to be put in place before the franchise could be safely conferred, raising the specter of socialism if the suffrage were too quickly extended.[16] Some even proposed an educational requirement, which, given the cost of education at the time, would have functioned as a property qualification. One member made the stakes clear that "universal, equal, and direct suffrage is intended to be used against our middle class in order to break its power."[17]

Despite these reservations, Liberals were powerless to stop suffrage expansion, which was adopted as part of the constitution of the North German Confederation and carried over to the Imperial Constitution. This episode was not entirely without victories for the Liberals. The status of parliamentary power in the new constitution was mixed. The Reichstag had the right to initiate legislation, though not unlike other representative bodies at the time, it shared this power with an unrepresentative legislative body—the Bundesrat, a heavily conservative federal council composed of representatives of the states.[18] Perhaps even more important, the Reichstag had the right to reject legislation.[19] This included the annual budget, which gave the Reichstag important leverage over imperial finances and was seen as a significant victory for Liberals.

The Reichstag did not, however, have any power over government formation or approval. This was not for lack of demand for such powers. At least two major proposals to establish ministerial responsibility—that is, to make government ministers responsible to the Reichstag—were debated and defeated.[20] In addition to this, and perhaps what undercut the power of the Reichstag most, was that the chancellor was granted the power to dissolve the Reichstag. This power of dissolution, and more so the threat of dissolution, played an important role in Reichstag politics. In the end, what prevailed was a form of constitutionalism rather than parliamentarism.[21] Alongside manhood suffrage, a national assembly was established whose assent was necessary for legislation but whose powers and independence remained significantly curtailed by the executive.

As this analysis demonstrates, the choice of institutions cannot be explained as a function of immutable antidemocratic impulses or a kind of German exceptionalism. Indeed, actors' preferences were forged *during* this critical juncture and displayed learning from outside examples. It was a highly contingent outcome, an experiment even, but one that would have significant and lasting consequences, leading quickly to party alignment along the regime dimension and, relatedly, to a misalignment of the two pivotal parties of the center on economic policy.

Early Party Formation and the Salience of the Regime Dimension

The choices made at this critical juncture would have important ramifications for party development, introducing a regime cleavage that would come to dominate Reichstag politics and over time would pull all parties into alignment along the regime dimension. The issue of parliamentary power would quickly manifest as a source of intense regime contention within the Reichstag. The common impression of the Imperial Reichstag, especially under Bismarck, is that of a docile body where debate was muted and contention limited.[22] It was anything but. From the start, parties clashed with each other and with Bismarck over a range of issues, the most volatile of which were those with implications for parliamentary rights and the regime question more generally. How does the regime question emerge in an unparameterized parliament? Often indirectly. The main wedge issues that emerged in these early years were over the military budget and taxation, areas where the chancellor sought to encroach on the Reichstag's right to review the federal budget, and areas that saw a strong and increasingly assertive effort not only to defend the rights of parliament but to expand them. Both issues would be recurring themes and vehicles of regime contention throughout the imperial period, joined in the 1880s by fights over colonial policy, which also provided an opening for challenges to the government and assertions of parliamentary power.

These challenges, of course, took place in a context where the Reichstag existed completely at the whim of the chancellor, who could dismiss it at any time. Indeed, the threat of dissolution was constant under Bismarck and later chancellors. On four occasions they made good on these threats, dissolving the Reichstag and calling for new elections in the hopes of obtaining a more compliant set of legislators. This happened in 1878, 1887, 1893, and 1906; each involved a significant clash over parliamentary power and increasingly assertive challenges to the executive. Far from hindering dissent, however, the threat of dissolution became part of the political game. The chancellor would dissolve when faced with serious challenges, and the opposition would use his actions to further their electoral campaigns—a badge of honor rather than the punishment it was intended it to be.

Why was there any opposition to parliamentarization in the Reichstag? The conflict between the chancellor and the Reichstag might not be surprising, but the conflict within the Reichstag requires further explanation. Why would parliamentarians not want greater power for themselves? In other words, why was there a regime cleavage at all? Certainly, some of this was ideological, as support for the monarchy remained strong among some conservative elements. But more than that was the threat parliamentarization posed as a result of mass suffrage. Suffrage transformed the prospect of parliamentarization from one that would give Liberals and Conservatives more power in relation to the Crown and the executive to one that could result in ceding all power to the masses.

The calculus here did not differ significantly from that in other cases. In the British Reform Act of 1832, for example, the push for parliamentarization aimed to strengthen Parliament vis-à-vis the Crown, while also establishing Parliament as the main vehicle for popular sovereignty, mediating between the masses and government. This balance was only possible in the UK because of the limitations on the franchise, which reinforced the dominance of Liberals and Conservatives. Without those safeguards, it was argued, the German parliament would become a tool of the masses. Rather than empowering parliamentarians in the Liberal and Conservative camps, it would lead to their decimation. As early as the 1870s, the main argument offered against the move to enhance parliamentary powers was that once the Catholics and Socialists had reached their full strength, parliament would become their instrument.[23] This was long before either group had much of a presence in parliament, as their growth had been hindered by the policies of the *Kulturkampf* and the antisocialist laws. But even at their height, these repressive systems faced significant opposition. And once they fell, it was feared, the Catholics and Socialists would rise.

These concerns drove the regime divide within the Reichstag from early on. At the epicenter of this divide were the German liberals. Originally unified under the Progressive Party, the liberals split in 1867 over the issue of parliamentarization in the constitution.[24] One faction, maintaining a staunch commitment to parliamentarization, remained within the Progressive Party. A second group broke off to form the National Liberal Party (NLP), adopting a position of accommodation toward the new constitution. They did so for the sake of establishing productive relations with the government and, perhaps more importantly, for the sake of national unification, long a goal of liberalism.[25]

NLP leadership maintained that this was not a capitulation on the question of parliamentarization, but rather a pragmatic outlook that a constitutional structure would provide opportunities for incremental reform.[26] This point was made most emphatically in 1867 by Eduard Lasker, the NLP leader who just a decade later would turn against the party over the issue of parliamentarization. But in these early years, he stressed the importance of unification and constitutionalism, which he was confident would lead to full parliamentarization in due course. "The source of all freedom is the security of the state," he maintained. "Only when Germany's full unity will be achieved, only then will freedom be gained. Not just for Germany but for all Europe. Until then, we remain subject to freedom's worst enemy, armed peace."[27] He argued for progressive development of the constitutional state, emphasizing that explicit constitutional laws brought less change than simple legislation.[28]

Lasker's pragmatism would quickly be put to the test. In fall 1867, Bismarck introduced a bill requesting an open-ended military budget, or an *Aeternat*. It would be the first of many confrontations on this issue. The constitution had taken the military budget out of the control of the Reichstag but also had set a fixed budget for military expenditures. Moving to an open-ended budget would have been a significant encroachment on the powers of parliament. First, the military budget already made up 70–75 percent of the federal budget.[29] Expanding it further would have reduced the funds available for other expenditures, and with it, the Reichstag's sphere of influence. Beyond that, an open-ended military budget would have effectively put the entire budget at the disposal of the chancellor, rendering meaningless the budgetary powers of the Reichstag. Protests immediately emerged from the Progressive Party and the left wing of the NLP, insisting that anything above what had been fixed would have to be subject to annual review along with other federal expenditures. At the head of the challenge to the military budget was Lasker, who maintained that the opposition was based not on the content of the legislation—they were willing to consider additional funds for the military—but on the grounds that it evaded the Reichstag's right to review.[30] The chancellor, wishing to avoid a split with the Liberals, at this time the largest party in the Reichstag and his closest allies, agreed to a compromise, setting a budget for four years.

The compromise avoided confrontation on this occasion but set the stage for many more, each of which would see the chancellor and the National Liberals move farther apart. They would clash again over the military budget in 1871 and in 1874.[31] On each occasion, Bismarck sought unlimited spending, and on each he was turned back. Ultimately, an agreement was reached that the Reichstag would review a *Septenate* military budget every seven years. Leading each of these challenges to Bismarck was Eduard Lasker, whose initial optimism persuaded Liberals to join Bismarck, and whose opposition became increasingly influential within the left wing of the party. The animosity between Bismarck and Lasker was well known and often on public display.[32]

Throughout the 1870s, the NLP held a dominant position as the largest party in the Reichstag, pivotal to the passage of any legislation. Therefore, the reformist impulse within the party was highly consequential and a source of significant irritation for Bismack. Tensions finally came to a head in 1877, when Bismarck introduced a tax bill that once again occasioned constitutional strife. In the constitution, the right to levy taxes was granted to state governments. The federal government could only implement tariffs.[33] Thus the attempt to levy federal taxes encroached on states' rights, but it also would create a source of revenue for the federal government out of reach of the Reichstag, and therefore it threatened to undermine the powers granted to them over imperial finances.

This led to an extended and highly volatile confrontation in the Reichstag, where the left wing of the NLP, led by Lasker, engaged in every kind of obstructionist tactic to block the bill and pressure their party to turn against Bismarck.[34] This time, however, the demands of reformers grew. In addition to insisting on Reichstag review, they made the acceptance of any tax bill conditional on the appointment of a finance minister who would be responsible to the Reichstag.[35] This, for the first time, moved the proparliamentarization camp from a defensive position to the offense, explicitly demanding reforms that would increase the powers of parliament. That the aim of the challenge was greater parliamentarization is clear from the internal deliberations of the NLP.[36] Negotiations would continue for months, with the NLP straining to keep the party together and find a solution that would satisfy both the government and reformers. Bismarck openly blamed Lasker for undermining the productive relationship between the NLP and the government and threatened the dissolution of parliament.

The opposition to this expansion of parliamentary power came not only from Bismarck, but also, and critically, from Conservatives and the right wing of the NLP, who insisted that the issue of parliamentary reform should not be linked to any piece of legislation. Repeatedly they warned reformers that those who sought the increase of parliamentary power should be prepared in the not too distant future to see it come under the control of the Catholics and Social-ists.[37] No doubt some of this resistance came from a weakness of party organization that plagued Conservatives and National Liberals, but in these early stages, it was a much more rudimentary analysis based on numbers fuel-ing fears that, once the parties of the masses reached their full potential, they would come to control the Reichstag.[38]

In the end, only a small part of the tax bill was passed; the rest died in com-mittee, but so too did demands for ministerial responsibility. Frustrated with the emboldened and uncooperative Liberals holding up his legislation, Bis-marck dissolved parliament and launched a vicious nationalist campaign tar-geting the NLP and seeking to rally friends of the Reich against Catholics and Socialists, whom he identified as *Reichsfeinde*, or enemies of the Reich.[39] The NLP suffered considerable losses during the election and was reduced from 128 to 99 seats. The loss meant that they were still the largest party in the Reich-stag, but only by a very slight margin.

In the next session, Bismarck returned with a bill introducing a collection of protectionist tariffs, containing a unique combination of industrial and agrarian protection. The bill, which would come to notoriously represent the "marriage of iron and rye" in the German political economy, served both substantive and strategic goals.[40] With Bismarck's tax bill defeated, the tariffs were needed to provide a new source of revenue for the federal government. But the combina-tion of industrial and agricultural protection was meant specifically to drive a wedge between the right wing of the NLP, which was generally protectionist, and the left, which supported free trade.[41] Bismarck's intention was to marginal-ize the left-wing reformers and be rid of their parliamentary challenges.

Bismarck did in fact succeed in dividing the party, but not on matters of economic policy. On the question of protectionism, the Left was ready to ac-quiesce, but again Lasker returned with the demand for ministerial responsi-bility as a condition for accepting any tariff outside the purview of the annual budget.[42] In the end, Lasker succeeded in convincing the party leadership to vote against the tariff bill, but the defection of the right wing left them without numbers and leverage. The tariff bill passed, leaving in its wake a very divided party. NLP leadership blamed the left wing for its loss of power and stature. Continued efforts of the left wing to push for greater parliamentary control were met with staunch opposition. In 1880 Lasker would lead the left wing, a third of the party at this point, to break off, first forming the Liberal Union (LV) and ultimately merging with the Progressives, now under the party label of the German Progress Party (DFP).[43]

The New Alignment

The merger with Lasker's group revitalized the progressive opposition. This group, which would come to be referred to as the Left Liberals, would anchor the proparliamentarization coalition in the Reichstag for the next decade.[44] In this coalition, the Left Liberals were joined by the Catholic Center Party (Zentrum) and the nascent Social Democratic Party (SPD). Their partners on the Left were quite familiar with being in the opposition, but ironically, they were rather ambivalent about the question of parliamentarization at first.[45] For the Zentrum, the official position of the party was in support of the monarchy. This was quite common at the time for confessional parties. Many, like the Zentrum, would later be converted to Christian democracy, but their early ideologies usually favored monarchies.[46] For the Socialists, the ambivalence similarly stemmed from ideology, but rooted in the particular brand of revolutionary Marxism they embraced—a doctrine that rejected participation in bourgeois governments and questioned the utility of parliamentary politics in achieving revolutionary goals.

Over the course of the 1880s both parties would be fully converted to the cause of parliamentarization, and by the turn of the century, they were leading the charge. For the Zentrum, the transformation had much to do with Bismarck's antagonistic politics and the policies of the Kulturkampf. The need to defend the Catholic minority from persecution pitted the party against the government almost as soon as the Reichstag was convened. The first of these policies came in November 1871, with the Pulpit Laws, which attached criminal penalties to electioneering by members of the Catholic Church. This attack on political Catholicism was soon followed by a cascade of laws that sought to limit the influence of the Catholic Church in German society, including laws targeting education policy, regulation of marriage, and the operations of Jesuit orders.[47]

Initially, the focus of the Zentrum was on liberalization rather than parliamentarization—removing the restrictions on political Catholicism and working with the government to dismantle, piecemeal, anti-Catholic legislation. These early struggles transformed the party, however, instilling both a deep mistrust of Conservatives and an affinity to other embattled constituencies within the Reich.[48] By the 1880s the Kulturkampf was already in retreat, but over the course of these battles, a new left wing in the party would come to share the opinion of the Left Liberals that, without parliamentary power to check the government, they had no means of securing any policies, and all victories were uncertain. This group regularly joined the opposition in advocating for democratizing reforms and greater parliamentary power.[49] They came to see parliamentary government as the only reliable protection against the government's arbitrary exercise of power and an alliance with Left Liberals and Social Democrats as the most promising route to this goal. By the late 1880s, this left wing of the Zentrum would represent a sizable faction, making it impossible for the party, as it had done on many occasions, to sit on the fence on matters related to parliamentarization.

For the Socialists as well, parliamentarization was not at first a goal because serious doubts existed within the socialist movement about the utility of parliamentary participation altogether. The struggle between reformist and revolutionary ideologies, which could be found within socialist parties across Europe, were especially intense among the German Social Democrats.[50] At the heart of these struggles was the question of whether participation in bourgeois governments would help or hinder the cause of social transformation. Ideological reservations about the utility of participation in bourgeois governments were compounded by several factors particular to the German context. First, the lack of strong parliamentary power, and especially the power to compel the government, reinforced the idea that this was a mechanism of social control rather than progress. Wilhelm Liebknecht, one of the movement's leading ideologues, famously opined that parliament was not a place where "history was made" but the "stage for comedy."[51] Second, for the Socialists, the political institutions of the empire fell short not only of parliamentarism, but also of constitutionalism, since even basic constitutional protections were not afforded to them. Declared enemies of the Reich by Bismarck, Socialist members of the Reichstag experienced open hostility and were regularly subjected to censure and arrest. Finally, the activities of socialist organizations were heavily curtailed by the antisocialist laws. These restrictions did not stop their electoral participation but transformed elections into a place of agitation rather than contestation.[52]

The official shift in the Socialists' position began with the Erfurt program of 1891, which aimed to balance radical theory with practical politics. For the latter, the party adopted an aggressive stance in favor of parliamentarization. Karl Kautsky, who anchored the revolutionary camp, was crucial to the transformation. In 1893 he published a pamphlet defending the utility of representative government in service of social transformation and integrating theories of republicanism within a Marxian socialist framing.[53] It signaled a shift in the parties' position—an embrace of its parliamentary role, which had grown considerably as the size of the party's Reichstag delegation had grown, and most importantly, a commitment to greater parliamentarization as a central goal in achieving its vision.[54] By the early 1900s the SPD would be a driving force behind the push for parliamentarization.[55]

The transformations of the 1880s produced a coalition of Left Liberals, Catholics, and Socialists that would form a formidable opposition in the Reichstag and a powerful force for parliamentarization. The first significant act of cooperation was the defeat of the 1887 military bill. The Left Liberals led the charge, now with Ludwig Bramberger at the helm after the death of Lasker in 1884. At stake in this was once again the right of the Reichstag to review the military budget. In this clash, Bramberger reminded his colleagues of the history and stakes of this conflict. Bismarck, he maintained, "has longed to achieve this goal for twenty years, with diplomacy, with power, with authority, with everything that is available to him. . . . Such a moment now appears to have come again. . . . Not to let this majority come into being, which blindly subordinates itself, and . . . abandons the empire and the entire welfare of the nation, that is our task."[56]

The opposition of the Left Liberals and Socialists was assured. But what made the defeat possible was that they were joined by the Zentrum. In the past, the Zentrum had stayed out of fights with clear parliamentary implications, focusing instead on liberalization, that is, on securing the political rights of the Catholic minority. By 1887 they had dismantled most of the anti-Catholic laws established by Bismarck. The Kulturkampf was defeated. But the experience had already convinced the left wing that liberalization would not be secure without parliamentarization. They succeeded in convincing party leaders to join the opposition. With the defeat of the military bill, the Reichstag was dissolved for the last time by Bismarck. The following election would see enhanced electoral cooperation among the new opposition bloc and a consolidation of the new alignment.

In these early stages of party formation, we find the beginnings of the coalitions that would form the core of the proparliamentarization, prodemocratization movement throughout the Wilhelmine period and into the Weimar Republic—what would come to be known as the Weimar Coalition. The peculiarities of this coalition were recognized from the start, and early party leaders struggled to keep it together.[57] On both sides, detractors referred to the alliance as "unholy," uniting the forces of secularization and the forces of political Catholicism to an extent that would not be seen anywhere else in Europe.[58] It speaks to the strength of the regime cleavage that during this formative period it trumped both the economic cleavage and the state-church cleavage, one of the dominant cleavages resulting from the national revolution.

On the Right as well, a new coalition would emerge. The same election of 1887 that saw the formation of a regime coalition on the Left also saw one emerging on the Right. This coalition consisted of traditional conservative forces, but they were joined now by the NLP. Having lost its left flank, the party sought to strengthen its ties to the Right and to the government, paving the way for this at the Heidelberg Conference in 1884, in which the party committed itself to support the government position in "areas of shared interests," particularly in the fight against the enemies of the Reich.[59] An electoral pact formed in 1887 would further tie the NLP to the right in a union known as the *Kartell*.

Roots of Economic Misalignment

This period ends not only with a realignment, but with what can be considered in comparison with other developing party systems at the time a *misalignment* of politics with respect to the economic policy dimension. This was especially true for the two pivotal parties of the center: the NLP, which moved to the right to join the conservatives, and the Zentrum, which moved to the left to join the Left Liberals and Socialists. This misalignment ran counter to trends in other emerging party systems at the time, which were consolidating along the economic dimension.[60] Along this spectrum, liberal parties typically made common cause with labor in pursuit of free trade policies that would benefit their respective constituencies.[61] Catholic parties typically aligned with conservatives in pursuit of protectionist policies that would benefit their respective constituencies, the most prominent example of which was the Belgian Catholic Party.[62]

Initially, both parties styled themselves in a manner similar to counterparts elsewhere in Europe: the National Liberals embraced liberalizing reform in both the political and economic realm, while the Zentrum party adopted a conservative economic agenda to serve its agrarian population as well as an official position in support of the monarchy, also consistent with Catholic parties. Yet, party development in the shadow of the regime question pushed both parties to prioritize regime preferences over other considerations.

Some have argued that the transformation of these two parties was so complete that this might not be considered a misalignment—that in fact the NLP *became* a conservative party, and the Zentrum *became* a liberal party. For example, James Sheehan has argued that the NLP's identity changed at this time.

He writes that even in regions with strong industrial interests such as the Ruhr, "the officials and businessmen who dominated party life increasingly saw themselves as a basically conservative political force with interests and values like those of the traditional right. Agrarians, *Mittelstand*, and industrialists all identified the pursuit of their own specific interests with the defense of German society against Social Democracy."[63] Similarly, Margaret Lavinia Anderson has argued that the Zentrum during this period was transformed into a liberal party, that it not only came to act as such, but also began to think of itself as a liberal party.[64]

Certainly, both accounts contain important insights, but they do not adequately appreciate differences *within* the parties. For example, while it is true that the right wing of the NLP embraced conservative political and economic views, moderates still remained a strong force within the party and would work throughout the Wilhelmine period and into the Weimar Republic to return the party to alignment along economic interests and to a coalition with the traditional parties of the Left. And while the left wing of the Zentrum was ascendant during this period, a strong faction continued to see it as a conservative party and worked to move it to the right. These intraparty conflicts suggest that the actors also understood themselves to be in a state of misalignment. Neither the identities nor the alignments of these parties were settled at this time, and struggles continued throughout the Wilhelmine period over both.

Episode 1: The Wilhelmine Reichstag and Liberalization without Parliamentarization

The year 1890 marks the end of the Bismarckian era and the beginning of a period of relative openness under Kaiser Wilhelm II. The antisocialist laws were allowed to expire, and many of the laws targeting Catholics were repealed. The easing of prohibitions on assembly and association was an important step in the liberalization of politics, which opened the political space to broader competition for the first time in the country's history. This was bolstered by a reduction in election fraud and the introduction of the secret ballot in the late nineteenth century.[65] Though voter suppression and fraud were still a crutch of the old guard, these obstacles to electoral competition were no longer enshrined in state policy.[66]

In this analysis, this period represents a test of the endurance of the repertoires of regime contention established in the Bismarckian era, as it introduced significant opportunities to reform coalitions. Perhaps the most significant change is that the liberalization of politics led to the rapid rise of the Social Democratic Party (SPD), which by 1912 was the largest party in the Reichstag.[67] This presented both a challenge and an opportunity for the Liberals to realign along the economic dimension. For the NLP, which under Bismarck adopted a progovernment position, making common cause with the Conservatives in defense of the empire, there was an opportunity to shift to the left. And indeed, there was a concerted push to achieve this. An alliance with the Social Democrats, with whom the Liberals shared overlapping electoral and economic interests, would have allowed it to pursue a free trade policy that would have served its commercial base and put it more in line with other liberal parties on the Continent. It also would have allowed it to reunite with left liberal parties, forming a bloc "from Basserman to Bebel," as was the vision of the forces of realignment, referring to the leader of the NLP and the leader of the SPD.[68]

For the Catholic Center Party (Zentrum) as well, this liberalization represented an important opening. Throughout much of the Bismarckian period, the party had positioned itself in opposition to the government parties. Though economically, it had more in common with the conservative parties, which similarly served rural constituencies with an interest in protectionist policies, the need to defend the Catholic population drove it into the opposition and led it to adopt a liberal stance on regime questions. The end of the Kulturkampf and the rise of the socialist threat would have offered an opportunity to move to the right, and there were in fact strong elements within the party pushing for a realignment along the economic dimension.

In addition to a test of the durability of coalitions established during the critical juncture, this period also provides a more precise test of the sequencing argument, because what the Wilhelmine era ushered in was precisely "liberalization" as Dahl would term it, an expansion of civil liberties that allowed increased political participation. Had the misalignment of the Bismarckian period been a function of the illiberal character of the regime alone, we would expect to see the regime dimension abate as these policies were reversed.

Analysis of the Wilhelmine period, however, reveals the misalignment to be persistent and even deepening within the party system, and especially within the NLP and the Zentrum, the two parties that could most directly affect a realignment. By the end of the Wilhelmine period, the NLP found itself again with the government coalition, and the Zentrum was not only in but often leading the opposition. As in the previous period, the regime question often entered the Reichstag indirectly. The issue of the military budget continued to be a major flare point, and in this period, a new and related issue of colonial policy would emerge as another wedge on which the proparliamentarization coalition could focus their efforts. To understand the dynamics driving these patterns, I examine the development of the two pivotal parties of the center, the NLP and the Zentrum, during this period.

The Rightward Drift of the National Liberals

For the NLP, 1890 presented both a challenge and an opportunity. The party had seen a steady decline in electoral support under Bismarck. Its vote share had decreased from 47 percent in 1871 to 23 percent in 1898, ground lost primarily to the SPD in urban centers. By 1890, the party was competitive only in small towns and semirural districts ceded by conservative partners in the Kartell.[69] These trends were alarming to most party members and empowered the younger members to push for greater liberalization of the party platform and a realignment to the left. Such a realignment would have brought it into line with other liberal parties on the Continent and allowed it to pursue economic policies through cooperation with the Left Liberals and SPD.

The first steps toward this came in 1891 with talk of a united liberal party, along with efforts to forge a "liberal Kartell" to coordinate candidacies among members of the NLP and the Left Liberals.[70] NLP leader Ernest Basserman warned that the defenders of liberalism could not afford to remain splintered and called for greater liberal unity.[71] In 1898 a group from within the NLP known as the Young Liberals pushed for a center-left alliance and advanced an agenda of "social liberalism," which would include suffrage reform, acceptance of inheritance taxation, and stronger ties with the working classes.[72]

This internal struggle within the NLP moved the government to act to preempt any realignment and keep the liberals within the conservative coalition. A campaign of Sammlungspolitik, literally "the politics of banding together," was launched to rally the bourgeoise parties. The rhetoric of the campaign borrowed heavily and self-consciously from Bismarck's precedent, but with a distinctive twist calibrated to the new political realities of the time.[73] This new formulation would focus entirely on the Socialists as the enemies of the Reich while bringing the Catholics into the government fold. The reason for this was simple: as of 1890 the Kartell parties no longer controlled a majority in the Reichstag. Any anti-Socialist coalition would have to include the Zentrum.

The campaign, launched under the leadership of Chancellor Bernhard von Bülow, was ostensibly aimed at defending the Reich's naval fleet. The defeat of two navy funding bills at the hands of the SPD was the rallying point for "friends of the Reich."[74] In appealing to the bourgeoise parties, Bülow attempted to strike a balance between industrial and economic interests. The government's platform called for "resistance to pure free trade and one-sided commercial interest . . . but resistance also to *excessive* protectionism, *compromise* between opposing interest[s] of trade and agriculture."[75] These concessions were enough to convince NLP party leadership to remain within the government coalition rather than risk an uncertain future with the opposition. At the party congress in 1900, the same Ernest Basserman who had called for liberal union a decade earlier revised his position, maintaining that continuing with the conservative Kartell would allow the NLP the greatest flexibility in its alliances, leaving open the possibility of tactical alliances with the Left Liberals, but rejecting cooperation with the SPD.[76]

That the alliance would undermine the NLP's economic interests was revealed as early as 1902 in a struggle with the government over a tariff overhaul. In the previous decade, the Liberals had chipped away at many of the protectionist tariffs introduced under Bismarck. This reduction in tariffs led to a boom in industry and clear economic benefits for the party's constituencies.[77] Now the government asked for their cooperation on a host of tariffs that would essentially undo this. To remain in good standing with their Kartell partners, the NLP complied. Party leadership strained to offer economic justification for their support of such openly protectionist policies.[78] NLP leaders such as Hermann Paasche instead reached for nationalist arguments, invoking the recurring theme of Sammlungspolitik. Each NLP member who spoke argued for the need for agriculture and industry to join on policies that would diminish "social democratic influences."[79] In the end, the NLP was able to solicit some concessions in the way of protection of domestic industry, but, by and large, the tariff reforms were seen as a coup for agrarian and *Junker* interests.

This episode reveals how repertoires of conflict and cooperation had deepened. In an earlier period, the NLP could maintain a traditional liberal position on economic matters while supporting the government on the regime question. On this occasion, however, economic interests were directly subverted to regime preferences, signaling a further stage in the party's evolution. And while this did not foreclose a path to center-left cooperation for the NLP, it did further entrench repertoires of conflict and cooperation based in regime contention. Despite the opportunities for realignment introduced in the 1890s, the NLP continued within the government bloc throughout much of the Wilhelmine period. The NLP's support of protectionist tariff policies ran counter not only to liberal doctrine but to the interests of many constituencies that would be served by a national liberal party.

Evolution of the Zentrum Party

The year 1890 also presented an opportunity to reform alliances on the Right. The easing of anti-Catholic Kulturkampf policies in the Wilhelmine period provided an opening for the Zentrum to embrace a conservative agenda more in line with its economic interests. Additionally, the campaign of Sammlungspolitik, which had closed the door to realignment for the NLP, opened one for the Zentrum. Throughout this period, the government ran a dedicated campaign to court the Zentrum and solidify an alliance of the bourgeois parties.[80] The growth of the party in this period helped to cement its pivotal position in any coalition.[81] By 1890 it was the largest party in the Reichstag, a position it would maintain until it was eclipsed by the SPD in 1912.

Within the Zentrum, a sizable contingent was in favor of realignment. This included both right-wing reactionaries, such as Peter Spahn and Count Hertling, and members of the Cologne wing, such as Karl Bachem, who aspired to establish the Zentrum as an interconfessional party.[82] To secure the support of the Zentrum for the government position, Chancellor Bülow offered several concessions, including the repeal of the Jesuit laws. One of the remaining codified features of the Kulturkampf, the Jesuit laws empowered the government to regulate the activity and residence of Jesuits and affiliated orders.[83] With these coalition-building compromises, Bülow was able to sway the Zentrum to join the government coalition from 1898 to 1903.[84]

This temporary realignment might have lasted were it not for the persistent efforts of an insurgent left wing under the leadership of Matthias Erzberger, who worked to establish an alliance with the Left based in their shared interest in promoting democratic reforms. Rejecting offers of protection from the government, Erzberger explicitly identified parliamentarization as the only reliable safeguard of the interests of the Catholic minority against government excesses.[85]

Beginning in 1906 Erzberger launched a full assault on the government, seeking to drive a wedge between the Conservatives and the Zentrum. Taking advantage of a series of scandals in the German colonies in southern Africa, Erzberger challenged the government's exclusive control of colonial policy. The scandals revealed severe mismanagement and abuse of power in the colonies that became a national embarrassment to Germany at a time when the

government was working to bolster its international standing.[86] Erzberger succeeded, over the vocal opposition of the Zentrum old guard, to convince the
party to vote against two consecutive funding bills to provide for extra troops
in the colonies. This led to both a parliamentary crisis and a crisis within the
party, as such budgetary requests were usually pro forma.

Much of the focus for Erzberger and his supporters was on the need for
oversight, specifically the desire to expand Reichstag control over colonial
affairs. Within the Imperial Constitution, all matters of foreign policy, including colonial administration, fell within the powers of the executive. Erzberger
insisted on the right of the Reichstag to weigh the causes of the uprising in
deciding on the budget, effectively asserting discretion in colonial management. Playing on the nationalist sentiment at the heart of Sammlungspolitik,
he maintained that only direct parliamentary oversight could safeguard imperial interests and insisted on the need to "legislate colonial affairs to ensure
their efficient management in the interest of the Reich."[87] He further argued
that such powers were essential to the principle of popular sovereignty, which
it was the responsibility of the Reichstag to uphold. "If we do not with all
determination insist on this first and highest right of popular representation,
we do not know where we are headed."[88] Beyond the rhetoric, there is much
to suggest that parliamentarization was the primary goal of the challenge, and
historians have maintained that the colonial scandals merely provided the
opening for a more fundamental challenge over the powers of parliament.[89]
A seemingly narrow struggle over foreign policy was opportunistically transformed into a significant moment of regime contention.

This episode marked a critical turning point for the Zentrum, with the steadily
increasing influence of Erzberger and the left wing pushing it more squarely
within the opposition.[90] For Erzberger, parliamentarization was the only way to
correct for an "unaccountable bureaucracy" and the mismanagement he argued
had besieged the state.[91] A series of subsequent scandals only helped increase
the political and rhetorical force of his message. As the left wing ascended, opportunities for cooperation with the conservatives became more elusive.

In this way, a period that began with significant opportunities for the
Zentrum to reform coalitions and join with Conservatives in pursuit of a
shared economic agenda ended with the party leading the opposition and reinforcing alignment along the regime dimension. The implications of this for
long-term political development are of a dual nature. Although undoubtedly, the
evolution of the Zentrum into a champion of parliamentarization was crucial to
the political transformation that brought about the Weimar Republic—indeed

it was a central figure in the Weimar Coalition—its position still left it in a state of misalignment in the party system with respect to economic policy, an issue that would pose ongoing challenges for coalition building and governance.

Weimar Continuities and Discontinuities

As the previous analysis has shown, legislative coalitions during the Wilhelmine period were heavily influenced by parties' orientations toward the regime question. Though this period saw considerable liberalization, in the absence of parliamentarization, the regime question remained at the center of legislative politics. In fact, these acts of liberalization intensified the regime contention by further catalyzing party formation and consolidating party positions along the regime dimension.

In 1918 another important opportunity arose for parties to pursue new alliances. Years of war and military defeat had fundamentally altered the political landscape, giving rise to new political forces on the Left and the Right. The burden of reparations and reconstruction placed economic issues at the center of Reichstag politics. And most notably, the introduction of parliamentarization as an essential feature of the regime transition removed an issue that had been a central vector of conflict in the Imperial Reichstag.

Of course, the advent of parliamentarization did not in itself eliminate the regime question. Conservative parties in particular would continue to contest the regime, and while engaging with the institutions of democracy, they never officially accepted them. The introduction of parliamentarization was consequential, however, especially for the two pivotal parties of the center. The NLP, now reconstituted as the Deutsche Volkspartei (DVP), adopted an accommodationist position with respect to the democratic republic. Under the leadership of Gustav Stresemann, the party abandoned its regime aspirations in favor of a more conventional liberal platform and sought out closer ties with the Left Liberals and the Socialists. For the Zentrum as well, this period presented important opportunities. Parliamentarization, one of its top priorities in the imperial period, was successful; the threat to the Catholic minority had largely been eliminated; and Catholics across the republic now enjoyed the full rights of citizenship.

These developments would free up both the DVP (former NLP) and the Zentrum to pursue policies more in line with their economic interests. Thus, for these two parties, which were key to any coalition, the period presented important opportunities to remedy the misalignment of the predemocratic period. And within both parties, powerful forces were pushing to bring about a realignment and leave behind "the old questions" of the regime.[92] Despite this, however, the period ends with both parties reverting to familiar repertoires of conflict and cooperation. The legacies of the imperial period continued to impede realignment along the economic dimension, leading to repeated legislative failure and executive encroachment.

Rigid Repertoires and the Challenge of Realignment, 1918–1932

The struggles within the DVP and Zentrum had a significant effect on coalition dynamics in the Weimar Reichstag. The period begins with the near hegemonic power of the Weimar Coalition, essentially a regime coalition, which consisted of the SPD, Zentrum, and the successor to the Left Liberals, the Deutsche Demokratische Partei (DDP). After that, we see movement back and forth between two types of coalitions, each representing an attempt at realignment along the economic dimension. One was a center-right coalition of the bourgeois parties, including the Zentrum, the DVP, and the successor to the Conservative Party, the Deutschnationale Volkspartei (DNVP). This Bourgeois Coalition dominated from 1920 to 1924 and again from 1924 to 1928. Another was a center-left coalition, referred to as a Grand Coalition, consisting of the SPD, Zentrum, DVP, and DDP. Grand Coalitions dominated for a brief but highly consequential period in 1924, then again from 1930 to 1932. Notably, in each period the Zentrum and DVP also moved back and forth, effectively driving the coalition patterns (see figure 1.7).[93]

The vacillation tracks with important changes within each party. For example, in the very early years of the republic, the Zentrum looked to the Left—its partners in the Weimar Coalition—for allies. With its regime objectives achieved, however, many voices emerged within the party seeking a realignment that would be more in line with its economic interests. The choice of Wilhelm Cuno to lead the party in 1922, a businessman and former director of the Hamburg-America line, and the Zentrum's role in the coalition of bourgeois parties during the first legislative period reflected the desire for a reorientation of the party and a realignment that better served its economic interests.[94] These forces would reappear throughout the life of the republic, often urging closer ties to the Right. The limiting factor was the DNVP, the reconstituted Conservative Party. Despite their shared economic interest, the inheritance of mistrust between the Conservatives and the

Zentrum made cooperation difficult and forming a government nearly impossible.[95]

For the DVP as well, the coalition patterns reflect important trends within the party, and a desired reorientation to the left. Much of this had to do with the unmatched skill of Gustav Stresemann. Widely considered one of Weimar's greatest statesmen, he carefully navigated the complicated terrain of party antagonisms to bring the Liberals closer to realignment. Both instances of Grand Coalitions in government were engineered by Stresemann.[96] He also delivered the support of the DVP for such controversial measures as the Dawes Plan, the Locarno treaties, and a host of other legislation aimed at promoting a liberal trade policy and peaceful relations with the West.[97] He struggled all along with right-wing industrialists who wished to return the Liberal Party to a conservative alliance. These struggles are reflected in the movement of the party back and forth between center-left and center-right alliances. His death in 1929 opened the door to a right-wing takeover and with it a rejection of cooperation with the Left, but for a time, there were strong indications that a new kind of political calculus was on the horizon for the party.

The ongoing misalignment of these parties on economic issues had important consequences for legislative politics. First, it led to the splintering of economic interest parties beginning in the 1920s.[98] This included the formation of the Business Party of the German Middle Classes (Wirtschaftspartei des deutschen Mittelstandes, WP), which emerged as a reaction to the DVP's inability to fully realign on economic policy and its continued cooperation with the Right.[99] The WP promised to be a voice for commercial interests that was independent of ideology.[100] Several agricultural parties also emerged to fight the alliance between agricultural and bourgeois interests, the most prominent of which was the German Peasant Party (Deutsche Bauernpartei, DBD), which threatened the conservatives' hold in rural areas.

Second, the continued misalignment on economic issues led to repeated legislative failure on the most pressing questions of the day, which often revolved around economic policy. The persistence of party antagonisms, formed around old patterns of regime contention, meant that often there simply were no viable legislative coalitions to support necessary policy. In times of crisis, this became debilitating and opened the door to executive encroachment, undermining parliamentary sovereignty. Below I examine two such critical episodes to illustrate legislative dynamics and how the inheritances of the predemocratic period led to such breakdowns. The two episodes show the weakness of both the center-left Grand Coalition and the center-right Bourgeois Coalition in managing economic policy.

Episode 2: The Crisis of 1923 and the Weakness of the Grand Coalition

The crisis of 1923 was brought on largely by the French invasion of the Ruhr Valley in February of that year. The occupation was aimed at extracting the reparations payments on which Germany had repeatedly defaulted. The crisis was compounded by the initial response of Chancellor Cuno, which was to encourage "passive resistance" of the occupation through strikes and general work stoppages. This led to a significant loss of productivity and hyperinflation, which plunged the country further into crisis. The Cuno government fell in August of that year, and Gustav Stresemann, leader of the DVP, assumed the chancellorship. His administration would last a brief but eventful 102 days, which would bring an end to the economic crisis but reveal the essential political weakness of legislative politics.

Stresemann succeeded in uniting a center-left Grand Coalition, which included the members of the Weimar Coalition along with the DVP. Given the dire circumstances, the Stresemann government set to work on currency stabilization, which they were able to accomplish with the introduction of the Rentenmark, a currency backed by mortgages at first and eventually tied to gold.[101] Stresemann also ended the policy of passive resistance, restoring productivity in the industrial hubs of the Ruhr.

One major political obstacle remained, however: to remedy the loss of revenue, there had to be a change to the Hours of Work Law to increase the permissible length of the workday in certain industries. Given that this was not a matter of regulation but of legislation, however, it had to go through the Reichstag. Though the cabinet, which included members of the DVP, SPD, Zentrum, and DDP, was united on the need for changes to the hours of work, the Reichstag delegations of the SPD and the DVP clashed over the solution. For the SPD the legislation introducing the eight-hour day was the result of fifty years of advocacy. It was one of the first acts of the SPD government on taking power in 1918, with as much symbolic significance as social impact. For the DVP, and especially the right-wing faction of industrial interests, the crisis was an opportunity to push for complete deregulation of the workday, or failing that, a return to the two-shift system of twelve-hour days.[102]

In an effort to navigate the chasm, Heinrich Brauns, who at the time was labor minister, offered an Hours of Work bill based on what he called the "sanitary maximum working day," by which he meant that the regulation would depend on the occupation and would "increase the working hours to the extent that seemed acceptable to health."[103] On balance this would have been a victory for the DVP since it gave industry leaders much leverage in setting the work hours. To the surprise of many, however, the DVP continued its opposition. As the crisis deepened, even the SPD Reichstag delegation grudgingly accepted the bill. The DVP delegation, on the other hand, in defiance of their party leadership, continued to push for complete deregulation.

Stresemann at the time maintained that the opposition within the DVP had less to do with policy and more to do with a desire to push the SPD out of the coalition and form a government of the bourgeois parties.[104] Indeed, party members openly called on him to "turn the Socialists out of the government."[105] Hugo Stinnes, who led the opposition to the Hours of Work bill in the Reichstag, expressed a desire to have Stresemann form a conservative government to move the legislation forward.[106] A similar sentiment was voiced by Paul Reusch, who labeled Stresemann the "Chancellor of Capitulation" and urged the party to bring down their own government.[107] The position of the DVP on the matter is rather revealing. Instead of taking the policy "win," they allowed their preference for coalition partners, based on repertoires of conflict and cooperation decades in the making, to drive their actions.

The DVP opposition was enough to defeat the Hours of Work bill. This effectively closed the door to a legislative solution. It was at this time that Stresemann offered the possibility of an Enabling Act to empower the cabinet to suspend parliamentary power and pass legislation independently. This is significant in that it was the first time an Enabling Act was used explicitly for legislative purposes.[108] Previously, these had been used to address exigent diplomatic or systemic needs that required an increase in executive power. The Enabling Act proposed at this time, however, was necessitated by a failure of legislative coalition building and was explicitly acknowledged as such.[109]

The dangers of using an Enabling Act in this way were widely known and fiercely debated. But by late September, the urgency of the matter had become clear to all. In a letter to labor minister Brauns, the minister of economic affairs Hans Von Raumer wrote, "One must be clear about the fact that the collapse of the German economy is inevitable if the problem of increase in labor productivity in mining is not solved immediately."[110] In cabinet meetings, the need for swift action was expressed by representatives of all parties, and after a cabinet reshuffle, all came out in support of an Enabling Act.[111] In a telling twist, the parties' Reichstag delegations also supported this. Whereas the government could not assemble a legislative majority on either the Left or the Right to support their Hours of Work bill, they received the two-thirds majority needed to pass the Enabling Act and take matters outside parliament.[112] Stresemann would later reflect on this moment and the abdication of parliamentary responsibility as one of the early signs of trouble in the republic, though he maintained there were no other viable options.[113]

Episode 3: The Crisis of 1929/30 and the Weakness of the Bourgeois Coalition

The next significant test of the Reichstag would follow the market crash of 1929, a crisis that would put the dysfunctionality of party politics fully on display. We know now that this crisis would end with the dissolution of parliament in September 1930, and new elections would see the rise of the Communist Party (KPD) and the Nazis (NSDAP), making legislation through regular parliamentary means all but impossible. But if 1930 signals the point of no return, as historians have suggested, it is important to understand how that point was reached.

A Grand Coalition under the leadership of Hermann Müller had been formed in the previous year but quickly succumbed to the pressure of the crisis, primarily due to antagonisms between the SPD and DVP. Stresemann's death in September of that year removed the primary obstacle to the right wing of the party, and under the leadership of Ernst Scholz, the party took an obstructionist stance toward all government proposals. When the Grand Coalition fell in March 1930, it was replaced by a minority government formed under the leadership of Heinrich Brüning of the Zentrum. The SPD declined to join the new government but continued to act as a "silent partner" to Brüning in the Reichstag.[114]

Brüning took office expecting that he would likely have to invoke executive powers to achieve his fiscal policies, but he made several concerted efforts to attain a parliamentary majority.[115] Encountering the same impasse between the SPD and DVP that his predecessor had, Brüning now looked to the Right to find a coalition to support his economic policies. The leader of the Zentrum's Reichstag delegation, Ludwig Kass, offered measured support for forging ties to the "non-Nationalist right," arguing that it would be an opportunity to "set the party free from Social Democratic pressures."[116]

Though the conservative party, the DNVP, was not included in the Brüning government, the choice of several cabinet ministers with close ties to the party signaled an opening to the right. The DNVP in return signaled its support for the new government and delivered the votes needed for it to survive a critical no-confidence vote introduced by the SPD. On matters of economic policy, the DNVP and the Zentrum could find much common ground, though the DNVP pushed for more agricultural subsidies than Brüning was willing to support.[117]

As negotiations continued, the country plunged further into economic crisis. Soaring unemployment led to increased pressure on the state's welfare system, and swift action was needed to meet rising demand for welfare provisions, especially unemployment benefits. Yet, there was fundamental disagreement over how this would be funded. The Left sought the enactment of various tax increases, while the Right insisted on increasing union dues.[118] Many attempts to pass a budget balancing these competing positions met with failure at the hands of one group or another.

When it ultimately became clear that there were no viable coalitions, Brüning sought and was granted emergency powers under Article 48. This would remove decisions not only from parliament, but from the cabinet as well, allowing legislation through presidential decree. In defending the decision, Brüning referred to the legislative failures of the Reichstag, stating that "the government has no more hope that parliament and the parties will fulfill their mission."[119] He maintained that the central task of parliament was to pass a budget, and having failed at that, the government had no choice but to act.[120]

The move to invoke Article 48 lost Brüning the support of the SPD, whose leader, Wilhelm Keil, objected, "Article 48 cannot possibly be used for enforcement of laws that the Reichstag does not want to approve. Such an application of Article 48 would be an abuse."[121] Brüning then appealed for support on the Right. The DNVP had no objections in principle to the use of Article 48, nor did they seek further economic concessions. Instead, what they asked in exchange for their support was Brüning's help in toppling the government of Otto Braun in Prussia. The final stronghold of the Weimar Coalition, Prussia had for some time frustrated the conservatives' efforts to make any electoral inroads. They hoped that Brüning could persuade the Prussian Zentrum party organization to abandon the government and put an end to SPD dominance in the region.[122]

There is no indication that Brüning considered this demand with any seriousness, as the cost of placating the conservatives would have meant losing the support of his own party.[123] When Brüning declined to act, the DNVP joined the SPD in its opposition to the use of Article 48. On July 18, by a narrow margin of seven votes, the Reichstag rejected the measure.[124] Seeing no path forward, Brüning immediately asked the president to dissolve parliament and call for new elections, a move he had threatened before and could not have known would effectively be the end of parliamentary government in the Weimar Republic.

Though it would not take its last gasp until 1933, some historians have dated the death of the republic at the crisis of 1930.[125] Whether or not this was in fact *the* critical turning point for the republic, it was a profoundly damaging turn for parliamentarism. New elections called for September 1930 would see the rise of the extreme flanks at the expense of the centrist parties and render impossible further legislative compromise. Subsequent governments would rule through presidential decree with little involvement of the Reichstag.

Looking back at the Weimar period, we find that neither the center-left Grand Coalition nor the center-right Bourgeois Coalition could navigate their way toward legislative solutions in times of crisis. This is because each represented a kind of misalignment that ignited repertoires of regime contention and sabotaged the possibility of compromise on substantive issues. It is important to stress that the legislative failures in this period were not random. This was not all-out fragmentation of the party system, as some have suggested. Rather it was a patterned breakdown reflecting decades of party development that disrupted typical economic coalition patterns in favor of regime alliance. Though some might see in these breakdowns simply a fight of democrats versus nondemocrats, where the latter got their wish, the struggles within the parties complicate this view. Moreover, the movement of parties back and forth belies this deterministic reading of German political development. Parties' positions and ideology were not fixed. The only thing that was "determined" was that the nature of political development would bring them to this point again and again, pitting regime coalitions against policy coalitions, and hindering progress on needed legislation. In times of crisis, this proved debilitating.

The German path of political development represents one of the most extreme cases of late parliamentarization among first wave democracies. In many ways it was the mirror opposite of the experience of the United Kingdom. In Germany, late parliamentarization increased the salience of the regime dimension for legislative politics and led to the formation of early coalitions animated by the logic of regime contention. Like the UK, the duration of the initial period of staggered sequencing—that is, the period in which either mass suffrage or parliamentarization was established but not both—lasted for over five decades, leading to rigid repertoires of conflict and cooperation. But in this case, the repertoires were rooted in regime contention.

With the regime question as an enduring vector of conflict, late parliamentarization introduced not only an additional issue dimension, but one that in many instances trumped others because of the existential stakes involved for parties. The salience of the regime dimension led to party misalignment, which made it difficult to forge legislative coalitions around other policy issues, the most critical of which throughout this period was economic policy. These dynamics, established at the critical juncture of institutional choice, survived three subsequent episodes that provided opportunities for realignment, the first at the turn of the century with the liberalization of the Wilhelmine period and the rise of the Social Democrats; the second after 1918, with the achievement of parliamentarization under the Weimar Republic; and the third during the economic crisis of the 1930s. In each instance, however, the legacies of party development in the shadow of the regime question led parties to revert to familiar repertoires of conflict and cooperation.

5

Simultaneous Introduction in France

THE DEVELOPMENT
OF MULTIPLE REPERTOIRES

IN MAY 1936, a cartel of Left parties known as the Front Populaire swept French elections, forming the first government under the leadership of the socialist party, Section Français de l'Internationale Ouvriére (SFIO). The coalition included not only Socialists and Radicals, but for the first time Communists as well. With Léon Blum, veteran socialist leader, at the helm, they undertook an ambitious agenda of social reform that provided robust welfare protections while stabilizing the economy. This coalition is also credited with keeping at bay the nascent fascist forces that had made their way onto the national political scene. Several things about this were remarkable. First, this was a viable coalition unified on economic matters. The inclusion of the Communists is especially noteworthy given their unsparingly critical posture toward government cooperation until this point. Despite the significant ideological differences between the parties, their ability to unite around a common program was unprecedented. And though the official governing coalition was short lived, the legislative coalition endured and succeeded in implementing what came to be known as the French New Deal, stabilizing the economy through one of the greatest crises of the interwar period.

That this was followed only a few years later by invasion and the rise of the Vichy government should not diminish the significance of what the Popular Front achieved. This episode in French history has received a great deal of attention in accounts of the interwar period, and the Popular Front is widely seen as the key factor keeping French democracy intact during this crucial episode. While the importance of the Popular Front is beyond doubt, however, the focus on this single example of solidarity has somewhat distorted the picture, as have exaggerated claims about its novelty. As Léon Blum recalled in his memoirs, "A political phenomenon such as the Popular Front did not suddenly grow up like a mushroom out of two Sunday polling days. It was linked to, and was in large measure a product of, that which went before it."[1] Indeed, this governing coalition was built on a long tradition of legislative cooperation, which made this moment possible. And it was in fact the *legislative* coalition of the Popular Front that carried through the economic agenda, even as the governing coalition began to fray.

This narrative contradicts the typical image of politics in the Third Republic as one of barely contained chaos.[2] It is true that there was a high level of government instability. Indeed, between 1870 and 1940, the republic saw eighty-seven different governments, each lasting on average no more than ten months, with a seemingly revolving door of over three hundred cabinet ministers.[3] This instability at the level of government coalitions, however, belies considerable stability in legislative coalitions and, starting in 1902, coalitions that began to approximate a Left–Right alignment on the economic policy dimension. These legislative coalitions represented a stabilizing force in French politics, with legislators and committee leadership outlasting most cabinets and premiers. Moreover, the availability of functional legislative coalitions allowed the country to face the economic crises of the interwar years with solutions rooted in legislative compromise rather than executive decree. Some have linked the strength of the legislative branch in France to the founding ideology of the Republican Party, but this was significantly enhanced by innovations in the organization and management of the party's legislative delegations at the turn of the century.[4]

The goal of this chapter is to understand the development of legislative coalitions in the Third Republic, with special attention to the role of institutional sequencing in shaping patterns of conflict and cooperation. As with the other cases, this chapter is organized around the critical juncture of institutional choice, as well as three subsequent episodes that tested the endurance of legislative coalitions. The critical juncture here is identified at the time of the founding of the Third Republic, which simultaneously introduced parliamentarization and mass suffrage. This simultaneity represented the failure of elites to manage the process of democratization through sequencing, but it did not signal an unqualified victory for democratizing forces. In fact, it resulted in a highly unstable equilibrium, as parliamentarization remained contested for the first decade of the republic, only to be secured in 1879.

The nature of the conflict led to the early formation of repertoires of regime contention, but the relatively short duration of this period of limbo meant that these repertoires did not become as entrenched or as rigid as those encountered in the German case. This could be seen in the first episode examined beyond the critical juncture. This episode was at the turn of the century and coincided with increased liberalization and the rise of the SFIO. In this period, critical choices made by party leaders within both the Radical Party and the SFIO paved the way for a center-left economic policy coalition in the tradition of Lib-Lab cooperation and pushed the party system toward alignment along the economic dimension beginning in 1902. It also ushered in a period in which multiple repertoires operated, allowing legislators to move between economic policy coalitions and regime coalitions as different challenges emerged. With the monarchist threat neutralized, and Republicans established as the dominant political force, parties began to embrace coalitions that cut against previous regime alliances and could help them pursue substantive policy objectives. By World War I, these coalitions began to take the shape of discernable center-left and center-right coalitions, the Bloc Nationale and the Cartel des Gauches.

A second episode testing the endurance of legislative coalitions can be identified immediately after World War I. At this time, the radicalization of labor threatened to undermine economic coalitions and return the party system to alignment exclusively along the regime dimension. Again, critical choices by party leaders preserved these economic coalitions and allowed the legislature to navigate some of the most difficult economic challenges of the postwar period. A third episode, brought on by the market crash and economic crises of the 1930s, again tested coalitions and ended with the Popular Front, a novel reconfiguration drawing on the multiple repertoires that had emerged throughout the course of the Third Republic. This periodization is presented in figure 5.1.

The path of simultaneous introduction in France was distinctive in many ways. Unlike the path of early parliamentarization in the UK, where policy coalitions emerged not long after parliamentarization, in France, regime contention continued to animate legislative politics well into the Third Republic. And in contrast to the path of late parliamentarization in Germany, where decades of primary regime contention entrenched repertoires of conflict and cooperation along the regime dimension, in France, repertoires of conflict and cooperation remained more flexible, and parties were capable of reforming coalitions away from the regime dimension and toward substantive policy

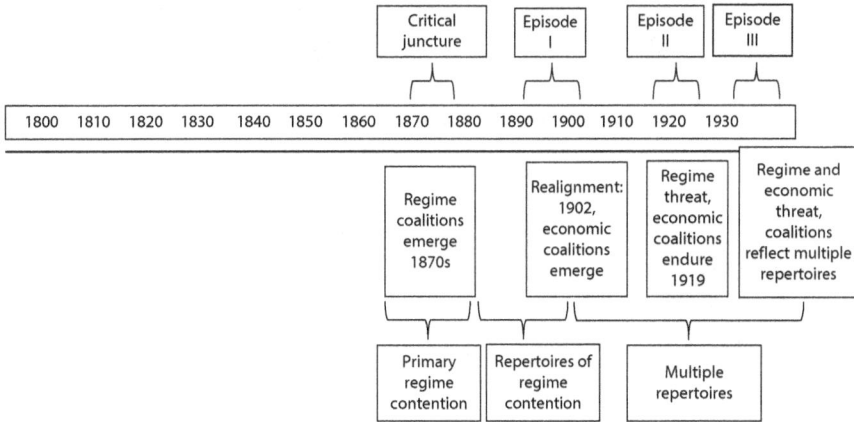

FIGURE 5.1. France timeline

coalitions. Importantly, the French case provides us with one of the clearest instances in which repertoires inherited from previous interactions are significantly altered or augmented. The realignment that took place at the turn of the century allowed for the emergence of repertoires of economic management alongside repertoires of regime contention. The development of multiple repertoires became a critical asset during the interwar period, as it allowed legislators to effectively respond to both economic and regime challenges.

Critical Juncture: The Founding of the Republic, 1870–1879

Most accounts of the French Third Republic date its origins to 1870, when Léon Gambetta declared a republican government to replace the fallen Second Empire.[5] On the heels of military defeat, this dramatic gesture came as close as any nineteenth-century European country would come to a watershed moment of democratization, sweeping away the old monarchical institutions and ushering in republican government. Significant as this moment was, however, Gambetta's declaration was more aspirational than actual. In no other case was the distinction between de jure and de facto parliamentarization so stark. While the constitutional laws of the Third Republic established a representative legislature with governing power, a long and uncertain road lay ahead, and republican government would not be secure in France for the next decade. Not until 1879, after the Seize Mai crisis, when Marshal Patrice de MacMahon, the monarchist first president of the republic, stepped down, can we speak of a decisive victory for parliamentary republican government. Until then, whether the republic would operate through presidential government, parliamentary government, or even constitutional monarchy was still very much an open question. Thus, for the purpose of this analysis, the intervening years between 1870 and 1879 constitute a continuation of the critical juncture, as well as a continuation of uncertainty regarding the fate of the republic.

Some have argued that this uncertainty carried through the entire Third Republic.[6] While it is true that conservative, and at times monarchical, forces did threaten regime stability throughout the life of the republic, this characterization diminishes the severity of the threat to parliamentary government in these early years and elides the fact that conservative and monarchical forces were dominant at the time the republic was established. Theirs was a vision of a presidential rather than a parliamentary republic, if not a full restoration of the monarchy.

The extended period of uncertainty between the founding of the republic and the Seize Mai crisis, when parliamentary government was more firmly established, left the country in limbo, with the regime question playing out in every arena of politics, shaping alliances and determining political strategy. The uncertainty of the 1870s also left institutional arrangements unsettled. Although both universal manhood suffrage and parliamentarization would ultimately be affirmed during this critical juncture, this outcome came about more by accident than by design. Republican government, in the words of historian J.P.T. Bury, entered through the "side door."[7] As in other cases, elites desired an asynchronic process where the institutions of democracy were staggered to moderate the impact. Only through the miscalculation of the monarchists and the strategic tradeoffs of the Republicans did simultaneous introduction, an outcome that neither group initially wanted, ultimately prevail.

The Uncertain Road to Securing the Republic

The early years of the republic were marked by conservative and monarchical dominance. Of the 645 members elected to the first National Assembly, 400 were monarchists.[8] Gambetta's proclamation of the republic in 1870 notwithstanding, the acceptance of republican government came about not as a result of victory from below but ironically, as a compromise between different monarchical forces competing for the crown.[9] Three competitors for the throne emerged in the wake of military defeat in 1871, each wishing to restore the monarchy, but none willing to yield to the others in their quest.[10] The main contenders were the Comte de Chambord, grandson of Charles the X, representing the Legitimist claim; and the Comte de Paris, grandson of Louis Phillip, representing the Orleanist claim. Two members of the Bonaparte family were also advanced at this time, but their claims were greatly weakened by Napoleon's defeat in the war. The competition between these different monarchical factions went on for years, while the National Assembly, also dominated by monarchists, kept the country in limbo.

The crisis seemed close to resolution in 1873, when it was agreed that the two Bourbon pretenders would establish a line of succession, with Chambord taking the throne first. A series of miscalculations and miscommunications, however, owing largely to the obstinance of Chambord, frustrated these efforts. With the continuation of the impasse, monarchists reluctantly accepted republican government to oversee the country's affairs until a resolution could be reached.[11] Adolphe Thiers, the moderate Republican who had been elected president, famously attributed the acceptance of republican government to the fact that "the republic is the form of government that divides us the least."[12] Importantly, it was intended as a placeholder until monarchical government could be restored.

Even with the acceptance of republican government, however, a great deal of ambiguity remained around the specific institutional configuration. Conservative and monarchical forces envisioned a form of presidential rather than parliamentary government. They sought a strong president who could act as a stand-in until monarchical power could be restored. And indeed, many aspects of the constitutional laws established in these early years were promulgated with the expectation of a restoration of the monarchy.[13] Even the term of the presidency—seven years—was set because it was thought to be an adequate amount of time to allow for the resolution of the dispute among the competing Bourbon houses.

Republicans were more focused on securing universal manhood suffrage above all else. They saw in this not just an institutional step toward democratization but one that could bring about further democratic reforms. This was most evident in the thinking of Léon Gambetta, who described the ballot as the "little paper" that was the republic itself.[14] For Gambetta, suffrage was a strategy to secure the republic. He firmly believed that the fate of the republic rested on persuasion of the masses, a task that Gambetta eagerly took up, earning himself the title of the traveling salesman of the republic.[15] This strategy was predicated on the long tradition of universal male suffrage, which in the history of France since the revolution had been upheld under both monarchical and republican government. Thus, the claim to represent the people was critical to political legitimacy for all forces, and under Gambetta's leadership, Republicans focused on success at the polls as a measure of this legitimacy.[16]

While the fate of parliamentary government remained uncertain throughout this period, Republicans knew that, given the history of manhood suffrage, which had attached to every form of government since the French Revolution, it would be difficult for the monarchists to resist this without turning the public against them and potentially toward the more radical left forces in the country. The history of the Paris Commune still loomed large at this time. The bloody insurrection, which left over 20,000 dead, represented the ongoing potential for violence and the strength of radical forces once mobilized. Though the Commune was handily put down, and many Communards were either jailed or sent into exile, the threat of popular uprisings remained, and the denial of manhood suffrage was precisely the kind of event that could trigger this.

While Republicans were confident in their ability to secure manhood suffrage, however, the fate of parliamentary government remained uncertain. In the balance was whether the republic would operate though presidential or parliamentary government. Two pressing issues were seen as decisive: first, whether the president would be directly elected, giving the office a popular mandate; and second, whether the president would have the power to dissolve parliament. Debate on these issues dragged on, not for months but years, until a resolution was finally reached in 1875.[17]

The solution in both cases was found in the Senate. The upper chamber, which was established as a conservative body, was to hold the balance between presidential and parliamentary power. On the issue of presidential elections, it was decided that the president would be elected indirectly by a two-thirds vote of the Senate.[18] This secured conservative influence over the office while stripping it of a popular mandate. On the issue of presidential prerogative, it was decided that the president would have the power to dismiss the lower chamber but only with the support of the Senate, thus falling short of full parliamentarization but still reining in the power of the president.[19] These two compromises came together to form a hybrid regime with elements of presidential and parliamentary government. The result was that parliamentary government was established but heavily curtailed by a president with significant and in many ways unprecedented powers. The first compromise would last well into the Fifth Republic (only in 1962 did France turn to direct election of the president), though the second would be successfully challenged just two years later in a confrontation that would first call into question and ultimately affirm the power of parliament.

The struggle over presidential and parliamentary power came to a head in 1877 during what came to be known as the Seize Mai crisis. The crisis was triggered when President MacMahon dismissed Republican prime minister Jules Simon and replaced him with Orleanist Albert de Broglie.[20] The question of ministerial responsibility was not yet settled in the new constitution. The conventional understanding was that the cabinet should reflect both the parliamentary majority and the office of the president as the representative of the country as a whole. How these dual mandates would be balanced and what would happen should the two conflict, however, was not clear. Technically, it was within the powers afforded to the president to dismiss ministers. But it was expected that the president would exercise this in consultation with parliament. MacMahon's failure to do so was seen as politically inflammatory and a signal that further executive encroachment was on the horizon.[21]

On May 16, 1877, Republicans in parliament, led by Georges Clemenceau, passed a vote of no confidence in the new government, asserting their own power over the cabinet. MacMahon then took the extraordinary action of dissolving parliament and calling for new elections. He did this with the support of the Senate, as was constitutionally required, and expected the new elections to allow him to replace the dissenting Republican faction with loyalists.[22]

The election in fact achieved the opposite. Though Republicans lost some seats, they remained in the majority and in fact expanded their geographic reach into rural locales. Much of this was thanks to the work of Gambetta, who had led Republican efforts in these regions long before the crisis. Indeed, many Republicans welcomed the confrontation with the president and looked to elections as an opportunity to show their strength throughout the country. The gamble paid off. By holding on to a majority in the Chamber of Deputies, Republicans were able to thwart MacMahon's aspirations to achieve a loyalist majority and force him to back down. He appointed a Republican, Jules Dufaure, as prime minister, in effect accepting the principles of ministerial responsibility to parliament.[23] MacMahon would resign two years later, marking the end of monarchist dominance in government. This would be the last time any president would attempt to dismiss parliament. Though this power remained within the constitutional laws, the office of the president was increasingly diminished to a figurehead, and parliament from this point became the central institution of the republic.

Repertoires of Conflict and Cooperation

With the establishment of parliamentary government alongside universal manhood suffrage in the first decade of the republic, the period of primary regime contention came to a close. Repertoires of conflict and cooperation based in this legacy of regime contention, however, continued to animate parties' positions and worked against the formation of typical center-left and center-right alliances along the economic policy dimension. This was reinforced by periodic regime challenges that were not monarchist per se but still heightened anxieties about the possibility of a monarchist threat. Nowhere was the complexity of this period more on display than during the Boulanger crisis. General Georges Boulanger was a former minister of war who in 1885 emerged on the political scene with a controversial program of constitutional reform, combining nationalist and populist appeals that attracted a large and diverse following that spanned the entire political spectrum.[24] He counted among his supporters both monarchists and socialists, who had little in common save for their hostility to the republic.[25] His ideas for constitutional reform remained rather vague; indeed, vagueness was in many ways the key to his broad appeal.[26] Historians have struggled to understand whether the movement belonged to the Left or the Right, with some identifying in it the roots of European fascism.[27] For monarchists, the appeal of Boulanger's attacks on democratic institutions is clear, but his economic agenda cut directly against their interests. For socialists as well, the relationship was fraught and reflected the internal struggle between revolutionary socialists, who rejected democratic participation, and reformists, who saw in it a vehicle for social progress.[28] In 1888, as Boulangists swept by-elections, Republicans in the Chamber of Deputies took up a campaign of republican defense, forming a regime coalition that brought together a wide array of political interests under the Republican bloc.[29]

The Republicans succeeded in 1888 in fending off the Boulangist threat, but the experience convinced them of the need for more aggressive actions. Beginning in 1899, Republicans, under the leadership of René Waldeck-Rousseau, engaged in a purge of government officers aimed at routing out the remnants of monarchism. This purge also coincided with the height of the Dreyfus affair, an event that once again divided the country and its political forces along regime lines.[30] The affair began in 1894 with accusations of treason against Captain Alfred Dreyfus, an officer in the French army. It lasted over a decade, with many dramatic turns, including revelations that documents had been forged in an apparent conspiracy against the general. By 1899, the affair had grown into a full-blown political scandal tinged with antisemitism and authoritarian nationalism.[31] In parliament, two sides emerged, identifying as Dreyfusards and Anti-Dreyfusards, the first representing a coalition of Radicals, moderate Republicans, and Socialists, and the second representing a coalition of forces that were, if not hostile to the republic, at least indifferent to it.[32] The affair was ultimately resolved in favor of General Dreyfus, but it further entrenched repertoires of regime contention well past the point at which the primary regime threat had been eliminated.

The complexities of political alliances in the early Third Republic reflect the ongoing influence of the regime question.[33] Yet the flexibility of repertoires in this case provided opportunities for political creativity, which actors would take advantage of to introduce a new coalitional calculus. In subsequent episodes, a significant shift would ultimately take place, and while it did not completely transform existing repertoires, it did augment them, enabling the formation of viable economic coalitions that allowed legislators to navigate multiple challenges. The availability of multiple repertoires would prove to be critical to legislative capacity and regime stability in the interwar period.

Episode 1: Tactical Liberalization and Party Realignment

The first test of the legislative alliances formed at the critical juncture in France came at the turn of the century, a period that provided significant opportunities to reform coalitions. This had to do with two important factors: First, and perhaps most important, is that parliamentarization and mass suffrage had been established for over two decades, and while the intervening years had seen episodic skirmishes with antirepublican forces, Republicans had prevailed. By 1902, the Republican bloc controlled two-thirds of the seats in the Chamber of Deputies, the monarchists had been eliminated, and a fractured conservative bloc controlled less than a third.[34]

Republican government at this time was ascendant. So too were the Socialists, and therein lay the dilemma for Republican forces. The Socialists presented an electoral threat as well as an ideological threat to the liberals. In fact, they had long been seen as a different kind of regime threat, at times even allied with the monarchists, as in the Boulanger affair. But the Socialists also represented an opportunity for a realignment that would support a liberal economic agenda.

The Socialists also faced a dilemma. An alliance with the liberals held opportunities for economic policies that would advance their social goals. But it meant cooperation with bourgeois governments, which compromised the regime objectives of their more radical members. This period therefore pitted reformist and revolutionary Socialists against each other. A realignment would ultimately take place, owing to the leadership and political creativity of two pivotal figures: René Waldeck-Rousseau, leader of the Republicans, and Jean Jaurès, leader of the Socialists. Together, they paved the way for a center-left coalition in the tradition of Lib-Lab cooperation and ultimately a party system realignment toward the economic dimension.

Liberalization and Shifting Legislative Coalitions

The Republican bloc came into the twentieth century dominant but seeking more permanent solutions to the lingering regime contention that infused almost every element of national politics and posed a major obstacle to progress on economic policy, the key component of which at the time was the income tax.[35] The need to fortify the republic against its detractors was still paramount, however, and the menu of options to accomplish this was significantly expanded with the rise of the Socialists in the Chamber of Deputies. While a significant faction of the Socialist camp held revolutionary antisystemic aspirations that would constitute a regime threat in their own right, a strong reformist faction had already come to the defense of the republic on numerous occasions. It was this group that the Republicans aimed to attract with new policies easing repressive practices that had prevailed since the founding of the republic.

Central to these efforts was the Law of Associations introduced in 1901 by Waldeck-Rousseau in an attempt to recruit Socialists to his "Cabinet of National Defense."[36] The act represented a mixed measure of liberalization. It allowed any citizen to form or join an association on the condition that such associations maintained no international ties or obligations. While most legislation of this sort served as blunt instruments of repression, this act held uncommon strategic precision. It successfully targeted for exclusion revolutionary socialists who looked abroad for leadership and direction, as well as representatives of the religious orders (the backbone of the monarchist movement), since they looked to the Vatican for leadership.[37] Importantly, this opened the door to the social democrats, the reformist branch of the socialist movement, who had shown themselves to be committed to the republic.[38]

This opening also strengthened the reformist socialists in parliament, offering a path forward for those wishing to embrace a more pragmatic orientation toward republican government. Recall that the Third Republic was established through one of the most profound acts of repression of the nineteenth century—Republican forces violently putting down the Paris Commune, a revolutionary uprising that lasted from March to May 1871. The exile, imprisonment, or execution of many Communards in the wake of the Commune left the labor movement disorganized and without its established leadership. Restrictions on the right of association further exacerbated this vacuum, weakening the labor movement as both a social force and a potential coalition partner. The easing of these restrictions promised to restore labor to the center of national politics, something the reformists within the movement had aspired to since the founding of the republic.

The opportunity to alter coalitions resulted in significant changes to the composition and organization of parties. In 1901, the Radical Republicans, led by Waldeck-Rousseau, broke off from the Republican bloc to form the country's first modern mass party. Until then, loose parliamentary groups were the main organizing feature of legislative politics.[39] The remaining Republicans formed the centrist Republican Federation, which would anchor the center-right coalition in parliament, bringing together Republicans who rejected cooperation with the Socialists and the reconstituted conservative parties. In the following year, a similar split would take place in the Socialist camp, forming the Socialist Party of France (PSF), under the leadership of Jules Guesde, and the French Socialist Party (POF), with Jean Jaurès at the helm. Though both factions supported parliamentary socialism, the first placed greater emphasis on revolutionary action and the latter on reform through existing structures. The embrace of reformist socialism by the Radical Republicans and acceptance of government cooperation by the reformist socialists made possible for the first time a coalition of the Left, known as the Bloc des Gauches. The resulting "Lib-Lab" alliance represented important concessions on the regime question from both sides, a transformation that would pave the way for more substantive policy-based legislative coalitions.[40] While regime anxieties were not fully eliminated, this period allowed actors to augment existing repertoires and usher in a period in which multiple repertoires operated.

The changes on the Left had consequences for the Right as well. Centrists who broke off to form the Republican Federation looked to find partners on the Right. This was now possible as a result of the weakening of the monarchist parties in the previous decade. The new conservative parties that emerged in their stead adopted an accommodationist position toward the republic, which made such a partnership possible. Again, concessions with respect to the regime question paved the way for coalitions to emerge in pursuit of substantive policy goals.[41] While this group was much smaller and less organized than the center-left Bloc des Gauches, it provided the framework for a center-right coalition forged along economic lines.

The combination of this center-right coalition and the center-left coalition between Radicals and Socialists allowed the country to move away from a pattern of "polarized pluralism," in which a centrist coalition of embattled Republicans held off the twin threats of monarchism and socialism.[42] A long road lay ahead, however, before stable legislative coalitions could be established. The following years witnessed an intricate dance between parties as they sought positions of accommodation that would allow for viable legislative coalitions. At many points, the temptation to fall back on familiar regime alliances was great, but the incentives provided by the institutional structure allowed parties to keep open multiple repertoires, making possible the formation of economic coalitions even when it required sacrificing ideological purity. This period would also reveal the critical role played by legislative coalitions in stabilizing the country amid ministerial turmoil and ever-changing government coalitions.

Délégation des Gauches: Formalizing Legislative Coalitions

The election of 1902 saw the first ever electoral pact among the Left parties. The Bloc des Gauches brought together Radicals, left Republicans, and reformist Socialists to contest elections as part of a coalition for republican defense. This electoral pact gave way to a coalition government representing the various Left parties and led by Waldeck-Rousseau. This alliance would see many incarnations throughout the life of the Third Republic, but on this first occasion, it met with immediate crisis and cabinet instability. Within a few weeks of the election, the head of government, Waldeck-Rousseau, stepped down because of a combination of personal and political challenges. A veteran Radical member whose leadership was critical to vanquishing the monarchist threat in the early decades of the republic and engineering the center-left coalition in the legislature, Waldeck-Rousseau was one of the backbones of the government, and his rapid departure threatened to undo the nascent coalition.

With the government coalition in jeopardy, members of the bloc convened a legislative committee known as the Délégation des Gauches. This was effectively a steering committee meant to keep the legislative coalition together as a means of stabilizing the government.[43] The Délégation comprised twenty-six members: seven Moderates, eight Radicals, six Radical Socialists, and five Socialists. The Radical MP Ferdinand Sarrien was chosen as the presiding officer, with the power to call meetings and set the agenda. At first, the work of the committee was ad hoc, but by 1903 a resolution was passed requiring a meeting of the Délégation before all major parliamentary votes.[44]

The strength and stability of this legislative coalition was remarkable. Faced with the potential collapse of its governmental coalition, the Délégation not only persisted, but helped to bolster the government of Émile Combes after Waldeck-Rousseau's departure. The Délégation has in fact been credited with extending the life of his government by several years. In the Chamber, it played a critical role in identifying policy compromises and managing the agenda to avoid areas of overt conflict. Unanimity of approval was required for any decision, and each group voted as a whole, which meant that each party, regardless of its size, effectively had a veto.[45]

Managing internal conflict among the groups was key to the success of the Délégation. A clear example of this can be seen in how the Délégation dealt with coal miners' strikes in 1902. Just two years earlier, the Socialists had been forced to vote against the government on a confidence vote related to strikes in Chalon-sur-Saône, in which three strikers had been killed in a confrontation with government troops. On this occasion, however, the Délégation was able to maintain coherence by offering a confidence vote with language that defended the right to work, to satisfy the Moderates, but also included promises of early consideration of laws concerning strikes, to satisfy the Socialists. In addition, the Socialists were invited to submit an amendment to the motion, calling for the government to evacuate the strike region, which was ultimately voted down but allowed the group to save face.[46] Indeed, the Délégation was so effective that critics charged that the government was forced to obey rather than guide its legislative majority. The premier admitted as much, stating that he attempted nothing without the previous consent of the Délégation.[47]

The Second International and the Social Democrats' Compromise

The rise of the Délégation revealed the increasing independence and importance of legislative coalitions in French politics. In maintaining the unity of the Left, the Délégation, of course, was not without its challenges. The greatest, perhaps, was the ongoing strife within the socialist camp, which remained divided, with the reformist POF included in the Délégation, and the revolutionary socialists of the PSF remaining in opposition. The main issue dividing the groups now was the question of government participation. The conflict had been brewing since 1899, with the ascension of Socialist MP Alexandre Millerand to the post of commerce minister under Waldeck-Rousseau's Cabinet of National Defense. Though Millerand had since withdrawn from the Socialist groups to form his own Independent Socialist Party, the two factions continued to clash over the question of cooperation with bourgeois governments. The issue would come to a head in 1902 when the reformist faction joined the electoral alliance of the Bloc des Gauches. That this would mean serving in cabinets alongside ministers who had taken part in the violent suppression of the Commune a few decades earlier alarmed many within the socialist movement. For a pragmatist such as Jean Jaurès, who led the POF, such ministerial cooperation was a necessary evil in the plight for social transformation. For Jules Guesde, leader of the PSF, on the other hand, such cooperation with bourgeois parties was anathema to the goals of parliamentary socialism.

Despite repeated challenges from the Left, the POF managed to hold its position and remained one of the most loyal of the groups in the Délégation, largely because of the skillful maneuvering and elegant oratory of Jaurès, who stressed the importance of legislative cooperation to advance socialist policies.[48] By 1904, however, tensions over Socialist participation reached a height, and divisions between the French Socialists was a central concern of the Congress of the Second International, held in Amsterdam in August 1904. Jaurès and the POF were heavily criticized during the congress, particularly by his intellectual rival and German counterpart Karl Kautsky, at the time a leading ideologue of Marxist revolutionary socialism.[49] Kautsky sought the affirmation of the Dresden resolution, passed the previous year, which held that "the congress rejects in the most energetic manner all revisionist efforts to change our tried and tested tactic based on the class struggle and to replace the conquest of power through lofty struggle against the bourgeoisie with a policy of making concessions to the established order." Kautsky maintained emphatically, "The social democracy cannot accept any government participation in a bourgeois society."[50] Jaurès responded with equally bitter reprobation, charging that it was not French reformism but German ideological purity and inactivity that was hurting the international labor movement:

What pressed so heavily upon the socialist-labour movement of the world . . . was not French reformism and the so-called watering down of the revolutionary principle of our faith; it was the deplorable inactivity, the political inefficiency, of German Social Democracy, our teachers in theory and organization, which paralyzed our international movement. What were they doing to turn the Reichstag into an efficient instrument of the German people? Nothing! How do they think to attain to their objective? Through the Reichstag? Quite an impossible assumption, and there was no evidence whatever that they were training the masses to resist, and manfully resist, the fatal policy of their government.[51]

Importantly, Jaurès maintained that Germany, a country where parliament had limited power to advance policy, could not dictate tactics of a country like France, where socialists, through government participation, could have a real impact on policy.[52] And indeed, at the time, government cooperation for the German SPD would have meant cooperation with the imperial government of the Kaissereich in a context where parliament had little power. Moreover, in the German context, parties did not govern; thus the question of government responsibility was not one with which the SPD had to seriously contend. Jaurès's emphasis on the absence of parliamentary power in Germany helps elucidate the impact of parliamentarization on parties' strategic behavior.

Ultimately, the revolutionary faction prevailed at the Amsterdam Congress. The Dresden resolution was upheld with an even more strongly worded Amsterdam resolution disavowing cooperation with bourgeois governments and barring ministerial participation by any Socialist Party member.[53] Further, the French factions were admonished to find a solution that would allow for the reunification of French socialism, a goal that was pursued at the Globe Congress held in Paris later that year.

While the affirmation of the Dresden resolution was undoubtedly a defeat for Jaurès's reformist visions on the international front, he won important concessions at the Globe Congress. There, he continued many of the arguments he had offered in the Amsterdam meeting, emphasizing the benefits gained from legislative cooperation and the unique position of French socialists to effect change through parliamentary means.[54] Though the congress could not contradict the International's decision on ministerial cooperation, Jaurès won an important concession on electoral coordination that would allow the SFIO to continue participating in the Bloc des Gauches.[55] This was a key victory, as participation in the bloc entailed not only electoral cooperation but agreement on a joint policy agenda. Electoral cartels were quickly becoming an important feature of legislative politics, delineating an identifiable Left from Right and adding structure and stability to the work of parliament. Jaurès and other reformists at the congress noted that the poor showing of the Socialists in the 1902 elections had resulted from their lack of participation in such electoral pacts.

With this, Jaurès arguably won a much greater victory than has been acknowledged by historians focusing on the defeat of his reformist vision in Amsterdam.[56] In the context of French politics, the SFIO's participation in legislative coalitions gave it as much if not more influence over policy outcomes than participation in the revolving door of French governing coalitions. The reformist logic proved compelling within the SFIO, and as the party organization grew, so did the hold of Jaurès's vision, which would remain dominant within the party until the Communist challenge at the Congress du Tours in 1920.[57]

With this compromise, the center-left legislative coalition of Radicals and Socialists was consolidated, and with it, the stability of the republic. Though the SFIO would forgo ministerial responsibility, the legislative coalition was a mechanism of coordination that enabled the passage of necessary policies. Out of the public eye, parties of the Délégation could often resolve conflicts more readily than official government parties, whose positions and compromises were heavily scrutinized. This was a coalition based on economic policy objectives. While it did not end regime contention or completely transform repertoires of conflict and cooperation based on this logic, it did provide an alternative principle of political competition and paved the way for new repertoires to emerge along the economic policy dimension. This would also lay the foundation for legislative compromise in the interwar period, when economic crisis and renewed regime challenges threatened to undo the alliances that had been forged in this episode.

Multiple Repertoires and the Multiple Challenges of the Interwar Period

The First World War presented an important test for the emerging legislative coalitions. Postwar politics saw the continued strength of the SFIO in national politics. In the election of 1919, the SFIO earned 21 percent of the vote, second only to the Republican Federation. Its rising electoral fortunes were amply evident and afforded it significant leverage as a coalition partner. This period also saw a marked radicalization of labor along the lines of that experienced in much of Europe following the Russian Revolution. This empowered the Socialists to pursue a bolder agenda, beginning with the implementation of the eight-hour workday in 1919. The public's appetite for social reforms only grew during the interwar years, assuring the Socialists a seat at the table in all fiscal matters.

The rise of the Socialists posed the greatest challenge to the Radical Party, the country's centrist liberal party, and the SFIO's legislative partners since 1902. After several decades in their shadow, the SFIO in the interwar period regularly outperformed the Radicals at the polls and would enter the legislature as a more powerful player. Whereas in Germany, the competition from the Socialists drove Liberals to the right and led them to embrace a more conservative economic agenda to protect their regime preference, in France, with the salience of the regime dimension diminished, the Radical Party would pivot further to the left to meet the socialists on common ground.

Cartel des Gauches and Bloc National: Consolidating Legislative Coalitions

Alongside the threat posed by the rise of the Socialists, Radicals also saw in this period an opportunity to strengthen an alliance of the Left despite their own declining electoral position. The rise of the French Communist Party at the Tours Congress in 1920 helped solidify this alliance, ridding the SFIO of its more radical elements, paving the way for a genuinely center-left politics, and giving both Socialists and Radicals incentives to maintain this. This cooperation would be formalized in the Cartel des Gauches, which would define the politics of the Left throughout the interwar period.

The increased stability of coalitions was also found on the Right, with the emergence of the Bloc National, representing a wide constellation of centrist and center-right parties.[58] Though this bloc housed a wide and ever-changing range of party labels, it brought together the successors to the Republicans, Progressives, and Opportunists of previous decades under banners such as the Republican Federation, the Democratic Republican Party, Action Libérale Populaire, along with several independent conservatives.[59] Though this group was heterogeneous ideologically, programmatically, they were united by a nationalist platform that was mostly directed at Germany and the desire to exact greater punitive measures following the war, as well as a defense of capitalism in the domestic economy, often expressed as anti-Bolshevism, targeting the radicalized labor movement of the interwar period.[60]

The Cartel des Gauches and the Bloc National were essentially electoral alliances devised to assist with coordination in elections. Given the two-round system in French elections, parties commonly formed electoral alliances with arrangements for one party to withdraw in the second round if only candidates of the other bloc remained, or to support candidates from the other party if their candidate was eliminated. These electoral alliances provided structure to legislative politics, since they implied an agreement to a given policy agenda that parties would offer in their campaign. But it should be stressed that the electoral alliances were in many ways a result rather than a cause of legislative cooperation. Indeed, a great deal of negotiation went into the articulation of the platforms around which the blocs would campaign. If electoral success was the goal, policy compromise was the vehicle that allowed these cartels to function.

Moreover, the electoral alliances clearly signaled a legislative coalition rather than a governing coalition. Especially on the Left, it was common, for example, for the SFIO to participate in an electoral alliance and commit to supporting the policies of the coalition but decline to participate in government. This happened in 1924 and 1932. This had much to do with the prohibition in the party's platform rejecting cooperation with bourgeois government.[61] But probably more important was the threat from its left flank, and from the ascendent Communist Party, if the party adopted too much of an accommodationist position toward the Radicals. Not until 1936 would the SFIO join in government as leaders of the Popular Front, and even this was only possible with Communist participation and support for the agenda of the Popular Front. Declining a role in government coalitions was for the SFIO a necessary political move. But it did not hinder legislative cooperation on the policy agenda advanced by the bloc.

Both the Bloc National and the Cartel des Gauches represented something novel in French politics: a clearly identifiable Left and Right. Moreover, while the platforms of both coalitions expressed distinct positions on social policy, foreign policy, and a range of other issue areas, the economic policy dimension dominated much of the interwar period and was the dimension around which the Left and the Right coalesced. While regime contention was never far from view during this period, legislative politics was polarized primarily along the economic dimension. Each coalition maintained a cohesive policy agenda, and each represented a distinct alternative to dealing with the many economic crises experienced in the interwar period. The Right typically responded to economic challenges with deflationary strategies (cutting government expenditures and encouraging prices to fall), fearing that deficits would lead to price inflation; and the Left responded with direct taxes and welfare benefits to promote demand-side recovery. For the Left, the economic crises were the result not of overproduction but underconsumption. The remedy according to Blum was to "increase the purchasing power of the masses."[62] These two logics of economic stabilization governed the interwar economy in France, providing legislative coalitions with an ideological organizing principle that could be exercised while in government or in opposition.

Two important episodes of economic crisis tested the stability of these alliances. Both centered on the budget: The first was in 1923–24 when the cost of reconstruction and the precipitous fall of the franc sent the economy into a tailspin, requiring decisive action to balance the budget, which only the legislature could do. Despite significant delays and obstruction, a budget was finally passed by the Bloc National, stabilizing the economy. The second was the crisis of 1936, which saw rising unemployment, inflation, and labor unrest following the market crash and global economic crisis. The effects of the Depression, slow to arrive in France but as severe in its impact, tested the stability of legislative coalitions as they had not been tested before. Ultimately, a coalition of the Left, now under the banner of the Popular Front, passed the French New Deal, restoring order and stabilizing the economy. That this was followed only a few years later by invasion and the rise of the Vichy government should not diminish the significance of what these legislative coalitions accomplished in maintaining viable parliamentary government throughout this period of extreme stress.

Episode 2: The Franc and the Crisis of 1924

The first test of the interwar period came in 1923 with an economic crisis that had its roots in war debt and the reconstruction efforts. In servicing its debt, France was heavily reliant on German war reparations, which ended abruptly in February 1923 when Germany declared it was unable to fulfill its obligations. Unable to reach a diplomatic solution and convinced that this was little more than a negotiating tactic on the part of the Germans wishing to exact more favorable conditions for reparations, France invaded the resource-rich Ruhr region. This move did little, however, to increase confidence in the French economy. From the start of the Ruhr occupation, the exchange value of the franc began to fall, with the rate of decline increasing rapidly in the closing months of 1923. The value of the franc was directly connected to the cost of living such that a depreciation of the franc would inevitably lead to inflation.[63] The government, relying on the restoration of German reparations, offered no fiscal response, ultimately leading to a panic at the French stock exchange in January 1924, signaling a full-fledged crisis.[64]

As the franc continued to fall, the crisis became apparent to all. Newspapers reported daily on the exchange rate, and the public's anxiety increased the threat of speculation and further decline. Maurice Bokanowski, rapporteur general of the Chamber's finance committee, described the mood as follows: "The anxiety reflected in conversations and on faces resembled the anguish caused in wartime by communiqués announcing bad news from our armies."[65]

This crisis offers important analytical leverage in that it spanned two governments, one of the Bloc National and another of the Cartel des Gauches, offering a window into the politics of legislative coalitions on the Left and the Right. It is also instructive in that it parallels the German crisis of 1923, also brought on by the invasion of the Ruhr. In France as well, the need to respond to a rapidly falling economy put a tremendous strain on the political system. And in France as well, leaders struggled to maintain their legislative coalitions and pass a budget that would end the crisis. But on this side of the conflict, legislators ultimately reached an agreement that allowed for a parliamentary resolution to the crisis.

At the time, the Bloc National, which had achieved a decisive victory in the first election after the war, held a majority of 412 out of 613 seats in the Chamber of Deputies. The government had at its disposal devaluation as the primary fiscal strategy to stabilize the currency. Devaluation, however, could only be expected to serve this purpose if the budget was balanced to ensure that the country could fulfill its expenditures. As budgetary matters required parliament's approval, this set in motion a five-week-long debate on how best to meet the challenges. Balancing the budget would require increasing revenue and decreasing expenditures.

The government proposed to achieve the first goal with an across-the-board 20 percent increase in all taxes.[66] The *double décime*, as it was called, had been previously debated in the Chamber but never garnered sufficient support, as it faced challenges on both the Left and the Right. The Left rejected the principle of a flat tax that treated different levels of income equally, preferring instead a progressive tax. The Right rejected the imposition of any direct income tax system, which they opposed ideologically as odious to French culture, preferring instead direct taxes on consumption.[67] Though a proposal for the double décime had failed as recently as 1920, the government revived it on this occasion largely because it was the simplest and most efficient way to increase revenue, but also because, unattractive as it was to many constituents, all other options would have been much less attractive.[68]

To achieve the second goal of reducing expenditures, the government turned to administrative reform. Government services and infrastructure had ballooned during the war, putting a significant strain on the budget. The Marín Commission had been established in 1922, under the leadership of Louis Marín, vice president of the Chamber, to identify areas of administrative reform that would reduce expenditures. Administrative reform proved a significant hurdle, as this would entail greater centralization of government function. The Marín Report, issued in December 1923, recommended shifting authority over the provision of services away from the arrondissement, or the electoral district, toward the department, a larger administrative unit not linked directly to elections or to the fortunes of legislators.[69] Investing the arrondissement with spending powers had created opportunities for rents that the move toward centralization would eliminate. As such, it posed a systematic threat to all incumbents, but especially to the Left, which had come to rely heavily on such spending as a means of meeting the needs of their constituents.

These complications meant that, while the government coalition of the Bloc National nominally held a decisive majority in the Chamber, identifying a viable legislative coalition to pass the budget was a different challenge. During the several weeks of debate that followed, the full range of ideological platforms were put on display. Socialists and Radicals dismissed the need for tax increases, insisting that the financial woes were linked to French foreign policy in the Ruhr. Members of the Right as well attempted to downplay the need for increased taxes, pushing instead for greater currency devaluation. The debate reflected political calculations as much as it did disagreements on economic policy, since elections were just a few months away, and no party wanted to be saddled with the record of highly unpopular taxes. A concession was ultimately made to secure the support of the Right among parties of the Bloc National. In exchange for their assent to the double décime, the government agreed to cede several government-held enterprises to private industry.[70]

On the question of administrative reform, there was less room to maneuver, as this affected all members whose incumbency rested on local control of state resources. Though the impact would have been greater on the Left, a significant number of MPs on the Right also protested. Unable to resolve the issue, the government fell on a no-confidence vote.[71]

New elections in May 1925 would see a sweeping victory for the center-left coalition of the Cartel des Gauches. On this, the first occasion of the cartel's electoral success, the SFIO declined to take a place in the government, ceding the premiership to Radical Édouard Herriot. While a great deal has been made of the failure to form a Socialist government at this time, it should be noted that the Socialists had signaled from early on that they would not participate in government.[72] This was in many ways welcomed by the Radicals. For the Socialists to join the cabinet, they would have required Vincent Auriol to be appointed finance minister as well as the adoption of a capital levy (tax on wealth), both of which were unacceptable to cartel partners.[73]

Declining to join the cabinet was an ideological statement, but as a matter of practical politics, the Socialists supported the policies of the Herriot government almost without exception. In fact, the Socialists took over the chairmanship of several committees in the legislature, including Auriol as head of the very powerful Chamber Finance Committee.[74] This was the first time a member of the SFIO was placed in such a prominent position. Despite the SFIO's absence from the governing coalition, the elevation of Auriol, a close ally of Léon Blum, head of the SFIO, to such a prominent position signaled significant accommodation among the cartel partners in the Chamber.[75]

This unity would quickly be tested as the economic crisis continued to embroil the country. The double décime tax increase had stabilized the economy for a time, but the price of the franc quickly began to drop immediately after the election. This was in part a reaction to the election of the cartel, and members of the SFIO took to calling it the "electoral franc," a reference to the political rather than economic forces at play in the value of the franc. Pointing in particular to the actions of the Bank of France, which had artificially propped up the franc to support the conservatives and quickly withdrew its support after the election, the Socialists charged that the bank was involved in a "reprisal" for the cartel's electoral success.[76]

If the victory of the cartel decreased confidence in the French economy at home, however, it increased it abroad, as it signaled a critical shift in French foreign policy on the Ruhr. The cartel had campaigned forcefully on bringing a peaceful end to the confrontation with Germany. This was a welcome development among France's close allies, especially the United Kingdom and the United States, where the invasion had been opposed from the start. The cartel's signaling of their intention in the Ruhr opened the door for financial assistance in the form of a substantial loan from J. P. Morgan, the terms of which were negotiated by Washington.[77] This loan was contingent, however, on the satisfactory resolution of the Dawes Plan, which would bring an end to the conflict in the Ruhr, with new reparations terms for Germany and a new settlement of interallied debt. On this occasion as well, the response to crisis required both executive action and legislative approval, particularly for the terms of the Dawes Plan. Though the legislative coalition remained intact and supportive of the foreign policy aims, the plan involved austerity measures that the Socialists especially would not countenance. To secure their support, the Herriot government offered a reduction of the double décime for the lowest income groups in the new budget, to be balanced with stricter enforcement of the income tax and new taxes on corporate wealth.[78] The Chamber voted in favor of the plan on August 23, 1924, by a margin of 336 to 204, with absolute discipline among the cartel partners.[79] With that, a legislative coalition of the Left passed a budget and one that, for the first time in the nation's history, the Socialists had played a leading role in shaping.

Critics of the French handling of the crisis have seen in this a failure, focusing on the fact that parties in parliament could not act more quickly.[80] Certainly the outcome may have been improved with faster action. The comparative perspective, however, with Germany facing a similar crisis, reveals the relative success of the French resolution and the significance of this being a *parliamentary* resolution with very limited independent executive action. In Germany, these same debates stretched for months and ended only with an Enabling Act empowering the executive to legislate in lieu of parliament. More importantly, in France, this episode lay the groundwork for future legislative cooperation in the crisis-ridden interwar period. The Bloc National and the Cartel des Gauches would continue to serve as a focal point of electoral and legislative politics, alternating in office and offering distinct policy programs in the coming years.

Episode 3: The Crisis of 1936

The next great test of legislative cooperation came in 1936 with another significant economic downturn. The effects of the Great Depression were slow to arrive in France. In fact, in 1929, the franc was in an especially strong position and the economy more stable than it had been in the previous decade.[81] The effects only began to manifest in 1931, and though less severe, they were longer lasting than in many other countries. While most of the world was well on the way to recovery by 1935, France was in the thick of its economic downturn.[82] The value of the franc dropped consistently between November 1935 and March 1936, leading to rising prices and a spike in unemployment. By April 1936, a general strike was called throughout the country, bringing industrial production in many sectors to a halt and threatening to damage the failing economy further.[83]

This labor unrest took place against the backdrop of rising fascist sentiment and right-wing violence, which, while infrequent, was symbolically powerful given the Nazi takeover in Germany.[84] Elections scheduled for May 1936 were explicitly focused on stabilizing the economy as a means of stabilizing the republic and defending against its detractors. It was in this context that the Popular Front emerged. The electoral alliance of Socialists and Radicals was by this point a familiar feature of French electoral politics, but on this occasion, they were joined by the Communists.

To be sure, this was an unprecedented occurrence, as the Communists' participation in the electoral pact implied ascent to a common program. And though it was never the intention of the Communists to join the government, they did commit their support to the Front's platform of economic justice and defense of democracy. This represented the most expansive alliance of the Left the country had ever seen. As unprecedented as this was, however, it should be stressed that the Popular Front was built on decades of legislative compromise and made possible by these long-standing repertoires of cooperation. Notably, it rested on the availability of multiple repertoires that allowed legislators to respond to both regime challenges and economic crisis. As Léon Blum reflected, "It was linked to, and was in large measure a product of, that which went before it."[85]

A large part of what made the Popular Front possible was the Communists' willingness to participate. This was significant not only because it added numbers to the cartel, but because it freed the SFIO to join in government, unfettered by the need to appease its Left flank. Just four years earlier, the Communists had refused any cooperation in government with the SFIO, which they labeled as "socialist fascists." Their refusal to join brought to power the National Unity government, a center-right coalition, but one that increasingly displayed fascist and authoritarian leanings, on occasion utilizing paramilitary forces to show strength, a development that led to widespread fears of democratic instability. The fascist takeover in Germany, partially enabled by the Communists' rejection of government participation, also loomed large. The French Communists' decision to join the Popular Front was remarkable in many ways, but importantly, it showed the availability of multiple repertoires at this time and the role of political creativity, on this occasion, on the part of Léon Blum, in navigating a seemingly impossible coalitional challenge.

The elections of 1936 saw a landslide victory for the Popular Front, with the SFIO as the largest party. In another first, the SFIO would not only join the government on this occasion, but would form the government under the leadership of Léon Blum. The challenges facing the new coalition were swift and severe. At the time they took office, the country had already experienced weeks of general strikes.[86] Emboldened by the victory of the first ever Socialist government, workers expanded their demands and intensified their recruitment efforts.[87] Demands included a forty-hour work week, wage increases, paid vacations, and mandatory collective bargaining. The new government undertook an intense period of negotiations between the Confédération Générale du Travail (CGT), a leading trade union organization, and the Confédération Générale de la Production Française (CGPF), the counterpart employers' association. In what came to be known as the Matignon Agreements (so named after the Hotel Matignon, at which they were signed), the government was able to get enough concessions from employers to convince workers to return. This included recognition of the right to strike, the removal of obstacles to union organization, and wage increases of 7–12 percent.

What made this resolution possible was the promise by the government to supplement these concessions with the provision of direct state benefits to meet the remaining demands of workers. To this end, the government undertook an expansive legislative project aimed at improving and expanding workers' benefits as well as their capacity for organization. This body of legislation would come to be known as the French New Deal, providing the foundations of the modern French welfare state. The Chamber took ten weeks to deliberate on the various components of the project. These deliberations would strain the coalition of the Popular Front to its limits, but in the end they delivered. Provisions for the forty-hour work week, paid vacation, and guarantees for collective bargaining were the centerpieces of a package that would remake the French domestic economy.

The Popular Front was in many ways also a regime coalition motivated by the goal of democratic preservation. This was clear from the start. But what is remarkable is that it also functioned effectively as a policy coalition and one that was able to expand its membership in a way that yielded concrete benefits in terms of economic policy. The availability of multiple repertoires meant that regime coalitions came to resemble economic coalitions. The two grew in tandem, and neither became overly entrenched. Again, the contrast with Germany is instructive. There, with a similar configuration of parties, the Communists prevented the viability of center-left coalitions, pushing the party system toward the pattern of polarized pluralism that would lead to repeated legislative failure. In both cases repertoires of conflict and cooperation enabled certain types of legislative coalitions and prevented others. The success of the center-left coalition in France would allow for the passage of legislation that would stabilize the economy and the country during a time of great turmoil. That the French government would fall to German invasion just a few years later should not detract from the fact that this and previous successful legislative coalitions maintained the strength of parliamentary government at a time in which other countries quickly reached for executive authority and decree powers.

The aim of this chapter is to show the effects of a particular path of institutional sequencing: the simultaneous introduction of mass suffrage and parliamentarization. In this case the critical juncture of institutional choice involved an expanded period of uncertainty. Despite the de jure parliamentarization of the regime in 1870, de facto parliamentarization—that is, the expectation and norm of parliamentary sovereignty—would not be secure until 1879. In the intervening years, the political system experienced a short but intense period of primary regime contention, which would lead to repertoires of conflict and cooperation in which party alliances were shaped by regime preferences. The short duration of regime contention, however, meant that these repertoires remained relatively flexible. The first episode that offered an opportunity to reform these alliances came at the turn of the century and would see repertoires significantly augmented, with center-left and center-right coalitions emerging along the economic dimension. A second episode in the 1920s presented threats to these emerging economic coalitions, as economic crisis and political radicalization on the Left would strain these alliances. But economic coalitions endured and helped stabilize both the economy and the political system throughout the interwar period. A final episode centered on the crisis of 1936 presented the ultimate test of legislative coalitions, as both regime threats and economic threats converged. On this occasion, the availability of multiple repertoires allowed legislators to successful identify coalitions to support necessary policy, fending off both executive encroachment and domestic threats to the regime.

Part II Conclusions

STRUCTURING SPACES AND ACTORS

THE THREE cases examined in part 2 represent three different modes of sequencing the two institutional pillars that were the focus of democratization in the first wave: parliamentarization and mass suffrage. Each mode of sequencing, chosen at a critical juncture of political development, had longstanding consequences for democratic politics, structuring political spaces and shaping the actors within them.

Perhaps the most instructive of the cases is the United Kingdom. As a model of democratization, its path has been so naturalized that it can be hard to see many features of the path itself. The received wisdom on the UK has focused on its gradualism as the key to stability. But we find here that it was not gradualism per se but a specific structuring of the political landscape that for much of the nineteenth century kept at bay regime contention by keeping out of legislative politics those who would challenge the status quo. Certainly, there was regime contention outside Parliament, but for the most part it remained outside. And this had a significant impact on political development throughout the nineteenth century, reducing the salience of the regime dimension in favor of the economic and leading to rigid repertoires of economic management that could not be dislodged, even at times of serious regime challenges, such as those introduced by the question of Irish Home Rule, which resurfaced regime contention time and again. But actors repeatedly rejected realignment along the regime dimension, reverting to familiar repertoires of economic management to identify friends and foes.

In addition, the actors involved, particularly parties, came to identify and align themselves in terms of their economic interests, another feature of political development in the United Kingdom that has been too readily naturalized. As the other cases demonstrate, it was not a given that parties would form and compete along the lines of their interests in an industrializing economy. But in the UK, this was the baseline resulting from the 1832 Reform Act. And as successive waves of suffrage expansion unfolded along economic lines, new parties were incorporated into the political system as class actors representing economic interests. They came into a political system that was already structured along the economic dimension and positioned themselves within this.

The reverse was true in the German case. There, the introduction of mass suffrage without parliamentarization led to an influx of new parties in the Reichstag. This intensified competition, as others have noted, but more importantly, it intensified it along the regime dimension. Dahl's original thesis on historical sequences maintained that in Germany, late parliamentarization meant that actors lacked practice in the "art of contestation." This analysis suggests that in fact they were highly skilled at the art of contestation, but those skills were formulated around repertoires of regime contention rather than economic management. In other words, delays in full parliamentarization did not halt party development and legislative politics; in fact, the introduction of mass suffrage accelerated it. But it did have the effect of orienting legislators toward questions of regime contention rather than economic policy. Throughout the imperial period, the regime question steadily pulled all political actors into its vortex, and parties increasingly began to identify and align themselves in terms of their regime preferences, despite ongoing efforts to realign along the economic dimension. It led to party fragmentation, particularly of the liberal forces, as splinter parties continually emerged to remedy the fact that the main liberal party was too taken with the regime question to properly address economic matters. Therefore, the salience of the regime dimension not only structured the political space but also shaped the actors within it.

This continued into the Weimar period, leading to political configurations that were suboptimal from a policy standpoint, but that made sense in view of the rigid repertoires of regime contention that had developed. A central thesis of this work is that to understand outcomes in Weimar, we need to look at the historical antecedents and the continuities across the threshold of regime transition. It also points to different temporalities for understanding political development, taking into account the asynchronic nature of institutional emergence. Democratic development in Germany did not begin with Weimar. It began with the introduction of mass suffrage in 1867. And the state of democratic politics at the time of the transition to Weimar was not "undeveloped," to borrow a phrase from the political economy canon.[1] Rather, it was highly developed, but it developed along lines that made governance exceedingly difficult, leading to repeated legislative breakdowns and ultimately executive encroachment.

Finally, turning to France, a case of simultaneous introduction of mass suffrage and parliamentarization, we find a path that had the potential to pull actors in the direction of either regime contention or economic management. The initial sequencing, as well as the prolonged and turbulent nature of the critical juncture of institutional choice, meant that although both institutional pillars were achieved by 1879, a great deal of residual regime anxiety would play out for the first decade of the Third Republic, as political forces aligned themselves, and many blatantly declared themselves in favor of the republic or against it. This might have led to the development of rigid repertoires of regime contention were it not for the tremendous acts of political creativity and the unmatched skill of Jean Jaurès in the Socialist camp and René Waldeck-Rousseau leading the Radicals. Starting at the turn of the century, they led their parties, and eventually the entire party system, toward a realignment along the economic dimension. Certainly, much residual regime contention would remain, but it was never allowed to take hold as it did in Germany. Rather, in France we see the emergence of multiple repertoires, as actors moved back and forth between regime coalitions and economic coalitions, and finally in the interwar period, through the political creativity of another Socialist Party leader, Léon Blum, a coalition that represented both regime and economic objectives. The path of France does not appear as stable as that of the United Kingdom, but it is noteworthy for a couple of reasons: (1) it did not involve the exclusionary dynamics that produced stability in the United Kingdom (the messiness of the French path may indeed be a virtue from a normative perspective); and (2) the inability to fully suppress regime contention led to the development of multiple repertoires, an orientation that, as I discuss in the concluding chapter, may be an important political resource for democracies embroiled in regime struggles today.

I turn in the concluding chapter also to a discussion of postwar development, which for the United Kingdom and France reflected a continuation of historical repertoires of conflict and cooperation, with the United Kingdom maintaining a stable Left–Right politics along the economic dimension, and France continuing its turbulent but democracy-preserving path of multiple repertoires into the Fourth and Fifth Republic. Germany, of course, experienced the greatest disruption to its political development, first with the Allied

176 PART II CONCLUSIONS

occupation, and then with continued Allied influence during the Cold War period. The main consequence of this was the suppression of the regime dimension through an exclusion not just of fascist actors on the Right, but importantly also of forces on the Left that might have unsettled the prevalent regime consensus. This yielded one of the most stable party systems in Europe in the postwar period, but again, stability came at the cost of exclusion. The tension between stability and inclusion, between governance and robust democratic defense, remains as relevant today as it has been historically. All three cases examined here offer important insights into how repertoires of conflict and cooperation have guided political development in the past and how we may utilize them today in service of both stable governance and democratic rejuvenation.

American Political Development

Part III Introduction

THE REGIME QUESTION
AND AMERICAN POLITICAL DEVELOPMENT

IN THE preceding chapters, I have developed a theoretical model to understand the emergence and persistence of the regime dimension in the politics of first wave democracies. It is a model very much built on the European experience. The concept of parliamentarization, the nature of the regime question, the choice of institutional sequencing—the key building blocks of the argument—all originate in the European experience of nation-state formation, and the resulting analysis yields a robust account of European political development. Given the great influence European democracies had on the rest of the world, this account holds import for the study of political development more broadly. But how exactly are we to understand this influence? And how might it inform our study of other contexts? Can this theoretical model help us explain outcomes in other places?

In part 3, I seek to take the insights gleaned from the European cases and expand the analysis to understand related process of political development in the United States. I choose to focus on the United States precisely because its political development throughout the nineteenth and early twentieth centuries was so intertwined with that of the European cases. In this far-flung former colony of a great European power, events in Europe were watched with great interest. European influence also arrived regularly through the influx of persons and ideas. And the influence flowed in the other direction as well. Its revolutionary origins and distinction as the only enduring republic of the Western world meant that the United States was highly influential in its own right. Events in the United States were watched closely in Europe, with both defenders and detractors of parliamentary government invoking it in turn as an example to emulate or avoid. Thus, incorporating the United States into the present analysis serves the important goal of historical understanding.

As important as the United States is to the present analysis, however, figuring out how to relate it to the other cases is a challenge. First, the United States does not fit neatly into the most-similar case design employed in the previous section. It is interconnected, to be sure, but that does not mean it bears enough of a resemblance that it can be slotted into a variable-based comparison with the other cases. To be clear, there are many instances in which the United States can fruitfully be combined in a most-similar case design with European cases, and indeed with many other cases as well.[1] The key issue to consider is whether there is a point of difference that may be theoretically relevant for the given research question. In this instance, there is. Given the divergent conditions of nation-state formation, and especially the absence of traditional monarchical and aristocratic institutions, theoretically relevant differences in the United States might affect the operation of the model and the variables within it. To include it in a most-similar case design would involve some conceptual stretching that could compromise confidence in our inferences.

The United States is also not a most-different case for many of the reasons noted.[2] As a settler colony, it had strong ties to Europe, most obviously to the UK but also to France, with which it shared a common revolutionary history and many political sympathies. Moreover, the United States may have broken with monarchical institutions, but it still very much had a monarchical tradition and history. And this influenced a great deal of thinking at the time of the founding and beyond. This means that the categories of European regime contention were quite familiar to the American public, and claims of exceptionalism notwithstanding, there was ongoing disagreement and anxiety about how different the United States actually was. Again, its interconnectedness confounds easy placement within variable-based Millian comparative schemes.

To incorporate the United States into the present analysis, I move to a different mode of inquiry and a different method of comparative analysis. I maintain the processual approach to the within-case analysis that is employed in other cases, using a critical juncture framework with an examination of repertoires to understand the impact of initial conditions on subsequent political development. Yet, rather than try to fit it within a nomothetically oriented case-based comparison, I engage in an evaluation of ideal types. This is a disciplined mode of open-ended inquiry that can advance both historical understanding and scientific knowledge.

This technique, pioneered by Max Weber, takes certain theoretical models and compares them to the observed social action in an evaluative exercise aimed at assessing the utility of the models.[3] It is a method of comparative analysis, but rather than comparing observations or cases to each other, it compares observations to the ideal type within a single case. The term "ideal type" has been widely used within the social sciences to connote various forms of abstractions. In this analysis it is used very narrowly, comparable to Weber's usage of the term within his historical and methodological writing.

The ideal type is understood to be a model of a historical person whose actions are animated by a specific set of motivations. The construction of the ideal type is meant to accentuate the characteristics to be evaluated, to exaggerate them even. It is a mental model of what the world would look like if actors were motivated exclusively by the ideal type: What would we expect to see? What kinds of actions would be consistent with the ideal type?

This approach is distinct from Millian case comparison in its methods and objectives. Within Millian case comparison, cases are compared to each other, and the inferences derived from the comparison should apply to a broader pool of cases defined by the scope conditions of the study.[4] In contrast, with an evaluation of ideal types, the case is compared to the ideal type, and the goal is to determine whether the ideal type can explain the observed social action in that case. This too involves generalization within the case examined but does not posit a broader set of cases to which the inferences apply.

Ideal types can be evaluated on their own or in comparison to others. The best example of the use of this approach comes from Weber himself. In his canonical work, *The Protestant Ethic and the Spirit of Capitalism*, he developed the ideal type of the Protestant ethic, animated by cultural as well as psychological factors related to early Calvinism and the doctrine of predestination, to account for a unique historical subjectivity and the emergence of a distinctive attitude toward labor and acquisition. The task of the analysis was twofold: first, to determine whether the ideal type can explain the observed social action; and second, to determine whether it can explain more than other ideal types. In his analysis, the Protestant ethic was contrasted to the ideal type of rational economic man, which dominated historical accounts of the period, and which Weber found inadequate to explain the observed social action, capitalist accumulation.[5] The ideal type of the Protestant ethic explained more of the observed action and therefore in this analysis held greater utility.

In the present analysis, the ideal type to be evaluated is a model of a historical person animated by regime considerations; in the context of the nineteenth and early twentieth centuries, this would be a historical person whose actions are motivated by anxieties over the status of representative government. The evaluation consists of a comparison of the model with the observed social action to determine whether the model can explain such action, whether it can explain as much as other ideal types, and whether it can potentially explain more.

In the context of US political development, where the most intense fights had to do with slavery and slave representation, other ideal types that have been advanced involve economic motivations and moral motivations. These are implicitly and explicitly compared at different points, but it is important to stress at the outset that ideal types are not understood to be mutually exclusive. On their own, each can capture only a dimension of social reality. This means that regime motivations, economic motivations, and moral motivations can and often do coexist. Indeed, by the turn of the century, economic motivations came to occupy a prominent place in US politics, *alongside* regime motivations. This duality had a significant impact on democratic development. Thus, the goal of the analysis will be not to refute these other motivations, but to illustrate that regime considerations, largely neglected in the study of US political development, were a powerful motivating force, and at key moments they can offer a better explanation of the observed action than other ideal types.

Conceptual Clarifications

Because the evaluation of ideal types involves the application of theoretical models derived from a different context, this evaluative exercise requires a translation or reinterpretation of some building blocks of the analysis.[6] Below I identify three key components and how they may be understood in the US context.

The regime question: The regime question, understood as a choice between different systems of government, was a powerful force in US political development throughout the nineteenth and early twentieth centuries. The specific binary posed in the US context, however, was different from the European case, as the main anxiety in the United States was not about the encroachment of the monarch, but rather about the aristocratic influence of wealthy slaveholders and property owners. Therefore, it was not a question of representative government or constitutional monarchy, as was the case in Europe, but rather representative government or oligarchy.

Parliamentarization: The concept of parliamentarization, understood as the empowerment of representative bodies, is broad enough that it can be fruitfully deployed in the United States. But here again the specific nature of the fight differed from those found in the European cases. As discussed in the introductory chapter, numerous conditions had to be met for a polity to be considered fully parliamentarized in the context of nineteenth- and early twentieth-century political development. A representative legislature would have to have (1) power over legislation; (2) independence from the Crown and aristocracy; (3) power over government formation; and (4) the ability to operate without the threat of dissolution. In the United States, the central issue at stake, and the institutional deficiency that called into question the full achievement of parliamentarization, was the slave representation, which disproportionately increased the power of wealthy slaveholders and property owners in the South. In the eyes of many at the time, this violated condition number 2. It is distinct from, but bears strong similarities to, the fight in the UK over the rotten boroughs. These were the target of the 1832 Reform Act in the UK and represented a similar institutional deficiency with respect to parliamentarization, though in the UK these rotten boroughs were thought to strengthen the Crown. Again, the struggle in the United States was distinct but highly relatable. Insofar as the slave representation was understood as the encroachment of an aristocratic element on the democratic representative body, as discussed extensively in the next chapter, it falls squarely within prevalent understandings of threats to parliamentarization at the time.

Sequencing: The sequencing of institutions at early stages of nation-state formation is posited in this analysis as a key factor in determining the salience of the regime question. With this key building block of the argument as well, the United States does not fit neatly into the modes of sequencing found in the European cases. I identify it as a path of "unsettled parliamentarization," which is not, strictly speaking, a sequence but a mode of vacillation between them. In some respects, the United States resembled the path of early parliamentarization in the UK: a representative legislature was granted governing power much earlier than mass suffrage was established. The institutional deficiencies with respect to the independence of the representative body from aristocratic influences, however, led to an unsettled path that at times ended up looking much more like Germany. In the United States therefore, parliamentarization was unsettled, not in the sense of being vulnerable to reversals—that was true of all democracies. Rather, it was unsettled in that the founding structures left considerable room for ambiguity and varied understandings of whether parliamentarization was actually achieved. This was compounded by the fact of western expansion, which unsettled matters even further and made it impossible for actors to settle into any status quo. This in itself was enough to ignite ongoing regime contention throughout the antebellum period and beyond.

This translation or reinterpretation of the conceptual building blocks of the analysis is not meant to suggest that this was all the same, or to force US struggles into European categories. Rather, it is to illustrate that a related story was unfolding in the United States. Part of what aided in this is that the actors involved were themselves engaged in processes of translation and frequently reached for European categories of regime contention as a means of making sense of their own situation. This sense making at times led *them* to view the conflicts as similar or even the same. As I aim to show in the following chapters, this led to patterns of regime contention that shared many of the dynamics of the European context and profoundly influenced US political development.

6

Roots of the Regime Question
in the United States

THE EMERGENCE OF REPERTOIRES
OF REGIME CONTENTION

THIS CHAPTER tells an unconventional story of US political development. It is one in which deep and enduring anxieties about the status of representative government led to ongoing regime contention similar to that which was unfolding across Europe. This is puzzling given the revolutionary origins of the United States and the absence of traditional monarchical and aristocratic institutions. One might expect that the break with its feudal past would have eliminated the regime question as such in the United States. And indeed, this is the prevalent narrative about US political development and the basis of many claims of exceptionalism.[1]

Yet we find in the United States throughout the nineteenth and twentieth centuries regime contention that closely approximated the fights over parliamentarization across Europe. These were struggles over core principles of democratic governance, particularly over the status of representative government. This mode of regime contention was related to but separate from struggles over the franchise—the focus of much work on democratic development in the United States.[2] And it was highly consequential throughout US political development, critically shaping the dynamics of party formation, legislative capacity, and democratic governance.

The different structural foundations in the United States meant that the categories of regime contention differed from those of the European context: a rising aristocracy, not a monarchy, was thought to pose the greatest danger to representative government in the United States; and the regime question pitted representative government not against the Crown, but against wealthy property owners. While the categories differed, however, these fights unfolded along lines similar to the European fights over parliamentarization. The reasons for this, I argue, are twofold: one institutional, and one ideational.

Institutionally, what triggered regime contention were institutional deficiencies in the US representative system that called into question whether the US political system was fully parliamentarized. As discussed in chapter 1, one of the key features of parliamentarization was that the democratic representative body (typically the lower chamber of the legislature) held independent governing power and could operate without interference from the Crown or the aristocracy. In the United States the biggest threat to this was from the disproportionate power granted to wealthy property owners in Congress as a result of the institution of slavery, especially "the slave representation"—the counting of the unfree, nonvoting slave population in the apportionment of congressional representatives. This was seen as an aristocratic arrangement that violated the democratic character of the House and jeopardized the republican character of the Constitution more generally. The affairs within slave states were not the key consideration; nor was it the morality of the institution of slavery or the actual representation of slaves that was at issue. Rather, regime contention centered on the disproportionate power given to wealthy slaveholding property owners as a result of the slave representation and claims that it represented an encroachment of aristocratic principles of governance on the democratic body.

Several "compromises" throughout the antebellum period were devised to manage the conflict, starting with the three-fifths clause adopted in the Constitution, which permitted the slave population to be partially counted at a ratio of three-fifths in congressional apportionment. This might have been enough to settle the matter and reduce regime contention were it not for western expansion, which repeatedly threw the balance of power into question and led to regime contention resurfacing throughout the antebellum period. This extended period of primary regime contention led to repertoires of conflict and cooperation based on regime considerations that would continue to shape legislative politics well past the Civil War.

The roots of regime contention also had an ideational component resulting from the influence of European ideas, persons, and events in the United States. Throughout the nineteenth and twentieth centuries, the histories of these two regions were very much intertwined, and events in Europe were highly influential in how actors in the United States would come to understand their own situation. At several important junctures, from the French and American Revolutions to the Revolutions of 1848 and the US Civil War, dense transnational networks facilitated the flow of ideas and often persons such that many actors in the United States came to see and understand their own conflicts through the lens of European regime contention. And as regime tensions intensified in Europe, anxieties rose in the United States.

While such equivalences may seem unwarranted, "reading history forward" in this case requires that we place events and words in context and understand fights as the actors understood them.[3] Recall that throughout much of the antebellum period, which saw the most intense regime contention in the United States, there existed no example of successful and durable republican government in Europe or elsewhere. The French Revolution, with its radical promise, failed not once but twice to establish a republic. The Revolutions of 1848 likewise promised to change conditions across Europe, only to be rebuffed by counterrevolutionary movements. The only reassurance Americans had of the security of their republic was that they had broken free from the feudal institutions that held Europe down. But if the slave representation was an aristocratic arrangement, as it was argued; if indeed it signaled an encroachment of the aristocratic principle on the democratic body—the representation of property and not of persons—then there was much less reason to be reassured. Indeed, stripped of the knowledge that democracy would endure (knowledge that we have and they did not), republican government in the United States appears much less secure throughout this period.

The fears driving regime contention in the United States have been too readily dismissed by historians, who often classify them as hyperbolic or even paranoid.[4] Typically, the conflict is characterized in sectional terms, with scholars identifying different root causes: economic conflict, moral conflict, cultural conflict, and so on. It was, of course, all of these things. But, as this analysis aims to show, it was also a conflict over the regime itself, particularly over the balance of republican and democratic elements relative to aristocratic and autocratic influences. To say that these conflicts contained a strong element of regime contention is not to say that they were not sectional, but simply to identify different roots of sectional conflict.

I maintain that regime contention was an essential component of actors' understanding of the conflict, coloring debates about federalism, slavery, economic interests, and a range of other issues. To be sure, the regime insecurities felt in the United States may seem unfounded to the contemporary observer. But they are there in the historical record. And to the actors involved, for whom the fate of the republican experiment was yet unknown, much evidence suggests that the fear was real, and it dominated the organization of politics for much of the nation's development. Therefore, a rigorous analysis of political development in this case requires that we take seriously the possibility of genuine regime contention and examine what role it may have had in motivating actions.

In making this argument, I am both drawing on and contrasting with the dominant understanding of US political development. Perhaps the strongest contrast is the view of regime contention advanced here, one that centers fights over the rules of the game as the object of the most intense conflict. Beyond that I maintain that this mode of regime contention was so strong and so persistent that it came to constitute a dimension of politics, that in fact the regime dimension dominated political organization throughout much of US political development, and that it never completely receded, a view that challenges prevalent understanding of alignment and realignment in US politics. The conceptualization of realignment offered here shares with proponents of alignment theory an appreciation of the importance of realignment for an understanding of US political development, but influenced by a comparative perspective, it offers a view of realignment that can better reflect both change and continuity over time.

An Evaluation of Ideal Types

To assess the role of regime considerations in US political development, I use an evaluation of ideal types. The logic of this approach is discussed in the introduction to part 3 of the book. Here I wish to clarify the objectives of the analysis. The specific ideal type to be examined here is a model in which actions are motivated by regime considerations. These regime considerations are not identical to those found in European struggles for parliamentarization, but they are highly analogous, having to do with the independent governing power of representative bodies.

In the United States, regime anxieties centered on the slave representation and what that meant in terms of the power of property versus persons. This was also intertwined with fights over states' rights and the power of the executive.[5] In many ways these were two sides of the same fight, with arguments for states' rights invoked, developed, and refined over the course of the antebellum period to defend the institutions of slavery on which the southern political economy was so heavily reliant. In this analysis, I focus on the slave representation, which I identify as the prime mover in regime struggles, and that which gives the clearest picture of the dynamics. I proceed with the understanding, however, that many other issues also figured prominently in these struggles and are embedded within the regime ideal type.

While the main objective of this evaluation is to show the utility of the regime ideal type, it should be stressed that ideal types are not understood to be mutually exclusive. On their own, each can capture only a dimension of social reality. This means that regime motivations may exist alongside economic motivations and moral motivations—other ideal types that have also been offered to explain fights over the slave representation. Therefore, the goal of the present analysis is not to refute other ideal types. I accept that all these motivations may have been at work. Rather, the goal is to show that regime considerations, largely neglected in the study of US political development, were a powerful motivating force and at key moments offer a better explanation of the observed action than other ideal types.

Specifically, I aim to show that (1) regime motivations, understood in terms of struggles over the power of representative bodies similar to those found in the European context, were an important and consequential factor in US political development; (2) that they can explain the observed social action—in this case, party development and legislative coalitions; and (3) that in some instances they can explain more of the observed social action than other noted motivations. This approach is uniquely suited to the examination of the United States. Precisely because the history of regime contention may have been "read out" of the secondary literature on US political development, a referential reading of this sort can help unearth important elements of the conflict.

Reconceptualizing Realignment in the United States

Examining political development through the lens of regime contention leads to a distinctive interpretation of party development and party system change in the United States, one that engages with questions of party alignment and realignment but does so in ways that are quite distinct from prevalent theories of alignment in the field of American political development. What I offer here is an account that understands alignment and realignment in terms of movement from one dimension to another. This implies both the displacement of salient issues and the reorganization of coalitions to achieve new objectives. Importantly, within this framework, realignment is understood not only with reference to what came immediately before, but in view of long-term political transformations. In the US context, given that early legislative coalitions were driven by the logic of regime contention, realignment is conceived as a move from politics organized along the regime dimension to that organized along the economic dimension, a move that I argue has never been fully achieved.

This conceptualization stands in contrast to the conventional understanding of electoral realignment in the United States. Rooted in the foundational work of V. O. Key Jr. and Walter Dean Burnham, a substantial literature has analyzed historical realignments in the United States, typically identifying five key realignments and corresponding party system change during the period examined here: the first in the 1820s, the second in the 1850s, the third in the 1890s, the fourth in the 1930s, and the fifth in the 1960s.[6] Most of the literature has been focused on identifying the precise timing and nature of realignments, examining critical elections, and understanding shifts in the electorate.[7] Important as this work has been to understanding US political development, within this literature the focus has been primarily on understanding the switch points—critical elections and moments of change that usher in new coalitions. Realignment is typically understood in terms of what came immediately before. Without a view of long-term political development, it can exaggerate change and miss important points of continuity.

This has been the subject of many critiques of alignment theory. Scholars have challenged both its historical interpretation of key episodes, such as the "system of 1896," as well as its theoretical claims of distinct periods in which the entire political system becomes ordered around a single logic.[8] Karen Orren and Stephen Skowronek, in particular, have offered a forceful challenge to alignment theory with the concept of institutional intercurrence, arguing that separate institutional arenas operate with their own logic and pace of political change that will invariably frustrate efforts at wholesale periodization or claims of realignment.[9]

My conceptualization of realignment takes on board many of the critiques. First, what I offer here is much more circumscribed, focusing exclusively on the alignment of parties in Congress.[10] It does not assume that the logic governing party alignment in legislatures extends beyond this institutional context, nor that broader political patterns are driving party alignment. Consistent with the principle of "multiple orders," I maintain that legislative party alignment follows its own logic.[11] Further, I argue that this logic is derived from early stages of political development and the repertoires that legislators acquire.

Second, and relatedly, this approach to party alignment does not adopt the same periodization as alignment theory, which posits at least five realignments over the course of the nineteenth and twentieth centuries. This view of realignment found in alignment theory is hard to reconcile with comparative perspectives. Given that realignments involve substantial political and social transformation, one would not expect them to be so frequent. For Lipset and Rokkan, party system alignment was deeply structural, rooted in social identities that are not easily amenable to change. Indeed, their canonical work is motivated by the puzzle of why there had been so little change in European party systems.[12] Following this work, scholars have continued to debate whether there has been genuine realignment in European party systems. Many have maintained that there has been no real realignment; that while parties have changed, party systems have not.[13] Those arguing that there has been realignment have rested those claims on significant structural shifts—globalization and Europeanization—leading to a breakdown of social formations and the emergence of a new dimension of politics.[14] In both cases, the understanding is that the bar for realignment is quite high, and the expectation is that they should be infrequent.

The perspective in this analysis does not strictly adhere to the structural view of realignment advanced by Lipset and Rokkan, offering instead the possibility of agentic routes to realignment with actors who seek to alter repertoires and reform coalitions. The historical institutionalist approach taken here, however, would still point in the direction of greater continuity and difficulty in altering repertoires after they have become entrenched. Thus the expectation is still that full realignments would be difficult to achieve and should be infrequent. In my analysis, the purported realignments of realignment theory represent important inflection points and even attempted realignments (see figure 6.1), but I see across these periods and party systems great continuity and a persistent struggle to realign away from the regime dimension toward the economic dimension, a process that is never fully achieved.

In my account of US political development, at no point does the regime dimension completely recede. That is to say, there is no full realignment. Rather, the regime dimension continues to operate and compete with the economic dimension. The only episode approaching full realignment is that which produced the New Deal party system. In this analysis, this is understood as a realignment not only or primarily in relation to what came before—the system of 1896—but in relation to long-term political development moving politics away from the regime dimension, which dominated antebellum politics, toward the economic dimension, which was the dominant logic of New Deal coalitions. Importantly, even the realignment of the 1930s rested on a

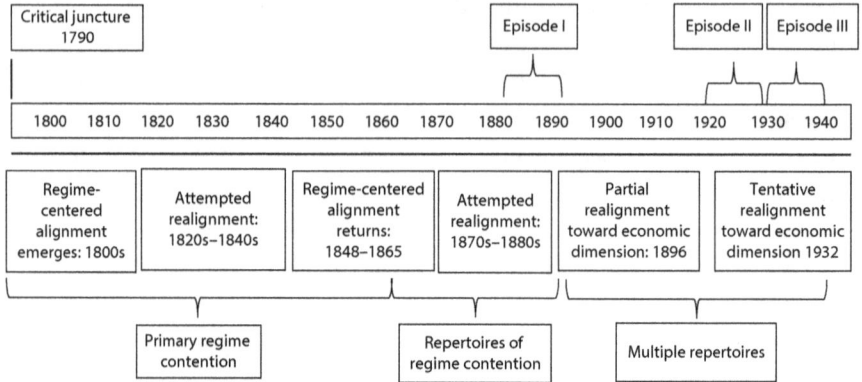

FIGURE 6.1. US timeline

suppression of regime contention, which would resurface once again in the 1960s. Thus, in this analysis the realignment is considered tentative. The messiness of this multidimensional political space led to a great deal of tumult but also proved to be a source of strength, as it allowed actors to develop multiple repertoires as they grappled with both regime and economic challenges. The availability of multiple repertoires increased legislative capacity while also allowing for significant periods of regime contention.

The concept of realignment remains important for an understanding of political development in the United States, and the conceptualization offered here renders it a more flexible and meaningful reflection of change and continuity. In each period there is significant change in legislative coalitions. Even in periods in which regime coalitions are said to return, they are not the same coalitions. Rather, what connects them is that they are organized around regime objectives and aligned along the regime dimension. The view of US political development that results from this reading is summarized in figure 6.1.

This chapter examines the first half of the timeline, beginning with the critical juncture of institutional choice at the time of the founding. The institutional configuration at this time reflected a choice to establish a republican constitution at the national level, but one in which the representation of propertied interests via the slave representation resulted in the encroachment of aristocratic influences within the democratic lower chamber. This led to ongoing regime contention and to legislative coalitions dominated by actors' preferences regarding the regime. A concerted attempt at realignment emerged during the period of Jacksonian democracy, which saw proto-economic coalitions emerging in Congress. This realignment might have succeeded were it not for the question of western expansion. The entry of new slave states disturbed the balance established at the time of the founding and enflamed regime contention. This could not be balanced by the addition of new free states, as the three-fifths clause gave slave states disproportionate representation in the House, and even though the population of free states grew much faster, the disproportionality of representation grew with every state added. Fears of the ascendance of the slaver power and the aristocratic influence of the southern states reached their peak in the 1850s, leading to a return to regime coalitions and ultimately war. The ongoing regime struggles during the antebellum period led to the formation of repertoires of regime contention that would carry over into the post–Civil War period. I begin in the next section with the critical juncture of institutional choice that sets these dynamics in motion.

Critical Juncture: A "Balanced Constitution"

The critical juncture of institutional choice in the United States came at the time of the founding, specifically, during the extensive deliberations over the Constitution between 1787 and 1790. The revolution had ushered in a period of heightened uncertainty and radical openness in which many possible paths were available to actors. Long before the British Reform Act of 1832 would establish the dominance of Parliament and even before the Estates General would give way to the French National Assembly, the US founders would debate one of the most robust instantiations of representative government in the modern history of the West. The revolutionary break with the traditional institutions of monarchy and aristocracy left the field wide open for experimentation, and the founders were well aware of this.

The critical nature of this moment in US history, and in the history of modern democracy more broadly, few would dispute. Whether it represents a critical juncture for the present analysis, however, needs to be further substantiated. Was this really a period of radical openness in terms of institutional choice? We know that there was genuine uncertainty about the extent of the franchise; that has been well documented. But was there uncertainty about parliamentarization? In the absence of an established monarchy and aristocracy, was the regime question really a question? Certainly the United States saw nothing like the confrontations between Parliament and the Crown that we find the UK, and the American Revolution had a much lower bar to displace its monarchy than did the French and certainly the German. In addition, despite the presence of feudal elements throughout the colonial period, a landed aristocracy never became entrenched in the same way in the United States. Given these differences, one might expect that representative government, with independent governing power vested in a democratic legislature— what in this analysis would be understood as full parliamentarization—was a foregone conclusion. Despite these differences, however, many aspects of European regime contention could be found in the United States during this critical juncture and were highly consequential for long-term political development.

The period between the Revolution and the ratification of the Constitution saw intense debates over the nature and purpose of representative government. The debates were open ended in that there was genuine uncertainty about institutional choice. And they were particularly heated with respect to the power of representative legislatures. The status quo going into the Constitutional Convention heavily favored representative government in which legislatures dominated. The immediate prerevolutionary period had seen an explosive democratization of legislatures. In state government particularly, legislatures had become the central organs of government, and legislatures themselves had become much more representative of the population.[15] At the national level as well, the legislature dominated. Under the Articles of Confederation, Congress was the main body of governance; the executive was little more than a coordinating committee, and the judiciary was not yet established as a national institution.

This did not mean, however, that the power of Congress was settled. In fact, the dominance of representative bodies in the prerevolutionary period produced a backlash. While the framers undoubtedly intended Congress to be a focal point of governance, the creation of a strong executive as well as a powerful upper chamber was offered as a means of balancing this, an attempt to temper the revolutionary fervor and rein in representative legislatures, which had come to dominate political life during the colonial period. In the debates over the Constitution, the struggle over the power of the legislature versus the executive reflected many of the concerns over parliamentary sovereignty found in the European context at the time, indicating that the regime question was very much central to the US founding and that many aspects of European regime contention shaped the contours of debate in the United States.

As with its European counterparts, the idea of a "balanced constitution" held powerful sway in the United States.[16] In this view, representative legislatures were broadly seen as the institutional organ that embodied the democratic principle, but ideas of good government typically sought to balance this with other elements less beholden to the whim of the demos. The typical formula contained some combination of a popular representative body, usually a legislative lower chamber representing the democratic element, with an executive representing the monarchical element, and a legislative upper chamber representing the aristocratic element. According to Gordon Wood, "Most American revolutionaries in 1776 had no intention of abandoning this celebrated theory of mixed or balanced government—even though they were throwing off monarchy and establishing republics. They still believed that their new republican state governments, although now elective, ought to embody the classic principles of monarchy, aristocracy, and democracy."[17] This trinity was expressed through different ideological formulations across the democratizing world; in the United States, it was captured within theories of republicanism that aimed to maintain a balance between the House of Representatives representing the democratic element, the president representing the monarchical element, and the Senate representing the aristocratic element.[18]

What precisely it meant to "balance" these different components, however, was the subject of significant contention. Given the dominance of Congress under the Articles of Confederation, many believed going into the Constitutional Convention that the status quo represented an imbalance—that it was too heavily weighted toward the democratic element.[19] Efforts to curtail the power of Congress and restore balance centered heavily on the design of the executive, which was frequently discussed in terms of its relationship to monarchies. In fact, a substantial literature has now documented the influence of monarchical thinking on the design of the US presidency.[20] While the Revolution radically broke with the institutions of monarchy, it could not completely dispense with the influence of monarchical thinking, which had deeply influenced the founders.[21] This should not be surprising. European monarchies were the closest available examples on which to model governing institutions. Where else were the founders to look for ideas about executive power? Furthermore, by this point, European monarchies had gone through many transformations, and most would no longer be considered absolute. In many countries, monarchs had come to function much like a constitutional executive.[22] It has been noted that in fact the powers granted the US president outstripped those of many European monarchs at the time.[23] While few seriously considered monarchy a viable option for the executive in the United States, the lines between the two were frequently blurred in ways that recalled many elements of European regime contention.[24]

The resulting constitution did indeed establish a strong executive and an upper chamber, both indirectly elected, to balance the democratic element, but it also affirmed the power of a national representative legislature, securing parliamentarization at the national level in all but one important respect: the influence of propertied interests in the House of Representatives via the slave representation meant that the Constitution fell short of full parliamentarization. Before moving on to that, however, I examine the fate of mass suffrage during this critical juncture.

Suffrage

Another significant choice that was made during this critical juncture was on the question of suffrage. By the time delegates to the Constitutional Convention got to this discussion, already the question had been narrowed because it was determined that both the president and the Senate would be elected indirectly. The question that remained had to do with elections to the House. We know now that the outcome of these debates would be a limited franchise following the parameters established within the states. This was a compromise of sorts, but not between defenders of universal suffrage and opponents. In fact, there were very few strong advocates of mass suffrage in the convention.[25] Even James Madison, who came the closest, stopped short of a full endorsement of universal suffrage. He saw it as perhaps inevitable but something to be delayed for as long as possible to curb its negative effects.[26] In the meantime, he maintained that "the freeholders of the country would be the safest depositories of republican liberty."[27] The prevailing consensus at the convention was that a broad franchise would be too great a risk. Most preferred to limit this to freeholders (property owners).[28] Delegates offered various arguments for limiting the franchise, rehearsing some of the prevalent themes of the time: the poor were too ignorant; they lacked a will of their own; if they combined, they would pose a threat to property; and, perhaps most prominent, the "stake in society" argument prevalent in the colonial period, which held that only those who held real property were sufficiently invested in the community and affected by the laws to be entrusted with the right of suffrage.[29]

The dilemma here was that a limited franchise would clash with states' regulations. There was a high level of variability in the extent of the franchise within the states, and some were close to full adult male suffrage. To adopt a limited franchise for national elections would mean that some electors who could vote in the states would be stripped of that right for national elections. It was feared that this might be enough for some to reject the federal Constitution. "The right of suffrage," it was maintained, "was a tender point, and strongly guarded by most of the state constitutions. The people will not readily subscribe to the National Constitution, if it should subject them to be disenfranchised."[30] The compromise that was ultimately reached was to align the national franchise with that in the states. It was a concession to expediency more than anything. Delegates did not wish to extend the franchise any further than necessary, and this allowed them to limit it in a way that was politically viable. The resulting suffrage arrangements left only about one in six adult white males eligible to vote.[31]

The Slave Representation and the Roots of Regime Contention

The adoption of limited suffrage in the United States could have potentially put the country on a path of early parliamentarization similar to that of the UK were it not for one particular defect of the Constitution—its acceptance of the institution of slavery and more importantly slave representation in the apportionment of congressional representatives. Both were associated with aristocratic power and seen as a threat to republican government. The source of regime contention on this matter, it should be stressed, was not the issue of suffrage, nor was it the subjugation of the slave population. Rather, it was about the concentration of power in the hands of wealthy slave owners. The association of slavery with aristocracy was commonplace. James Madison had offered the logic as follows: "In proportion as slavery prevails in a State, the Government, however democratic in name, must be aristocratic in fact. The power resides in a part instead of the whole: in the hands of property, not of number."[32] Property versus numbers was the essence of the divide— not who was included in the polity, but how much power was wielded by each of its constituent parts. Basing representation so heavily in favor of property in the slave states, according to Madison, is what rendered them aristocratic.

What was most threatening, however, was not the nature of representation within the slave states, but how this would affect national representation. Slave states wanted to have the unfree slave population (considered by them as property) counted in the apportionment of seats in the House of Representatives. Not only would this give them disproportionate influence in the House, that influence would be based on the property in enslaved persons they held.[33] This was different from the property qualifications for suffrage that were prevalent at the time. Those qualifications placed a bar on suffrage, but once this bar was passed, all would be granted equal power. The slave representation was substantially different in that it gave slave owners collectively disproportionate power based on property in enslaved persons. Such an arrangement, it was argued, would throw off the supposed balance of the mixed constitution. It represented the encroachment of aristocratic or oligarchical principles on the House, the body that was to represent the democratic element of the Constitution.

This was a central theme of many challenges to the Constitution. The charge of aristocratic intent was commonly leveled, particularly by northern antifederalists, who saw in the design of the Constitution a retreat from the principles of the Revolution.[34] The slave representation in particular was seen as decisively tipping the scales, an "ill-boding prelude," as one commentator described it, "soaring to the summit of aristocracy."[35] Critics claimed that under the proposed Constitution, the House would be a "pretended concession to democracy" and would easily succumb to aristocratic influences, which would hold disproportionate power.[36] In legislation it was argued that "one southern man with sixty slaves, will have as much influence as thirty-seven free men in the eastern states."[37] This disproportionate influence of property was at the heart of regime contention and would come to form the basis of enduring regime anxieties centered on the "slave power" that would pervade national politics throughout the antebellum period.[38]

The apportionment of the slave states was one of the fiercest debates of the Constitutional Convention, and it ended with one of the convention's most famous and notorious "compromises," the three-fifths clause, which stipulated that the apportionment of seats would be "determined by adding to the whole Number of free Persons . . . three fifths of all other Persons."[39] The three-fifths ratio was not arbitrary. It was calculated based on the existing populations and calibrated to bring the representation of free states and slave states to parity. The formula gave slave states thirty seats, and free states thirty-one.[40] It quickly drew criticism from delegates of free states. One of the most outspoken critics of the clause was Gouverneur Morris, who argued that it enhanced "the most prominent feature in the aristocratic countenance of the proposed Constitution." Specifically, it engendered the "vassalage of the poor," "the favorite offspring of Aristocracy."[41] Others, such as Governor Elbridge Gerry of Massachusetts, argued that, in granting greater representation to property, the provision revealed aristocratic intent.[42]

Importantly, the confrontation over the slave representation took place not only between supporters and opponents of slavery but among its opponents as well, who divided in this period along lines that would continue to animate politics throughout the antebellum period—abolition versus antislavery.[43] The crucial distinction was that the abolitionist position saw no possibility of accommodating slavery and no means of coexistence in a union with the slave states; the antislavery position, on the other hand, took a pragmatist stance, seeking a gradual end to slavery through various limitations.[44] This divide frequently overlapped with the divide on the national question, with abolitionists gravitating toward the antifederalist position, and federalists embracing an antislavery agenda, seeking concessions and compromises on the slave representation for the sake of union.[45]

The logic animating the antislavery federalists' position can be seen in the writings of Madison, for example. While he acknowledged the regime concerns associated with slavery, he argued that the accommodation of slavery was needed for the sake of union. In Federalist 54 Madison made a specific plea for the three-fifths clause on the basis of political expediency, imploring readers, "Let the compromising expedient of the Constitution be mutually adopted."[46] But perhaps more importantly, he saw the limitations on slavery imposed in the Constitution, particularly the ban on the transatlantic slave trade, which would take effect after twenty years' time, as sufficient to contain slavery so that it would come to a natural end. A passage from Federalist 42 makes these expectations clear. In it Madison touted the proposed ban as a great accomplishment, "a point gain in favor of humanity, that a period of twenty years may terminate forever, within these States, a traffic which has so long and so loudly upbraided the barbarism of modern policy, it will receive a considerable discouragement from the federal government, and may be totally abolished, by a concurrence of the few States which continue this unnatural traffic, in the prohibitory example which has been given by so great a majority of the Union."[47]

The view expressed by Madison and other antislavery federalists held that slavery was a vestige of the past, and as southern economies modernized, proponents of slavery would come to recognize this and adapt. This view was reinforced even by proslavery federalists, such as Charles Pickney, who opposed the ban but argued that "if the Southern States were let alone, they will probably of themselves stop importations."[48] And indeed one of the central themes of debates at the convention and in the push for ratification was whether it was reasonable to expect slavery to end on its own, with many antislavery federalists arguing that this was indeed a reasonable expectation and that the ban on the transatlantic slave trade would seal its fate.[49] The accommodation of slavery at this time might not have been possible were it not for the expectation that it would, in due course, come to an end. To put it differently, antislavery federalists were willing to put questions of national unification above the regime question, but only because they saw concessions on the latter as temporary.

The compromise on the three-fifths clause was indeed an expedient, and there may not have been any other route to ratification. But it was an unstable equilibrium from the start. This compromise was built for 1787. While antislavery federalists had claimed and hoped that slavery would die out on its own, we now know that the limitations on the transatlantic slave trade proved grossly inadequate and even counterproductive in containing slavery. States like South Carolina and Georgia, in fact, brought in more slaves in these twenty years than in any previous twenty-year period.[50] And by 1808 there were enough enslaved persons to fuel the domestic slave trade, which had not been banned, and to support further western expansion of slavery, which the Constitution provided no means of regulating.[51]

Of course, actors at the time did not have this knowledge. This helps us understand why such a compromise on the regime question was acceptable to them, and why, over the course of the antebellum period, and with every act of western expansion, regime anxieties grew.[52] This was driven by fear that the "slave power," understood as an illegitimate and disproportionate power based on wealth and property in enslaved persons, would come to dominate national politics and undo the republican character of the Constitution. This fear would repeatedly resurface the regime divide, driving party formation and political development throughout the antebellum period.[53]

It should be noted at the outset that the regime anxieties associated with the slave power, a focal point of this analysis, touch on questions of the "slave power thesis," or "slave power conspiracy," as it is sometimes referred to. This is the idea, which circulated in many antislavery and abolitionist circles, that slaveowners were seeking a takeover of the federal government to protect and expand slavery. The slave power thesis has received a great deal of scholarly attention, much of it skeptical, and I do not here take it at face value. Skeptics have characterized it as no more than idle conspiracy theory, attributing it to the "paranoid style" that pervaded antebellum politics.[54] Others have set aside the more outlandish conspiratorial elements of the slave power rhetoric and acknowledged that a credible threat was at the heart of claims of southern domination.[55] Eric Foner maintained that there was "much truth" in the charge. Richard Sewell has argued that even if the claims at the heart of the thesis were at times exaggerated, they "were by no means baseless."[56] And others have demonstrated in a nonsensationalist way the presence of institutions of aristocracy and feudalism at the founding and beyond.[57]

The analysis offered here does not presume to settle this debate but focuses instead on the actual function of the slave representation and how it drove regime anxieties, whether or not slaveowners in fact held the intentions attributed to them. What is important for the present analysis is that the three-fifths clause *did* disproportionately advantage property—an institutional arrangement that was correctly associated with aristocratic government. And the incorporation of new states compounded this problem. Whatever we might think of the language used, the analysis of the situation was in many ways accurate. Whether the slave states had these aristocratic or oligarchical ambitions, this anxiety was persistent throughout the antebellum period, driving many aspects of national politics.

The First Party System
and the Emergence of Regime Coalitions

Early party development in the United States reveals the impact of the unsettled state of parliamentarization. A compromise that would become obsolete by the time of the first congressional elections, in which already two states were added to the union, the slave representation continued to be a source of intense regime contention.[58] Efforts to alter the status quo began in the first sessions of the First Congress.[59] And throughout the first decade of the republic, the question and its regime implications were injected into a wide array of debates that seemingly held little relation to it. A proposal to place a tax on slaves was introduced to a routine tariff bill, leading to acrimonious exchanges. A debate on how to deal with fraudulent land claims was turned into an indictment of the indolence of the southern planter. An accord negotiated with Britain was called into question because of violations of the Treaty of Paris regarding compensation for slaves removed from the colonies. These were not mere passing skirmishes; each led to weeks-long debates and negotiations.[60]

By the 1800s the loosely organized factions of the House would assemble themselves into two parties, the Federalists and the Democratic-Republicans.[61] Until this point, the slavery debate had not clearly mapped onto party lines or even onto the geographic divide of North versus South. This would quickly change. Between 1800 and 1820 several events would put the fragile equilibrium of the slave question to the test and resurface many aspects of regime contention associated with the slave power. The Louisiana Purchase of 1803, the expiration of the constitutional protection of the slave trade of 1808, the War of 1812, and finally the expansion of 1820 into Missouri and Kansas—each of these events threw into flux the status quo established in the Constitution.[62] The disproportionate influence of the slave states was being evidenced not only in the House, but also extended to the election of the president, and even to party caucuses, enflaming regime contention and pushing parties to adopt adversarial positions on the slave question.[63]

Party leaders knew the issue held existential implications for both sides that would threaten not only their political goals but the union itself. They worked to keep the issue out of the House, but it frequently found expression elsewhere. Direct challenges to the three-fifths clause came as early as 1804. On the heels of the Louisiana Purchase, the state of Massachusetts proposed a constitutional amendment to "repeal the federal ratio" and base apportionment instead on free inhabitants. It warned that the union could not "harmoniously exist for a long period" unless all free citizens were given "equal political rights and privileges in the Government, so that a minority of free Citizens may not govern a majority, an event, which on the principles of representation now established, has already happened, and may always happen."[64] Another proposal emerged out of the Hartford Convention in 1814, a series of meetings among northern Federalists opposing the War of 1812.[65] In addition to repealing the three-fifths clause, the convention sought to establish a two-thirds vote in the House for the admission of new states. Neither proposal was considered by Congress, but they added fuel to what by 1819 would become a raging fire.

The Missouri Crisis of 1819 was the first time the threat of western expansion was made clear. The controversy centered on whether Missouri would be admitted without restrictions on slavery. The Constitution offered no clear answer as to Congress's power to restrict slavery in new states, rendering it a purely political battle between pro- and antislavery forces. The stakes could not have been higher. The question of slavery, as many representatives reminded the House, was the question of union. This was made explicit in many remarks. Charles Pickney of South Carolina, for example, opined that he could not conceive of "any question, but the one which respects slavery, that can divide us."[66]

But for the antislavery contingent, the stakes were just as high. Rufus King, the outspoken senator from Massachusetts, dedicated two lengthy speeches to the topic, in which he identified the three-fifths clause as the most significant source of grievance. The principle of equality, he maintained, was a "vital

principle in our theory of government." Referencing the apportionment compromise reached in the Constitution, he continued, "the departure from this
principle in the disproportionate power and influence allowed to the slaveholding states was a necessary sacrifice to the establishment of the Constitution." The effects of this concession were "obvious in the preponderance which
it has given to the slaveholding states." Though he did not wish to disturb this
agreement, which he recognized was a necessary condition for the ratification
of the Constitution, he insisted that it was intended only for the original states,
and that "the extension of this disproportionate power to the new States would
be unjust and odious."[67]

In the political press the charge was put more plainly. William Duane, editor of the Philadelphia-based *Aurora*, identified the slave representation as the
"most odious of all the aristocracies that human cupidity had ever devised,"
the extension of which would undermine "the rights of the free people of this
union."[68] In state legislatures, the debate raged as well. One senator from New
Hampshire opined that slavery was incompatible with democracy, as "it de-
generates to aristocracy, to monarchy, and perhaps despotism itself."[69] Governor Oliver Wolcott of Connecticut warned his legislature that "a diversity of
habits and principles of government" was growing in the nation, giving greater
influence to an "aristocratic order."[70]

Were these sentiments sincere? Were politicians merely cynically resurrect-
ing the language of regime contention from the founding to advance other
goals—religious or moral ideals, economic interests, or simple power seeking?
To be sure, multiple motivations could be found for the use of such rhetoric,
but once again, regime considerations have been too quickly dismissed in the
literature. Though concerns about threats to republican government are abun-
dantly found in these exchanges, subsequent historical interpretations have
dismissed them as insincere polemics or ignored them altogether.[71] In some
accounts, descriptions of the charges of aristocratic aspirations are often qualified with terms like "supposed" and "so-called."[72] Some have pointed to the
apathy displayed by many within the antislavery movement to the actual conditions of slaves to suggest that the use of such rhetoric was insincere. But that
is precisely the point that must be stressed. The regime contention at this time
revolved around not the welfare of slaves, but the institution of slavery and
what that did to national representation.[73] It was emphatically not about the
inclusion of the slave population within the republic, but about the distribution of power among the free white population. This is not to say that there
were no actors for whom regime considerations and moral considerations

coincided, but simply that these two motivations were independent of each other, and for the antislavery movement, as distinct from the abolitionist movement, the regime considerations were the primary motivation.[74]

Accounts of the actors involved in these struggles reveal that they very much understood them in terms of regime contention, which from the beginning centered on the question of the slave representation and the disproportionate power it gave to aristocratic over republican principles. This regime discourse was consistently found and highly effective. Even skeptics of the slave power thesis have puzzled over how very potent the regime discourse was, especially in the North.[75] It would continue to be the most effective way of igniting antislavery sentiment and mobilizing antislavery forces throughout the antebellum period and the Civil War. Whatever the intent of those articulating these ideas, they clearly resonated with the public, and this is perhaps the most important factor in understanding the emerging regime cleavage.

The Missouri Crisis in 1819 would make clear to all that the question of the slave representation was the most critical divide in US society and the most compelling force in US politics, highly volatile with the potential to unravel the union. It would also establish the sectional divide between North and South that would shape US political development for over a century.[76] This sectional cleavage, to be sure, had many other factors animating it, but at its core was regime contention, specifically fears of the impact of the slave representation on republican government. The compromise that was ultimately reached would allow Missouri to be admitted without restrictions on slavery while admitting Maine as a free state, a stopgap that would do little to diffuse regime contention, as it did nothing to remedy the disproportionality of the ratio of slave representation. The next period saw concerted efforts at realignment, which would be held back repeatedly by the question of western expansion and the crisis of representation that invariably accompanied it.

Jacksonian Democracy and Attempted Realignment

With the Missouri Compromise offering a reprieve from the fight over slave representation, the Jacksonian period saw the first concerted efforts at realignment along the economic dimension. Economic matters, which had been subverted to regime considerations in the previous decades, emerged in the late 1820s as a new organizing principle of politics. This was fueled by several structural changes. With the rise of manufacturing industries in the United States, the economy began to more closely resemble those of its European counterparts, creating a constituency for commercialization that spanned the political spectrum and pushed to transcend regime coalitions. Related to this, as industry grew, we find the beginnings of class stratification in the United States.[77] By the 1820s this was very apparent, especially in the urban centers of the Northeast. This too helped to push matters of economic management to the forefront of politics. The twin demands of promoting industrial growth and managing the conditions of labor created constituencies of economic interests resembling the class-based coalitions that defined the Left–Right spectrum in much of Europe. Indeed, the two most contentious issues of the period—the chartering of the national bank and tariff policy—both pushed economic considerations to the center of national politics, mobilizing different groups along their interests in an industrializing economy.

Of course, a different set of regime questions could be found throughout this period, which is well known for its dramatic transformation of the franchise.[78] Throughout the 1820s and 1830s, state after state held constitutional conventions, successively eliminating property and tax qualifications.[79] By 1840 only three states, Rhode Island, North Carolina, and Virginia, still had any sort of property qualifications, and these too were eliminated by 1856. Remarkable as this suffrage expansion was, it did not at the time interrupt the formation of economic policy coalitions. This is because, similar to the UK, working-class incorporation aligned with class-based economic coalitions.[80] In other words, *this* was not the regime question that threatened alignment because the struggle over suffrage polarized parties along similar lines to those over economic policy. In addition, the nature of suffrage expansion in the United States, especially the competition with western states, where new settlers could easily acquire property and gain the vote, pushed both parties to embrace suffrage expansion. Finally, expansion of the franchise in the United States did not involve a fight within Congress, as suffrage laws remained the purview of the states. All these factors combined to reinforce the prevailing regime consensus, which allowed parties to pivot to economic matters.

Starting in the 1830s, a new class-based economic logic could be found in the coalitions that made up the two major parties. Within the Democratic Party, the focus was on the protection of workers, both agrarian small farmers and industrial laborers, whereas the Whigs sought to fashion a coalition of wealthy property owners in the South and in the North. Modeled after the British Whig Party, Whigs in the United States similarly represented many liberal capitalist ideals central to industrialization and economic growth. The

Democrats, steeped in agrarianism, fought the rise of industrial society, in which they saw perils for all workers.[81] Importantly, both parties pushed against the sectionalism of the previous period and the regime contention it engendered. Both strove to be national parties appealing to different combinations of northern and southern interests.[82]

Jacksonian Democrats went to great pains to minimize the divisions over slavery and make wealth the dividing line in politics. Instead of the slave power, Jacksonians railed against the "money power."[83] This new money power and industrial society more generally were thought to lead to a degradation of labor, both economically and politically, leaving propertyless industrial laborers beholden to their employers.[84] At the heart of all this was the banking system, which, according to Jacksonians, made it possible for the wealthy owners of property and industry to accumulate the surplus value of labor.[85] Jackson's refusal to recharter the Second Bank of the United States cemented this issue as the focal point of the growing economic cleavage.[86]

In this fight, the language of regime contention from the previous era shifted and became fused with the prevalent economic discourse. A commentary by William Leggett, editor of the *New York Evening Post* and widely regarded as a spokesman for Jacksonian democracy, demonstrates how democracy and aristocracy during this period came to be understood in economic terms: "The one party is for a popular government, the other for aristocracy. The one party is composed, in a great measure, of the farmers, mechanics, laborers, and other producers of the middling and lower classes . . . and the other of the consumers, the rich, the proud, the privileged, of those who, if our Government were converted to an aristocracy, would become our dukes, lords, marquises, and baronets."[87] The social theory undergirding much of this discourse closely resembled the nascent socialist philosophies circulating in Europe at the time.[88] What is most significant is that this discursive shift joined economic and political categories in ways that would enable class-based economic coalitions and alignment along the economic dimension.

Bank policy was only one area of economic contention. Similar struggles could be seen in tariff policy, which saw at least three major changes between the 1820s and 1840s. Jacksonian Democrats typically pushed to lower tariffs to aid agricultural interests, while Whigs promoted protectionism as a means of advancing commercialization and securing domestic markets for nascent industry.[89] The radical shifts in policy reflect the high levels of polarization around these issues, and the fact that the polarization was around economic policy is significant. Actors in this struggle were focused not on changing the political system but on the distributive politics of the country. This suggests that realignment was a real possibility during this period.

The fragility of the realignment, however, was evident on every occasion in which policy touched on the question of slavery. This could be seen, for example, during the 1832 Nullification Crisis, in which South Carolina rejected a tariff imposed by the federal government.[90] In debates on the tariff, southern Democrats broke with their party, charging that northerners were trying to attack the institution of slavery by impoverishing the South. Of the protective tariff, John Calhoun argued, "it is one of the great instruments of our impoverishment, and if persisted in must reduce us to poverty or compel us to an entire change of industry."[91] The implications of tariff policy for the question of slavery meant that these battles were always infused with an element of regime contention. As free trade came to be equated with proslavery, antislavery groups and abolitionists also weighed in on the debate, pushing for greater protectionism and creating divisions within the Jacksonian Democrats.[92]

And of course, nothing was more threatening to the fragile economic coalitions and the regime consensus on which they were based than the question of western expansion. The debate over slavery intensified throughout the 1840s, leading to many political confrontations within Congress. This was ignited by a series of decisions governing how new states would be incorporated into the union following the US-Mexico War. The controversy reached as far back as 1846, with the start of the war and the United States' annexation of Texas. Anticipating a battle over the slavery question, the antislavery members of Congress (at this point mostly Democrats but with a number of Whigs as well) mobilized to prevent the admission of more slave states, proposing the Wilmot Proviso, which would have banned slavery in any territory gained in the war. The proposal failed, leading to an intensification of the conflict.[93]

Once again, the regime question would return to the center of national politics, with parties moving to coalitions organized along the regime dimension. This shift centered very much on the rise of the Republican Party and the regime-centered coalition it assembled, one that saw the expansion of slavery as a direct threat to the republic.

The Return of Regime Contention

By the 1850s, the question of western expansion was a full-blown national crisis. A "compromise," reached in 1850 and modeled after the Missouri Compromise of 1820, attempted to settle the dispute by balancing the number of slave and free states in the western territories. But this did little to lessen the perceived threat of the expansion of slavery. The problem, as it was understood, was not simply one of balancing the number of free and slave states, but rather the balance of power between them. This balance was established in the Constitution in very explicit terms. The three-fifths ratio had been chosen because it would at the time lead to a balance of representation between the slave and free states in the House. In 1790, this ratio yielded thirty representatives for slave states and thirty-one for free states, still disproportionate to the free white population of each state, but maintaining a balance of power in the House.[94] Many at the time of the founding feared that this would give too much power to the slave states, but they accepted the compromise expecting that the institution of slavery would die out relatively soon. The Constitution did not account for the continuation, much less the expansion, of slavery.

By 1850, the three-fifths clause gave southern states an additional thirty seats over what they would have had without including slaves in the apportionment.[95] While the population explosion in the North ensured that free states still held the majority in the House, the disproportionality in the representation of the free white population was a continued source of contention. The slave power thesis, a feature of US politics since the founding, gained an expansive following in the 1850s. Fears, particularly among northerners, that the representative advantage of the three-fifths clause allowed slave states to dominate the union were joined once again and even more forcefully with the discourse of regime contention and charges that the aristocratic institutions of the slave states posed a dire threat to the republic.[96]

The admission of new slave states exacerbated fears of the slave power no matter how symmetrically they were accepted with free states. The so-called compromises would keep the number of slave and free states even, maintaining balance in the Senate, but in the House, this would amplify the disproportionality introduced by the three-fifths clause. It was argued that with every slave state admitted, even if a corresponding free state was admitted, the aristocratic element increased exponentially. Senator William Seward, speaking of the requirements of republican government, maintained, "Slavery is incompatible with all of these; and, just in proportion to the extent that it prevails in a republican state, just to that extent it subverts the principle of democracy, and converts the state into an aristocracy or a despotism."[97] The characterization of slave states as aristocratic and even monarchical was common and often unceremonious at this time.[98]

The intensity of these confrontations made it impossible to keep together the coalitions that parties had forged around national economic interests. Trying to cater to both northern and southern interests became exceedingly difficult. Both parties transformed into Janus-faced organizations, saying one thing to their northern constituents and another to the southern.[99] And both parties' tacit acceptance of the expansion of slavery left little recourse to the antislavery movement within them. As early as 1848 the party system began to fracture, with new third-party challengers emerging, the most significant of which was the Free Soil Party, which drew antislavery factions from both parties to it. But the Kansas-Nebraska Act of 1854 would be the final undoing of the second party system and its attempted realignment. This was yet another act of western expansion, adding one slave state and one free state to the union, but doing nothing to counter the disproportionality of representation. In addition, it would repeal a provision of the Missouri Compromise of 1820 that prohibited the introduction of slavery above the 36th parallel separating North from South.[100] With the passage of the Kansas-Nebraska Act, any consensus that had existed over slavery was shattered. And, as with earlier periods of regime contention, the power of slave states was pitted directly against the viability of republican government.

The *Republicans'* Party

In the wake of the passage of the Kansas-Nebraska Act, the antislavery movement in Congress intensified, leading to a brief period of party fragmentation and rising third-party challenges. The Free Soil Party would form the core of the coalition that established the Republican Party in 1854, essentially a regime coalition that put the preservation of republican government ahead of other considerations. The Republican Party became the focal point of a political shift that fully reorganized the party system around the regime question. Even the choice of names—symbolic but significant—stressed that this was the *Republicans'* party.[101] The first party platform made this link explicit:

> Resolved, That in view of battling for the first principles of republican government, and against the schemes of aristocracy the most revolting and oppressive with which the earth was ever cursed, or man debased, we will co-operate and be known as REPUBLICANS until the contest be terminated.[102]

Within the Republican Party and within the antislavery movement more generally, the threat of the slave aristocracy, or the "slaveocracy" as it was known, would become a common battle cry.[103] Campaigning for the Republican Party, Senator Seward offered, "The Republican party declares that, by means of recent treacherous measures adopted by Congress and the President of the United States, the constitutional safeguards of citizens, identical with the rights of human nature itself, are undermined, impaired, and in danger of being overthrown. It declares that if those safeguards be not immediately renewed and restored, the Government itself, hitherto a fortress of republicanism, will pass into the hands of an insidious aristocracy, and its batteries be turned against the cause which it was reared to defend."[104] The impressive Republican returns in the election of 1856 suggest that the public overwhelmingly responded to these ideas.

Despite the abundant evidence that the regime question was central to the antislavery movement and more generally to the political transformations of the 1850s, the historiography of this period has tended to dismiss such claims as hyperbole, exaggeration, or even cynical manipulation of long-standing regime anxieties for political gain. While the role of slavery in inflaming sectional conflict during this period is widely acknowledged, the connection to regime contention generally is not.[105] Within the literature, the prevalent interpretation of the political transformations taking place are structural. Eric Foner's foundational work, for example, connected antislavery to the ideology of free labor, which had deep roots in US history and became especially influential during the Jacksonian period, out of which the movements that made up the Republican Party emerged. Foner attributed the rise of the free labor ideology to the rapid structural change experienced in this period and the social unease and status anxiety that resulted from it.[106]

Some have disputed this interpretation, and indeed a growing body of research has asserted that slavery as a political system, not as an economic system, was most threatening. Scholars have pointed to the fact that northern Democrats, for example, did not embrace the free labor ideology, despite being situated within industrial society.[107] Others have identified within the northern antislavery agenda more imperialist aims to supplant the southern aristocratic political economy.[108] Perhaps the most forceful rebuttal of the structural argument has come from Michael Holt, who identified in the 1850s a distinct political fight and revival of the slave power thesis, to which neither of the major political parties could adequately respond.[109] Though he does not use the language of regime contention, Holt essentially makes the case that the political transformation of the period in which the rise of the Republican Party was central was in fact about the nature of the regime and the threat that slavery posed to republican government. William Gienapp's work also stresses the very political character of the crises of the 1850s and the importance of the slave power thesis as the essential key to understanding Republican ideology.[110]

The analysis offered here supports the latter interpretation. Without disputing the influence of free labor ideology, this analysis points to an important and determinative role for regime contention in the political transformations underway. To support this claim, in the next section I offer another important piece of evidence that is not considered in the works noted above—the European influence on the US conflict. Throughout the 1830s and 1840s, an influx of ideas and persons from Europe helped to reinforce the threats to republican government. This was especially true following the Revolutions of 1848, which saw a wave of uprisings throughout Europe asserting parliamentary sovereignty against traditional monarchical and aristocratic institutions. Most US observers saw an affinity to these revolutionaries and shared their disappointment as counterrevolutions reversed their advances only a year later. The reversals helped to underscore the dangers to republican government throughout the Western world and, claims of exceptionalism notwithstanding, in the United States as well.

The correspondence of political upheaval in Europe with the crisis brewing in the United States reinforced the regime stakes of the conflict over slavery. This context is essential in understanding not only the nature of the conflict, but also why during this period it became so volatile. Those pointing to the enduring impact of the slave power thesis have not been able to explain why the response in this instance was so explosive, other than a vague sense of a straw breaking the proverbial camel's back. Bringing in the influence of events in Europe helps to explain why in the 1850s conflicts over slavery became an immediate and existential regime crisis.

Fuel to the Fire: European Influence in the US Conflict

European influence in the US conflict could be seen in several important areas. The first was through the vast network of activists and reformers that connected the United States and Europe. This was especially true within the antislavery movement, which in the United States and in Europe drew a strong connection between the institution of slavery and the regime question. In the UK, for example, the antislavery movement, strongly connected to the Chartists movement, was motivated by similar considerations that the institution of slavery strengthened the power of the landed aristocracy versus the commercial class. This issue figured prominently in debates over parliamentarization in the UK, and in fact, the abolition of slavery was one of the first acts of Parliament after parliamentarization was achieved: the Slavery Abolition Act was passed in 1833 in the UK, just one year after the passage of the Great Reform Act of 1832.[111] The antislavery movement in the UK would subsequently merge with the British Chartist movement, further blurring the lines between antislavery and regime contention.

By the 1840s, there was a great deal of cooperation between the US antislavery movement and the British Chartist movement. Regular exchanges between reformers on both sides of the Atlantic reinforced the similarities between US and European struggles, and the conviction that the institution of slavery posed a significant threat to republican government.[112] Henry Clark Wright, a prominent abolitionist reformer, made explicit connections, arguing that "the Aristocracy of England resemble the slaveholders of America exceedingly."[113] Wendell Phillips, another prominent abolitionist, framed the threat of slavery in similar terms: "Slavery has deeper root here than any aristocratic institution has in Europe."[114] These ties helped reinforce the regime stakes of slavery for US reformers.

Another important source of ideational transference was the intellectual influence of European commentators who frequently weighed in on US affairs. Of course, one of the most influential of these commentators, Alexis de Tocqueville, was also one of the foremost progenitors of the idea of American exceptionalism. In his now famed treatise *Democracy in America*, we find little of the regime contention taking place in the United States. Instead, he drew a sharp contrast between the United States and Europe, stressing the uniquely egalitarian nature of American political culture. Forceful in his claims regarding the strength of US democracy, he dismissed the possibility of aristocracy in the United States or comparisons between the United States and European aristocracy.[115]

As influential as this work has been subsequently, Tocqueville's claims were sharply disputed by his European contemporaries.[116] Francis Grund, a German emigrant and a prominent journalist in the United States, forcefully rebuffed Tocqueville's view of US democracy and his dismissal of slavery as representing an aristocratic influence. In a series of satirical essays under the title "Aristocracy in America," he offered a contrasting view, highlighting the affinities between slaveholding society and European aristocracy.[117] Views of the American conflict from Europe also reinforce the significance of regime contention.[118] James Stirling, a Scottish Chartist, insisted that the source of the conflict was not slavery per se but the tensions between the democratic political culture in the North and the aristocratic political culture in the South. His understanding of this aristocracy was put in terms of the state of slaveholding, "a fraction of the population monopolizing the principal property of the community."[119] Stirling stressed that what made these states aristocratic was not that they held slaves, but that there was no equality in slaveholding, not the subjugation of slaves, but their disproportionate subjugation by a few.

What is most remarkable in these exchanges is not only the different interpretations of the US political system, but also the extent to which Europeans were working out their own regime struggles in and through the US experience. A French aristocrat, a German radical, and a Scottish Chartist each brought their own struggles to the US conflict and infused it with their own objectives. Certainly, it was in the interests of reformers to blur the lines between the European and American conflicts, as it was in the interest of conservatives to make the contrast more stark. But whether they emphasized similarities or differences, they saw and helped to shape the conflict through the lens of European regime contention.

A final and critical factor in the ideational transference that took place between the United States and Europe was the massive influx of European, particularly German, émigrés following the Revolutions of 1848. Fleeing persecution at the hands of counterrevolutionaries, hundreds of thousands of Germans arrived in the United States after 1848, bringing the regime contention of Europe directly to US shores.[120] The Forty-Eighters, as the German émigrés were called, quickly entered the political scene. Many flocked to the newly formed Free Soil Party, the precursor to the Republican Party.[121] Established in 1848 out of an antislavery coalition from both major parties, the Free Soil Party was seen as the closest American counterpart to the 1848 European revolutionaries.[122] Forty-Eighters saw the US conflict very much in terms of regime contention. One of the those Forty-Eighters, a prominent author and journalist who would come to edit the New York daily *Abendzeitung*, wrote, "The problem of slavery is not the problem of the Negro. It is the eternal conflict between a small privileged class and the great mass of the non-privileged, the eternal struggle between aristocracy and democracy."[123] The Forty-Eighters would play an important role in US politics, especially in the rise of the Republican Party, in terms of the formation of its ideology and in its early electoral success.[124]

The influence of events in Europe is rarely mentioned in accounts of this period. But this context is critical to understanding not only the nature of the conflict in the United States, but also why in the 1850s it became so volatile. The groundwork for regime contention around the issue of slavery had already been laid in previous periods. But this was reinforced and given heightened urgency throughout the 1830s and 1840s by the influx of European ideas and refugees. And by the 1850s the United States had witnessed the only other experiments in republican government violently put down. One can easily see how this might have blurred the lines between the struggles taking place on both sides of the Atlantic. Whether they *were* actually fighting the same fight, or close enough to merit the regime anxiety that resulted in the United States, the widespread circulation of these ideas meant that in the public imagination, the threat to republican government became a reality and, in politics, a powerful motivating force.

In the 1850s, as in 1820, the fragile regime consensus was dramatically disrupted by the question of slavery's expansion and the increased disproportionality in representation that would result from it. But this time, the fight unfolded in a context where republican government was everywhere under attack. US political development at this time cannot be understood without this reference point. Viewed in this light, there can be no doubt that, for the founders of the Republican Party, the regime stakes of slavery were a critical consideration. Their success signaled the return of US politics and the party system to alignment along the regime dimension.

Regime contention has been an enduring feature of US political development from the start. While the democratization of the United States has typically been viewed in terms of struggles over the franchise, the analysis in this chapter illustrates that struggles over the rules of the game and the status of representative government have also been central to the evolution of US democracy. The revolutionary nature of its founding suggests that this should not have been the case. Yet, the deficiencies with respect to parliamentarization, particularly the slave representation, which introduced an oligarchic and, in the view of many, aristocratic element into the lower chamber, led to ongoing contention, which over the course of the antebellum period drew all political forces into alignment along the regime dimension. The fact that some significant elements of parliamentarization were achieved at the time of the founding, particularly those securing the power of Congress versus the executive, helped to mitigate this and meant that the United States could avoid the rigid repertoires of regime contention found in other cases of late parliamentarization, particularly in Germany. But the deficiencies in the representative form and the duration of primary regime contention meant that repertoires of regime contention, though less rigid than those found in Germany, would continue to animate politics well past the Civil War, the point at which the reasons that gave rise to them had been ostensibly eliminated. These dynamics are examined in the next chapter.

7

The Persistence of Regime
Contention in the United States

THE DEVELOPMENT
OF MULTIPLE REPERTOIRES

IN THIS chapter, I examine the repertoires of conflict and cooperation that
persisted after the regime question had been ostensibly settled with the decisive defeat of the South and the eradication of the slave representation. The
period provides three episodes that offered significant opportunities to reform
coalitions and realign along the economic dimension, each resulting in mixed
success but ultimately leading to the development of multiple repertoires of
conflict and cooperation.

The first episode came after the Civil War, with attempts to alter coalitions as
early as the 1870s, and factions from each party seeking to move past the war and
its divisions to promote an agenda of industrialization and economic growth.
This intensified in the 1880s as rising unrest among industrial and agrarian workers presented challenges to the dominant parties. Addressing these challenges
and the legislative incapacity that plagued Congress would require a change in
legislative coalitions and alteration of the repertoires of conflict and cooperation
inherited from earlier stages of regime contention. The push to reform coalitions
would persist until the 1890s, when probusiness forces succeeded in elevating
economic matters to the forefront of national politics. A partial realignment
would be achieved in 1896, with parties moving toward economic coalitions. The
realignment remained constrained, however, by established repertoires of regime contention, which limited the geographic reach of parties. The Republican
Party was able to forge a viable economic coalition, bringing together business
interests, labor, and wealthy farmers, but was confined to northern and western

states. The Democratic Party identified an economic base of small farmers but operated almost exclusively in southern states. During this period, we begin to see multiple repertoires operating; that is, repertoires of regime contention and repertoires of economic management were available to actors.

The second episode that provided an opportunity for realignment came during the interwar period. While the availability of multiple repertoires helped Progressive era coalitions effectively navigate the early decades of the twentieth century, these coalitions began to show their vulnerabilities under the pressures of war and the economic crises of the 1920s. In particular, the Republican Party coalition that combined regional economic interests could not respond to the demands of farmers and industrial workers. Forging more coherent economic coalitions would have required the nationalization of the party system. Efforts to establish national economic coalitions, however, necessitated a reckoning with the southern question, which threatened to resurface regime contention once again. The inability to reform coalitions during this period led to decreased legislative capacity and ultimately the transference of certain powers to the executive, most notably budgetary powers.

The third episode that provided an opportunity to reform coalitions came after the market crash of 1929. As in other cases, the economic crisis put tremendous pressure on legislators to identify viable coalitions to support necessary economic policy. At this time, actors would deliberately set aside the regime question, accepting the democratic transgressions of the Jim Crow South, to forge the national economic coalitions that would serve as the basis of the New Deal party system. This realignment, I contend, can only be considered tentative—resting on a suppression rather than a resolution of regime contention, and ultimately leading to a resurfacing of regime contention in the postwar period. Still, it was highly consequential in strengthening legislative capacity in the interwar period and in helping the United States endure the tumultuous years of economic crisis. The impact of this shift on legislative function is examined through the politics of budgets, which, as in the other cases, became the measure of legislative success and failure in the interwar period.

Episode 1: Post–Civil War Conflict and the Partial Realignment of 1896

The defeat of the South during the Civil War brought to a close a critical period of primary regime contention in the United States. With the abolition of slavery, the contest between the republican visions held in the North and the aristocratic leanings of the South was seemingly settled in favor of the former. It was not settled permanently, of course, and the political system of the Jim Crow South, beginning in the 1890s, would restore elements of these aristocratic arrangements through other means. The post–Civil War period, however, represents the end of the institutions that had driven regime contention in the antebellum period. As such, it offers the first test of coalition patterns established during the critical juncture in that it contained significant opportunities for parties to reorganize coalitions along the economic dimension. In addition to the political changes that eliminated the root cause of regime contention, the post–Civil War period also saw rapid industrialization, which brought with it significant economic challenges. As in other cases, the rise of labor, in industrial and agrarian circles, would precipitate a crisis, pushing parties to organize in ways that would allow them to address the most pressing economic issues. While no nationally competitive independent labor parties formed in the United States, rising labor unrest pushed both parties to grapple with the challenges of managing an industrializing economy. These pressures created strong incentives to set aside alliances based on the logic of regime contention and to pursue coalitions based in shared economic interests.

The opportunities, however, competed with the constraints imposed by a history of intense regime contention and the trauma of the Civil War. For several decades after the war, repertoires of conflict and cooperation based in the logic of regime contention would continue to dominate national politics and legislative coalitions, posing significant obstacles to effective governance. For Congress, politics during the Gilded Age has frequently been described in terms of the "politics of stalemate," reflecting the pervasiveness of legislative incapacity during this period.[1] Throughout this period, factions within each party pushed for realignment along the economic dimension and attempted to forge coalitions to promote economic policies over regime and sectional considerations. These factions, rooted in a probusiness economic growth mindset, would ultimately succeed by the turn of the century in forcing a *partial* realignment.[2]

Intraparty Factions and Antecedents of Realignment

The immediate post–Civil War period saw a continuation of prevalent patterns of regime coalitions but also early indications that the dominance of the regime imperative would be challenged. As early as 1872 a group within the Republican Party would break off to form the Liberal Republican Party. The probusiness group was eager to see their party move on from its wartime mindset, especially from the patronage politics that had proliferated, to pursue a more aggressive agenda of economic growth.[3] Though the effort was short lived, with most Liberal Republicans rejoining the Republican Party by 1876, it did signal the instability of the party's coalition, which had been based on the logic of regime contention.

A more significant challenge to the prevailing regime coalitions came in 1877, with the "compromise" that effectively ended Reconstruction.[4] The so-called compromise was forged by factions within both parties and involved the Democrats' conceding the disputed presidential election of 1876 in exchange for economic investment in the South and withdrawal of many northern military units from the southern states. The election had resulted in a political stalemate between Rutherford B. Hayes of the Republican Party and Samuel Tilden of the Democratic Party. In several of the southern states, the outcome was disputed, leaving both candidates short of the necessary majority in the Electoral College. Tilden had won the popular vote and was significantly ahead of Hayes in the Electoral College vote count, with 184 uncontested votes compared to Hayes's 165 votes. A total of 185 votes were needed for victory. The nation would hang in limbo for months, with various attempts to resolve the impasse, including the appointment of an election commission to adjudicate a resolution to the various state disputes and identify a winner.[5]

The final resolution came in March, a full four months after the election, with a purported compromise in which the Democrats would accept Hayes as president in exchange for various concessions to the southern states. According to C. Vann Woodward, this included important political concessions, the most significant of which would be to return the remaining three states still under military control—Florida, Louisiana, and South Carolina—to home rule. It meant the withdrawal of most US troops from the South and autonomy to deal with the Black population within those states, effectively bringing an end to Reconstruction. In addition to these political concessions, however, the compromise included a significant commitment to the economic rejuvenation of the South, including an investment in industrialization and the construction of a second transcontinental railroad.[6]

The most significant part of this resolution for the purposes of the present analysis is the coalition that brought it to fruition. Within the Republican and Democratic ranks, this included business-minded legislators who saw an opportunity to move past the Civil War period of regime contention and pursue new economic opportunities.[7] Foremost among them was Hayes, who had both publicly and privately expressed sympathy for the condition of the South, especially the men of property, who had been stripped of the basic rights of self-governance. Woodward characterized Hayes as "an old Whig, like many Southern leaders who now called themselves Democrats or Conservatives, that dreamed of breaking down the sectional barrier between men of property and reviving the antebellum political alliance between conservatives of North and South."[8] For Hayes there was a need for solidarity among the propertied interests of the country in the face of rising economic challenges.[9]

The old Whig ties played a significant role in the reconstitution of political allegiances during this period. The antebellum Whig Party had been based on a coalition of propertied economic interests in the North and South. Once the party was dissolved, many joined the Republican Party; some, particularly in the South, joined the Democrats; and others held no party affiliation at all, but still the ties were there.[10] They were associational ties in that many of the same figures returned to the national scene but in opposing parties, and they were also economic ties rooted in a common interest in economic growth and industrialization. In considering a Democrat to join his Republican cabinet, for example—one of the purported points of compromise in 1877—Hayes favored John C. Brown, governor of Tennessee and vice president of the Texas and Pacific Company, also a former Whig. The other contender was David M. Key, another southern Democrat of the "Whig leaning and internal improvement leaning."[11] Key was ultimately selected and given the role of postmaster general in Hayes's cabinet, an influential position given its access to patronage.

The tenuous economic linkages once housed within the Whig Party resurfaced in this period, pushing factions within each party to once again seek changes to party coalitions that would allow them to better serve economic interests. The emerging economic coalitions, however, came into direct conflict with the repertoires of conflict and cooperation inherited from the previous era of regime contention. In fact, the compromise of 1877 and the end of Reconstruction produced a considerable backlash that split the Republican Party into two distinct factions: the Stalwarts, representing radical republicanism, took a hard line on Reconstruction to stamp out any vestige of the old southern power base; the Half-Breeds, who were moderate Republicans, adopted a more conciliatory tone toward the South and sought to move the party toward a more aggressive economic agenda.[12]

The divide between the two factions would deepen after the compromise of 1877, which Stalwarts saw as a capitulation and betrayal of both Republican principles and of southern Republicans. Many of the Stalwarts, themselves Republicans hailing from southern states, saw the end of Reconstruction as a threat to their own viability.[13] Sometimes derisively referred to as "waving the bloody shirt" of fallen soldiers, they sought to keep alive within the Republican Party the history of wartime antagonism and the continuing specter of a regime threat in the South.[14] The antipathy between the two factions was at points intense. In 1880, this led to a faceoff in the Republican Party Convention between the Stalwarts, who supported Ulysses S. Grant for a third nonconsecutive term, and the Half-Breeds, supporting James Blaine, a probusiness reformer. In that contest, James Garfield would emerge as a dark horse, not technically affiliated with either faction, though his association with Blaine connected him to the Half-Breeds. Garfield would win the nomination and ultimately the presidency, which he held for only a few months before he was assassinated by a disaffected Stalwart.[15]

While Republicans dominated Congress, divisions between these two factions contributed to a highly dysfunctional party dynamic within and between parties. In fact, the period is known for its endemic legislative incapacity, originating not only from the highly obstructionist Democratic Party, which sought only to limit the role of government, but also from the divisions within the Republican Party, which split on matters big and small. This proved debilitating throughout the 1880s and became a major impediment to dealing with the growing unrest among industrial and agrarian laborers. The next section examines how efforts of party leaders to deal with this resulted in the partial realignment of the 1890s.

Legislative Incapacity and the Transformations of the 1890s

The crisis of legislative incapacity was a common theme of the political press and a common lament of party leaders throughout the 1880s. This was especially problematic for Republicans, who had a much more aggressive agenda during this period but whose ambitions were consistently frustrated by an obstructionist Democratic minority and dissenters within their own party.[16] One particular episode that put legislative dysfunction on display was the Geneva Award—a settlement of $15 million for a wartime dispute between the United States and Great Britain over a captured war vessel. The settlement was granted to the United States in 1872, but Congress failed for over a decade to disburse the funds, unable to even reach an agreement as to whom it should be given. Beyond the substantive disagreement, there was also a dizzying array of dilatory tactics that sent the legislation to committee on numerous occasions only to return months later with little changed and no progress made. It was considered the epitome of legislative dysfunction at the time.[17]

The breakdown of legislative capacity would have been a challenge under any circumstances, but at this time, it was compounded by mounting pressures from economic instability and labor unrest, which had built up throughout the 1880s.[18] Depression among western farmers and deteriorating conditions among northern laborers were pressing problems that saw no remedy within the fragmented Congress. Action on the tariff was one of the most pressing issues, as it affected the conditions of both industrial and agrarian labor.[19] But repeated efforts at tariff reform had ended in failure. The inability of parties to respond to these pressures produced a crisis of governance that proved dangerous from within and from without. A populist movement growing within the Democratic Party and a progressive movement gaining ground among Republicans demanded immediate action on economic matters from their respective parties, at times breaking off to challenge them.

The response to this crisis came in the 1890s, originating with an entrepreneurial group of Republican leaders who would set out to address this legislative incapacity and in the process set the party system on a track toward realignment.

The System of 1896

The system of 1896, as it has been subsequently called, holds a special status in the study of US political development.[20] According to Schattschneider, "The establishment of the alignment of 1896 is perhaps the best example in American history of the successful substitution of one conflict for another."[21] It represented a reorientation of politics from the old Civil War and Reconstruction cleavage, based in sectional and regime preferences, toward a new cleavage based on interests within an industrializing economy. The election of 1896 embodied this new ethos—a victory for Republican William McKinley, running on a protectionist platform and bringing together a coalition of pro-business manufacturers, wealthy farmers, and labor. While the new coalitions remained constrained geographically by old sectional divisions, and thus represent in this analysis only a partial realignment, this period was highly consequential in moving the US party system toward the economic dimension.[22] It also ushered in a period in which multiple repertoires of conflict and cooperation operated, offering greater flexibility in dealing with different challenges.

In examining the political transformation of this period, we can identify a series of decisions and actions, particularly among Republican Party leadership, that paved the way and demonstrated considerable political creativity in reforming coalitions. This began in 1890 with a group of entrepreneurial Republican leaders who would introduce revolutionary changes, reshaping their party along with the broader political landscape. The Fifty-First Congress is perhaps best known for the dramatic institutional changes brought about with the introduction of the Reed rules, a set of majority-building measures enacted by Republican Speaker of the House Thomas Reed to limit obstruction and to facilitate the building of legislative majorities.[23] Perhaps the most consequential of these measures was Reed's move to end the practice of the "vanishing quorum," whereby members would refuse to respond to the roll call, denying the chamber of the half plus one quorum needed to do business. Following a decade of endemic legislative incapacity, these institutional fixes were seen as a way of taming legislative politics so that Republicans could pursue their ambitious agenda.

While the Reed rules have received a great deal of attention among students of legislative politics for their impact on congressional institutions, much less attention has been devoted to the substantive agenda Republicans associated with the Reed rules and what was at stake in terms of policy.[24] An examination of the broader context of the Fifty-First Congress indicates that these rule changes were in fact a key component of the realignment underway.

At the top of the Republican agenda in the Fifty-First Congress was the McKinley Tariff, a set of protectionist measures engineered by Congressman William McKinley, at the time head of the Ways and Means Committee. McKinley and Reed were the two highest-ranking Republican House members and worked closely during this period. McKinley was a strong advocate of Reed's rule changes, speaking forcefully in favor on several occasions.[25] Reed reciprocated with zealous support of McKinley's tariff policy, strongarming it through several legislative hurdles. The level of coordination between the two suggest that both the rules reform and the tariff were part of a common agenda centered on economic reform and party building.[26]

The importance of the Reed rules to the passage of the McKinley Tariff, and the broader realignment at this time, cannot be overstated.[27] Reed's rules were key not only to ending Democratic obstruction, but also to imposing discipline on Republican legislators. The opposition's use of the vanishing quorum had given cover to Republican dissenters. The party was plagued with divisions, which would not necessarily appear in the voting because dissent could be expressed through absence. Party leaders constantly struggled to keep their members in the chamber and in Washington, as members would regularly travel back to their constituencies to avoid contentious votes.[28] With the introduction of the Reed rules, any break within the Republican ranks was much more transparent.

This is significant because the issue of the tariff had been a point of contention not only between Democrats and Republicans, but within the Republican Party as well. Though the Republican Party since its founding had positioned itself as the party of protection, in the 1870s it had moved away from this position, accepting broad reductions in tariffs to accommodate the demands of southern Republicans.[29] This was consistent with the desire of the "old guard" after the Civil War to maintain a Republican presence in the South, but it ran against the economic interests of the industrial North, where the party was dominant.[30] Throughout the 1870s and early 1880s a quiet consensus kept the issue of the tariff out of the national spotlight. This all changed with the panic of 1883. The depression that followed brought with it major labor unrest and renewed the push within the Republican Party for higher tariffs to protect industry and labor. Despite holding a sizable majority in the Forty-Seventh Congress, however, Republicans were unable to push this through.[31]

Among the considerations that held Republicans back from aggressive protectionist policies at the time, a crucial factor was the knowledge that embracing protectionism would mean losing the South.[32] Some might argue, and many did at the time, that the South had already been lost: by 1890 there were no Republican senators from southern states, and in the House, only a handful of southern Republicans remained.[33] For the old guard, however, still animated by repertoires of regime contention, maintaining some southern presence was crucial. The compromise of 1877 had diminished that significantly, but southern Republicans had been appeased with concessions on the tariff. Eliminating these concessions meant completely ceding the South to the Democrats, and for many that was still a dangerous proposition. For this reason, Republicans made no progress on the tariff question even when they held the majority.[34] As late as 1888, Benjamin Harrison, the Republican president, adopted a more conciliatory tone, pledging no tariff increases during his term.[35]

The divisions within the party could also be seen in the fact that the other major piece of legislation advanced by the party during this session was the Federal Elections bill. Also known as the Lodge bill, after Henry Cabot Lodge, one of its main proponents, it would have established federal regulations for elections, aimed specifically at protecting the rights of Black voters. The Federal Elections bill and the McKinley Tariff reflected different approaches to party building: one focused on preserving and expanding the Republican Party's presence in the South; the other on fortifying ties between the northern and western states.[36] The two bills also reflected different ideological orientations, one that continued to be animated by the logic of regime contention, and another that sought to move away from this to forge new economic coalitions. At first, both pieces of legislation were pushed together by Republican leadership, but it quickly became apparent that each involved a different political calculus and explicit tradeoffs.[37]

The debates over these measures among Republicans revealed how much the decision of the party's direction rested on legislators' assessment of whether the old politics of regime contention could safely be abandoned—that is, whether ceding the South to the Democratic Party would pose a threat to republican government. James Blaine, the Half-Breed and former presidential candidate at the heart of the 1880 nomination struggle, opined that moving in an economic direction was the party's best chance. He sought to reassure his nervous co-partisans that there was little to fear from the South: "Any effort to unite the Southern States upon issues that grow out of the memories of war," he insisted, would fail. The "Southern Commonwealths are learning to vindicate civil rights, and adapting themselves to the conditions of political tranquility and industrial progress."[38] The second part, at least, was demonstrably false, as Jim Crow laws were already emerging in the South. But others agreed that the regime threat posed by the southern states—understood as a threat to republican government and not a question of inclusion—had dissipated. As one senator put it, "The old issues are largely settled."[39]

Proponents of the Elections bill stressed that electoral strategy should take precedence. Henry Cabot Lodge argued, "There is another matter, more important than any tariff can ever be . . . a fair ballot throughout the length and breadth of the land."[40] Lodge stressed the strategic priority of the Elections bill—that in increasing the power of Republicans in the South, it would facilitate other policy objectives. Meanwhile, others such as Representative Green B. Raum returned to the regime stakes of the bill, insisting that "talk of economics is only invoked to detract from the political conditions in the south."[41] Charles Boutelle similarly argued, "I should also place the establishment of political and civil rights and the vindication of the ballot as the foremost issue—taking precedence of merely material and economic questions." Then he conceded, "I suppose I am behind the times."[42]

Ultimately, the McKinley Tariff would pass, while the Lodge bill would fail, both at the hands of Republicans. Democrats were opposed to both and were prepared to filibuster in the Senate. The McKinley Tariff was rescued through a compromise that included delaying consideration of the Elections bill and ultimately sacrificing it altogether for a Silver bill supported by western Republicans.[43] The choice, and the direction of the party, was clear. The Reed-McKinley revolution in 1890 was a radical departure, requiring the party to embrace an economic imperative over a regime imperative.

In addition to overcoming the ideological resistance of the Republican old guard, key to McKinley's success was showing Republicans a path forward to a stronger coalition between the northern and western states. This had to do with the specific nature of the McKinley Tariff, which protected manufactured goods from competition while carefully admitting duty free certain items needed for agriculture.[44] McKinley, from Ohio, a state that carried all the complexity of industrial and agrarian economies combined, was able to identify a new way to thread the needle on the tariff to gain the support of wealthy western farmers.[45] With these coalition-building compromises, the McKinley Tariff passed along strict party lines. Given the level of dysfunction seen in the previous decade, this was a considerable achievement.

Republicans would not see the fruits of their efforts immediately. The election of 1892 saw the Democrats take the House amid widespread public opinion that the Republicans had overreached, with portrayals of Reed as czar and McKinley as Napoleon.[46] The following years, however, would see a major economic boom, which, rightly or wrongly, was attributed to the McKinley Tariff and helped solidify his coalition. He was elected governor of Ohio in 1892 and spent the following years traveling the Midwest bolstering support for the tariff. Democrats in Congress could do little to stop the momentum of the Reed-McKinley revolution. An attempt to repeal the tariff with the Wilson-Gorman Tariff Act was heavily blundered, yielding little in terms of actual tariff reduction and adding for the first time a very unpopular income tax to replace the lost revenue. Even the Reed rules, which Democrats had initially rejected, were ultimately accepted and used by Democrats to manage legislative dynamics.[47]

By 1896, the return of the Republicans to power was a foregone conclusion. The McKinley Tariff represented a new economic and political calculus, bringing together industrial and agrarian producers as well as laborers. It would be the basis of his victory in the election in 1896, forging a Lib-Lab coalition in the tradition of the British Liberal Party. This coalition would be expanded and fortified in the following decades, as progressive leaders deepened ties with labor and strategically balanced protectionism with concessions to western agricultural interests, following McKinley's formula. The cost of these triumphs was, as anticipated, ceding any presence in the South. For the following decades, the country would see the rise of one-party rule, with

Republicans dominating in the North and West, and Democrats in the South. It would also see the rise of an elaborate system of exclusion in the South through the propagation of Jim Crow laws and policies that introduced by other means the distortions of representation that had been the source of regime contention in the antebellum period.

Thus, the system of 1896 would not do away with regime contention but introduced a period in which multiple repertoires were available to legislators, facilitating greater efficacy in governance. The legislative incapacity of the Gilded Age was replaced with a highly productive legislature, mostly under the leadership of Republican progressives who passed key economic legislation, introducing new regulations aimed at improving the condition of labor, regulating trusts, and introducing the first major income tax. The ability to identify legislative coalitions to support such policies reflects the salience of the economic policy dimension at this time. The partial realignment of 1896 did more than just promote a set of issues to the national scene; it reoriented parties toward the economic dimension. The transformation of legislative politics that came about with this reorientation would also help stabilize legislative coalitions and facilitate governance in the following decades. Nonetheless, the fact that these economic coalitions remained constrained by a sectional logic would lead to instability during tumultuous years of the interwar period.

Interwar Politics and the Push for Full Realignment

The interwar period provides more opportunities to examine the stickiness of legislative coalitions. The partial realignment of 1896 moved both parties toward organizing around economic issues, but legislative coalitions remained constrained by repertoires of regime contention that restricted the national reach of each party and introduced a misalignment of certain interests. These Progressive era economic coalitions, though always tenuous and fraught with competing interests, for a time held and would prove to be highly successful engines of economic and social policy from the 1890s through the 1910s.

During the interwar period, however, these coalitions would become strained, particularly within the Republican Party. The war had revealed the vulnerabilities of coalitions combining industrial, agricultural, and labor interests. The ambitions of business, the economic precarity of the farmer, and the radicalization of labor placed different and often incompatible demands on economic management. This led to much greater legislative instability and difficulty in dealing with the economic crises of that period.[48]

The political instability of the period also threatened to inject regime contention once again into party politics, in ways both new and old. First, the radicalization of labor brought with it the same regime anxieties found in the European cases. With the shadow of the Bolshevik Revolution looming large, the language of autocracy for the first time would enter public discourse, often attached to the labor movement.[49] Accommodating labor interests became increasingly difficult within Progressive era coalitions, especially after the economic crisis of 1929. The second factor that held the potential to resurface regime contention was that the reconfiguration of coalitions necessary to correct for the misalignment of the Progressive era would have required the nationalization of parties, and this would bring the southern question—that is, the exclusionary practices and undemocratic institutions of the southern states—back into focus.

The radicalization of labor and the persistence of the southern question both held the potential to heighten the salience of the regime dimension. Instead, however, the period saw a realignment *within* the economic dimension, a reshuffling of alliances that maintained the primacy of economic policy and set aside regime contention once again. This deepened ties among northern and southern workers, both industrial and agrarian, but left largely untouched the "authoritarian enclaves" of the South.[50] The New Deal coalition represented a decision to set aside, and in many respects suppress, the regime question in favor of an economic agenda, this time on a national scale.

The strength of economic coalitions at the time had significant implications for policy, specifically for the ability of Congress to respond to the demands of economic management in times of crisis. I examine two such episodes in the interwar period, both involving management of the budget. One came immediately after the First World War, to address the crisis of rapidly rising debt, and ends with the Budget and Accounting Act of 1921, which handed significant budgetary power over to the executive. This took place in a context where Progressive era economic coalitions were fraying, and divisions within parties resulted in repeated legislative failure. While the transference of power to the executive solved the budget problem, in this analysis, it signals legislative weakness. The final episode comes after the market crash of 1929, with another effort to get the budget under control, culminating with the Economy Act of 1933, which introduced significant measures of austerity to produce a balanced budget. This episode, taking place in a context where national economic coalitions for the first time dominated legislative politics, represents a successful legislative resolution to the crisis and signals legislative strength.

Although the evolution of the budget process in the United States differs from the European cases, in the interwar period it became a focus of intense national discussion and scrutiny, offering an important test of governance and legislative function.

Episode 2: Economic Crisis and the Budget and Accounting Act of 1921

In the United States, as in other cases, the politics of budgets became the litmus test of legislative capacity in the interwar period. This has been obscured by the fact that until 1921, the United States lacked a unified budget process. Indeed, it lacked any kind of national budget. Prior to this, what prevailed was a highly decentralized process whereby departments sent requests directly to Congress, to be taken up by one of many committees entrusted with appropriations and approved piecemeal.[51] There was no office in charge of reconciling expenditures, and no point at which outlays were examined alongside revenues. This had long been a point of grievance among Progressive reformers, who had for over a decade pushed for a national budget. This was critical to the Progressives' visions of responsible government and efforts to move politics toward greater transparency to avoid the influence of bosses and party machines.[52]

Although this was a pet cause of Progressive reformers, the issue did not receive significant national attention until after the war, when suddenly the crisis of the national debt took center stage. Wartime spending had increased the national budget exponentially. In 1916 the federal budget was less than $800 million. By 1919 it was over $18 billion. Revenues did not come close to covering this, and by 1920 the deficit stood at $25 billion.[53] In addition to the costs of the war itself, there were significant costs at home.[54] Foremost among these was maintaining programs that helped deal with the economic dislocation of the war and others that supported veterans' benefits. The government also faced new economic stressors at home, particularly in maintaining food supply. The need to keep food costs low for consumers conflicted with the needs of producers, especially western farmers, who had faced dramatic economic hardships throughout the war.[55] The imbalance was corrected with subsidies provided by the federal government during the war, on which farmers became dependent after the war.[56]

When the Sixty-Sixth Congress took office in 1919, calls for a unified national budget process were widespread across the political spectrum. That some action had to be taken was clear, but what actually resulted from these deliberations has been the subject of much scholarly attention and puzzlement. The Budget and Accounting Act of 1921 established for the first time a national budget process, but also took the extraordinary step of giving the executive, for the first time, a direct role in this process. The president was given the responsibility of assembling and proposing the national budget.

Many things were striking about this. First, the transfer of budget authority seemed to have been mostly supply side.[57] In other words, there was no strong push from the executive for such power. What would induce a legislature to hand over any authority over the budget to the executive? The all-sacred power of the purse was one of the foremost powers granted to Congress, and one of the essential functions of legislatures across the democratic world. Yes, establishing a national budget was a necessity, but they could have done so and kept that process in Congress.[58] Moreover, if it were about the urgency of passing a specific budget, that could have also been accomplished through normal legislative channels, given that unified Republican government prevailed at the time.

In trying to understand this puzzling move, scholars have offered two main justifications. Some have pointed to the recognition of legislative incapacity and inefficiency—that Congress was too corrupt and decentralized to execute this task.[59] Other have focused on the idea of presidential representation—that the president, as the only official elected by the entire country, was seen as the only person in a position to hold the nation's various and competing interests in the balance.[60] Certainly both themes can be found in debates on the budget question at the time, and an ideational shift regarding the role of the presidency, starting with the Progressive era, undoubtedly made such a transfer of power more palatable. Still, the question remains, why at this time? And even more important, why did this happen specifically with respect to the budget? It is rare that legislators so readily accept their own ineptitude as grounds for relinquishing power, and rarer still that they would willingly hand power to the executive to remedy their own shortcomings. Yet, the budget question was different.

The key to understanding this puzzling decision lay in the connection between its two main components—centralization and executive leadership. It was the creation of a unified budget process that made delegation to the president especially attractive. This is because establishing a unified budget process in Congress would have put a great strain on the Republican Party's already fragile legislative coalition. Such a process would make the spending excesses more apparent and put pressure on party leaders to curtail their members' budget requests. It is telling that the executive did not want or ask for this power. Indeed, authority over budgets in the interwar years was not something to be envied, as it often required dramatic reductions of expenditures, cutting welfare programs, subsidies, and entitlements. This put anyone in charge of the budget in a very unpopular position. Handing over authority to the executive to produce a balanced budget allowed Congress to also transfer much of that conflict.

In addition to these considerations, there is also reason to believe that Republican Party leaders were not confident that they could in fact produce a balanced budget. That is, they did not believe they could identify a legislative coalition to support it given the divisions that had already emerged within the party regarding economic policy.[61] These divisions are hard to detect on the appropriations side because spending was easy, and it was also done behind closed doors. To see the divisions within the Republican coalition, we need to look at the other side of the balance sheet to the struggle over taxation.

A central component of the Republicans' agenda at this time was to lower taxes, which had skyrocketed during the war. By 1919 the top bracket paid 63 percent income tax, and some corporate income was taxed as high as 80 percent.[62] To satisfy the business interests within their coalition, Republicans consistently worked to chip away at these rates. These efforts had been frequently thwarted by a new congressional faction known initially as the agricultural and progressive bloc, or as it would come to be known, the farm bloc.[63] This interparty faction combined representatives of farming interests from both parties, and from both western and southern states.[64] Importantly, the farm bloc consisted of many Republican members who would consistently join with Democrats to defeat tax reductions.[65] The dissension of the farm bloc was devastating for the party and proved a significant obstacle to maintaining a coherent economic policy agenda.[66]

The divisions over tax reductions revealed an important crack in the Republican Party's legislative coalition, one that would have proved just as lethal to any attempt to produce a balanced budget. The reduction of taxes to serve business interests would have affected a critical source of revenue, necessitating the implementation of severe austerity measures affecting the same programs the farm bloc had fought to preserve. It is evident from debate on the Budget and Accounting Act that this was at the top of Republicans' considerations in supporting the act. The tax question came up in almost every speech, with many legislators indicating that the act would help to lower taxes.[67]

Viewed in the broader context of fiscal policy, the Budget and Accounting Act can be seen as a result of both past and anticipated legislative failure rooted in divisions within existing economic coalitions, divisions that were in many ways the result of the constrained coalition making of the 1890s. While the party had achieved a realignment along the economic dimension, it was only a partial realignment, as repertoires of conflict and cooperation reflecting a history of sectional divisions and regime contention limited the reach of co- alitions. The Progressive era economic coalitions were viable for a time, but war and economic crises demonstrated their vulnerabilities. The combination of business interests with labor and agricultural interests was not sustainable in the postwar economy. These pressures would come to a head after the eco- nomic crisis of 1929 and ensuing depression, pushing parties to rethink coali- tions once again.

Episode 3: Political Transformation and the Making of New Deal Coalitions

As Progressive era coalitions began to fray, factions within both parties pushed to establish coalitions based on *national* economic interests. Such efforts posed significant perils, as they would open up opportunities for regime contention to resurface. National coalitions would ostensibly require a reckoning with the southern question once again, either committing to reforming the exclusion- ary institutions of the South or accepting them. In the political shift that took place in 1932, the choice was neither. Rather, the New Deal coalition was es- tablished on a mix of avoidance and suppression of regime contention on the southern question. This allowed viable economic coalitions to operate during the critical interwar years but left significant regime contention barely under the surface.[68]

In this analysis, the New Deal era comes closer than any to achieving full realignment. This is understood not only, or primarily, in terms of what came immediately before, but in view of the long-term transformation from coali- tions organized along the regime dimension to coalitions organized along the economic dimension. Indeed, in terms of what came before, the change was not so dramatic, as there was a great deal of continuity with Progressive era coalitions. Moreover, some of the most critical shifts were underway long before 1932. This can be seen in the transformation of two important constitu- encies: the labor vote and the Black vote. Both groups, at earlier stages, had ties to the Republican Party, and their shift to the Democratic Party made the New Deal coalition possible.

In the case of labor, the move to the Democratic Party was not without precedent. Though labor had been a significant part of the Republican Party coalition during the Progressive era, as a voting bloc, it remained largely noncommittal, often supporting third parties, and in some regions, the Democratic Party.[69] The Republican Party also displayed some ambivalence toward labor, and in some regions, outward hostility.[70] What was most significant in this shift was not so much labor's move away from the Republican Party, but the strengthening of its ties to the Democratic Party, which for a time it had also kept at arm's length.

This shift culminated in the decision of some labor organizations, particularly the Congress of Industrial Organizations, to formalize its relationship with the Democratic Party during this period, reversing a decades-long ban on engagement with partisan politics that had been established by the American Federation of Labor.[71] This prohibition had been motivated by ideological commitments to trade unionism, but also by strategic motivations, as it left open the possibility of an independent labor party, or at the very least independent labor candidates. Thus, strengthening ties with the Democratic Party was significant, not, strictly speaking, in terms of a realignment of labor, but in terms of its acceptance for the first time of an alignment within the existing party system.[72]

In the case of the Black vote, the ties with the "party of Lincoln" had been much stronger, but even those had begun to fray during the Progressive era, reflecting the increasing skepticism of Black voters about the ability and intent of the Republican Party to promote the cause of Black equality.[73] The disillusionment with the Republican Party was articulated most forcefully by W.E.B. Du Bois as early as 1906. On the heels of the Niagara Movement Declaration of Principles, Du Bois penned "An Address to the Nation," challenging "the failure of the Republican Party in Congress at the session just closed to redeem its pledge of 1904 with reference to suffrage conditions at the South." He maintained that the failure "seems a plain, deliberate, and premeditated breach of promise, and stamps that party as guilty of obtaining votes under false pretense."[74]

Du Bois would become one of the most consistent and powerful voices challenging the emerging regime consensus and reminding the American public time and again of the unresolved regime questions in the South.[75] But he also saw the strategic advantage of Black voters breaking away from the Republican Party and occasionally aligning with the Democratic Party, a view that was shared by other prominent intellectuals at the time. T. Thomas Fortune, the civil rights leader and influential editor of the *New York Age*, as early as 1886 had warned of the dangers of the Black vote becoming captured by the Republican Party.[76]

At first these dissenting views were at the margins. But as the Republican Party's failures to act on crucial issues of Black political equality and physical safety accumulated, they increasingly gained traction.[77] By the 1920s a significant rift had emerged between the party and Black voters, and in 1924, the NAACP convention adopted a resolution encouraging Black voters to disregard party labels and maintain their independence in the upcoming elections.[78] The push for an independent Black vote was driven by disappointment with both parties and growing frustration with the limitations of party politics more generally. As Du Bois put it in 1928, "No attempt to liberalize either the Republican or the Democratic Party, or to start a new third-party movement, can succeed as long as the present disfranchisement of the Negro supports a Solid South."[79] The collusion of the Democratic and Republican Parties left Black voters few good options in addressing the southern question.

The hope for a truly independent Black vote never fully materialized. Instead, the move away from the Republican Party brought Black voters increasingly to the Democratic Party, a move that held no further hope of advancing Black equality but the promise of protection from the harshest consequences of the market crash and subsequent Depression. Even for those most directly affected by the exclusionary policies of the Democratic Party, the economic imperative proved compelling. Black voters who were offered and received no relief from the Jim Crow South shifted to the Democratic Party for the economic relief it promised.[80]

These shifts allowed for a new political calculus and new coalitional politics affirming the primacy of economic policy. The Democratic Party's New Deal coalition was an economic one based on a heavily redistributive agenda targeting embattled farmers and labor for relief from the Depression. The Republican Party responded by leaning into its probusiness base across the country. This coalition allowed it to maintain a more cohesive economic agenda rooted in fiscal conservatism and opposition to the New Deal.[81] For the first time in US history, national economic coalitions would come to dominate politics.

While the factors contributing to the realignment were decades in the making, in many respects the shift itself was rapid. Scholars of realignment typically point to 1928 and 1932 as critical elections and the points at which we see the most significant shifts, no doubt a result of the equally rapid pace of the economic crisis.[82] A small window into the broader shift could be found, for example, in the transformation of Illinois's first district in urban Chicago. Long a stronghold for Republicans, this predominantly Black working-class district in 1928 elected Oscar De Priest, a Black Republican. In 1932, he was defeated by Arthur Mitchell, a Black Democrat who campaigned heavily on New Deal economic policy. Mitchell would become the first Black Democrat elected to office in the United States.[83]

Building and maintaining the Democratic Party's New Deal coalition required a self-conscious choice to put aside, and often suppress, regime contention and tolerate the "authoritarian enclaves" that had become even more entrenched in the southern states.[84] In fact, New Deal politics carefully steered away from the southern question to maintain the support of white southerners.[85] The quiescence of the Democratic Party on the southern question, while dissonant with the received mythology of New Deal liberalism, is not difficult to understand. After all, the party had long represented southern interests, working actively to protect the exclusionary institutions of the South. As long as Roosevelt and other northerners did not threaten this order, the southern Democrats, who formed a large base in the party, were satisfied. And indeed, they did not, at least not at the level of Democratic Party elites. Party leadership consistently avoided discussions of race and exclusion in the South.[86]

This is not to say that the status of the South was settled by any measure. In fact the suppression of the regime question meant that the realignment on which it was predicated was always tentative, and indeed fractures in the prevalent economic coalitions could be seen as early as the 1940s. But for the critical period of the 1930s, the realignment, however tentative, was significant. It provided the basis for reliable and identifiable economic policy coalitions on the Left and the Right, something that was critical for increasing legislative capacity during a time of crisis. Below I examine a key episode in which this increase in legislative capacity was crucial for both an effective response to the economic crisis and the endurance of representative government.

Budget Crisis of 1933

The realignment of 1932 would prove to be one of the most consequential in US history. It was a realignment *within* the economic dimension that self-consciously suppressed the regime question, establishing national coalitions that affirmed the primacy of economic policy.[87] The Republican Party concentrated its efforts on business interests, which had always been central to its coalition but now became its focus on a national scale. The Democratic Party, arguably returning to its roots in the era of Jacksonian democracy, assembled a national coalition of labor and farming interests, but with an agenda updated for an industrialized economy.[88] Importantly, the realignment would also usher in a process of nationalization of the electorate and of parties that would move the political system away from the old sectional divide. All these changes would help the United States navigate the economic crises of the 1930s, one of the most critical tests of governance the country would encounter.

The New Deal era would lead to a tremendous federal response, supported by a highly productive Congress that could be relied on to produce viable coalitions to support economic policy. Moreover, these coalitions could be identified on both the Right and the Left; they represented distinct and cohesive interests within the economy and supported policies that reflected those interests. The flurry of activity during President Roosevelt's storied first one hundred days can attest to that.

One episode offers an important test of the viability of legislative coalitions at this time—the Economy Act of 1933, which introduced dramatic cuts to the federal budget. It was the second piece of legislation to be introduced by the Roosevelt administration, submitted to Congress only days after the Emergency Banking Act. The Economy Act differed from the bulk of New Deal legislation, which typically involved spending programs and easily won the support of congressional Democrats. The Farm Relief Act, the Industrial Recovery Act, the Emergency Relief Act—these were the acts that defined the New Deal coalition and passed with overwhelming majorities. Yet, significant elements of fiscal conservatism in New Deal policies required a different economic calculus.[89] The Economy Act was one such example. It would introduce a cut of $500 million (approximately 30 percent of the federal budget), primarily targeting federal agencies and veterans' pensions. It remains the biggest budget cut in US history.[90]

In making the case to Congress, Roosevelt stressed that the country was on the road to bankruptcy, and action on the budget was essential to economic recovery, especially to restore the faith of creditors in the US economy. The act was also referred to as "An Act to Maintain the Credit of the United States," underscoring the connection to the banking crisis. The US economy, though not as roughly battered as its European counterparts, was held hostage to the same economic logic whereby fiscal austerity became the measure of credit worthiness. The same pressures to produce balanced budgets that drove European legislatures to the brink emerged in the United States as well and proved equally contentious.[91]

Compared to the Emergency Banking Act, which was passed in four hours, debates over the Economy Act defied the sense of urgency Roosevelt projected, dragging on for weeks. Once again, the politics of budgets serves as an important test of legislative success and failure. In an episode that recalled many aspects of German Chancellor Brüning's search for a legislative coalition to support the budget of austerity of 1930, Roosevelt commenced his own search, first looking to the Left and his own party. There he found strong opposition from congressional Democrats, who declared the austerity measures to be too harsh and disproportionately placed on pensioners. After several futile attempts to bring Democrats on board, Roosevelt looked to the Right. There, he found support among Republicans who, along with some centrist Democrats, would form the basis of the center-right coalition that passed the Economy Act and many other measures of New Deal policy leaning toward fiscal conservatism. The accomplishment was remarkable not only in comparison to the struggles of Germany at the time, but also in comparison with the United States' recent history. A similar act had been proposed in the previous session by President Hoover, who also wished to cut $500 million from the budget. It made little progress in Congress and died in committee.[92] After realignment, there were more avenues for legislative success. When the center-left New Deal coalition could not be relied on to support the act, Roosevelt moved to the right.

Roosevelt continued to move back and forth throughout his presidency, looking to different coalitions to support different policies.[93] This has led scholars to characterize the New Deal Congress as docile and bending to Roosevelt's will.[94] What it actually reveals is that Congress was functional in a way it had not been in some time, and with respect to economic coalitions, more than it had ever been. Roosevelt had something that no previous president had in the United States, a Congress with coherent coalitions on the Left and the Right organized around competing economic interests. Congress as a whole did not bend to his will; rather, different coalitions responded effectively to different parts of his program.[95] The availability of viable coalitions, both center-left and center-right, made it possible for Roosevelt to promote his recovery agenda.

The path of the United States, as this analysis demonstrates, was an unsteady one, with the regime dimension rising and falling in salience throughout the country's history. The partial realignment of 1896, which paved the way for multiple repertoires, and the realignment of 1932, which allowed for the formation of national economic policy coalitions, helped stabilize the economy and representative government throughout the tumultuous years of the interwar period. Neither, however, eliminated regime contention; they merely suppressed it and augmented repertoires of regime contention with repertoires of economic management. The emergence of multiple repertories became a lifeline for a country struggling with ongoing regime challenges but needing to navigate the economic crises of the interwar period. As the concluding chapter discusses, the suppression of the regime dimension would continue in the United States and elsewhere in the immediate postwar period, giving way to what has been viewed as the golden age of Left–Right politics. This historical moment in the present analysis, however, represents only a reprieve from underlying regime contention, which has returned once again to the politics of the United States and other established democracies.

Part III Conclusions

AMERICAN POLITICAL DEVELOPMENT IN THE MIRROR OF EUROPE

THE PRECEDING analysis has self-consciously sought to understand US political development in view of related processes in Europe, a comparative perspective that offers unique purchase on key dynamics of nineteenth- and early twentieth-century US politics. This "sideways" reading of US history, I contend, is useful and indeed necessary because the two regions were so intertwined throughout this period. Through an evaluation of an ideal type, that of actors motivated by regime anxieties and preferences, I have sought to illustrate the persistent impact of regime contention on US political development, with many of the categories of European regime struggles invoked and applied in the US context. At the heart of this contention were concrete institutional deficiencies, specifically the slave representation, which called into question the status of representative bodies and the full achievement of parliamentarization. Regime anxieties were reinforced by the influx of European ideas and persons, bringing to US shores many of the fights of Europe. In addition, the actors themselves were involved in processes of "translation" as a means of making sense of their own situation. They frequently reached for European categories of regime contention in ways that blurred the lines between the two contexts and at times made their struggles appear to be one.

While regime considerations were certainly not the only motivations at work, without taking them into account, we miss a great deal that might help us understand key moments in US political development. I highlight here a few areas in which a sensibility toward the dynamics of regime contention in the United States proves especially fruitful.

Party system change: The first is the view of party system change that emerges from this analysis. Informed by comparative perspectives on realignment, I offer a conceptualization of realignment as movement from one dimension to another. The leads to an understanding of party system change that departs from prevalent theories of realignment, which posit at least five realignments over the course of the nineteenth and twentieth centuries. In my analysis, these shifts represent important changes in coalitions, but not realignments. I see across these periods and party systems great continuity and a persistent struggle to realign away from the regime dimension toward the economic dimension, a process that is never fully achieved. In this view the first party system began in a state of flux and then gravitated toward alignment along the regime dimension as conflicts over western expansion and its implications for the slave representation intensified. The second party system saw an attempted realignment, with national parties that worked to set aside the growing sectional and regime divide to forge coalitions based on economic policy objectives. This might have succeeded were it not for the question of western expansion, which again in the 1850s brought the system back to alignment along the regime dimension and ushered in a new party system. This alignment would survive until the 1890s, when a new set of party leaders worked to move the system to alignment along the economic dimension and succeeded, at least partially, in doing so. The fourth party system saw a decided move toward parties based on economic coalitions, though it remained constrained geographically by the sectional divide born of old regime struggles. The fifth party system in this analysis represents a more complete realignment along the economic dimension, and the first time in US politics that viable national coalitions based on economic interest were established, but one which relied on suppression rather than resolution of regime contention.

The Revolutions of 1848: The influence of European political development on corresponding processes in the United States is evident throughout this analysis. But at no point was this more consequential than it was following the Revolutions of 1848. These revolutions created strong political sympathies within the US public, and the counterrevolutions that violently put them down created significant anxieties over the status of representative government. Unfolding while political tensions over the slave representation in the United States were escalating, the Revolutions of 1848 had a profound impact in the United States, leading actors to increasingly view their own struggles in terms of European regime contention. The Free Soil Party, founded that year, was often likened to the European republican forces leading the revolutions, and the Republican Party established just a few years later would further reinforce this connection to the republican cause in name and in substance. In the wake of 1848, regime anxieties were inflamed in the United States like at no point before. The slave representation was always understood along the lines of regime contention, an encroachment of the aristocratic principle within the democratic representative legislature. But by the 1850s, this was transformed into an existential threat. There can be no doubt that events in Europe had a strong role in this, as did the massive influx of European émigrés, mostly German political dissidents fleeing persecution in Europe. The Forty-Eighters, as they were called, flooded the Republican Party, bringing with them a heightened sense of regime anxiety and an urgent need to defend republican government. These connections are evident in the historical record but infrequently explored in the secondary literature. The analysis offered here points to the need for more research on this period, with a view to understanding the connections between events in the United States and Europe and taking seriously the regime anxieties that were everywhere heightened as a result of 1848.

The political transformations of the 1890s: Another major inflection point in US history comes in the 1890s, a period known for the transformation of legislative politics and the adoption of the Reed rules, a set of majority-building measures enacted by Republican Speaker of the House Thomas Reed to limit obstruction and facilitate the building of legislative majorities. Here as well, viewing these events through the lens of regime contention leads to a new way of thinking about the political transformations underway. This was a key turning point, which pitted regime-oriented Republicans seeking to strengthen their hold on the South against economically oriented Republicans working to reform coalitions to advance economic policy objectives. One group, led by Henry Cabot Lodge, endorsed the Federal Elections bill, or the Lodge bill, as a means of protecting Black voters and the position of the Republican Party in the South. Another group, led by William McKinley, pushed for a Tariff bill, forsaking the South for the promise of a new economic coalition within the Republican Party. This moment put regime concerns directly in conflict with economic concerns, and the outcome, passage of the McKinley Tariff and rejection of the Lodge Bill, reflected the triumph of economic over regime concerns within the Republican Party and in the party system more broadly.

The New Deal party system: Finally, turning to the New Deal party system, celebrated for its substantive achievements, the increase in legislative capacity, and the general stability it ushered in, we find a different story alongside the conventional view. It was a party system built on the suppression of the regime dimension rather than on an actual resolution of regime contention. In fact, what made the New Deal coalition possible as a national coalition based on economic interests was the acceptance among northern Democrats of the exclusionary practices of the Jim Crow South. Again, we find that stability in this case came at the cost of exclusion, a theme that was evident in the European cases as well, and especially in the United Kingdom. The ability to suppress the regime dimension in the United States, however, was never as thorough as it was in the UK, where the suppression happened early in the process of party development through the exclusion of certain political forces. This took place at such an early stage in the UK that it shaped the political landscape and the actors within it. Not so in the United States. By the 1930s, the actors were already established and had accumulated repertoires of regime contention that continued to operate, even as new repertoires of economic management were emerging. As a result, the suppression of the regime dimension during the New Deal era was successful for a time, but never stable. Party leaders were able to maintain coalitions along the Left–Right economic policy dimension, but they could do so only by keeping off the agenda anything that might ignite regime contention and minimizing the influence of dissenting factions within their own party. These struggles would continue under the surface through much of the postwar period, until the civil rights movement ultimately unraveled the New Deal party system. Tumultuous as this period was, however, it resulted in the development in the United States of multiple repertoires of conflict and cooperation, and an ability to move between them, an important political resource that, as discussed in the concluding chapter, may be of value in contemporary regime struggles.

A focus on the politics of regime contention helps shed new light on key events in US history. The historical interpretations offered here are meant not to displace others, but to illustrate the utility of the ideal type of regime motivations in understanding social actions. Because ideal types are not mutually exclusive, and because actors can hold multiple and overlapping motivations, we can conclude that the regime-oriented ideal type captures an important element of social reality without denying the role played by other ideal types. Its value lies precisely in its contributions to historical understanding, that it can lead us to view certain events in a different way and note things that might otherwise have been missed. The insights offered here, along with others found within these chapters, attest to the significant role of regime contention in US political development and the need for further exploration along these lines.

Conclusion

THE REGIME QUESTION, THEN AND NOW

THIS BOOK has offered an account of the history of regime contention in Western democracies that challenges the ways in which we tend to think about political development in the West. Scholarship on the topic has typically focused on inclusion as the measure of democratization, with the assumption that, except in aberrant cases, there was broad agreement about the rules of the game, and only the extent of the franchise was in dispute. The history of regime contention offered in this study demonstrates that critical and fundamental disagreements, not only about inclusion but about the rules of the game, have shaped much of European and American political development.

The regime question, I argue, far from being a matter settled at founding moments is a foundational question of democratic politics, which returns repeatedly, forcing democratic publics to answer anew, how shall we govern ourselves? It contains within it multitudes of questions: What are the rules that will guide the competition for power? What will be the constraints on such power? Who will have a seat at the table? What are the boundaries of the political community? And, perhaps most crucially in the context of modern democracies, what will be the status of representative government? The regime question is one that is so fundamental to the establishment and maintenance of political order that, like the national question (shall we function as one?) and the economic question (how shall we distribute resources?), it can never truly be eliminated. And much like the national and economic questions, it also endures as a critical dimension of democratic politics. The salience of the regime dimension waxes and wanes depending on the circumstances, but it resides continuously within the political system. And at various stages in the political development of Western democracies, the regime dimension has served as the primary organizing principle of democratic politics, dividing democracies on the very structures they are built on and shaping the oppositional forces on both sides of the divide.

For much of the postwar period, the regime dimension appeared to recede, leaving the impression that a new stage of political maturity had arrived, and fights over these old questions were settled. Today its salience has increased once again, along with alarm over the political turbulence it has ushered in. In this chapter, I seek to situate the postwar period and the current moment in the broader history of regime contention in Western democracies. To this end, I extend the analysis of the book to examine postwar development, as this is the period to which the current moment is most directly compared. What I offer here is by necessity only a sketch of postwar political development. It is intended to offer an alternative historical interpretation of this period to better situate the current moment of regime contention. This exercise holds value, I contend, because an erroneous interpretation of this period has led to a skewed view of both the past and the present.

I contend that, when viewed in terms of long-term historical processes of political development, it is the postwar period—the so-called "golden age" of Left–Right politics—that appears to be the exception, as was the apparent regime consensus it was built on. Particularly in cases that previously had strong repertoires of regime contention, this consensus was the result of concerted political engineering and often the suppression of regime contention to produce and maintain a centrist Left–Right politics along the economic dimension. An unstable equilibrium from the start, this golden age ended in fragmentation as another dimension began to disrupt existing coalitions, a trend that started in the 1970s and accelerated in the 1990s. At first identified with cultural values, among them authoritarian versus liberal values, today we can more readily identify this "new" dimension as the regime dimension of old. The specific regime questions associated with this developmental stage have shifted, but the regime dimension endures, and fights over the status of representative government remain central. In this view, the current moment of regime contention represents not a break with prior trajectories of political development, but a new instantiation of fights found in previous eras.

The chapter is organized as follows: I begin with the immediate postwar period, 1945–1970, in which the salience of the regime dimension decreased, and relatively stable party systems became organized along the Left–Right economic policy dimension. I argue that on closer examination, we find that there was in fact a great deal of variation in the success of Left–Right politics during this period, and where it did succeed, it was either a continuation of long-established patterns, as in the UK, or the result of the suppression of regime contention, as in Germany and the United States. Second, I examine the period from the 1970s to the early 2000s, in which we begin to see the crumbling of coalitions and a different dimension arising, disrupting the typical Left–Right spectrum. Scholars of the period have identified specifically the rise of a cultural dimension representing a set of values separate from the class-based identification of the earlier period. Within this cultural dimension we already see elements of regime contention, the nature of which could not be fully appreciated during this transitional period. The last period I examine spans the early 2000s to the current moment, in which we see much more vividly the resurgence of the regime dimension. It brings with it both the unfinished business of older periods of regime contention and a new set of questions related to the status of representative government. I end with some reflections on what earlier episodes of regime contention can tell us about the present.

1945–1970: The Golden Age of Left–Right Politics

The immediate postwar period saw an unprecedented reorganization of politics within and between Western democracies. Much of this was achieved through the implementation of an elaborate political and economic system known as the liberal international order. In part a reaction to the catastrophic political failures that had led to the war, but also driven by Cold War imperatives, the political reorganization of the postwar period aimed to secure a system of liberal capitalist democracy across the Western world.[1] Out of these efforts emerged an apparent regime consensus, which allowed for the stabilization of politics and party systems along the Left–Right economic policy dimension in many countries.[2]

Closer examination of the period, however, reveals several important things. The first is that there was in fact a high level of variation in the success of stable Left–Right politics, much of which tracked with prewar patterns of political development. In the United Kingdom and much of northern Europe, where the path of early parliamentarization produced more rigid repertoires of economic management, Left–Right politics was sustained and even strengthened. In France, Left–Right politics did emerge but was always fragile. Much like the interwar period, the inability to fully suppress regime contention in France led to ongoing instability, though the availability of multiple repertoires facilitated democratic resilience. And in much of southern Europe, where regime contention continued to undermine the push for tidy Left–Right politics, much more fragmented party systems prevailed.[3]

The second significant aspect of this period is that where stable Left–Right politics prevailed in previously conflicted party systems, it was often the result of concerted political engineering. In many respects this reflected Cold War objectives that necessitated not only the suppression of the regime dimension but also the narrowing of the economic dimension to smaller questions of economic management within a capitalist system. In many places, this required an exclusionary politics that targeted those forces that might actively engage in regime contention or disrupt prevalent coalitions. In Europe, this meant the systematic exclusion not only of fascist antisystemic forces, but also of economic actors that dissented from the capitalist order, especially Communist and Social Democratic parties that did not adopt accommodationist platforms. And in the United States, this was achieved through the exclusion of racial minorities and the suppression of the southern question, which threatened to undo the New Deal party system.

Viewed in this light, the apparent regime consensus of the postwar period, as well as the centrist Left–Right politics it was built on, appears highly unstable. It also belies significant continuities in the dynamics of regime contention throughout this period. Below I offer a closer look at these dynamics in Germany and in the United States, as these were the cases with the strongest repertoires of regime contention historically and saw the most concerted efforts to suppress regime contention in the postwar period.

German Reconstruction

Postwar Germany was the site of massive reconstruction efforts, not only in terms of state structures, which had been decimated during the war, but critically, in terms of the political landscape. The latter took the shape of concerted political engineering aimed at forging a stable centrist Left–Right politics out of the highly polarized German political system. While the immediate postwar efforts focused on eliminating regime threats on the Right, this quickly bled into Cold War imperatives to exclude regime dissenters on the Left. This included a campaign of "national defense" aimed at solidifying the position of the center-right coalition led by the Christian Democratic Union (CDU).[4] In Germany, as in much of Europe, the Christian Democrats emerged as the dominant political force in the postwar period, the face of government, and the main champions of the ascendent liberal democratic capitalist order.[5] And with fascist successor parties and political currents contained by the end of the Allied occupation in 1949, they turned their attention to what they considered extreme elements on the Left. The Right warned that the Communist Party (KPD) and the Social Democratic Party (SPD) could not be trusted to defend democracy in light of their associations with and perceived sympathies toward the Soviet Union. In this context, defending democracy meant defending the parliamentary majorities of center-right governments.[6]

To secure parliamentary majorities, these coalitions relied not only on appeals to voters, but also on a host of institutional safeguards that were introduced in the early stages of party system formation to weed out extreme parties. This included, for example, the addition of a threshold for elections to the German parliament and the switch to the two ballot system, both introduced in 1953.[7] The 5 percent threshold would impose a high barrier to entry for smaller parties, and the two ballot system would reduce the proportionality of representation, also hindering the access of smaller parties.[8] Both were strongly opposed by the Social Democrats and their partners on the Left, and both passed with the support of the Christian Democrats' center-right coalition.[9] Ironically, the same power-consolidating institutional changes we now associate with the populist challenges to contemporary democracy were first employed in the postwar period to secure the liberal order, internationally and domestically, against "extreme opinion," which included much of the Left.

As important as these efforts were to securing center-right coalitions, they were also critical in remaking the political landscape of the Left. This was accomplished by the exclusion of the Communist Party, de facto at first and later through a formal party ban, as well as the marginalization of the Social Democratic Party. Only after the Social Democrats had moderated their position and accommodated themselves to the emergent liberal order were they welcomed into government. The party's official shift in platform came in 1959.[10] It followed a decade of decline in electoral politics, and perhaps more importantly, the ban on the Communist Party in 1956, which left it without its main partner in opposition.[11] The moderation of its platform paved the way for the SPD to join a coalition with the CDU in 1966. It was the first time in the postwar period that the Social Democrats were in government and the first time since the Weimar Republic that they were part of a Grand Coalition with the Christian Democrats. With both center-left and center-right coalitions fortified in this way, Germany emerged with one of the most stable party systems in all of Europe. Indeed, in the postwar period, it has served as the model of political moderation and party system stability. But it was the suppression of regime contention, through the exclusion of antisystemic actors on the Right as well as regime dissenters on the Left, which made this apparent moderation and stability possible.[12]

Postwar United States and the New Deal Coalition

Though the regime challenge was quite different, the postwar golden age of Left–Right politics in the United States was similarly marked by a suppression of the regime dimension to protect the economic coalitions forged in the interwar period. This was not based on genuine regime consensus or the elimination of the source of regime contention. Rather, the New Deal party system and the Left–Right politics it embraced required legislators to set aside the southern question and tolerate the Jim Crow system, which had returned by other means the exclusionary politics and distortions of representation that had once led the country to civil war.[13]

The challenges of the southern question were not new of course; nor was the Jim Crow system. It had its roots in the failures of Civil War Reconstruction and was strengthened by the decision of the Republican Party in the 1890s to turn away from the South to forge new coalitions centering economic policy.[14] After that point, the southern political landscape began to significantly transform. The system of 1896, which paved the way for both major parties to move toward economic coalitions, also opened the door for southern states to develop elaborate systems of exclusion and segregation. The Jim Crow system touched on almost every aspect of public life, from schools to workplaces to voting booths, and extended into private life to regulate marriage and even recreational activities. And of course, the most significant of these restrictions from a regime perspective was the suppression of voting rights for Blacks and poor whites.

The politics of Jim Crow gave rise to a new set of regime questions centering democratic inclusion and civil rights. But it also resurfaced old regime questions, as it essentially brought the old aristocratic principle of representation in through the back door. By disenfranchising Blacks and poor whites, the Jim Crow system reintroduced the essential problem of the slave representation— it increased the power of wealthy southern whites. This was no longer linked to the principle of property and thus was not vulnerable to the same charge of aristocratic influence, but it functioned in a similar way. It meant that the voting power of wealthy southern whites was greater than that of any other constituency and increased their representation in the national legislature.[15] As early as the 1930s, critics such as W.E.B. Du Bois referred to it as a system of "rotten boroughs," explicitly framing it in the old terms of regime contention.[16] These challenges, however, were drowned out by the pressures of the economic crises of the 1930s and the Second World War, which solidified the New Deal party system and the exclusionary politics on which it was built.

By the postwar period, the South was a fortress, and its maintenance required only the continued collusion of the dominant parties. As Schickler has noted, "National party elites—that is, the leaders of political institutions of national scope, such as the president, top congressional leaders, and national party chairs—feared the disruptive potential of civil rights issues for their respective partisan coalitions."[17] This was especially threatening to the Democratic Party, which housed the most diverse coalition. Within the party, two increasingly antagonistic factions regularly squared off: racial liberals, especially union leadership and African American representatives, dominated one powerful wing of the party; and racial conservatives, mostly southern Democrats, the other.[18]

Keeping this coalition together was a constant struggle for party leaders. This is the reason they were not only slow to take up the issue of reform, but on many occasions, actively worked against it. This took the form of diluting party platforms, suppressing the dissent of racial liberals, and blocking legislation that would antagonize southern Democrats.[19] On the occasions in which national leadership did seek to intervene, they were often turned back by the opposition of southern Democrats. This happened on many occasions with anti–poll tax and antilynching legislation.[20] It is noteworthy that the main interventions in the politics of the Jim Crow South throughout this period came not from Congress but from the courts.[21]

The New Deal coalition did hold through the 1960s, but the cracks within it were apparent from much earlier. Again, a period that has been naturalized in the history of political development as the heyday of party system stability in the United States appears to be anything but. While party leadership worked to keep divisions at bay, the exclusionary politics that kept the system together produced ongoing challenges.[22] By the 1960s these challenges ultimately moved the Democratic Party to embrace the civil rights agenda. This move would reconfigure legislative coalitions and move the party system back toward the regime dimension, updated for a new era, but with many of the marks of earlier stages.

The Crumbling of Coalitions: 1970s–2000s

Perhaps just as important as what happened in the postwar period have been subsequent interpretations of what happened. Scholarship on party systems and social cleavages has tended to naturalize this period and the economic coalitions that appeared to lend it stability. Struggles over distributive politics were viewed as the norm within advanced industrialized democracies, ordering politics in ways that, while at times contentious, lent stability to democratic governance. Much of this framing was advanced in the work of Marxian scholars, who saw in the primacy of economic matters and in the postwar coalitional dynamics the work of productive class struggle.[23] The rise of social democracy, albeit in a moderate fashion, throughout western Europe helped to reinforce this image.

By the 1970s, to the dismay of many, these party systems began showing signs of strain. The biggest shift in Europe came from the decline in class voting, along with the decreasing power of unions.[24] In the United States similar trends were seen and were compounded by the struggles over civil rights, which ultimately broke apart the New Deal party system.[25] Along with these changes, the process of European unification and the easing of Cold War tensions also worked to remake the political landscape, diminishing the salience of the economic dimension and allowing other issues to surface. By the 1990s, traditional Left–Right politics was everywhere disrupted by numerous issues that were generally lumped under the label of "cultural values."[26]

Many cast this as an outgrowth of modernization. Terry Clark and Seymour Martin Lipset, in trying to understand the decline in class voting and identification, attributed it to structural changes. Specifically, they argued that greater affluence was producing different bases for social stratification and with it a "decline in traditional authority, hierarchy and class relations."[27] Ronald Inglehart framed the shift in terms of a hierarchy of needs. Having satisfied first order material needs, Western societies, he contended, had moved on to postmaterial values.[28] Others saw the shift in less progressive terms. Kriesi and his collaborators attributed it to unfettered globalization and neoliberal growth, which undermined the traditional bases of both center-left and center-right support, producing instead identification in terms of the "winners" and "losers" of these economic transformations.[29] And Hooghe and Marks linked the shift to the process of Europeanization, which created a nationalist backlash and divided populations along cosmopolitan and nativist lines.[30]

One thing was clear: the economic dimension was receding, and a new one was taking its place. At the time the fissures began to emerge, many attributed them to shifts in cultural values. One of these cultural values was democracy, and the new dimension identified by scholars highlighted this, contrasting authoritarian with liberal (alternately called libertarian) values.[31] Authoritarian values included respect for authority, obedience, social control, and hierarchy, whereas liberal values emphasized individual freedoms and civil liberties.[32] At the time, however, this was not conceived as a regime cleavage per se. That is, it was understood to reflect not regime preferences but rather attributes that produced a certain kind of attitudinal disposition or mode of identification within a democratic political system.

Ironically, this line of research had its roots in the idea of the "authoritarian personality" advanced in the 1950s by Theodor Adorno and his team of collaborators, who sought to identify the psychological basis of regime preferences and specifically the personality type that would lend itself to supporting authoritarian regimes.[33] While this work, and especially the Freudian analysis of personality types it rested on, fell out of favor by the 1970s, its influence can still clearly be seen in research on the cultural shift.[34] Yet within the literature on cultural values, perhaps overly confident about the consolidation of Western democracies, the authoritarian-libertarian dimension did not reflect regime preferences.

Today this has begun to shift, and scholars have tentatively started identifying a regime dimension representing divergent regime preferences. With decades of political development obscured from view, however, today this dimension presents itself as new and even more alarming for its novelty. The work in this study suggests that it is not new. Rather, it has been there from the start, though its salience has waxed and waned depending on the circumstances.

The Resurgence of the Regime Dimension

The fact that regime contention has returned to established democracies has led many to call into question the extent to which these democracies were actually consolidated.[35] In fact, it should call into question the very idea of consolidation. Understood as a dimension of democratic politics, and not something that rests outside, the regime dimension presents us with different temporalities and theoretical expectations. While there may be circumstances that reduce the salience of the regime dimension, and periods in which it recedes from politics, it must be understood as an enduring feature of democratic politics. Without this understanding, we are left in a state of political disorientation when it does emerge, without the tools or resources to productively engage it.

But is what we see today really the same regime dimension? Are we fighting the same fights? Surely many aspects of the regime question are transformed. Today this is no longer a fight between parliamentarism and constitutional monarchy. Nor is it, strictly speaking, a fight between democracy and

autocracy. Rather, the most common way in which the regime question mani-
fests today is as a fight between different conceptions of democracy: one
steeped in the liberal tradition of pluralist competition and institutional constraints, and others, of varied ideological leanings, posing challenges to liberalism and pushing for more unitary government structures that carry out the
specific will of a specific notion of "the people." Often adopting a populist style
of politics, new actors have emerged on the Left and the Right, articulating
multiple economic and social grievances, and importantly, questioning
whether the established rules of the game can deliver on their demands. Indeed, some identify the existing representative institutions, and especially the
rules of pluralist competition, as obstacles to the fulfillment of democracy and
push for executive aggrandizement to remedy this.[36]

Still at the heart of the regime question today is the status of representative
government, the role of legislatures—the "power of parliaments"—to govern
and to operate independently of encroachment. What we see today is indeed
the same regime question, updated for a new millennium. Legislatures remain
at the center of regime contention because they are democracy's key representative bodies, the primary vehicles of pluralist competition, and the institutions most capable of checking the power of executives. And legislative
capacity—the ability to identify viable coalitions to pass responsive policy—
remains a key factor in their ability to do so.[37]

To be sure, the regime challengers today are also transformed. This is not
the same Right nor the same Left of the prewar period. But these challengers
occupy the space left vacant by them and long suppressed by postwar politics
and Cold War imperatives. Having emerged in a context in which history had
ostensibly ended and democratic political systems were ascendant, regime
challengers today cannot but speak the language of democracy, though they
speak it in a different register. Whether through the Left populism of Latin
America or the Right populism of the United States and Europe, regime challengers today seek to upend the centrist politics of the postwar period, laying
bare its failures to produce both equitable distributive outcomes and responsive government.[38] They push back directly against the rules of the game, with
power-consolidating institutional changes and a rejection of the constraints at
the heart of liberal constitutionalism.[39] And they do so in the name of democracy. In this way, regime challengers push the system toward alignment along
the regime dimension.

Defenders of the established political order have responded in kind, forming regime coalitions of their own, centering principles of defensive

democracy, and purporting to offer a "third way." These coalitions stress that they are neither on the Left nor on the Right. In France, Emmanuel Macron's "neither left nor right" campaign was praised for its ability to halt the progress of far right parties.[40] In the United States, an anti-Trump alliance of Democrats and Republicans, operating under the label No Labels, mobilized to head off another Trump presidency.[41] Where regime challenges are more advanced, we see more explicit regime coalitions, such as Hungary's opposition alliance.[42] The analysis in this book suggests that what these coalitions are actually doing is organizing along the regime dimension, and once the regime dimension becomes salient, a stable Left–Right politics becomes exceedingly difficult.

The development of such coalitions, while reassuring to some in terms of the strong prodemocracy stance they display, presents its own set of problems. First, in terms of the structure of the conflict, these trends are concerning. The resulting coalitional configurations begin to look a lot like Sartori's polarized pluralism, where a centrist coalition attempts to hold off challenges from both the Left and the Right. This is an unstable position at best. As the analysis of this book shows, during periods of heightened regime contention, democracy is imperiled not by the designs of regime challengers, but because the nature of the conflict itself can be debilitating for effective governance. Responsive legislatures have been and remain democracy's best defense and the best way to strengthen representative government against the push for unitary power. The rise of these centrist coalitions of democracy defense does not help in this respect. Historically, such coalitions have been exceedingly difficult to sustain and ineffective at governing.[43] They may in fact endanger the thing that is most needed to defend representative institutions—legislative capacity. Already, we see this with the increasing legislative gridlock across established democracies and the difficulty of identifying viable legislative coalitions to support governments and policies.[44]

Second, in terms of the substance of the problem, these trends are also worrying. Today, regime contention brings with it democratic contention; that is, there is disagreement about the very meaning of democracy. This means that the claims of these coalitions to defend democracy enter contested political space. In these contests, the particularity of their visions is quickly revealed. The preservationist impulse of these centrist coalitions reflects a vision of democracy that may not be able to accommodate the politics of the current moment. Moreover, the democratic arrangements they protect are in fact very historically particular. They come from a specific set of circumstances and the struggles associated with them. Seemingly unaware of the particularity of their positions, these actors seek to maintain the constrained ideological space of the postwar period. In their own way, such coalitions also seek to suppress regime contention by asserting visions of democracy that exclude much of the Left and the Right.

The history of European and American political development presented in these pages suggests that the key to long-term democratic endurance will not be in resisting or suppressing regime contention—often it is necessary for democracy's preservation and vital to the protection of particular groups within it—but rather, in keeping open multiple repertoires of conflict and cooperation that offer flexibility in responding to challenges as they emerge. We saw this in the cases examined here. Aside from the path of early parliamentarization, which produced rigid repertoires of economic management—a path that was unavailable to many in the first wave, and none beyond that— the political conditions that proved most conducive to democratic preservation were in cases where multiple repertoires emerged. This was the case in France and the United States. Both followed unsteady paths that were fraught with ongoing regime contention, but they endured. The availability of multiple repertoires was critical to that. This remains the most viable strategy for much of the democratic world.

Embracing multiple repertoires requires that we separate out the substance of our conflicts from the structure of the conflict. While the substance of the conflict will be settled in the confrontation between different political forces, confrontations in which we will make political claims and advocate for specific outcomes, the structure of the conflict, and the prospects for long-term democratic endurance, rests on our collective ability to navigate the demands of democratic governance. In these transitional moments, we may find that the true heroes are the "politicians"—those who in the Weberian sense embrace an "ethics of responsibility" and a spirit of political creativity.[45] They are the political brokers, the protectors of possibilities, who resist ideological rigidity to facilitate the movement from one status quo to another, navigating coalitional politics such as to produce effective governance that also accommodates a changing democratic landscape. And we may find that we are all called on to be occasional politicians, moving between repertoires to advance both democracy and democratic stability.[46]

Regime contention undoubtedly presents perils. But it also presents opportunities. The present moment holds important opportunities to rebuild coalitions—on the Left and on the Right—in a way that can address the needs of democratic publics, and to reenvision democracy in a way that can strengthen confidence in representative institutions and pluralist competition. Harnessing these opportunities for the future requires a proper orientation to both past and present, one that understands the regime question as an enduring feature of democratic politics and appreciates that the "rules of the game" are not settled at founding moments, but rather involve ongoing struggles within democratic publics.

APPENDIX

TABLE A.1. Weimar Governments

Elections	Government formation	Chancellor	Party	Reichstag seats (%)
Jan. 1919	Feb. 1919	Scheidemann	SPD	78
	June 1919	Bauer	SPD	60
	March 1920	Müller	SPD	78
June 1920	June 1920	Fehrenbach	Zentrum	37
	May 1921	Wirth	Zentrum	45
	Nov. 1922	Cuno	Independent	41
	Aug. 1923	Stresemann	DVP	59
	Nov. 1923	Marx	Zentrum	37
May 1924	June 1924	Marx	Zentrum	29
Dec. 1923	Jan. 1925	Luther	Independent	56
	Jan. 1926	Luther	Independent	35
	May 1926	Marx	Zentrum	35
	Jan. 1927	Marx	Zentrum	49
May 1928	June 1928	Müller	SPD	61
Sept. 1930	March 1930	Brüning	Zentrum	35
July 1932	June 1932	Papen	Zentrum	6
Nov. 1932	Dec. 1932	Schleicher	Independent	9
March 1933	Jan. 1933	Hitler	NSDAP	43

Gray background: minority government. No background: majority government.
I consider only Weimar governments here because prior to 1919, there was no party government; rather government was formed exclusively by the executive still operating as a constitutional monarchy.

TABLE A.2. UK Governments

Parliament	Year	Prime minister	Party	Seats held (%)
11th	1832	Earl Grey	Whig	67
11th	1832	Viscount Melbourne	Whig	67
11th	1834	Sir Robert Peel	Conservative (minority)	29
12th	1835	Viscount Melbourne	Whig	58
13th	1837	Viscount Melbourne	Whig	52
14th	1841	Sir Robert Peel	Conservative	56
14th	1846	Lord John Russell	Whig (minority)	42
15th	1847	Lord John Russell	Whig (minority)	46
16th	1852	Earl of Derby	Conservative (minority)	43
16th	1852	Earl of Aberdeen	Whig-Peelite (coalition)	49.5
17th	1857	Viscount Palmerston	Whig	58
18th	1859	Earl of Derby	Conservative (minority)	46
18th	1859	Viscount Palmerston	Liberal	54
19th	1865	Earl of Russell	Liberal	56
19th	1865	Earl of Derby	Conservative (minority)	44
19th	1866	Benjamin Disraeli	Conservative (minority)	44
20th	1868	William Ewart Gladstone	Liberal	59
21st	1874	Benjamin Disraeli (Earl of Beaconsfield from 1876)	Conservative	54
22nd	1880	William Ewart Gladstone	Liberal	54
23rd	1885	William Ewart Gladstone	Liberal (minority)	48
23rd	1885	Marquess of Salisbury	Conservative (minority)	37
24th	1886	Marquess of Salisbury	Conservative-Unionist Coalition	51
25th	1892	William Ewart Gladstone	Liberal (minority)	40
25th	1894	Earl of Rosebery	Liberal (minority)	40
26th	1895	Marquess of Salisbury	Conservative and Liberal Unionist Coalition	61
27th	1900	Marquess of Salisbury	Conservative and Liberal Unionist Coalition	60
27th	1902	Arthur Balfour	Conservative and Liberal Unionist Coalition	60
28th	1906	Henry Campbell-Bannerman	Liberal	59
28th	1908	H. H. Asquith	Liberal	59
29th	1910 (Jan.)	H. H. Asquith	Liberal (minority)	41
30th	1910 (Dec.)	H. H. Asquith	Liberal (minority)	41

(continued)

Parliament	Year	Prime minister	Party	Seats held (%)
30th	1916	David Lloyd George	Liberal (minority)	41
31st	1918	David Lloyd George	Coalition Liberal	74
32nd	1922	Bonar Law	Conservative	56
33rd	1923	Ramsay MacDonald	Labour (minority)	31
34th	1924	Stanley Baldwin	Conservative	67
35th	1929	Ramsay MacDonald	Labour (minority)	47
36th	1931	Ramsay MacDonald	National Government	67

Light gray background: coalition government. Dark gray background: minority government. No background: majority government.

TABLE A.3. France Governments

Prime minister	Start of term	End of term	Party	Seats in the Chamber of Deputies (%)
Jules Armand Dufaure	Feb. 19, 1871	May 24, 1873	Opportunist Republicans	35
Albert, duc de Broglie	May 25, 1873	May 22, 1874	Monarchist	62
Ernest Courtot de Cissey	May 22, 1874	March 10, 1875	Monarchist	62
Louis Buffet	March 10, 1875	Feb. 23, 1876	Monarchist	62
Jules Armand Dufaure	Feb. 23, 1876	Dec. 12, 1876	Opportunist Republicans	35
Jules Simon	Dec. 12, 1876	May 17, 1877	Opportunist Republicans	74
Albert, duc de Broglie	May 17, 1877	Nov. 23, 1877	Monarchist	25
Gaëtan de Rochebouët	Nov. 23, 1877	Dec. 13, 1877	Monarchist	30
Jules Armand Dufaure	Dec. 13, 1877	Feb. 4, 1879	Opportunist Republicans	60
William Waddington	Feb. 4, 1879	Dec. 28, 1879	Opportunist Republicans	60
Charles de Freycinet	Dec. 28, 1879	Sept. 23, 1880	Opportunist Republicans	60
Jules Ferry	Sept. 23, 1880	Nov. 14, 1881	Opportunist Republicans	60
Léon Gambetta	Nov. 14, 1881	Jan. 30, 1882	Opportunist Republicans	75
Charles de Freycinet	Jan. 30, 1882	Aug. 7, 1882	Opportunist Republican	75
Charles Duclerc	Aug. 7, 1882	Jan. 29, 1883	Opportunist Republicans	75
Armand Fallières	Jan. 29, 1883	Feb. 21, 1883	Opportunist Republicans	75
Jules Ferry	Feb. 21, 1883	April 6, 1885	Opportunist Republicans	75
Henri Brisson	April 6, 1885	Jan. 7, 1886	Radical Republicans	55
Charles de Freycinet	Jan. 7, 1886	Dec. 16, 1886	Opportunist Republicans	55
René Goblet	Dec. 16, 1886	May 30, 1887	Radical Republicans	55
Maurice Rouvier	May 30, 1887	Dec. 12, 1887	Opportunist Republicans	55
Pierre Tirard	Dec. 12, 1887	April 3, 1888	Opportunist Republicans	55
Charles Floquet	April 3, 1888	Feb. 22, 1889	Opportunist Republicans	55

Name			Party	
Pierre Tirard	Feb. 22, 1889	March 17, 1890	Opportunist Republicans	61
Charles de Freycinet	March 17, 1890	Feb. 27, 1892	Opportunist Republicans	61
Émile Loubet	Feb. 27, 1892	Dec. 6, 1892	Opportunist Republicans	61
Alexandre Ribot	Dec. 6, 1892	April 4, 1893	Opportunist Republicans	61
Charles Dupuy	April 4, 1893	Dec. 3, 1893	Opportunist Republicans	48
Jean Casimir-Perier	Dec. 3, 1893	May 30, 1894	Opportunist Republicans	48
Charles Dupuy	May 30, 1894	Jan. 26, 1895	Opportunist Republicans	48
Alexandre Ribot	Jan. 26, 1895	Nov. 1, 1895	Opportunist Republicans	48
Léon Bourgeois	Nov. 1, 1895	April 29, 1896	Radical Republicans	26
Jules Méline	April 29, 1896	June 28, 1898	Opportunist Republicans	48
Henri Brisson	June 28, 1898	Nov. 1, 1898	Radical Republicans	40
Charles Dupuy	Nov. 1, 1898	June 22, 1899	Opportunist Republicans	40
Pierre Waldeck-Rousseau	June 22, 1899	June 7, 1902	Opportunist Republicans	40
Émile Combes	June 7, 1902	Jan. 24, 1905	Radical-Socialist Party	57
Maurice Rouvier	Jan. 24, 1905	March 12, 1906	Democratic Republican Alliance	57
Ferdinand Sarrien	March 12, 1906	Oct. 25, 1906	Radical-Socialist Party	57
Georges Clemenceau	Oct. 25, 1906	July 24, 1909	Independent	49
Aristide Briand	July 24, 1909	March 2, 1911	Republican-Socialist Party	54
Ernest Monis	March 2, 1911	June 27, 1911	Radical-Socialist Party	54
Joseph Caillaux	June 27, 1911	Jan. 21, 1912	Radical-Socialist Party	54
Raymond Poincaré	Jan. 21, 1912	Jan. 21, 1913	Republican Democratic Party	54
Aristide Briand	Jan. 21, 1913	March 22, 1913	Republican-Socialist Party	54
Louis Barthou	March 22, 1913	Dec. 9, 1913	Republican Democratic Party	54
Gaston Doumergue	Dec. 9, 1913	June 9, 1914	Radical-Socialist Party	54
Alexandre Ribot	June 9, 1914	June 13, 1914	Republican Federation	63
René Viviani	June 13, 1914	Oct. 29, 1915	Republican-Socialist Party	63

(continued)

TABLE A.3. (*continued*)

Prime minister	Start of term	End of term	Party	Seats in the Chamber of Deputies (%)
Aristide Briand	Oct. 29, 1915	March 20, 1917	Republican-Socialist Party	63
Alexandre Ribot	March 20, 1917	Sept. 12, 1917	Republican Federation	63
Paul Painlevé	Sept. 12, 1917	Nov. 16, 1917	Republican-Socialist Party	63
Georges Clemenceau	Nov. 16, 1917	Jan. 20, 1920	Independent	63
Alexandre Millerand	Jan. 20, 1920	Sept. 24, 1920	Independent (National Bloc)	53
Georges Leygues	Sept. 24, 1920	Jan. 16, 1921	Republican, Democratic and Social Party (National Bloc)	53
Aristide Briand	Jan. 16, 1921	Jan. 15, 1922	Republican-Socialist Party	53
Raymond Poincaré	Jan. 15, 1922	June 8, 1924	Republican, Democratic and Social Party (National Bloc)	53
Frédéric François-Marsal	June 8, 1924	June 15, 1924	Republican Federation (National Bloc)	53
Édouard Herriot	June 15, 1924	April 17, 1925	Radical-Socialist Party (Cartel des Gauches)	38
Paul Painlevé	April 17, 1925	Nov. 28, 1925	Republican-Socialist Party (Cartel des Gauches)	38
Aristide Briand	Nov. 28, 1925	July 20, 1926	Republican-Socialist Party (Cartel des Gauches)	38
Édouard Herriot	July 20, 1926	July 23, 1926	Radical-Socialist Party (Cartel des Gauches)	38
Raymond Poincaré	July 23, 1926	July 29, 1929	Democratic Alliance (National Union)	46
Aristide Briand	July 29, 1929	Nov. 2, 1929	Republican-Socialist Party	42
André Tardieu	Nov. 2, 1929	Feb. 21, 1930	Democratic Alliance	46
Camille Chautemps	Feb. 21, 1930	March 2, 1930	Radical-Socialist Party	42
André Tardieu	March 2, 1930	Dec. 13, 1930	Democratic Alliance	46
Théodore Steeg	Dec. 13, 1930	Jan. 27, 1931	Radical-Socialist Party	42
Pierre Laval	Jan. 27, 1931	Feb. 20, 1932	Independent	NA
André Tardieu	Feb. 20, 1932	June 3, 1932	Democratic Alliance	46
Édouard Herriot	June 3, 1932	Dec. 18, 1932	Radical-Socialist Party (Cartel des Gauches)	46

Name	Start	End	Party	
Joseph Paul-Boncour	Dec. 18, 1932	Jan. 31, 1933	Republican-Socialist Party (Cartel des Gauches)	46
Édouard Daladier	Jan. 31, 1933	Oct. 26, 1933	Radical-Socialist Party (Cartel des Gauches)	46
Albert Sarraut	Oct. 26, 1933	Nov. 26, 1933	Radical-Socialist Party (Cartel des Gauches)	46
Camille Chautemps	Nov. 26, 1933	Jan. 30, 1934	Radical-Socialist Party (Cartel des Gauches)	46
Édouard Daladier	Jan. 30, 1934	Feb. 9, 1934	Radical-Socialist Party (Cartel des Gauches)	46
Gaston Doumergue	Feb. 9, 1934	Nov. 8, 1934	Radical-Socialist Party	46
Pierre-Étienne Flandin	Nov. 8, 1934	June 1, 1935	Democratic Alliance	NA
Fernand Bouisson	June 1, 1935	June 7, 1935	Independent	NA
Pierre Laval	June 7, 1935	Jan. 24, 1936	Independent	NA
Albert Sarraut	Jan. 24, 1936	June 4, 1936	Radical-Socialist Party (Popular Front)	57
Léon Blum	June 4, 1936	June 22, 1937	French Section of the Workers' International (Popular Front)	57
Camille Chautemps	June 22, 1937	March 13, 1938	Radical-Socialist Party (Popular Front)	57
Léon Blum	March 13, 1938	April 10, 1938	French Section of the Workers' International (Popular Front)	57
Édouard Daladier	April 10, 1938	March 21, 1940	Radical-Socialist Party	57
Paul Reynaud	March 21, 1940	June 16, 1940	Democratic Alliance	NA
Philippe Pétain	June 16, 1940	July 11, 1940	Independent	NA

Gray background: minority government. No background: majority government.

ACKNOWLEDGMENTS

EVERY BOOK is a journey. This one began in a different place than it ended. It began with an important but narrower set of questions. It addressed itself more toward the guild and less toward the world. As I wrote it, the world changed, and the book changed. The historical struggles over the regime question that I was chronicling had resurfaced, altered but too similar to ignore the familiar patterns. The resurgence of the regime question demanded a dialogue between past and present, across conventional geographic areas, traversing various research traditions and theoretical paradigms, and requiring new methodological tools. This journey has been as challenging as it has been rewarding, and it would not have been possible without the help, guidance, and support of many fellow travelers who have contributed to this work in important ways.

I am grateful for the support of colleagues who have engaged with the work at many stages of its development. Several in particular have offered a close reading and significant feedback on different versions of the manuscript. In the first full reading of the manuscript, Sheri Berman, Michael Bernhard, Steve Hanson, and Daniel Ziblatt contributed significantly to developing the arc of the book and pushed me to refine the empirical and theoretical claims. I could not have asked for more thoughtful, challenging, and rigorous interlocuters. A second group of generous readers also helped me refine and sharpen the analysis in important ways. My thanks to Devin Caughey, Sara Chatfield, Adam Hilton, Nicole Mellow, Chloe Thurston, and Emily Zackin for taking up the work and providing their insights on key themes. A hearty crew of department colleagues offered a close reading and significant feedback on the manuscript in the final stretch. My gratitude to Adam Dahl, Andrew March, Raymond La Raja, Jesse Rhodes, Dean Robinson, Fred Schaffer, Regine Specter, and special thanks to Timothy Pachirat who gave copious, detailed, and very helpful comments on multiple drafts.

In addition to these groups, several individuals have commented on and made significant contributions to the development of the book. Eric Schickler commented on two separate drafts, and at both times engaged the work with great enthusiasm and a critical eye that helped with the "translation" of concepts and mechanisms central to the comparative analysis of US political development. Kathleen Thelen provided extensive feedback and pushed the question of repertoires and theories of political change in ways that have benefited the work on many different levels. Conversations with Nicolas Jabko helped hone my claims about political creativity and opened an important avenue of theoretical development. Early collaborations with Stephanie Chan helped develop my thinking on how to conceptualize and measure legislative coalitions. Paul Frymer's incisive comments helped to sharpen my arguments about realignment. Many others have lent their valuable help and expertise along the way. My appreciation to David Art, David Bateman, Valerie Belu, Giovanni Capoccia, Daniel Carpenter, Volha Charnysh, Fatih Cetin, Ali Cirone, Ann Daly, Matthias Dilling, Graham Dodds, Augustin Goenaga, Jeff Kopstein, Marcus Kreuzer, Cathie Jo Martin, Christopher Sebastian Parker, Svend-Erik Skaaning, Dawn Teele, and Jan Toerell for their support throughout the process.

Two individuals in particular have shaped my thinking and intellectual development in immeasurable ways. Rogers Smith has from the start cultivated my curiosity about both comparative politics and American political development and appreciated the distinctive perspective I bring as a "boundary dweller," straddling multiple fields and disciplinary traditions. On this manuscript he offered important feedback on the theoretical framework and pushed me on several key points of historical interpretation. Rudra Sil encouraged my pursuit of unconventional comparisons and helped to create intellectual space and a productive framework for comparative area studies. His feedback has helped broaden my approach to comparison in ways that directly contributed to the analysis in this work. Their mentorship dates back to graduate school, but their continued steadfast support and critical challenges as well as their intellectual leadership have helped create the space that this work occupies.

Parts of this work have also been presented and benefited from the engagement of participants in workshops at the University of Bremen; Aarhus University; Lund University; the University of California, Berkeley Comparative Politics Colloquium; the University of California, Berkeley, Historical Social Science Workshop; Oxford University Politics Colloquium; and Concordia University Comparative Politics Workshop. In addition, various presentations at the annual meeting of the Council for European Studies, the American Political Science Association, and the Midwest Political Science Association have benefited the development of the work.

Thanks also to the team at Princeton University Press for their support and careful shepherding of the manuscript through many stages: Alena Chekanov, Eric Crahan, Jess Herdman, Sara Lerner, Bridget Flannery-McCoy, and Melanie Mallon. Four anonymous reviewers offered important feedback that greatly improved the manuscript, along with the series editors, who helped to further refine the theoretical framework and empirical analysis.

In addition to the above, I am fortunate to have had by my side friends, colleagues, and friend/colleagues who have helped to sustain me throughout. Norma Akamatsu, Sonia Alvarez, Ivan Ascher, Angelical Bernal, Anna Branch, Barbara Cruikshank, Yasmine Daifallah, Cedric De Leon, Carlene Edie, Hind Elkalai, Kathy Forde, Jane Gordon, Lewis Gordon, Nader Hebela, Larisa Layug, Jennifer Lundquist, Julia Lynch, Eryn MacDonald, Tatishe Nteta, Isabel Perera, MJ Peterson, Deena Said, Jillian Schwedler, Libby Sharrow, Mary Summers, Caroline Summers-Smith, Linda Tropp, and Melissa Wooten have provided support, encouragement, intellectual engagement, spiritual fortitude, and so much more. And special thanks to Jimi Ojelade, who has seen this work through many stages, and listened to me as I excitedly talked through half-baked ideas, setbacks, breakthroughs, and everything in between. My gratitude also goes to members of the Third Spaces Writing Group: Judyie Al-Bilali, Kiran Asher, Sonya Atalay, Richard Chu, Lorraine Cordeiro, Isabel Espinal, Maria Galano, Tara Mandalaywala, Sindiso Minisi-Weeks, Joya Misra, Youngmin Moon, Alice Nash, and Caroline Yang.

My deepest gratitude goes to my family, without whose love and support none of this would be possible. Special thanks to my parents, Farouk and Eslah, my first teachers and most cherished mentors, who modeled for me from very early on a critical view toward the political, along with hope for the good it can do. Thanks also to my brother, Ahmed, whose natural curiosity, understated confidence, deep wisdom, and good humor always inspire me. My extended and growing family network has provided equal parts support and distraction as needed. My thanks to Gladys, Haris, Chris, Matt, Elisa, Annie, Ivan, Jim, Sue, and with fondest memories, Ken. My thanks also to my sweet family both within and beyond these shores, whose boisterous laughter, unconditional love, and light-hearted irreverence is the perfect antidote to anyone ever taking themselves too seriously.

Finally, to my children, Leyla and Noor—my beautiful night and my bright light, my dearest companions, my endless questioners, my greatest source of wonder, joy, and resilience—this book is dedicated to you, with love and appreciation for all you do to support and inspire me.

NOTES

Introduction: The Regime Question

1. Pippa Norris and Ronald Inglehart, *Cultural Backlash: Trump, Brexit, and Authoritarian Populism* (Cambridge: Cambridge University Press, 2019); Marc Hetherington and Jonathan Weiler, *Authoritarianism and Polarization in American Politics* (Cambridge: Cambridge University Press, 2009); Hanspeter Kriesi, "Restructuration of Partisan Politics and the Emergence of a New Cleavage Based on Values," *West European Politics* 33, no. 3 (2010): 673–85; Robert Ford and William Jennings, "The Changing Cleavage Politics of Western Europe," *Annual Review of Political Science* 23 (2020): 295–314.

2. Seymour Lipset and Stein Rokkan, "Cleavage Structures, Party Systems, and Voter Alignments," in *Party Systems and Voter Alignments*, ed. Seymour Lipset and Stein Rokkan (London: Free Press, 1967); Stefano Bartolini and Peter Mair, *Identity, Competition and Electoral Availability: The Stabilization of European Electorates, 1885–1985* (Cambridge: Cambridge University Press, 1990).

3. According to Juan Linz and Alfred Stepan, democracy is consolidated when it becomes the "only game in town." Juan Linz and Alfred Stepan, *Problems of Democratic Transition and Consolidation: Southern Europe, South America, and Post-Communist Europe* (Baltimore, MD: Johns Hopkins University Press, 1996), 5.

4. Similar insights have been offered on the nature of the regime cleavage in new and emerging democracies. See Kenneth Greene, "Dominant Party Strategy and Democratization," *American Journal of Political Science* 52, no. 1 (2008): 16–31; Kenneth Roberts, "Historical Timing, Political Cleavages, and Party-Building in Latin America," in *Challenges of Party-Building in Latin America*, ed. S. Levitsky, J. Loxton, B. Van Dyck, and J. Domínguez (Cambridge: Cambridge University Press, 2016), 51–75; and Dan Slater, "Democratic Careening," *World Politics* 65, no. 4 (2013): 729–63.

Chapter 1. The Regime Question and the First Wave

1. Important exceptions include Charles Tilly, "Parliamentarization of Popular Contention in Great Britain, 1758–1834," *Theory and Society* 26, nos. 2–3 (1997): 245–73; and Markus Kreuzer, "Parliamentarization and the Question of German Exceptionalism: 1867–1918," *Central European History* 36, no. 3 (2003): 327–57. There is a growing literature on the determinants of parliamentarization, but its role in the process of democratization is underexplored in historical context.

2. Sheri Berman, *Democracy and Dictatorship in Europe: From the Ancien Régime to the Present Day* (Oxford: Oxford University Press, 2019), especially chapters 3–5.

3. Ann Swidler, "Culture in Action: Symbols and Strategies," *American Sociological Review* 51, no. 2 (1986): 273–86.

4. Lipset and Rokkan, *Party Systems and Voter Alignment.*

5. Stefano Bartolini and Peter Mair, "Policy Competition, Spatial Distance and Electoral Instability," *West European Politics* 13, no. 4 (1990): 1–16.

6. The transformation of confessional parties to interdenominational Christian Democratic parties exemplifies this. See Stathis Kalyvas, *The Rise of Christian Democracy in Europe* (Ithaca, NY: Cornell University Press, 1996); and Matthias Dilling, *Parties Under Pressure: Institutional Choices, Factionalism, and the Politics of Party Adaptation* (Chicago: University of Chicago Press, 2024).

7. Lipset and Rokkan observe that "the *party systems* of the 1960s reflect, with few but significant exceptions, the *cleavage structures* of the 1920s." Lipset and Rokkan, *Party Systems and Voter Alignment*, 50.

8. Bartolini and Mair, "Policy Competition, Spatial Distance and Electoral Instability."

9. For contemporary western Europe, many have questioned the durability of economic alignments and the freezing thesis, noting the emergence of new value-based cleavages as well as those arising out of Europeanization. See, for example, Russell Dalton, Scott Flanagan, and Paul Beck, *Electoral Change in Advanced Industrial Democracies: Realignment or Dealignment?* (Princeton, NJ: Princeton University Press, 1984); Mark Franklin, Thomas Mackie, and Henry Valen, eds., *Electoral Change: Responses to Evolving Social and Attitudinal Structures in Western Countries* (New York: Cambridge University Press, 1992). In new democracies a substantial literature has identified a wide array of different dimensions found in early stages of party formation, many of them linked to distinctive patterns of predemocratic political development. See Herbert Kitschelt, Z. Mansfeldova, R. Markowski, and G. Tóka, *Post-Communist Party Systems: Competition, Representation, and Inter-Party Cooperation* (Cambridge: Cambridge University Press, 1999); Michael Coppedge, "The Evolution of Latin American Party Systems," in *Politics, Society, and Democracy: Latin America*, ed. S. Mainwaring and A. Valenzuela (Boulder, CO: Westview Press, 1998), 171–206; and R. Dix, "Cleavage Structures and Party Systems in Latin America," *Comparative Politics* 22, no. 1 (1989): 23–37.

10. Notably, many scholars of emerging democracies have identified a regime cleavage in new democracies, especially in post-Communist contexts, but tend to treat this as idiosyncratic or a failure of consolidation. Herbert Kitschelt, "Formation of Party Cleavages in Post-Communist Democracies: Theoretical Propositions," *Party Politics* 1, no. 4 (1995): 447–72, https://doi.org/10.1177/1354068895001004002; and Anna Grzymala-Busse, "Coalition Formation and the Regime Divide in New Democracies: East Central Europe," *Comparative Politics* 34, no. 1 (2001): 85–104.

11. See Arend Lijphart, "The Cleavage Model and Electoral Geography," in *Developments in Electoral Geography*, ed. Ron Johnston, Fred M. Shelley, and Peter J. Taylor (London: Routledge, 2014).

12. Hans Daalder, "Parties, Elites and Political Developments in Western Europe," in *Political Parties and Political Development*, ed. Joseph LaPalombara and Myron Weiner (Princeton, NJ: Princeton University Press, 1966), 66–67.

13. Center-periphery and state-church relations continued to shape politics in many first wave democracies, most commonly those that experienced late unification and those with large religious minority populations. Even in England, however, where the economic policy dimension dominated from the mid-nineteenth century, fights along the national dimension were never fully extinguished. The issue of Irish Home Rule, in particular, continued to resurface these tensions well into the twentieth century. In the United States as well, center-periphery relations remained strained, as demonstrated by the ongoing fights over states' rights, which animated politics throughout the nineteenth century. And in many instances, the national dimension came to overlap either the economic or the regime dimension in ways that have obscured its continued influence. These qualifications notwithstanding, however, in few first wave democracies was the national dimension the dominant organizing principle of national politics beyond the mid-nineteenth century. See Kalyvas, *Rise of Christian Democracy in Europe*; Daniel Ziblatt, *Conservative Parties and the Birth of Democracy* (Cambridge: Cambridge University Press, 2017); and Forrest McDonald, *States' Rights and the Union: Imperium in Imperio, 1776–1876* (Lawrence: University Press of Kansas, 2000).

14. For an important treatment of analogous processes in the United States, see Daniel Carpenter's *Democracy by Petition: Popular Politics in Transformation, 1790–1870* (Cambridge, MA: Harvard University Press, 2021).

15. Tilly, "Parliamentarization of Popular Contention in Great Britain."

16. Giovanni Capoccia and Daniel Ziblatt, "The Historic Turn in Democratization Studies," *Comparative Political Studies* 43, no. 8–9 (2010): 931–68; Daniel Ziblatt, "How Did Europe Democratize?," *World Politics* 58, no. 2 (2006): 311–38.

17. Barrington Moore, *Social Origins of Dictatorship and Democracy* (Boston: Beacon Press, 1966); Charles Tilly, *Coercion, Capital, and European States, AD 990–1992* (Cambridge, MA: Wiley, 1992).

18. Kreuzer, "Parliamentarization and the Question of German Exceptionalism"; Deborah Boucoyannis, "No Taxation of Elites, No Representation: State Capacity and the Origins of Representation," *Politics and Society* 43, no. 3 (2015): 303–32; Deborah Boucoyannis, *Kings as Judges: Power, Justice, and the Origins of Parliaments* (Cambridge: Cambridge University Press, 2021); Alexandra Cirone and Brenda Van Coppenolle, "Bridging the Gap: Lottery-Based Procedures in Early Parliamentarization," *World Politics* 71, no. 2 (2019): 197–235; José Antonio Cheibub and Bjørn Erik Rasch, "Constitutional Parliamentarism in Europe, 1800–2019," *West European Politics* 45, no. 3 (2022): 470–501, https://doi.org/10.1080/01402382.2020.1870841; Michael Koß, *Parliaments in Time: The Evolution of Legislative Democracy in Western Europe, 1866–2015* (Oxford: Oxford University Press, 2018); Adam Przeworski, Tamar Asadurian, and Anjali T. Bohlken, "The Origins of Parliamentary Responsibility," in *Comparative Constitutional Design*, ed. Tom Ginsburg, 101–37 (Cambridge: Cambridge University Press, 2012).

19. Boucoyannis, *Kings as Judges*.

20. Capoccia and Ziblatt, "Historic Turn in Democratization Studies"; Ziblatt, "How Did Europe Democratize?"

21. This includes Robert Dahl's highly influential argument on sequencing in *Polyarchy*, as well as other foundational works that address the issue of historical sequences: Robert Dahl, *Polyarchy: Participation and Opposition* (New Haven, CT: Yale University Press, 1970); Leonard Binder and Joseph LaPalombara, eds., *Crises and Sequences in Political Development* (SPD-7)

(Princeton, NJ: Princeton University Press, 1971); Nancy Bermeo and Philip Nord, *Civil Society before Democracy: Lessons from Nineteenth-Century Europe* (New York: Rowman and Littlefield, 2000); Guillermo O'Donnell and Philippe Schmitter, *Transitions from Authoritarian Rule: Tentative Conclusions about Uncertain Democracies* (Baltimore, MD: Johns Hopkins University Press, 2013); Linz and Stepan, *Problems of Democratic Transition and Consolidation*; Paul Pierson, "Not Just What, but When: Timing and Sequence in Political Processes," *Studies in American Political Development* 14, no. 1 (2000): 72–92. The argument also builds on scholarship that has demonstrated the importance of institutional choice for long-term regime stability in the interwar period. See Michael Bernhard, *Institutions and the Fate of Democracy: Germany and Poland in the Twentieth Century* (Pittsburgh, PA: University of Pittsburgh Press, 2005); and Markus Kreuzer, *Institutions and Innovation: Voters, Parties, and Interest Groups in the Consolidation of Democracy, France and Germany* (Ann Arbor: University of Michigan Press, 2001).

22. See especially Sydney Verba, "Sequences and Development," in Binder and LaPalombara, *Crises and Sequences in Political Development*, chapter 8.

23. Dahl, *Polyarchy*, 36–42.

24. For a useful breakdown of components of Dahl's notion of contestation, see Michael Coppedge, Angel Alvarez, and Claudia Maldonado, "Two Persistent Dimensions of Democracy: Contestation and Inclusiveness," *Journal of Politics* 70, no. 3 (2008): 632–47, https://doi.org/10.1017/s0022381608080663. Measures of legislative effectiveness and executive constraints in particular speak to parliamentarization as a distinct feature.

25. The impact of liberalization on the process of democratization was a central feature of O'Donnell and Schmitter's *Transitions from Authoritarian Rule* and other works in the transitions school that presume the "democracy game" begins with an opening of the authoritarian regime. See O'Donnell and Schmitter, *Transitions from Authoritarian Rule*; Linz and Stepan, *Problems of Democratic Transition and Consolidation*; and Adam Przeworski, *Democracy and the Market* (Cambridge: Cambridge University Press, 1991). Later scholarship has more explicitly looked at the sequencing of liberalization and participation. Because the path of early parliamentarization is no longer a viable option for contemporary democracies, it is not considered in these works. See Richard Rose and Doh Chull Shin, "Democratization Backwards: The Problem of Third-Wave Democracies," *British Journal of Political Science* 31, no. 2 (2001): 331–54, https://doi.org/10.1017/S0007123401000138; Sheri Berman, "How Democracies Emerge: Lessons from Europe," *Journal of Democracy* 18, no. 1 (2007): 28–41, https://doi.org/10.1353/jod.2007.0000; Thomas Carothers, "How Democracies Emerge: The 'Sequencing' Fallacy," *Journal of Democracy* 18, no. 1 (2007): 12–27, https://doi.org/10.1353/jod.2007.0002; and Edward D. Mansfield and Jack Snyder, "Exchange: The Sequencing 'Fallacy,'" *Journal of Democracy* 18, no. 3 (2007): 5–9, https://doi.org/10.1353/jod.2007.0047.

26. Leon Epstein, *Political Parties in Western Democracies* (London: Transaction Publishers, 1980), 19–20; Susan Scarrow, "The Nineteenth-Century Origins of Modern Political Parties: The Unwanted Emergence of Modern Political Parties," in *Handbook of Party Politics*, ed. R. S. Katz and W. Crotty (New York: Sage, 2006), 17.

27. The term "right parties" typically refers to traditional liberal and conservative parties that emerged prior to working-class incorporation. They are typically classified as parties of the "right," as they would find themselves to the right of the median voter after suffrage expansion.

28. Other indicators were also consulted, including questions about the powers of the executive to appoint cabinet members as well as the possibility that legislatures would question or censure the executive. Given the variation in constitutional design across cases, however, sometimes these indicate differences of procedure rather than differences in the status of parliamentarization.

29. Robert Locke, *French Legitimists and the Politics of Moral Order in the Early Third Republic* (Princeton, NJ: Princeton University Press, 1974), 252–64.

30. Vernon Bogdanor, *The Monarchy and the Constitution* (London: Clarendon Press, 1995).

31. The specific V-Dem measures I reference include lower chamber legislates in practice (v2lglegplo); percentage indirectly elected (v2lginello) + malapportionment (v3elmalalc); head of government appointed by legislature (v2ex_legconhog); head of state appoints cabinet in practice (v2exdfcbh); and head of state dissolution in practice (v2exdfdshs).

32. In France, for example, many features of parliamentarization are identified as having been achieved in 1830 with the establishment of the Second Republic; however, the reversals of the Second Empire represent a significant discontinuity in the present study precisely because they would have disrupted the development of actors' repertoires. Thus, the more relevant dates for the present analysis are 1870, 1875, and 1879, with the establishment of the Third Republic, the constitutional laws, and the Seize Mai crisis. These events and their relevance for parliamentarization are discussed in much greater detail in chapter 5.

33. This is particularly challenging with different practices related to the appointment and dismissal of ministers as well as votes of no confidence.

34. Stefano Bartolini, *The Political Mobilization of the European Left, 1860–1980: The Class Cleavage* (Cambridge: Cambridge University Press, 2000); Adam Przeworski and John Sprague, *Paper Stones: A History of Electoral Socialism* (Chicago: University of Chicago Press, 1986).

35. Andreas Schedler has described this in the context of electoral institutions. I use it here more broadly to apply to the major building blocks of democracy. Andreas Schedler, "Elections without Democracy: The Menu of Manipulation," *Journal of Democracy* 13, no. 2 (2002): 36–50, https://doi.org/10.1353/jod.2002.0031.

36. On perceptions of these revolutions in the politics and political thought of nineteenth-century Europe, see Seamus Deane, *The French Revolution and Enlightenment in England, 1789–1832* (Cambridge, MA: Harvard University Press, 1988); Jennifer Mori, *Britain in the Age of the French Revolution: 1785–1820* (London: Routledge, 2014); and R. R. Palmer, *The Age of the Democratic Revolution: A Political History of Europe and America, 1760–1800* (Princeton, NJ: Princeton University Press, 1959).

37. Piecemeal reform was the strategy not only of conservatives, as has been frequently noted, but of liberals as well. While the latter are often associated with democratizing efforts because of their strong advocacy of parliamentarization in many cases, they were also strong advocates of restricting suffrage as well as various other exclusionary safeguards that were part of the menu of manipulation. David Bateman, *Disenfranchising Democracy: Constructing the Electorate in the United States, the United Kingdom, and France* (Cambridge: Cambridge University Press, 2018); Dawn Teele, *Forging the Franchise: The Political Origins of the Women's Vote* (Princeton, NJ: Princeton University Press, 2020); Amel Ahmed, *Democracy and the Politics of Electoral System Choice: Engineering Electoral Dominance* (Cambridge: Cambridge University Press, 2013).

38. According to Kathleen Thelen, rational choice institutionalism tends to emphasize institutions as coordinating mechanisms used to generate and maintain equilibria among actors. Such a view can overstate the proximate impact of institutions on behavior and elide the long-term consequences. Peter Hall and Rosemary Taylor similarly make the point that historical institutionalism "rejects the traditional postulate that the same operative forces will generate the same results everywhere in favor of the view that the effect of such forces will be mediated by the contextual features of a given situation often inherited from the past." Kathleen Thelen, "Historical Institutionalism in Comparative Politics," *Annual Review of Political Science* 2, no. 1 (1999): 371; Peter Hall and Rosemary Taylor, "Political Science and the Three New Institutionalisms," *Political Studies* 44, no. 5 (1996): 941.

39. Giovanni Capoccia has referred to this as *distal causation*, whereby "decisions and development in the distant past can have a long-lasting effect on institutional arrangements." Giovanni Capoccia, "Critical Junctures and Institutional Change," in *Advances in Comparative Historical Analysis*, ed. James Mahoney and Kathleen Thelen (Cambridge: Cambridge University Press, 2015).

40. Swidler, "Culture in Action," 273–86. Michèle Lamont and Laurent Thévenot use a similar framework in their comparative study of repertoires of evaluation in France and the United States. See Michèle Lamont and Laurent Thévenot, *Rethinking Comparative Cultural Sociology: Repertoires of Evaluation in France and the United States* (Cambridge: Cambridge University Press, 2000).

41. Charles Tilly, "Repertoires of Contention in America and Britain, 1750–1830" (University of Michigan CRSO Working Paper 151, 1977); Charles Tilly, *Popular Contention in Great Britain, 1758–1834* (Boulder, CO: Paradigm, 1995).

42. The importance of "founding coalitions" has long been noted by numerous scholars of political development. The addition of the framework of repertoires here helps to account for why some are stickier than others. See Arthur Stinchcombe, "Social Structure and Organizations," in *Handbook of Organizations*, ed. James March (Chicago: Rand McNally, 1965); Ziblatt, *Conservative Political Parties and the Birth of Modern Democracy in Europe*. Steve Hanson has offered an important historical institutionalist account of party development, which similarly links predemocratic development with regime outcomes but focuses on the role of ideology. Stephen Hanson, *Post-Imperial Democracies: Ideology and Party Formation in Third Republic France, Weimar Germany, and Post-Soviet Russia* (Cambridge: Cambridge University Press, 2010).

43. This understanding of flexibility in repertoires draws on both traditional structural analysis, as exemplified in the work of Charles Tilly, and pragmatists' theories of social action found in recent scholarship in the field of contentious politics and beyond. See Tilly, "Repertoires of Contention in America and Britain"; Tilly, *Popular Contention in Great Britain*; Charles Tilly, *Regimes and Repertoires* (Chicago: University of Chicago Press, 2010); Robert Jansen, "Situated Political Innovation: Explaining the Historical Emergence of New Modes of Political Practice," *Theory and Society* 45 (2016): 319–60, https://doi.org/10.1007/s11186-016-9272-0; Gerald Berk and Dennis Galvan, "How People Experience and Change Institutions: A Field Guide to Creative Syncretism," *Theory and Society* 38, no. 6 (2009): 543–80; and Gerald Berk, Dennis Galvan, and Victoria Hattam, *Political Creativity: Reconfiguring Institutional Order and Change* (Philadelphia: University of Pennsylvania Press, 2013).

44. Giovanni Sartori, *Parties and Party Systems: A Framework for Analysis* (Cambridge: Cambridge University Press, 1976), 132–39.

45. For a useful discussion of these economic perspectives, especially the attitudes toward debt and austerity and the fixation on the gold standard that contributed to the crisis, see Barry Eichengreen and Richard Portes, "Debt and Default in the 1930s: Causes and Consequences," *European Economic Review* 30, no. 3 (1986): 599–640; Ben Bernanke, *Non-monetary Effects of the Financial Crisis in the Propagation of the Great Depression* (No. w1054, National Bureau of Economic Research, 1983); and Jacopo Ponticelli and Hans-Joachim Voth, "Austerity and Anarchy: Budget Cuts and Social Unrest in Europe, 1919–2008," *Journal of Comparative Economics* 48, no. 1 (2020): 1–19.

46. Moore, *Social Origins of Dictatorship and Democracy*.

47. Gregory Luebbert, *Liberalism, Fascism, or Social Democracy: Social Classes and the Political Origins of Regimes in Interwar Europe* (Oxford: Oxford University Press, 1991).

48. Sheri Berman, *The Social Democratic Moment* (Cambridge, MA: Harvard University Press, 1998).

49. Ziblatt, *Conservative Political Parties*.

50. Ponticelli and Voth, "Austerity and Anarchy," 1–19.

51. Erika Simmons and Nicholas Rush Smith, "Communication across Contexts: How Translation Can Benefit Comparative Area Studies," in *Advancing Comparative Area Studies,* ed. Ariel Ahram, Patrick Köllner, and Rudra Sil (Oxford: Oxford University Press, 2025).

52. James Mahoney and Dietrich Rueschemeyer, eds., *Comparative Historical Analysis in the Social Sciences* (Cambridge: Cambridge University Press, 2003); James Mahoney and Kathleen Thelen, eds., *Advances in Comparative Historical Analysis* (Cambridge: Cambridge University Press, 2015); Ariel Ahram, Patrick Köllner, and Rudra Sil, eds., *Comparative Area Studies: Methodological Rationales and Cross-Regional Applications* (Oxford: Oxford University Press, 2018); Marcus Kreuzer, *The Grammar of Time* (Cambridge: Cambridge University Press, 2023).

53. Rudra Sil, "Triangulating Area Studies, Not Just Methods: How Cross-Regional Comparison Aids Qualitative and Mixed-Method Research," in Ahram, Köllner, and Sil, *Comparative Area Studies*, 225–46.

54. Amel Ahmed, "American Political Development in the Mirror of Europe: Democracy Expansion and the Evolution of Electoral Systems in the 19th Century," in Ahram, Köllner, and Sil, *Comparative Area Studies*, 103–18; Amel Ahmed, "The Utility of Comparative Area Studies for Historical Analysis," *Qualitative and Multi-Method Research* 18, no. 1 (2020): 7–10.

55. Giovanni Capoccia and Daniel Kelemen, "The Study of Critical Junctures," *World Politics* 59, no. 3 (2007): 341–69; Kreuzer, *Grammar of Time*, 147–58.

56. Thelen, "Historical Institutionalism in Comparative Politics," 371; Hall and Taylor, "Political Science and the Three New Institutionalisms," 941.

57. On the uses of such counterfactual episodes in historical institutionalist analysis, see Evan Lieberman, "Causal Inference in Historical Institutional Analysis," *Comparative Political Studies* 34, no. 9 (2001): 1011–35.

58. Early approaches to critical juncture analysis associated with the "punctuated equilibrium" model understood the self-reinforcing mechanism as a function of equilibria, whereby dominant actors had no strong incentive to alter the status quo. Later articulations of critical juncture analysis have moved to a framework of path dependence, where the self-reinforcing

mechanism is seen as a function of the increasing returns to actors from continuing along a certain path, which, along with mechanisms such as positive feedback loops, can lead to institutional lock-in. Walter Powell and Paul DiMaggio, eds., *The New Institutionalism in Organizational Analysis* (Chicago: University of Chicago Press, 1991); Randall Calvert, "Rational Actors, Equilibrium, and Social Institutions," in *Explaining Social Institutions*, ed. Jack Knight and Itai Sened, 57–93 (Ann Arbor: University of Michigan Press, 1995); Paul Pierson, "Increasing Returns, Path Dependence, and the Study of Politics," *American Political Science Review* 94, no. 2 (2000): 251–67, https://doi.org/10.2307/2586011; Paul Pierson, "'Policy Feedbacks' and Political Change: Contrasting Reagan and Thatcher's Pension-Reform Initiatives," *Studies in American Political Development* 62 (1992): 359–90, https://doi.org/10.1017/S0898588X00001012.

59. The charge of stability bias has been most forcefully wielded against early models of punctuated equilibrium. Even path-dependent approaches, however, while importantly developing a dynamic and processual understanding of how institutions become reinforcing, have been vulnerable to the criticism of stability bias. See Wolfgang Streeck and Kathleen Thelen, eds., *Beyond Continuity: Institutional Change in Advanced Political Economies* (Oxford: Oxford University Press, 2005); Thelen, "Historical Institutionalism in Comparative Politics," 369–404; and James Mahoney and Kathleen Thelen, "A Theory of Gradual Institutional Change," in *Explaining Institutional Change: Ambiguity Agency and Power*, ed. James Mahoney and Kathleen Thelen (Cambridge: Cambridge University Press, 2010), 8.

60. Amel Ahmed, "Crossing the Boundaries of Comparison: Comparative Historical Analysis and Comparative Area Studies," in Ahram, Köllner, and Sil, *Advancing Comparative Area Studies*.

61. While context is important to a great deal of historical analysis, a contextualist approach aims to foreground the subjectivity of actors as the key to historical understanding. In this tradition, scholars have emphasized the importance of getting an accurate reading of "what actors were actually fighting about." See Giovanni Capoccia and Daniel Ziblatt, "The Historical Turn in Democratization Studies," *Comparative Political Studies* 43, nos. 8–9 (2010): 940. Some have argued for a subjective understanding of time itself, maintaining that time operates differently in different contexts. See Anna Grzymala-Busse, "Time Will Tell?," *Comparative Political Studies* 44 (2011): 1267–97.

62. Paul Pierson, *Politics in Time: History, Institutions, and Social Analysis* (Princeton, NJ: Princeton University Press, 2004); Amel Ahmed, "Reading History Forward" *Comparative Political Studies* 43, nos. 8–9 (2010): 1059–88; Capoccia and Ziblatt, "Historical Turn in Democratization Studies."

63. For a detailed discussion of this approach, see Amel Ahmed, "What Can We Learn from History? Competing Approaches to Historical Methodology and the Weberian Alternative of Reflexive Understanding," *Polity* 54, no. 4 (2022): 734–63; Thomas Burger, *Max Weber's Theory of Concept Formation: The Methodological Status of the Ideal Type* (Durham, NC: Duke University Press, 1972); and Ryan Saylor, "Why Causal Mechanisms and Process Tracing Should Alter Case Selection Guidance," *Sociological Methods and Research* 49, no. 4 (2020): 982–1017.

64. Following the Weberian tradition of evaluating ideal types, "theoretical models" refers to models of historical persons whose actions are animated by certain motivations. In this analysis, the ideal type to be evaluated stipulates motivations based on regime preferences.

65. Ryan Saylor, "Causal Explanation with Ideal Types: Opportunities for Comparative Area Studies," in Ahram, Köllner, and Sil, *Advancing Comparative Area Studies*.

66. Ian Lustick, "History, Historiography, and Political Science: Multiple Historical Records and the Problem of Selection Bias," *American Political Science Review* 90, no. 3 (1996): 605–18; Cameron Thies, "A Pragmatic Guide to Qualitative Historical Analysis in the Study of International Relations," *International Studies Perspective* 3, no. 4 (2002): 351–72.

67. According to Gregory Luebbert, British-style Lib-Labism was the key to democratic survival in the interwar period. Luebbert, *Liberalism, Fascism, or Social Democracy.*

68. Berman, *Social Democratic Moment.*

69. Erich Matthias and Rudolph Morsey, eds., *Der Interfaktionelle Ausschuss 1917/18* (Düsseldorf: Droste, 1959).

70. Roll call analysis is based on an original dataset of votes in the House of Commons and in the German Reichstag for the period of 1918–36. Network analysis utilizes methods developed in collaboration with Stephanie Chan. For a discussion of the data and methods, see Amel Ahmed and Stephanie Chan, "Continuities and Discontinuities of Political Development," Working Paper.

71. The classical statement on this comes from Ferdinand Hermens, who attributed instability to the proportional representation system adopted as part of the Weimar constitution. Yet, the Weimar party system had its roots in the Imperial Reichstag, which operated as a multi-member system. A highly useful modification of the institutionalist argument has been offered by Michael Bernhard, who demonstrates the endogeneity of institutional choice. Markus Kreuzer has also offered a modification of the argument, focusing on how institutions shape party adaptation and responsiveness. Ferdinand Hermens, *Democracy or Anarchy? A Study of Proportional Representation* (South Bend, IN: University of Notre Dame, 1941); Bernhard, *Institutions and the Fate of Democracy*; Kreuzer, *Institutions and Innovation.*

72. For a systematic comparison of the German and French systems, see Lauri Karvonen, *Fragmentation and Consensus: Political Organization and the Interwar Crisis in Europe* (Boulder, CO: Social Science Monographs, 1993); and Lauri Karvonen and Sven Quenter, "Electoral Systems, Party System Fragmentation and Government Instability," in *Authoritarianism and Democracy in Europe, 1919–39*, ed. D. Berg-Schlosser and J. Mitchell (London: Palgrave Macmillan, 2002), https://doi.org/10.1057/9781403914231_8.

73. Robert Self, *Evolution of the British Party System: 1885–1940* (London: Taylor and Francis, 2014).

74. Lee Drutman and Timothy Lapira identify this period in US legislative politics as the ideal type of "parochial patronage," a disordered system with little capacity to advance a systematic policy agenda. See Lee Drutman and Timothy LaPira, "Capacity for What?," in *Congress Overwhelmed*, ed. Timothy M. LaPira, Lee Drutman, and Kevin Kosar (Chicago: University of Chicago Press, 2020).

75. Dirk Berg-Schlosser and Gisèle De Meur, "Conditions of Democracy in Interwar Europe: A Boolean Test of Major Hypotheses," *Comparative Politics* 26, no. 3 (1994): 253–79, https://doi.org/10.2307/422112; Jørgen Møller, Svend-Erik Skaaning, and Agnes Cornell, *Democratic Stability in an Age of Crisis: Reassessing the Interwar Period* (Oxford: Oxford University Press, 2020).

76. Stephen Schuker, *The End of French Predominance in Europe: The Financial Crisis of 1924 and the Adoption of the Dawes Plan* (Chapel Hill: University of North Carolina Press, 1976); Eberhard Kolb, *The Weimar Republic* (London: Taylor and Francis, 2012), 59–65.

77. Leonard Gomes, *German Reparations, 1919–1932: A Historical Survey* (London: Palgrave Macmillan, 2010).

78. Ekkart Zimmerman, "Government Stability in Six European Countries during the World Economic Crisis of the 1930s: Some Preliminary Considerations," *European Journal of Political Research* 15, no. 1 (1987): 23–52; Ekkart Zimmermann and Thomas Saalfeld, "Economic and Political Reactions to the World Economic Crisis of the 1930s in Six European Countries," *International Studies Quarterly* 32, no. 3 (1988): 305–34.

Chapter 2. A Historical Institutionalist Approach to Legislative Coalitions

1. Tiberiu Dragu and Michael Laver, "Legislative Coalitions with Incomplete Information," *Proceedings of the National Academy of Sciences* 114, no. 11 (2017): 2876–80, https://doi.org/10.1073/pnas.1608514114.

2. Pierson, *Politics in Time*.

3. David Austen-Smith and Jeffrey Banks, "Elections, Coalitions, and Legislative Outcomes," *American Political Science Review* 82, no. 2 (1988): 405–22, https://doi.org/10.2307/1957393; David Austen-Smith and Jeffrey Banks, "Stable Governments and the Allocation of Policy Portfolios," *American Political Science Review* 84, no. 3 (1990): 891–906, https://doi.org/10.2307/1962771; David P. Baron, "A Noncooperative Theory of Legislative Coalitions," *American Journal of Political Science* 33, no. 4 (1989): 1048–84, https://doi.org/10.2307/2111120; David P. Baron and Daniel Diermeier, "Elections, Governments, and Parliaments in Proportional Representation Systems," *Quarterly Journal of Economics* 116, no. 3 (2001): 933–67, https://doi.org/10.1162/00335530152466278; Michael Laver and Norman Schofield, *Multiparty Government: The Politics of Coalition in Europe* (Ann Arbor: University of Michigan Press, 1998); Massimo Morelli, "Demand Competition and Policy Compromise in Legislative Bargaining," *American Political Science Review* 93, no. 4 (1999): 809–20, https://doi.org/10.2307/2586114; Lanny Martin and Georg Vanberg, *Parliaments and Coalitions: The Role of Legislative Institutions in Multiparty Governance* (Oxford: Oxford University Press, 2011); Thomas Saalfeld, "Intra-Party Conflict and Cabinet Survival in 17 West European Democracies, 1945–1999," in *Intra-Party Politics and Coalition Governments*, ed. Daniela Giannetti and Kenneth Benoit (London: Routledge, 2008), 169–86; Michael F. Thies, "Keeping Tabs on Partners: The Logic of Delegation in Coalition Governments," *American Journal of Political Science* 45, no. 3 (2001): 580–98, https://doi.org/10.2307/2669240.

4. Exceptions include Lanny W. Martin and Georg Vanberg, "Coalition Policymaking and Legislative Review," *American Political Science Review* 99, no. 1 (2005): 93–106, https://doi.org/10.1017/S0003055405051518; Mark P. Jones, Wonjae Hwang, and Juan Pablo Micozzi, "Government and Opposition in the Argentine Congress, 1989–2007: Understanding Inter-Party Dynamics through Roll Call Vote Analysis," *Journal of Politics in Latin America* 1, no. 1 (2009): 67–96, https://doi.org/10.1177/1866802X0900100104; and Scott Morgenstern, "Organized Factions and Disorganized Parties," in *Patterns of Legislative Politics: Roll-Call Voting in Latin America and the United States*, ed. Scott Morgenstern (Cambridge: Cambridge University Press, 2003).

5. Kaàre Strøm, *Minority Government and Majority Rule* (Cambridge: Cambridge University Press, 1990).

6. On opposition parties: G. Bingham Powell, *Elections as Instruments of Democracy: Majoritarian and Proportional Visions* (New Haven, CT: Yale University Press, 2000), 32; and Thomas Saalfeld, "Members of Parliament and Governments in Western Europe: Agency Relations and Problems of Oversight," *European Journal of Political Research* 37, no. 3 (2000): 353–76, 365, https://doi.org/10.1111/1475-6765.00517. On government parties: William Patterson and David Southern, *Governing Germany* (New York: Norton, 1991).

7. Lanny Martin and Georg Vanberg, "Parties and Policymaking in Multiparty Governments," *American Journal of Political Science* 58, no. 4 (2014): 979–96.

8. This norm was formalized in the Second International through a resolution passed in 1904 prohibiting ministerial cooperation in any bourgeois government. Daniel De Leon, *Flashlights of the Amsterdam International Socialist Congress* (New York: New York Labor News Company, 1905); James Young, *Socialism Since 1889: A Biographical History* (London: Pinter, 1988); Albert S. Lindemann, *A History of European Socialism* (New Haven, CT: Yale University Press, 1938), 157.

9. Frederick Craig, ed., *British Electoral Facts, 1832–1987* (London: Parliamentary Research Service, 1987).

10. These included, for example, the Aberdeen coalition of 1852 between Whigs and the Conservative-Liberal Unionist Alliance, which had more longevity but in which the Liberal Unionists remained very much independent of the government, cooperating primarily on the question of Irish Home Rule but little else. See Timothy Peacock, "Myths, Methods and Minorities," in *The British Tradition of Minority Government* (Manchester: Manchester University Press, 2018), 1–23.

11. John G. Heinberg, "The Personnel of French Cabinets, 1871–1930," *American Political Science Review* 25, no. 2 (1931): 389–96, https://doi.org/10.2307/1947667.

12. Gilles Candar, "Bloc des gauches et gouvernements radicaux (1902–1914)," in *Histoire des gauches en France*, ed. Jean-Jacques Becker and Gilles Candar, 215–26 (Paris: La Découverte, 2004).

13. In the context of the French Third Republic, Mildred Schlesinger has shown that throughout the interwar years, ministerial instability belies a great deal of stability in legislative coalitions. Mildred Schlesinger, "Legislative Governing Coalitions in Parliamentary Democracies: The Case of the French Third Republic," *Comparative Political Studies* 22, no. 1 (1989): 33–65.

14. The canonical articulation of this perspective comes from the work of David Mayhew, especially "Congressional Elections," which offers an account of legislative behavior based on incumbency interests in reelection. This view is later elaborated in *Divided We Govern*, where Mayhew finds little evidence that unified party control of government yields much greater legislative success than divided government. David Mayhew, "Congressional Elections: The Case of the Vanishing Marginals," *Polity* 6, no. 3 (1974): 295–317, https://doi.org/10.2307/3233931; David Mayhew, *Divided We Govern: Party Control, Lawmaking, and Investigations, 1946–1990* (New Haven, CT: Yale University Press, 1991).

15. Particularly influential has been William Riker, *The Theory of Political Coalitions* (New Haven, CT: Yale University Press, 1962); and William Riker and Peter C. Ordeshook, *An Introduction to Positive Political Theory* (Englewood Cliffs, NJ: Prentice-Hall, 1973).

16. Riker's work has also been highly influential in the study of governing coalitions within parliamentary systems. David P. Baron and John A. Ferejohn, "Bargaining in Legislatures," *American Political Science Review* 83, no. 4 (1989): 1181–1206, https://doi.org/10.2307/1961664;

Anna Bassi, "A Model of Endogenous Government Formation," *American Journal of Political Science* 57, no. 4 (2013): 777–93, https://doi.org/10.1111/ajps.12031; Itai Sened, "A Model of Coalition Formation: Theory and Evidence," *Journal of Politics* 58, no. 2 (1996): 350–72, https://doi.org/10.2307/2960230.

17. Riker, *Theory of Political Coalitions*, 47; David H. Koehler, "Legislative Coalition Formation: The Meaning of Minimal Winning Size with Uncertain Participation," *American Journal of Political Science* 19, no. 1 (1975): 27–39, https://doi.org/10.2307/2110691; Barbara Hinckley, "Coalitions in Congress: Size and Ideological Distance," *Midwest Journal of Political Science* 16, no. 2 (1972): 197–207, https://doi.org/10.2307/2110055.

18. Robert L. Butterworth, "A Research Note on the Size of Winning Coalitions," *American Political Science Review* 65, no. 3 (1971): 741–45, https://doi.org/10.2307/1955518; Kenneth Shepsle, "On the Size of Winning Coalitions," *American Political Science Review* 68, no. 2 (1974): 505–18, https://doi.org/10.1017/S0003055400117332.

19. Shepsle, "On the Size of Winning Coalitions"; Russell Hardin, "Hollow Victory: The Minimum Winning Coalition," *American Political Science Review* 70 (1976): 1202–14.

20. Michael Weingast, "Between Theoretical Elegance and Political Reality: Deductive Models and Cabinet Coalitions in Europe," in *Coalitional Behaviour in Theory and Practice: An Inductive Model for Western Europe*, ed. Geoffrey Pridham (Cambridge: Cambridge University Press, 2009), 41; Robert Axelrod, *The Evolution Of Cooperation* (New York: Basic Books, 1984); L. Dodd, *Coalitions in Parliamentary Government* (Princeton, NJ: Princeton University Press, 2016); Baron, "Noncooperative Theory of Legislative Coalitions"; Hinckley, "Coalitions in Congress." The political effects argument has also been applied within parliamentary settings for both oversized and minority coalition governments: see also Anna Bassi, "Policy Preferences in Coalition Formation and the Stability of Minority and Surplus Governments," *Journal of Politics* 79, no. 1 (2017): 250–68; Marjorie Randon, "Incumbency and the Minimum Winning Coalition," *American Journal of Political Science* 17, no. 3 (1973): 631–37, https://doi.org/10.2307/2110749.

21. A formal presentation of the theory of universalism is found in Barry R. Weingast, "A Rational Choice Perspective on Congressional Norms," *American Journal of Political Science* 23, no. 2 (1979): 245–62, https://doi.org/10.2307/2111001.

22. Hall and Taylor, "Political Science and the Three New Institutionalisms"; Keith Krehbiel, *Pivotal Politics: A Theory of U.S. Lawmaking* (Chicago: University of Chicago Press, 1998); Gregory J. Wawro and Eric Schickler, *Filibuster: Obstruction and Lawmaking in the U.S. Senate* (Princeton, NJ: Princeton University Press, 2007); Gregory J. Wawro and Eric Schickler, "Where's the Pivot? Obstruction and Lawmaking in the Pre-Cloture Senate," *American Journal of Political Science* 48, no. 4 (2004): 758–74, https://doi.org/10.1111/j.0092-5853.2004.00100.x.

23. Supporting these claims, Wawro and Schickler have found evidence that coalition size increased after the 1917 passage of the cloture rule formalizing the filibuster. See Wawro and Schickler, "Where's the Pivot?"; Wawro and Schickler, *Filibuster*.

24. David Rohde, *Parties and Leaders in the Postreform House* (Chicago: University of Chicago Press, 1991); D. Roderick Kiewiet and Mathew D. McCubbins, *The Logic of Delegation* (Chicago: University of Chicago Press, 1991).

25. Gary W. Cox and Mathew D. McCubbins, *Legislative Leviathan: Party Government in the House* (Berkeley: University of California Press, 1993); Gary W. Cox and Mathew D. McCubbins, *Setting the Agenda: Responsible Party Government in the U.S. House of Representatives* (Cambridge: Cambridge University Press, 2005).

26. Thelen, "Historical Institutionalism in Comparative Politics."

27. Cox and McCubbins, *Legislative Leviathan*; Rohde, *Parties and Leaders in the Postreform House*. See also Ruth Bloch Rubin's recent work on intraparty organizations, which applies a collective action framework: Ruth Bloch Rubin, *Building the Bloc: Intraparty Organization in the U.S. Congress* (Cambridge: Cambridge University Press, 2017).

28. Hall and Taylor identify three distinct institutionalisms that have had a significant impact on the study of politics: historical institutionalism, rational choice institutionalism, and sociological institutionalism.

29. Kathleen Thelen and Sven Steinmo, "Historical Institutionalism in Comparative Politics," in *Structuring Politics: Historical Institutionalism in Comparative Analysis*, ed. Sven Steinmo, Kathleen Thelen, and Frank Longstreth (Cambridge: Cambridge University Press, 1992), 7.

30. Pierson, *Politics in Time*; Hall and Taylor, "Political Science and the Three New Institutionalisms."

31. Thelen, "Historical Institutionalism in Comparative Politics," 371.

32. Pierson, *Politics in Time*; Thelen, "Historical Institutionalism in Comparative Politics."

33. Grzymala-Busse, "Time Will Tell?"

34. Pierson, "Not Just What, but When."

35. William Sewell, "Three Temporalities," in *Logics of History: Social Theory and Social Transformation* (1990; Chicago: University of Chicago Press, 2005).

36. Hall and Taylor similarly make the point that historical institutionalism "rejects the traditional postulate that the same operative forces will generate the same results everywhere in favor of the view that the effect of such forces will be mediated by the contextual features of a given situation often inherited from the past." Hall and Taylor, "Political Science and the Three New Institutionalisms," 941.

37. Capoccia and Kelemen, "Study of Critical Junctures."

38. Paul Pierson, "The Limits of Design: Explaining Institutional Origins and Change," *Governance* 13, no. 4 (2000): 475–99, 493, https://doi.org/10.1111/0952-1895.00142.

39. Karen Orren and Stephen Skowronek, "Institutions and Intercurrence: Theory Building in the Fulness of Time," *Nomos* 38 (1996): 111–46; Alexandra Kelso, *Parliamentary Reform at Westminster* (Manchester: Manchester University Press, 2013); Rubin, *Building the Bloc*; Schickler, *Disjointed Pluralism*.

40. This may also reflect a divide within the study of US politics, which has dominated the study of legislative coalitions, between behavioralists and institutionalists. Because coalition formation is taken to be a kind of behavior rather than an institutional structure, the lens of institutionalism has not been applied.

41. Powell and DiMaggio, *New Institutionalism in Organizational Analysis*; Avner Greif, "Contract Enforceability and Economic Institutions in Early Trade: The Maghribi Traders' Coalition," *American Economic Review* 83, no. 3 (1993): 525–48; Calvert, "Rational Actors, Equilibrium, and Social Institutions."

42. Pierson, "Increasing Returns, Path Dependence, and the Study of Politics"; Pierson "'Policy Feedbacks' and Political Change."

43. Pierson, *Politics in Time*, 135.

44. Capoccia and Kelemen, "Study of Critical Junctures," 351.

45. Ruth Berins Collier and David Collier, *Shaping the Political Arena* (Princeton, NJ: Princeton University Press, 1991); Ronald Aminzade, "Historical Sociology and Time," *Sociological Methods and Research* 20, no. 4 (1992): 456–80, https://doi.org/10.1177/0049124192020004003; James Mahoney, "Path Dependence in Historical Sociology," *Theory and Society* 29, no. 4 (2000): 507–48.

46. Capoccia, "Critical Junctures and Institutional Change," 174.

47. Mahoney and Thelen, "Theory of Gradual Institutional Change," 8.

48. Mahoney and Thelen offer a power-distributional model that provides a mechanism for endogenous institutional change, moderating the continuity bias of much historical institutionalist work. In any given episode, they contend, outcomes will depend on the relative power afforded to defenders of the status quo and the extent to which targeted institutions afford opportunities for discretion and interpretation. In addition to this, they consider the type of change agent that emerges in a given context as an important factor in determining the pattern of institutional change. Mahoney and Thelen, "Theory of Gradual Institutional Change," 23.

49. Larry Eugene Jones, *German Liberalism and the Dissolution of the Weimar Party System, 1918–1933* (Chapel Hill: University of North Carolina Press, 2017), 320–22.

50. Daniel Brower, *The New Jacobins: The French Communist Party and the Popular Front* (Ithaca, NY: Cornell University Press, 1968), 190–95.

51. Swidler, "Culture in Action"; Lamont and Thévenot, *Rethinking Comparative Cultural Sociology.*

52. The conceptualization of repertoires used here draws from both traditional structural analysis and pragmatists' theories of social action. Structuralist accounts, such as those found in the work of Charles Tilly, placed a great deal of emphasis on the structure of the conflict in shaping repertoires and determining their flexibility, that is, how easily they could be altered. This tended to produce a rather rigid view of repertoires as unchanging, especially under highly repressive conditions. Against this structuralist view, however, later scholarship has sought to highlight the role of political creativity in the development and transformation of repertoires. For the structuralist view, see Tilly, "Repertoires of Contention in America and Britain"; and Tilly, *Popular Contention in Great Britain.* For more agentic accounts, see Jansen, "Situated Political Innovation"; Berk and Galvan, "How People Experience and Change Institutions"; Berk, Galvan, and Hattam, *Political Creativity.* For a helpful discussion of the role of repertoires in shaping behavior, see Nicolas Jabko, "Contested Governance: The New Repertoire of the Eurozone Crisis," *Governance* 32, no. 3 (2019): 493–509, https://doi.org/10.1111/gove.12389. See also Tomás Gold, "Contentious Tactics as Jazz Performances: A Pragmatist Approach to the Study of Repertoire Change," *Sociological Theory,* 40, no. 3 (2022): 249–71, https://doi.org/10.1177/07352751221110625.

Part II Introduction. The Regime Question
and European Political Development

1. Also known as John Stuart Mill's method of difference, this approach is commonly used to understand variation among similarly situated cases. Alexander George and Andrew Bennett, *Case Studies and Theory Development in the Social Sciences* (Cambridge, MA: MIT Press, 2005).

2. Many of the foundational works in the field of historical political development, including those of Barrington Moore, Alexander Gerschenkron, and Gregory Luebbert, treat these as most-similar cases. More recently as well, Daniel Ziblatt has employed this approach in

comparing the United Kingdom and Germany. It is precisely the similarity within the structural conditions at early stages of political development that allow them to draw robust inferences about divergent outcomes. See Moore, *Social Origins of Dictatorship and Democracy*; Luebbert, *Liberalism, Fascism, or Social Democracy*; and Ziblatt, *Conservative Political Parties*.

3. On the role of within-case analysis in a comparative case design, see George and Bennet, *Case Studies and Theory Development in the Social Sciences*, 179.

Chapter 3. Early Parliamentarization in the United Kingdom: The Dominance of Repertoires of Economic Management

1. Capoccia and Ziblatt, "Historic Turn in Democratization Studies."

2. The influence of the French Revolution on reformers in England is discussed in E. P. Thompson, *The Making of the English Working Class* (1968; Harlow, UK: Penguin, 2013). Also see Albert Goodwin, *The Friends of Liberty: The English Democratic Movement in the Age of the French Revolution* (London: Hutchinson, 1979); H. T. Dickinson, ed., *Britain and the French Revolution, 1789–1815* (London: MacMillan, 1989); and Jenny Graham, *The Nation, the Law and the King: Reform Politics in England, 1789–99* (Lanham, MD: University Press of America, 1999).

3. For accounts of the conservative backlash, see Ian Christie, *Stress and Stability in Late Eighteenth-Century Britain: Reflection on the British Avoidance of Revolution* (1956; New York: Clarendon Press of Oxford University Press, 1984); T. Schofield, "Conservative Political Thought in Britain in Response to the French Revolution," *Historical Journal* 29, no. 3 (1986): 601–22; Matthew Grenby, *The Anti-Jacobin Novel: British Conservatism and the French Revolution* (Cambridge: Cambridge University Press, 2001); and Arthur Burns and Joanna Innes, eds., *Rethinking the Age of Reform: Britain 1780–1850* (Cambridge: Cambridge University Press, 2003).

4. John Cannon, *Parliamentary Reform, 1640–1832* (Cambridge: Cambridge University Press, 1973); Michael Brock, *The Great Reform Act* (London: Hutchinson, 1973); David Moore, *The Politics of Deference: A Study of the Mid-Nineteenth Century English Political System* (Hassocks: Harvester Press, 1976); Richard W. Davis, *Political Change and Continuity, 1760–1885: A Buckinghamshire Study* (Hamden, CT: Archon, 1972); Frank O'Gorman, *Voters, Patrons and Parties: The Unreformed Electoral System of Hanoverian England, 1734–1832* (Oxford: Oxford University Press, 1989).

5. John Phillips and Charles Wetherell, "The Great Reform Act of 1832 and the Political Modernization of England," *American Historical Review* 100, no. 2 (1995): 411–36; E. Evans, *The Great Reform Act of 1832* (London: Routledge, 1994); Bingham Powell Jr., "Incremental Democratization: The British Reform Act of 1832," in *Crisis, Choice, and Change: Historical Studies of Political Development*, ed. Gabriel A. Almond, Scott Flanagan, and Robert Mundt (Boston: Little, Brown, 1973).

6. The act as watershed in suffrage expansion is a fairly common view. For a recent articulation, see T. S. Aidt and R. Franck, "How to Get the Snowball Rolling and Extend the Franchise: Voting on the Great Reform Act of 1832," *Public Choice* 155 (2013): 229–50. Those who maintain that the results of franchise expansion at this time were modest include Norman Gash, *Politics in the Age of Peel: A Study in the Technique of Parliamentary Representation, 1830–1850* (New York: Longman, 1953); E. A. Smith, *Reform or Revolution: A Diary of Reform in England, 1830–32*, (London: Stroud, 1992); and John Dinwiddy, *From Luddism to the First Reform Bill: Reform in*

England 1810–1832 (Oxford: Oxford University Press, 1986). Even those who claim that the act was a watershed moment often do so with reference to later events that it would usher in: see Phillips and Wetherell, "Great Reform Act of 1832"; and Derek Beales, "The Electorate before and after 1832: The Right to Vote and the Opportunity," *Parliamentary History* 11, no. 1 (1989): 139–50.

7. Sewell, "Three Temporalities."

8. On the Reform Act as elite concession, see B. Morrison, "Channeling the Restless Spirit of Innovation: Elite Concessions and Institutional Change in the British Reform Act of 1832," *World Politics* 63, no. 4 (2011): 678–710; Sean Lang, *Parliamentary Reform 1785–1928* (London: Routledge, 1999); Ellis Archer Wasson, "The Great Whigs and Parliamentary Reform, 1809–1830," *Journal of British Studies* 24, no. 4 (1985): 434–64; and Joseph Hamburger, *James Mill and the Art of Revolution* (New Haven, CT: Yale University Press, 1963).

9. See correspondence between the king and Lord Grey. *Reform Act, 1832: Correspondence of the Late Earl Grey with His Majesty King William IV* (London: Murray, 1867). In addition, E. A. Smith's *Reform or Revolution* contains a useful review of newspaper articles, personal correspondences, and political publications that reveal the various dimensions of public debate on the issues.

10. Angus Hawkins, "'Parliamentary Government' and Victorian Political Parties, c. 1830–c. 1880," *English Historical Review* 104, no. 412 (1989): 638–66, 652.

11. Tilly, "Parliamentarization of Popular Contention in Great Britain"; Richard Huzzey and Henry Miller, "Petitions, Parliament and Political Culture: Petitioning the House of Commons, 1780–1918," *Past and Present* 248, no. 1 (2020): 123–64.

12. In fact, the Crown was considered to be part of the legislative power of the state, along with the Houses of Lords and Commons.

13. Jeremy Black, *George III: America's Last King* (New Haven, CT: Yale University Press, 2008), 401. The measure specifically would have allowed Catholics to serve in the military, counteracting the Test Act. Though the monarch did not actually veto the legislation, his intention to do so led the cabinet (Earl Grey in particular, who had introduced it to the Commons) to withdraw it. See also Eugene Forsey, *The Royal Power of Dissolution of Parliament in the British Commonwealth* (Oxford: Oxford University Press, 1943).

14. Tilly, "Parliamentarization of Popular Contention in Great Britain." In 1834, William IV attempted to replace the Whig prime minister Lord Melbourne with Conservative leader Robert Peel. See Ian Newbould, *Whiggery and Reform, 1830–1841: The Politics of Government* (London: MacMillan, 1990).

15. Christie, *Stress and Stability*; Archibald S. Foord, "The Waning of 'The Influence of the Crown,'" *English Historical Review* 62, no. 245 (1947): 484–507.

16. Christie, *Stress and Stability*, 147.

17. Dinwiddy, *From Luddism to the First Reform Bill*.

18. The role of patronage was much disputed at the time, as the political consequences of this claim were closely tied to the reform agenda. Even those disputing the Crown's influence, however, could not deny the role of patronage but only insist that it did not affect all MPs. See John Ranby, *An Inquiry into the Supposed Increase of the Influence of the Crown, the Present State of that Influence, and the Expediency of a Parliamentary Reform* (London, 1811).

19. Brian Hill, *Early Parties and Politics in Britain 1688–1832* (London: Macmillan, 1966).

20. John Keene, *The Life and Death of Democracy* (New York: Norton, 2009), 504–5; Thomas Oldfield, *Representative History of Great Britain and Ireland* (London: Baldwin, Chaddock, and Joy, 1816).

21. Dinwiddy, *From Luddism to the First Reform Bill*, 192–94.

22. Lord John Russell, *An Essay on the History of the English Government and Constitution* (1823), 403, quoted in Dinwiddy, *From Luddism to the First Reform Bill*.

23. Samuel Whitbread, quoted in Dinwiddy, *From Luddism to the First Reform Bill*, 190.

24. See *Reform Act, 1832: Correspondence of the Late Earl Grey with His Majesty King William IV* (London: Murray, 1867), especially correspondence from December 2–15, 1831.

25. Gash, *Politics in the Age of Peel*, 24–25.

26. Russell, Hansard Parliamentary Debate, March 9, 1931, quoted in Gash, *Politics in the Age of Peel*, 24.

27. See Ertman on 1832 as a critical juncture: Thomas Ertman, "The Great Reform Act of 1832 and British Democratization," *Comparative Political Studies* 43, nos. 8–9 (2010): 1000–1022, https://doi.org/10.1177/0010414010370434.

28. Karl Polanyi, *The Great Transformation: The Political and Economic Origins of Our Time* (1957; Boston, MA: Beacon Press, 2001), 124.

29. On the absence of established parties prior to 1832, see O'Gorman, *Voters, Patrons and Parties*; and John A. Phillips and Charles Wetherell, "The Great Reform Bill of 1832 and the Rise of Partisanship," *Journal of Modern History* 63, no. 4 (1991): 621–46. http://www.jstor.org/stable/2938583.

30. The labels Conservatives and Liberal were an innovation at the time. Both groups grew out of the Tory party, with the Conservatives label introduced by Peel as an attempt to rebrand the Tory party and focus its agenda on conservation of the constitutional order against democratic encroachment. The Liberal Party label was later introduced by leaders such as Gladstone who sought to stake out a liberal position on economic matters but still maintained a conservative attitude toward democratic reform. According to Halévy, the term Liberal only came into use in 1847 and only to describe Conservative MPs who maintained a liberal attitude toward economic matters. Élie Halévy, *The Triumph of Reform: The History of the English People in the Nineteenth Century, 1830–1841* (London: Ernest Benn, 1961).

31. Lewis Namier, *The Structure of Politics and the Ascension of George III* (London MacMillan, 1929).

32. D.E.D. Beales, "Parliamentary Politics and the 'Independent' Member 1820–1860," in *Ideas and Institutions of Victorian Britain*, ed. R. Robson (Oxford: Oxford University Press, 1967), 1–19. Gary Cox, *The Efficient Secret: The Cabinet and the Development of Political Parties in Victorian England* (Cambridge: Cambridge University Press, 1987), also attributes this to parliamentarization but through a different mechanism. He argues that the rise of cabinet government strengthened parties by decreasing the power of individual MPs. See also J.A.W. Gunn, ed., *Factions No More: Attitudes to Party in Government and Opposition in Eighteenth-Century England* (London: Routledge, 1972). Gunn provides a selection of primary sources showing the gradual embrace of party as an instrument of political action during this period.

33. Norman Gash offers a comprehensive account of party composition and alignment, stressing the importance of the regime dimension not only in party positions but in actors

understanding of the very purpose of party. See Norman Gash, *Reaction and Reconstruction in English Politics, 1832–1852* (Oxford: Clarendon, 1965).

34. For detailed analysis of party alignment in the decade after reform, see David Close, "The Formation of a Two-Party Alignment in the House of Commons between 1832 and 1841," *English Historical Review* 84, no. 331 (1969): 257–77.

35. Ian Newbould, "The Emergence of a Two-Party System in England from 1830 to 1841: Roll Call and Reconsideration," *Parliaments, Estates and Representation* 5, no. 1 (1985): 25–32; W. O. Aydelotte, "The House of Commons in the 1840s," *History* 39, no. 137 (1954): 249–62; Valerie Cromwell, "Mapping the Political World of 1861: A Multidimensional Analysis of House of Commons' Division Lists," *Legislative Studies Quarterly* 7, no. 2 (1982): 281–97; T. A. Jenkins, *Parliament, Party and Politics in Victorian Britain* (Manchester: Manchester University Press, 1996).

36. Gash, *Reaction and Reconstruction*, 148.

37. Austen Mitchell, *The Whigs in Opposition, 1815–1830* (Oxford: Oxford University Press, 1967).

38. Gash, *Reaction and Reconstruction*, 146.

39. Henry Donaldson Jordon, "The Political Methods of the Anti-Corn Law League," *Political Science Quarterly* 42, no. 1 (1927): 58–76; J. L. Hammond and Barbara Hammond, *The Age of the Chartists: A Study of Discontent, 1832–54* (London: Longmans, Green, 1930).

40. Michael Lusztig, "Solving Peel's Puzzle: Repeal of the Corn Laws and Institutional Preservation," *Comparative Politics* 27, no. 4 (1995): 393–408.

41. Ian Newbould, "Sir Robert Peel and the Conservative Party, 1832–1841: A Study in Failure?," *English Historical Review* 98, no. 388 (1983): 529–57.

42. According to Gash, this role of Peel as party destroyer was in no way antithetical to Peel as party builder from decades earlier. In both cases the party was an instrument to achieve the primary goal of preserving the traditional order. In earlier decades, building up the party was necessary to deliver a majority to support the government in political conservation, and with the repeal of the Corn Laws, breaking up the party served these same goals. Norman Gash, "Peel and the Party System, 1830–1850," *Transactions of the Royal Historical Society* 1 (1951): 47–69.

43. Gash, "Peel and the Party System," 58.

44. There is disagreement about the exact number of Peelites at the time. According to the *Times*, in 1847, this group numbered approximately 117, a third of the party. Among them, approximately 40 identified explicitly as Peelite, while others affiliated as free trade Conservatives or Liberal Conservatives. See J. B. Conacher, *The Aberdeen Coalition, 1852–1855* (Cambridge: Cambridge University Press, 1968), 4; and J. B. Conacher, *The Peelites and the Party System, 1846–1852* (London: David and Charles, 1972), 111–13. Moreover, there is fundamental confusion about party labels at this time, to the extent that it was not even clear which coalition had the majority. Much of this had to do with the ambiguity of the Peelite affiliation. The confusion was so widespread that, according to Jones, no one really knew the extent of the Conservative victory in 1852. See Wilbur Jones, *The Peelites, 1846–1857* (Columbus: Ohio State University Press, 1972), 140. As Conacher notes, "*The Times* gave the ministry 284 safe seats, and the Liberal opposition, including the Radicals and the Irish Brigade, 309 seats, while it listed separately the names of fifty-eight 'Liberal Conservatives', but not all of these could be called Peelite. Bonham, Peel's former party manager, counted fifty 'Peelites', but Sir John Young, the former

Conservative chief whip, only found thirty four and his names were not all the same as Bonham's" (5). Party labels aside, however, Jones estimates that the Peelites could count on approximately one hundred votes on fiscal matters; *Peelites*, 152.

45. Jones, *Peelites*, 152.

46. H. Matthew, "Disraeli, Gladstone, and the Politics of Mid-Victorian Budgets," *Historical Journal* 22, no. 3 (1979): 623–24.

47. Quoted in Matthew, "Disraeli, Gladstone, and the Politics of Mid-Victorian Budgets," 631.

48. Quoted in Matthew, "Disraeli, Gladstone, and the Politics of Mid-Victorian Budgets," 627.

49. December 17, 1852; see Conacher, *Aberdeen Coalition*; and Jones, *Peelites*, 145.

50. Conacher, *Aberdeen Coalition*, 7.

51. Quoted in Conacher, *Aberdeen Coalition*, 8.

52. Jones, *Peelites*, 148.

53. Gary W. Cox, "The Development of a Party-Orientated Electorate in England, 1832–1980," *British Journal of Political Science* 16, no. 2 (1986): 187–216; John Vincent, *The Formation of the Liberal Party, 1857–1868* (London: Constable, 1966); John Vincent, *Poll-Books: How Victorians Voted* (Cambridge: Cambridge University Press, 1968).

54. Hawkins, "'Parliamentary Government' and Victorian Political Parties," 643.

55. Hugh Stephens, "The Changing Context of British Politics in the 1880s: The Reform Acts and the Formation of the Liberal Unionist Party," *Social Science History* 1, no. 4 (1977): 486–501; Bernard Ostry, "Conservatives, Liberals, and Labour in the 1880's," *Canadian Journal of Economics and Political Science* 27, no. 2 (1961): 141–61. See also E.E.H. Green, *The Crisis of Conservatism: The Politics, Economics and Ideology of the Conservative Party, 1880–1914* (London: Taylor and Francis, 2005).

56. This period has been referred to as one of realignment. See Hugh Stephens, "Partisan Realignment and Electoral Arrangement in Britain: The MacDonald-Gladstone Pact of 1903," *Journal of Political Science* 9, no. 2 (1982): article 3. While it does bear similarities to other realignments in terms of the reshuffling of MPs and interparty alliances, it does not constitute a full realignment in this analysis as it does not move parties to a different issue dimension, but rather shifts them along the same one.

57. Hansard, April 8, 1886; known as the First Home Rule Bill.

58. Though no formal electoral pact was made, Conservatives decided not to oppose the approximately 148 Liberal Unionist candidates running in that election, opening the door for future cooperation. T. A. Jenkins, "Hartington, Chamberlain and the Unionist Alliance, 1886–1895," *Parliamentary History* 11, no. 1 (1992): 108–38. See also Stephens, "Partisan Realignment and Electoral Arrangement in Britain," 81.

59. Peter Fraser, "The Liberal Unionist Alliance: Chamberlain, Hartington, and the Conservatives, 1886–1904," *English Historical Review* 77, no. 302 (1962): 53–78; Wesley Ferris, "The Candidates of the Liberal Unionist Party 1886–1912," *Parliamentary History* 30, no. 2 (2011): 142–57.

60. Two important studies that detail the origins of the party highlight its heterogeneous economic bases, with the Irish question serving as its organizational focus for the first decade of its existence: Peter Davis, "The Liberal Unionist Party and the Irish Policy of Lord Salisbury's Government, 1886–1892," *Historical Journal* 18 (1975): 85–104; W. C. Lubenow, "Irish Home Rule and the Great Separation in the Liberal Party in 1886: The Dimensions of Parliamentary Liberalism," *Victorian Studies* 26 (1983): 161.

61. Gordon Goodman, "Liberal Unionism: The Revolt of the Whigs," *Victorian Studies* 3, no. 2 (1959): 173–89; Gregory Phillips, "The Whig Lords and Liberalism, 1886–1893," *Historical Journal* 24, no. 1 (1981): 167–73.

62. G. R. Searle, *The Liberal Party: Triumph and Disintegration, 1886–1929* (London: Macmillan International, 1992).

63. Wallace Notestein, "Joseph Chamberlain and Tariff Reform," *Sewanee Review* 25, no. 1 (1917): 44–46.

64. Peter Fraser, "Unionism and Tariff Reform: The Crisis of 1906," *Historical Journal* 5, no. 2 (1962): 149.

65. Fraser, "Unionism and Tariff Reform," 151; Douglas Irwin, "The Political Economy of Free Trade: Voting in the British General Election of 1906," *Journal of Law and Economics* 37, no. 1 (1994): 80.

66. Douglas, "Political Economy of Free Trade," 83.

67. Goodman, "Liberal Unionism"; Fraser, "Unionism and Tariff Reform."

68. John Fair highlights the cross-class composition of the original Liberal Unionists and challenges the class reading of Liberal Unionists as something that emerged out of the party's disintegration rather than origins. John Fair, "From Liberal to Conservative: The Flight of the Liberal Unionists after 1886," *Victorian Studies* 29, no. 2 (1986): 291–314.

69. A. Jones, *The Politics of Reform, 1884* (Cambridge: Cambridge University Press, 1972); Jennifer Hart, *Proportional Representation: Critics of the British Electoral System, 1920–1945* (Oxford: Clarendon, 1992); Ahmed, *Democracy and the Politics of Electoral System Choice.*

70. D. J. Rossiter, R. J. Johnston, and C. J. Pattie, *The Boundary Commission: Redrawing the U.K.'s Map of Parliamentary Constituencies* (Manchester: Manchester University Press, 1999); M. Chadwick, "The Role of Redistribution in the Making of the Second Reform Act," *Historical Journal* 19, no. 3 (1976): 665–83.

71. Henry Pelling, *Origins of the Labour Party* (Oxford: Oxford University Press, 1965).

72. Frank Bealey, "The Electoral Arrangement between the Labour Representation Committee and the Liberal Party," *Journal of Modern History* 28, no. 4 (1956): 353–73, 354.

73. *Report of the First Annual Conference of the Labour Representation Committee Held in the Cooperative Hall, Downing Street Manchester, Friday February 1st 1901.*

74. *Report of the First Annual Conference.*

75. Fair, "From Liberal to Conservative," 307–8.

76. This special cross-class coalition is offered in Barrington Moore's foundational work as the explanation of the strength of British democracy. The importance of the interparty alliance is affirmed in Gregory Luebbert's work as well. See Moore, *Social Origins of Dictatorship and Democracy*; and Luebbert, *Liberalism, Fascism, or Social Democracy.*

77. David Powell, "The Liberal Ministries and Labour, 1892–1895," *History* 68, no. 224 (1983): 408–26.

78. G.D.H. Cole, *British Working Class Politics, 1832–1914* (London, 1941), 72; Bealey, "Electoral Arrangement," 353.

79. Quoted in David Powell, "The New Liberalism and the Rise of Labour, 1886–1906," *Historical Journal* 29, no. 2 (1986): 369–93; memorandum, March 13, 1903, Viscount Gladstone Papers, B. L. Add MSS 46 106, fo. 9.

80. Michael Bentley, *The Climax of Liberal Politics: British Liberalism in Theory and Practice, 1868–1918* (Baltimore, MD: Edward Arnold, 1987), 1.

81. The Lords' efforts to exploit the association between the Liberal and Labour Parties to heighten anxiety over the socialist threat also aimed to highlight the regime stakes of the conflict. Corrine Weston, "The Liberal Leadership and the Lords' Veto: 1907–1910," in *Peers, Politics and Power: House of Lords, 1603–1911*, ed. Clyve Jones and David Lewis Jones (London: Bloomsbury Academic, 1986).

82. Dorey Kelso, *House of Lords Reform since 1911: Must the Lords Go?* (London: Palgrave Macmillan, 2011), 20–24.

83. Anthony Stewart, *The Ulster Crisis: Resistance to Home Rule, 1912–1914* (Belfast: Blackstaff, 1997), 45.

84. Timothy Bowman, *Carson's Army: The Ulster Volunteer Force, 1910–22* (Manchester: Manchester University Press, 2007).

85. Jeremy Smith, "Bluff, Bluster and Brinkmanship: Andrew Bonar Law and the Third Home Rule Bill," *Historical Journal* 36, no. 1 (1993): 161–78, 162.

86. Andrew Taylor, *Bonar Law* (London: Haus, 2006), 48.

87. Ziblatt, *Conservative Parties*, 155.

88. James Doherty, *Irish Liberty, British Democracy: The Third Irish Home Rule Crisis, 1909–14* (Chapel Hill, Ireland: Cork University Press, 2019); Ziblatt, *Conservative Parties*, 155.

89. H.C.G. Matthew, R. I. McKibbin, and J. A. Kay, "The Franchise Factor in the Rise of the Labour Party," *English Historical Review* 91 (1976): 727; M. Hart, "The Liberals, the War, and the Franchise," *English Historical Review* 97 (1982): 381; D. Tanner, "The Parliamentary Electoral System, the 'Fourth' Reform Act and the Rise of Labour in England and Wales," *Bulletin of the Institute of Historical Research* 56 (1983): 213.

90. Quoted in John Shepherd and Keith Laybourn, *Britain's First Labour Government* (London: Palgrave Macmillan, 2006), 16; Earl of Oxford and Asquith, *Memories and Reflections* (Boston, 1928), 27–28.

91. Ramsay MacDonald, *Parliament and Revolution* (New York, 1920), 21.

92. Christine White, *British and America Commercial Relations with Soviet Russia, 1918–1924* (Chapel Hill: University of North Carolina Press, 1992), 112–14.

93. Quoted in White, *British and America Commercial Relations with Soviet Russia*, 110. See also Harvey Wish, "Anglo-Soviet Relations during Labour's First Ministry (1924)," *Slavonic and East European Review* 17, no. 50 (1939): 390. Sources on the benefits of trade for UK: Louis Fischer, *The Soviets in World Affairs*, vol. 2 (New York: Vintage, 1960), 466; A. Santalov and L. Segal, eds., *The Soviet Union Year Book* (London, 1928), 68; editorial, "Economic Revival in Russia," *Nation* 6 (February 19, 1924); *Ministry of Labour Gazette* 32, nos. 1–9 (1924); *The Board of Trade, Statistical Abstract for the United Kingdom* 74, no. 99 (1924): 318–19, 322–23.

94. Quoted in White, *British and America Commercial Relations with Soviet Russia*, 110. See also Wish, "Anglo-Soviet Relations during Labour's First Ministry," 390.

95. White, *British and American Commercial Relations with Soviet Russia*, 109–10.

96. White, *British and American Commercial Relations with Soviet Russia*, 192.

97. Quoted in Marjorie Clark, *The British Labour Government in Contemporary Opinion* (Berkeley: University of California Press, 1925). See also H. Hessell Tiltman, *J. Ramsay MacDonald* (New York, 1929).

98. Asquith, *Memories and Reflections*, 24.

99. George Dangerfield, *The Strange Death of Liberal England* (Stanford, CA: Stanford University Press, 1966), 22 and chapters 2, 7; Wish, "Anglo-Soviet Relations during Labour's First Ministry," 389–403.

100. Charles Mowat, "The Fall of the Labour Government in Great Britain, August, 1931," *Huntington Library Quarterly* 7, no. 4 (1944): 356; Great Britain, Committee on National Expenditures, Report, Cmd. 3920 (1931).

101. Neil Ridell, *Labour in Crisis: The Second Labour Government, 1929–1931* (Manchester: Manchester University Press, 1999).

102. Keith Laybourn, *Britain on the Breadline: A Social and Political History of Britain 1918–1939* (London: Sutton, 1998), 21–25.

103. The exact term "Enabling Act" was used and would have functioned in a manner very similar to that in the German case, establishing the cabinet as the primary legislative body and bypassing Parliament.

104. S. Cripps, *Can Socialism Come by Constitutional Means?* (London, 1934), 14; G.D.H. Cole, *A Plan for Britain* (London, 1932), 37; Roger Eatwell and Anthony Wright, "Labour and the Lessons of 1931," *History* 63, no. 207 (1978): 38–53.

105. Lansbury memo, "Cabinet Crisis of 1931," early September 1951, Lansbury Papers 25 III n.

106. Christopher Hood and Rozana Himaz, *A Century of Fiscal Squeeze Politics: 100 Years of Austerity Politics and Bureaucracy in Britain* (Oxford: Oxford University Press, 2017).

107. Cecil T. Carr, C. W. Duret Aubin, Arthur S. Quekett, and A. Denis Pringle, "British Isles," *Journal of Comparative Legislation and International Law* 15, no. 2 (1933): 1–34.

Chapter 4. Early Mass Suffrage in Germany: The Dominance of Repertoires of Regime Contention

1. Sartori, *Parties and Party Systems*, 132–39.

2. Proponents of the "Sonderweg thesis" include Volker Berghahn, *Imperial Germany, 1871–1914* (Oxford: Oxford University Press, 1994); Hans-Jürgen Puhle, "Parlament, Parteien und Interessenverbande 1890–1914," in *Das kaiserliche Deutschland*, ed. Michael Stürmer (Düsseldorf: Droste Verlag, 1970); Hans Mommsen, *The Rise and Fall of Weimar Democracy* (North Carolina: University of North Carolina Press, 1996); Ralph Dahrendorf, *Society and Democracy in Germany* (Garden City, NY: Doubleday, 1969); Fritz Fischer, *From Kaiserreich to Third Reich* (Boston: Allen and Unwin, 1986); and Talcott Parsons, "Democracy and Social Structure in Pre-Nazi Germany," in *Essays in Sociological Theory* (Glencoe, IL: Free Press, 1954).

3. Hans-Ulrich Wehler, *The German Empire, 1871–1918* (Warwickshire, UK: Leamington Spa, 1985), 355–56.

4. A variation on this thesis has been offered by Gunther Roth, who argued that "negative integration" produced an alternative political subculture, particularly within the socialist movement, which suppressed the democratic impulse during the imperial period. Guenther Roth, *The Social Democrats in Imperial Germany* (Totowa, NJ: Bedminster Press, 1963).

5. Mark Hewitson, "The Kaiserreich in Question," *Journal of Modern History* 73, no. 4 (2001): 725–80; Markus Kreuzer, "Parliamentarization and the Question of German Exceptionalism: 1867–1918," *Central European History* 36, no. 3 (2003): 327–57, https://doi.org/10.1163

/156916103771006034; David Blackbourn and Geoff Eley, *The Peculiarities of German History: Bourgeois Society and Politics in Nineteenth-Century Germany* (Oxford: Oxford University Press, 1984), https://doi.org/10.1093/acprof:oso/9780198730583.001.0001; David Blackbourn, *Class Religion and Local Politics in Wilhelmine Germany* (New Haven, CT: Yale University Press, 1980); Geoff Eley, *Reshaping the German Right: Radical Nationalism and Political Change after Bismarck* (Ann Arbor: University of Michigan Press, 1991); Richard Evans, *Rethinking German History* (London: Unwin Hyman, 1981).

6. Margaret Lavinia Anderson, *Practicing Democracy: Elections and Political Culture in Imperial Germany* (Princeton, NJ: Princeton University Press, 2000); Margaret Anderson, "An Exchange on the Kaiserreich: Reply to Volker Berghahn," *Central European History* 35, no. 1 (2002): 83–91; Stanley Suval, *Electoral Politics in Wilhelmine Germany* (Chapel Hill: University of North Carolina Press, 1985).

7. Manfred Rauh, *Die Parlamentarisierung des Deutschen Reichs* (Düsseldorf: Droste Verlag, 1977); Wolfgang Böckenförde, "Der deutsche Type der konstitutionellen Monarchie im 19. Jahrhundert," in *Recht, Staat, Freiheit*, ed. Ernst Böckenförde (Frankfurt am Main: Suhrkamp, 1999); Thomas Nipperdey, *Deutsche Geschichte, 1866–1918* (Munich: C. H. Beck, 1992); Gerhard Ritter, *Der Berliner Reichstag und die politische Kultur der Kaiserzeit* (Berlin: Humboldt-Universität, 1999).

8. Helmut Smith, "When the Sonderweg Debate Left Us," *German Studies Review* 31, no. 2 (2008): 225–40; Jurgen Kocka, "German History before Hitler: The Debate about the German Sonderweg," *Journal of Contemporary History* 23, no. 1 (1988): 3–16.

9. Erich Eyck, *Bismarck and the German Empire* (1950; New York: Allen and Unwin, 1964), 115.

10. Edgar Feuchtwanger, *Bismarck: A Political History* (London: Taylor and Francis, 2014), 96; Charles Seymour and Donald Frary, *How the World Votes* (Springfield, MA: C. A. Nichols, 1918), 26–27.

11. These meetings were made public when Bismarck was asked about them on the floor of the Reichstag during debates on the anti-Socialist laws in 1878. Bismarck spoke of Lassalle warmly and stated that they shared an interest in protecting the masses but differed on how socialism was best achieved, Lassalle preferring a democratic socialism while Bismarck's vision was for state socialism. Eyck, *Bismarck and the German Empire*, 115; James Headlam, *Bismarck and the Foundation of the German Empire* (1899; London: Putnam, 2007), 255–56; Feuchtwanger, *Bismarck*, 94–96. See also Eduard Bernstein, *Ferdinand Lassalle as a Social Reformer* (London: S. Sonnenschein, 1893), 167.

12. Headlam, *Bismarck and the Foundation of the German Empire*, 140.

13. Grant Roberston, *Bismarck* (New York: Holt, 1919), 242; William M. Sloane, "Bismarck as a Maker of Empire," *PSQ* 15, no. 4 (1900): 647–66, 648, https://doi.org/10.2307/2140466.

14. Alan S. Kahan, *Liberalism in Nineteenth-Century Europe: The Political Culture of Limited Suffrage* (London: Palgrave Macmillan, 2003), 142; Eyck, *Bismarck and the Foundation of the German Empire*, 118.

15. James Sheehan, *German Liberalism in the Nineteenth Century* (Chicago: University of Chicago Press, 1978); Luebbert, *Liberalism, Fascism, or Social Democracy*.

16. Waldeck, *Stenographische Berichte über die Verhandlungen des Deutschen Reichstags* (Munich: FB&C Limited Stenographishe Berichte), March 27, 1867, 390–92.

17. Grumbrecht, *Stenographische*, March 28, 1867, 423–32.

18. Nipperdey, *Deutsche Geschichte.*

19. Anderson, *Practicing Democracy*, 10.

20. Two bills were introduced, one by Carl Ausfeld and another by Eduard Lasker. James Harris, *A Study in the Theory and Practice of German Liberalism: Eduard Lasker, 1829–1884* (New York: University Press of America, 1984), 77–78.

21. Sheri Berman has likened this to a kind of "soft authoritarianism," underscoring that neither the powers of Parliament nor the constraints on the executive were insignificant. Sheri Berman, "Modernization in Historical Perspective: The Case of Imperial Germany," *World Politics* 53, no. 3 (2001): 431–62. On constitutionalism versus parliamentarism, see also Andreas Biefang and Andreas Schulz, "From Monarchical Constitutionalism to a Parliamentary Republic: Concepts of Parliamentarism in Germany since 1818," in *Parliament and Parliamentarism: A Comparative History of a European Concept*, ed. Pasi Ihalainen, Cornelia Ilie, and Kari Palonen, 62–80 (London: Berghahn, 2016), https://doi.org/10.1515/9781782389552-007.

22. Biefang and Schulz, "From Monarchical Constitutionalism to a Parliamentary Republic," 73.

23. John Flynn, "At the Threshold of Dissolution: The National Liberals and Bismarck 1877/1878," *Historical Journal* 31, no. 2 (1988): 319–40.

24. While early scholarship tended to attribute the initial split to structural divisions within the liberal movement, subsequent research has shown that in fact the economic composition of the two parties did not differ in any significant way; both contained a balance of industrial and landed interests, and each composed approximately 20 percent of both parties from 1867 to 1884. Lenore O'Boyle, "Liberal Political Leadership in Germany, 1867–1884," *Journal of Modern History* 28, no. 4 (1956): 338–52, 341.

25. On the connection between liberalism, commercialization, and national unification, see Daniel Ziblatt, *Structuring the States: The Formation of Italy and Germany and the Puzzle of Federalism* (Princeton, NJ: Princeton University Press, 2006), 34–35, 40–44.

26. Gordon Mork, "Bismarck and the 'Capitulation' of German Liberalism," *Journal of Modern History* 43, no. 1 (1971): 59–75.

27. Jürgen Schlumbohm, *Der Verfassungskonflikt in Preussen 1862 bis 1866* (Göttingen: Vandenhoeck u. Ruprecht, 1970).

28. Adolf Laufs, "Eduard Lasker und der Rechtsstaat," *Der Staat* 13, no. 3 (1974): 365–82.

29. Hans-Ulrich Wehler, *The German Empire 1871–1918* (London: Berg, 1985), 150.

30. Harris, *Theory and Practice of German Liberalism*, 74.

31. John Flynn, "The Split in the German National Liberal Caucus over the Military Budget Bill of 1871," *Historical Journal* 25, no. 3 (1982): 687–95; A.J.P. Taylor, *Bismarck: The Man and the Statesman* (London: Knopf Doubleday, 1967), 95–96.

32. Harris, *Theory and Practice of German Liberalism*, 78; Gordon Mork, "Eduard Lasker (1829–1884): Thoughts on the Relevance of Studying Obscure, Dead Politicians," *Centennial Review* 15 (1971): 273.

33. Otto Pflanze, *Bismarck and the Development of Germany: The Period of Consolidation, 1871–1880* (1990; Princeton, NJ: Princeton University Press, 2014), 445–47.

34. This is carefully documented in Flynn, "At the Threshold of Dissolution."

35. Flynn, "At the Threshold of Dissolution," 327–28.

36. Hienz Edgar Matthes, "Die Spaltung der Nationalliberalei Partei" (PhD diss., Kiel University, 1953), 65–66.

37. Flynn, "At the Threshold of Dissolution," 329.

38. Ziblatt offers this argument in relation to conservative parties, but it was true of both Conservatives and National Liberals at the time. Ziblatt, *Conservative Political Parties.*

39. Detlev Peukert, *The Weimar Republic* (London: Allen Lane, 1987), 50; Otto Pflanze, *Bismarck and the Development of Germany* (Princeton, NJ: Princeton University Press, 1992), 339–408.

40. Cheryl Schonhardt-Bailey, "Parties and Interests in the 'Marriage of Iron and Rye,'" *British Journal of Political Science* 28, no. 2 (1998): 291–332.

41. Pflanze, *Bismarck and the Development of Germany,* 353–55.

42. Elizabeth Nuebel, *Zollpolitik; Socialistengesetz und Steuerreform also Kampfmittel in Bismarcks Ringen mit dem Liberalismus, 1873–1979* (Gelsenkirchen: Fost, 1934).

43. Harris, *Theory and Practice of German Liberalism,* 109–11.

44. For a useful genealogy of the various liberal and left liberal parties, see Alasdair Thompson, *Left Liberals, the State, and Popular Politics in Wilhelmine Germany* (Oxford: Oxford University Press, 2000), 27.

45. Berman, *Social Democratic Moment.*

46. Noel Cary, *The Path to Christian Democracy: German Catholics and the Party System from Windthorst to Adenauer* (Cambridge, MA: Harvard University Press, 1996).

47. Joseph Lowry, *Big Swords, Jesuits, and Bondelswarts: Wilhelmine Imperialism, Overseas Resistance, and German Political Catholicism, 1897–1906* (London: Brill, 2015), especially chapter 2.

48. It was not only the anti-Catholic laws they resisted. They also offered unwavering opposition to the antisocialist laws. On several occasions, Ludwig Windthorst, founder of the party and its leader in the Reichstag, chastised the Conservatives on their support of such policies, proclaiming that a government cannot defeat ideas with force. John Zeender, "Ludwig Windthorst, 1812–1891," *History: The Journal of the Historical Association* 77, no. 250 (1992): 237–55, 247.

49. Edgar Feuchtwanger, *Imperial Germany, 1850–1918* (London: Taylor and Francis, 2002), 87–90. See also Alphonse De Valk, *The Centre Party in the Reichstag: Its Relations with Bismarck, 1878–1887* (Toronto: University of Toronto Press, 1965).

50. Berman, *Social Democratic Moment.*

51. Quoted in Anne Heyer, *The Making of the Democratic Party in Europe, 1860–1890* (Zurich: Springer International, 2022), 13, from *Protokolle der sozialdemokratischen Arbeiterpartei* (Glaushütten im Taunus: D. Auvermann, 1870).

52. Jonathan Sperber, "The Social Democratic Electorate in Imperial Germany," in *Between Reform and Revolution: German Socialism and Communism from 1840 to 1990,* ed. David Barclay and Eric Weitz (London: Berghahn, 2009), 167; Anderson, *Practicing Democracy.*

53. Karl Kautsky, *Karl Kautsky on Democracy and Republicanism,* trans. Ben Lewis (1893; Chicago: Haymarket, 2019).

54. Elfi Pracht, *Parlamentarismus und deutsche Sozialdemokratie 1867–1914* (Pfaffenweiler: Centaurus Verlag, 1990); Heyer, *Making of the Democratic Party in Europe,* 215–28; Andrew G. Bonnell, "Socialism and Republicanism in Imperial Germany," *Australian Journal of Politics and History* 42, no. 2 (1996): 192–202, https://doi.org/10.1111/j.1467-8497.1996.tb01362.x.

55. Detlef Lehnert, *SPD und Parlamentarismus: Entwicklungslinien und Problemfelder 1871–1990* (Cologne: Böhlau Verlag, 2016), especially chapters 3 and 4.

56. Quoted in Stanley Zucker, *Ludwig Bamberger: German Liberal Political and Social Critic, 1823–1899* (Pittsburgh, PA: University of Pittsburgh Press, 1975), 205.

57. Zeender, "Ludwig Windthorst," 237–55.

58. Ernst Schraepler, "Die politische Haltung des liberalen Bürgertums im Bismarckreich," *Geschichte in Wissenschaft und Unterricht* 5 (1954): 532–65, 534–35.

59. Brett Fairbairn, *Democracy in the Undemocratic State: The German Reichstag Elections of 1898 and 1903* (Toronto: University of Toronto Press, 1997), 162.

60. Lipset and Rokkan, *Party Systems and Voter Alignments*; Bartolini and Mair, *Identity, Competition and Electoral Availability*.

61. Andrew Gould, *The Origins of Liberal Dominance: State, Church, and Party in Nineteenth-Century Europe* (Ann Arbor: University of Michigan Press, 1999).

62. Kalyvas, *Rise of Christian Democracy in Europe*; Ellen Evans, *The Cross and the Ballot: Catholic Political Parties in Germany, Switzerland, Austria, Belgium and the Netherlands, 1785–1985* (Boston: Humanities Press, 1999).

63. Sheehan, *German Liberalism*, 259.

64. Margaret Lavinia Anderson, *Windthorst: A Political Biography* (Oxford: Oxford University Press, 1982).

65. Isabela Mares, *From Open Secrets to Secret Voting: Democratic Electoral Reforms and Voter Autonomy* (Cambridge: Cambridge University Press, 2015).

66. Daniel Ziblatt, "Shaping Democratic Practice and the Causes of Electoral Fraud: The Case of Nineteenth-Century Germany," *American Political Science Review* 103, no. 1 (2009): 1–21; Ziblatt, *Conservative Political Parties*.

67. Thomas Kühne, *Dreiklassenwahlrecht und Wahlkultur in Preussen, 1867–1914* (Düsseldorf: Droste Verlag, 1994).

68. The framing is typically attributed to Friedrich Naumann, who led the movement to unite the Left. Beverly Heckert, *From Bassermann to Bebel* (New Haven, CT: Yale University Press, 1974); James Mote, "Friedrich Naumann: The Course of a German Liberal" (PhD diss., University of Colorado Department of History, 1971).

69. Fairbairn, *Democracy in the Undemocratic State*, 104–6.

70. Fairbairn, *Democracy in the Undemocratic State*, 157; Thompson, *Left Liberals, the State, and Popular Politics*.

71. Heckert, *From Bassermann to Bebel*, 29–30.

72. Sheehan, *German Liberalism*, 267.

73. Geoff Eley, "Sammlungspolitik, Social Imperialism and the Navy Law of 1898," *Militärgeschichtliche Zeitschrift* 15, no. 1 (1974): 29–64, 30–31, https://doi.org/10.1524/mgzs.1974.15.1.29.

74. Eley, *Reshaping the German Right*, 90–94.

75. Quoted in Fairbairn, *Democracy in the Undemocratic State*, 71.

76. Heckert, *From Bassermann to Bebel*, 44–47.

77. Kenneth Barkin, *The Controversy over German Industrialization* (Chicago: University of Chicago Press, 1970); Cornelius Torp, "The 'Coalition of Rye and Iron' under the Pressure of Globalization: A Reinterpretation of Germany's Political Economy before 1914," *Central European History* 43, no. 3 (2010): 401–27, 413–15.

78. Jonathan Wright, *Gustav Stresemann, Weimar's Greatest Statesman* (Oxford: Oxford University Press, 2002), 28.

79. Barkin, *Controversy over German Industrialization*, 229.

80. David Blackbourn, "The Political Alignment of the Centre Party in Wilhelmine Germany," *Historical Journal* 18, no. 4 (1975): 821–50, 821–22, https://doi.org/10.1017/S0018246X00008906.

81. David Blackbourn, "Class and Politics in Wilhelmine Germany: The Center Party and the Social Democrats in Württemberg," *Central European History* 9, no. 3 (1976): 220–49.

82. Noel Cary, *The Path to Christian Democracy: German Catholics and the Party System from Windthorst to Adenauer* (Cambridge, MA: Harvard University Press, 1996), 128; Klaus Epstein, *Matthias Erzberger and the Dilemma of German Democracy* (Princeton, NJ: Princeton University Press, 1959), 3; Margaret Lavinia Anderson, "Interdenominationalism, Clericalism, Pluralism: The Zentrumsstreit and the Dilemma of Catholicism in Wilhelmine Germany," *Central European History* 21, no. 4 (1988): 350–78, 352.

83. Lowry, *Big Swords, Jesuits, and Bondelswarts*, 185.

84. Fairbairn, *Democracy in the Undemocratic State*.

85. See Matthias Erzberger, *Politik und Völkerleben* (Paderborn: Druck und Verlag Ferdinand Schöningh, 1914).

86. Anderson, "Interdenominationalism, Clericalism, Pluralism"; Klaus Epstein, "Erzberger and the German Colonial Scandals, 1905–1910," *English Historical Review* 74, no. 293 (1959): 637–63.

87. Erzberger, *Stenographische*, January 16, 1906, 591.

88. Erzberger, *Stenographische*, January 16, 1906, 591.

89. Anderson, "Interdenominationalism, Clericalism, Pluralism"; Epstein "Erzberger and the German Colonial Scandals."

90. John Lowry, "African Resistance and Center Party Recalcitrance in the Reichstag Colonial Debates 1905/6," *Central European History* 39, no. 2 (2006): 244–69, 244.

91. Erzberger, *Politik und Völkerleben*, 28.

92. Gustav Stresemann, *Gustav Stresemann: His Letters, Diaries, and Papers* (New York: Macmillan, 1935), 305.

93. Note that movement to the left represents a misalignment of the Zentrum, whereas the opposite is true for the DVP.

94. Gerald Feldman, *The Great Disorder: Politics, Economics, and Society in the German Inflation, 1914–1924* (Oxford: Oxford University Press, 1997), 490–92.

95. There were only two exceptions to this: under Hans Luther in 1925 and under Marx in 1927. Each lasted for only a few months before succumbing to party antagonisms between the Zentrum and DNVP. See Richard Evans, *The Coming of the Third Reich* (New York: Penguin, 2004), 295–97.

96. Wright, *Gustav Stresemann*.

97. Kolb, *Weimar Republic*, 53–101.

98. Larry Jones, "The Dying Middle: Weimar Germany and the Fragmentation of Bourgeois Politics," *Central European History* 5, no. 1 (1972): 23–54, 35–36.

99. Larry Jones, "Inflation, Revaluation, and the Crisis of Middle-Class Politics: A Study in the Dissolution of the German Party System, 1923–28," *Central European History* 12, no. 2 (1979): 143–68, 164, https://doi.org/10.1017/S0008938900022330.

100. Sigmund Neumann, *Die Parteien der Weimarer Republik* (Stuttgart: Kohlhammer, 1965), 28–40.

101. Wright, *Gustav Stresemann*, 172.

102. Gerald D. Feldman, *Iron and Steel in the German Inflation, 1916–1923* (Princeton, NJ: Princeton University Press, 1977), 430.

103. Brauns, Bundesarchiv, Kabinett Stresemann, vol. 1, doc. no. 97.

104. Stresemann, *Gustav Stresemann*, 152.

105. Stresemann, *Gustav Stresemann*, 144.

106. Feldman, *Iron and Steel in the German Inflation*, 411, 430.

107. Feldman, *Iron and Steel in the German Inflation*, 396.

108. Kolb, *Weimar Republic*, 161.

109. Kolb, *Weimar Republic*, 163.

110. Raumer, Bundesarchiv, Kabinett Stresemann, vol. 1, doc. no. 86.

111. Brauns, Bundesarchiv, Kabinett Stresemann, vol. 1, doc. no. 97.

112. *Stenographische*, October 14, 1923.

113. Stresemann, *Gustav Stresemann*, 425–26.

114. James McSpadden, "'A New Way of Governing': Heinrich Brüning, Rudolf Hilferding, and Cross-Party Cooperation during the Waning Years of the Weimar Republic, 1930–1932," *Central European History* 53, no. 3 (2020): 584–612, https://doi.org/10.1017/S0008938919000943.

115. Evans, *Rethinking German History*, 250; Kolb, *Weimar Republic*, 166; Bundesarchiv, Kabinett Brüning, vol. 1, doc. no. 6; William Patch, *Heinrich Brüning and the Dissolution of the Weimar Republic* (Cambridge: Cambridge University Press, 2006), 88–90; Larry Jones, *German Liberalism and the Dissolution of the Weimar Party System, 1918–1933* (Chapel Hill: University of North Carolina Press, 1988), 364.

116. Evans, *Rethinking German History*, 360.

117. Patch, *Heinrich Brüning*, 89; Jones, *German Liberalism*, 364.

118. Kolb, *Weimar Republic*, 82.

119. Patch, *Heinrich Brüning*, 80.

120. Brüning, *Stenographische*, April 3, 1930, 4769.

121. Keil, *Stenographische*, July 15, 1930, 6379.

122. Dietrich Orlow, *A History of Modern Germany: 1871 to Present* (London: Pearson, 2012), 35–39.

123. Patch, *Heinrich Brüning*, 94; Evans *Rethinking German History*, 366–67.

124. *Stenographische*, July 18, 1930, 1310.

125. Bracher, "Parteienstaat, Präsidialsystem, Notstand"; Werner Conze, "Brunings Politik unter de Druck der grossen Krise," *Historische Zeitschrift* 199 (1964): 529–50, 542–50; Rosenberg, *History of the German Republic*, 211.

Chapter 5. Simultaneous Introduction in France: The Development of Multiple Repertoires

1. Léon Blum, 1942, quoted in Julian Jackson, *The Popular Front in France: Defending Democracy, 1934–1938* (Cambridge: Cambridge University Press, 1988), 17.

2. The chaos narrative is found in countless accounts on the Third Republic that note party system fragmentation, with an average of six to nine effective parties in each legislative period; instability of party labels, with parties continually rebranding between elections; and frequent party switching by legislators. See Jack Hayward, *Fragmented France: Two Centuries of Disputed Identity* (Oxford: Oxford University Press, 2007).

3. Heinberg, "Personnel of French Cabinets," 389–96; Auguste Soulier, *L'instabilité ministérielle sous la Troisième République (1876–1936): Bibliothèque d'Histoire politique et constitutionnelle* (Paris:

Sirey, 1942); Mogens Pedersen, "Review of *Research on European Parliaments*: A Review Article on Scholarly and Institutional Variety," *Legislative Studies Quarterly* 9, no. 3 (1984): 505–29.

4. Charles Benoist, *La réforme parlementaire* (Paris: Plon-Nourrit et Cie, 1902); A. Esmein, *Éléments de droit constitutionnel* (Paris: Recueil Sirey, 1927); Rudolf Winnacker, *The "Délégation Des Gauches" and Its Critics* (Ann Arbor: University of Michigan Press, 1937).

5. William Fortescue, *The Third Republic in France: Conflicts and Continuities* (London: Routledge, 2017), 5–7.

6. Perhaps the strongest claims along these lines are offered by historian William Shirer, who has linked the fall of the Third Republic in 1940 to this originary moment of regime ambivalence: William Shirer, *The Collapse of the Third Republic: An Inquiry into the Fall of France in 1940* (New York: Rosetta, 1969).

7. J.P.T. Bury, *Gambetta and the Making of the Third Republic* (London: Longman, 1973), 235.

8. Jean-Marie Mayeur and Madeleine Rebérioux, *The Third Republic from Its Origins to the Great War, 1871–1940* (Cambridge: Cambridge University Press, 1984), 8–9.

9. Robert Gildea, *The Third Republic from 1870–1914* (London: Longman, 1988), chapter 3.

10. This competition has been extensively documented, with most historians in agreement that, save for the intransigence of the Comte de Chambord, the monarchy may have easily been restored in these early years. See Frank Brabant, *The Beginning of the Third Republic in France: A History of the National Assembly* (New York: MacMillan, 1972); Marvin L. Brown, *The Comte de Chambord: The Third Republic's Uncompromising King* (Durham, NC: Duke University Press, 1967); René Rémond, *Les Droites en France* (Paris: Aubier, 1982); and Robert R. Locke, *French Legitimists and the Politics of Moral Order in the Early Third Republic* (Princeton, NJ: Princeton University Press, 1974).

11. J.P.T. Bury, "Gambetta and the Revolution of 4 September 1870," *Cambridge Historical Journal* 4, no. 3 (1934): 263–82.

12. Benjamin Martin, *Years of Plenty, Years of Want: France and the Legacy of the Great War* (Ithaca, NY: Cornell University Press, 2013), 48.

13. There was no codified constitution, but a series of constitutional laws passed in 1875 provided the foundation for a constitutional framework. See Karl Loewenstein, "The Demise of the French Constitution of 1875," *American Political Science Review* 34, no. 5 (1940): 867–95.

14. James Lehning, *To Be a Citizen: The Political Culture of the Early French Third Republic* (Ithaca, NY: Cornell University Press, 2001).

15. Philip Nord, *The Republican Moment: Struggles for Democracy in Nineteenth-Century France* (Cambridge MA: Harvard University Press, 1995), 135.

16. Bury, *Gambetta and the Making of the French Third Republic*, 140–41; Joseph Reinach, *Discours et plaidoyers politiques de M. Gambetta* (Paris: G. Charpentier, 1883); Bateman, *Disenfranchising Democracy*, 295–320.

17. Robert Atkinson, "Principle and Pragmatism: The Origins and Development of the Presidency in the Early Third Republic, 1871–1875" (PhD diss., Duke University, 1982).

18. David Thomson, *France: Empire and Republic, 1850–1940—Historical Documents* (London: Palgrave Macmillan, 1968), 57–68.

19. Thomson, *France*, 57–68.

20. Alan Grubb, *The Politics of Pessimism: Albert de Broglie and Conservative Politics in the Early Third Republic* (Wilmington: University of Delaware Press, 1996).

21. Some have referred to the Seize Mai as a coup, pointing to the monarchists' encroachment across a range of government offices: Maurice Reclus, *Le Seize Mai* (Paris: Hachette, 1931), 53–54; Fresnette Pisani-Ferry, *Le Coup d'etat Manqué du 16 mai 1877* (Paris: R. Laffont, 1965); Locke, *French Legitimists*, 224–26.

22. Emile Louis Gustave Deshayes de Marcère, *Histoire de la République de 1876–1879*, vol. 2, *Le Seize Mai Et La Fin de Septennat* (New York: Forgotten Books, 2017).

23. Locke, *French Legitimists*, 256–62.

24. Robert Fuller, *The Origins of the French Nationalist Movement, 1886–1914* (New York: McFarland, 2014).

25. Judith Stone, *Sons of the Revolution: Radical Democrats in France, 1862–1914* (Baton Rouge: Louisiana State University Press, 1996), 130; Kevin Passmore, *The Right in France from the Third Republic to Vichy* (Oxford: Oxford University Press, 2013), 46.

26. Jacques Néré, *La crise industrielle de 1882 et le mouvement boulangiste* (Paris: Éditeur inconnu, 1959), 22–23.

27. Zeev Sternhell, *La droite révolutionnaire, 1885–1914: Les origines françaises du fascisme* (Paris: Editions du Seuil, 1978).

28. Patrick Hutton, "Popular Boulangism and the Advent of Mass Politics in France, 1886–1890," *Journal of Contemporary History* 11 (1976): 85–106.

29. Frederick Seager, *The Boulanger Affair: The Political Crossroads of France* (Ithaca, NY: Cornell University Press, 1968), 174.

30. Piers Read, *The Dreyfus Affair: The Scandal that Tore France in Two* (London: Bloomsbury, 2012).

31. George Whyte, *The Dreyfus Affair: A Chronological History* (New York: Palgrave MacMillan, 2005).

32. Wayne DeJohn, *The Dreyfus Affair and the Chamber of Deputies, 1897–1899* (Madison: University of Wisconsin Press, 1976).

33. On the ongoing influence of regime contention in the early decades of the Third Republic, see François Goguel, *La politique des partis sous la IIIe Republique* (Paris: Editions de Seuil, 1958).

34. Gerald Friedman, "Capitalism, Republicanism, Socialism, and the State: France, 1871–1914," *Social Science History* 14, no. 2 (1990): 151–74, https://doi.org/10.1017/S014555320002071X.

35. Robert Kaplan has identified the struggle over the tax as one of the most pressing of the early twentieth century in France, and that which motivated the realignment. Others have disputed this, maintaining that it was the Dreyfus affair and the ongoing antirepublican threat represented in the Dreyfus affair. This analysis does not aim to adjudicate between these two views, but rather accepts both motivations as significant. What is important for present purposes is the difficulty encountered in resolving economic issues, which led to high levels of legislative dysfunction prior to realignment. Robert Kaplan, *Forgotten Crisis: The Fin-de-Siecle Crisis of Democracy in France* (Oxford: Berg, 1995); James F. McMillan, *Dreyfus to De Gaulle: Politics and Society in France, 1898–1969* (London: Edward Arnold, 1985); Judith Stone, *The Search for Social Peace: Reform Legislation in France, 1890–1914* (Albany: State University of New York Press, 1985).

36. On Waldeck-Rousseau's strategy, see Malcolm Partin, *Waldeck-Rousseau, the Cabinet of Republican Defense, and the Law of Associations of 1901* (Durham, NC: Duke University Press, 1960).

37. The Law of Associations was followed in 1903 and 1904 with laws that further diminished the activities of the church in education and civil matters. The restrictions on the church significantly diminished not only the influence of the monarchists but the resources they had at their disposal. Gilles Le Béguec, "Le parti," in *Histoire des Droits in France*, vol. 2, ed. Jean-François Sirinelli (Paris: Gallimard, 1992); Fortescue, *Third Republic in France*, 64–65.

38. The law of associations allowed any citizen to form an association but required that it be composed entirely of French citizens and that it have no foreign obligations; thus all churches had to change their ties to the Vatican or face dissolution. Peter McPhee, *A Social History of France 1780–1914* (London: Palgrave MacMillan, 2003); Magali della Sudda, "Associations and Political Pluralism: The Effects of the Law of 1901," in *Pluralism and the Idea of the Republic in France*, ed. Julian Wright and H. S. Jones (London: Palgrave Macmillan, 2012).

39. Le Béguec "Le parti"; David Hanley, *Party, Society, and Government: Republican Democracy in France* (New York: Berghahn, 2002), 33.

40. Kaplan, *Forgotten Crisis*.

41. Passmore, *The Right in France*; W. D. Irvine, *French Conservatism in Crisis: The Republican Federation in France* (Baton Rouge: Louisiana State University Press, 1979); Jean Vavasseur-Desperriers, *Associations politiques et groupes parlementaires* (Nancy, France: Presses Universitaires de Nancy, 2000).

42. Sartori characterized party systems with centrist coalitions, or "polarized pluralism," as inherently unstable, as the centrists had to constantly fend off the pull of their extreme flanks on the Left and Right. Giovanni Sartori, "European Political Parties: The Case of Polarized Pluralism," in *Political Parties and Political Development*, 137–76 (1966; Princeton, NJ: Princeton University Press, 2015).

43. Maurice Larkin, *Church and State after the Dreyfus Affair: The Separation Issue in France* (London: Palgrave Macmillan, 1974), 106.

44. Rudolf A. Winnacker, *The Bloc and the Délégation Des Gauches* (Cambridge MA: Harvard University Press, 1933).

45. Gilles Candar, "Bloc des gauches et gouvernements radicaux (1902–1914)," in *Histoire des gauches en France*, vol. 2, ed. Jean-Jacques Becker, 215–26 (Paris: La Découverte, 2005).

46. Winnacker, *Bloc and the Délégation Des Gauches*, 459.

47. Winnacker, *"Délégation Des Gauches" and Its Critics*, 79.

48. Julien Bouchet, "Jaurès au temps du combisme," *Cahiers Jaurès* 211, no. 1 (2014): 31–52.

49. De Leon, *Flashlights*; James Young, *Socialism since 1889* (London: Print Publisher, 1988); Albert Lindmann, *A History of European Socialism* (New Haven, CT: Yale University Press, 1983), 157.

50. Quoted in Raymond Buell, *Contemporary French Politics* (London: D. Appleton, 1920).

51. Quoted in Max Beer, *Fifty Years of International Socialism* (Geneva: Minkoff Reprint, 1978).

52. Michael Harrington, *Socialism: Past and Future* (New York: Arcade, 2011), 74.

53. De Leon, *Flashlights*.

54. *Compte Rendu Analytique du 1er & 2e Congrès Nationaux, Tenus à Paris en Avril 1905 et à Chalon-sur-Saone en Octobre 1905* (Paris: Au siège du Conseil National, n.d.).

55. *Compte-rendu du 5° Congrès du parti radical et radical-socialiste* (Paris, July 1905).

56. Geoffrey Kurtz, *Jean Jaurès: The Inner Life of Social Democracy* (University Park: Pennsylvania State University Press, 2014), 126; Harvey Goldberg, *The Life of Jean Jaures* (Madison: University of Wisconsin Press, 1968), 329–30.

57. Frédéric Cépède, "La SFIO des années 1905–1914: Construire le parti," *Cahiers Jaurès* 187–88, no. 1 (2008): 29–45. See also Gerald Friedman, *State-Making and Labor Movements: France and the United States, 1876–1914* (Ithaca, NY: Cornell University Press, 1998); and Rosemonde Sanson, "Centre et gauche (1901–1914): l'Alliance républicaine démocratique et le Parti radical-socialiste," *Revue d'histoire moderne et contemporaine* 39, no. 3 (1992): 493–512.

58. Passmore, *The Right in France.*

59. Action Française, a monarchist party, which by 1919 was a highly anachronistic entity, maintained a following based on its appeal to conservative social policies of natalism and preservation of the traditional family. See S. Wilson, "The 'Action Française' in French Intellectual Life," *Historical Journal* 12, no. 2 (1969): 328–50.

60. Passmore, *The Right in France*, 206–14; Benjamin Martin, *France and the Après Guerre, 1918–1924: Illusions and Disillusionment* (Oxford: Oxford University Press, 1999), 50–51.

61. Mildred Schlesinger, "The Cartel des Gauches: Precursor of the Front Populaire," *European Studies Review* 8, no. 2 (1978): 211–34; Tony Judt, "The French Socialist and the Cartel des Gauches of 1924," *Journal of Contemporary History* 11, no. 2–3 (1976): 199–215; D. G. Wileman, "What the Market Will Bear: The French Cartel Elections of 1924," *Journal of Contemporary History* 29, no. 3 (1994): 483–500.

62. Quoted in Jackson, *Popular Front in France*, 162.

63. Schuker, *End of French Predominance in Europe*, 48, 66.

64. W. A. McDougall, *France's Rhineland Policy, 1914–1924: The Last Bid for a Balance of Power in Europe* (Princeton, NJ: Princeton University Press, 1978), 286–92.

65. Bokanowski in *Journal officiel de la République française: Débats parlementaires*, January 25, 1924, 274.

66. Richard Kuisel, *Capitalism and the State in Modern France: Renovation and Economic Management in the Twentieth Century* (Cambridge: Cambridge University Press, 1983).

67. In fact, a direct system of taxation only began to emerge in France during the war and was institutionalized in 1920. See Schuker, *End of French Predominance in Europe*, 68; François Albert, "Chronique politique," *Revue politique et parlementaire* 34, no. 3 (1920): 136–40; and Edgard Allix and Marcel Lecerclé, *L'impôt sur le revenu, impôts cédulaires et impôts général: Traité théorique et pratique* (Paris: Rousseau, 1926).

68. For a discussion of these debates, see Albert, "Chronique politique"; and F. François-Marsal, "Impôts réels ou impôts personnels," *Revue politique et parlementaire* 34, no. 1 (1920): 13–26. One less attractive option, for example, was a capital levy, but its impact was not well understood and would have likely gotten even more opposition from the Right. Other measures, such as improving enforcement of tax collection, sale of state enterprises, stricter controls on currency operations, and increasing the cost of postal and telegraph services were all considered but would not provide either sufficient revenue or savings to balance the budget. Schuker, *End of French Predominance in Europe*, 60–65; *Histoire politique de la Troisième République*, vol. 4, *Cartel des gauches et union nationale: 1924–1929* (Paris: Presse universitaires de France, 1959), 400–15.

69. "Premier Rapport de la Commission des Réformes, instituée par le décret du 3 aout 1922," in *Journal Official*, Annexe, Documents administratifs, December 10, 1923, 885–953.

70. Goguel, *La politique des parties*, 198. See *Journal Official*, Débats, February 18–21, 1924, 876–914.

71. *Journal Official*, Session Ordinaire, Chambre 1924, 326–38; Otto Kirchheimer, "Decree Powers and Constitutional Law in France under the Third Republic," *American Political Science Review* 34, no. 6 (1940): 1104–23, https://doi.org/10.2307/1948192; Herbert Tingsten, *Les pleins pouvoirs: L'expansion des pouvoirs gouvernementaux pendant et après la grande guerre* (Paris: Librairie Stock, 1934); Walter R. Sharp, *The Government of the French Republic* (New York: D. Van Nostrand, 1938), 133–37; Karl Lowenstein, "The Balance between Legislative and Executive Power," *University of Chicago Law Review* 5, no. 4 (1938): 566.

72. Several have pointed to the events of 1924 as evidence of weakness on the Left: Jean-Noël Jeanneney, *Leçon d'histoire pour une gauche au pouvoir, la faillite du Cartel 1924–1926* (Paris: Seuil, 1977); William Irvine, *French Conservatism in Crisis* (Baton Rouge: Louisiana State University Press, 1979), 104. On not participating in government, see Judt, "French Socialist and the Cartel des Gauches."

73. Georges Lachapelle, *Le credit public* (Paris: Persée, 1932), 228–30.

74. Schlesinger, "Cartel des Gauches," 225.

75. Daniela Neri-Ultsch, *Sozialisten und Radicaux—eine schwierige Allianz: Linksbündnisse in der Dritten Französischen Republik 1919–1938* (Munich: R. Oldenbourg Verlag, 2005).

76. Schuker, *End of French Predominance*, 128–31; Martin, *France and the Après Guerre*, 248–49.

77. Schuker, *End of French Predominance*, 130–35.

78. Schlesinger, "Cartel des Gauches," 227; Georges Lachapelle, *Les Finances de la IIIe République* (Paris: E. Flammarion, 1937), 121–29; Martin Wolfe, *The French Franc between the Wars, 1919–1939* (New York: Columbia University Press, 1951), 35–36.

79. Bonnefous, *Histoire politique de la Troisième République*; Neri-Ultsch, *Sozialisten und Radicaux*, 127–28.

80. Schuker, *End of French Predominance in Europe*, 61.

81. Alfred Sauvy, "The Economic Crisis of the 1930s in France," *Journal of Contemporary History* 4, no. 4 (1969): 21–35, https://doi.org/10.1177/002200946900400402.

82. Jackson, *Popular Front in France*, 20.

83. Adrian Rossiter, "Popular Front Economic Policy and the Matignon Negotiations," *Historical Journal* 30, no. 3 (1987): 663–84.

84. An especially critical episode that held the attention of the nation happened on February 6, 1934. Right-wing demonstrators gathered at the Palace de la Concorde, protesting the newly formed Radical government of Édouard Daladier and parliamentary government more generally.

85. Blum, 1942, quoted in Jackson, *Popular Front in France*, 17.

86. Rossiter, "Popular Front Economic Policy."

87. Georges Lefranc, *Histoire du Front Populaire, 1934–1938* (Paris: Payot, 1963).

Part II Conclusions. Structuring Spaces and Actors

1. World systems theory has contrasted the idea of "undeveloped" with that of "underdeveloped." While the latter term is a little too loaded for my liking, the contrast is useful in illustrating the erroneous temporalities that might lead us to take as the start of the process of democratic development something that is actually in the middle. An asynchronic view of

democratization must consider that democratic development begins well before the acquisition of all the requisite institutions.

Part III Introduction: The Regime Question and American Political Development

1. Ahmed, *Democracy and the Politics of Electoral System Choice*; Bateman, *Disenfranchising Democracy*; Cathie Jo Martin and Duane Swank, *The Political Construction of Business Interests* (Cambridge: Cambridge University Press, 2012); Didi Kuo, *Clientalism, Capitalism, and Democracy* (Cambridge: Cambridge University Press, 2018); Robert Lieberman, *Shaping Race Policy: The United States in Comparative Perspective* (Princeton, NJ: Princeton University Press, 2011); Dawn Teele, *Forging the Franchise* (Cambridge: Cambridge University Press, 2020); Richard Bensel, *The Founding of Modern States* (Cambridge: Cambridge University Press, 2022); Anthony W. Marx, *Making Race and Nation: A Comparison of South Africa, the United States, and Brazil* (Cambridge: Cambridge University Press, 1998); Sven Steinmo, *The Evolution of Modern States: Sweden, Japan, and the United States* (Cambridge: Cambridge University Press, 2010); Kathleen Thelen, *How Institutions Evolve* (Cambridge: Cambridge University Press, 2004); Debra Thompson, *The Schematic State* (Cambridge: Cambridge University Press, 2016).

2. A most-different case follows the model of Mill's method of agreement. It is useful in explaining similar outcomes among cases with highly divergent originary conditions. George and Bennet, *Case Studies and Theory Development in the Social Sciences*.

3. For a discussion of this approach, see Ahmed, "What Can We Learn from History?"; and Burger, *Max Weber's Theory of Concept Formation*.

4. George and Bennett, *Case Studies and Theory Development*, 153–56; John Gerring, "What Is a Case Study and What Is It Good For?," *American Political Science Review* 98, no. 2 (2004): 341–54.

5. Max Weber, *The Protestant Ethic and the Spirit of Capitalism* (1904; London: Routledge, 1992), 12–15.

6. Simmons and Smith, "Communication across Contexts."

Chapter 6. Roots of the Regime Question in the United States: The Emergence of Repertoires of Regime Contention

1. A classical statement of US exceptionalism is found in Louis Hartz's thesis that a radical rupture with European political structures led to an exceptional liberal political culture in the United States. This has been challenged now by numerous scholars, including works that show the presence of feudal structures well into the nineteenth century, as well as the illiberal impact of racial hierarchies in US political development. See Louis Hartz, *The Liberal Tradition in America* (New York: Harcourt, 1955); Karen Orren, *Belated Feudalism: Labor, the Law, and Liberal Development in the United States* (Cambridge: Cambridge University Press, 1991); and Rogers Smith, "Beyond Tocqueville, Myrdal, and Hartz: The Multiple Traditions in America," *American Political Science Review* 87, no. 3 (1993): 549–66.

2. A rich body of scholarship has sought to understand the politics of enfranchisement and disenfranchisement in the democratization of the United States. Important as these works are

for our understanding of US political development, the exclusive focus on the franchise as the measure of US democracy can obscure the equally critical struggles that took place over the terms of contestation and the status of representative government. On the politics of the franchise, see Alexander Keyssar, *The Right to Vote* (New York: Basic Books, 2000); Bateman, *Disenfranchising Democracy*; and Teele, *Forging the Franchise*.

3. On the theme of reading history forward, see Pierson, *Politics in Time*; Ahmed, "Reading History Forward"; Capoccia and Ziblatt, "Historical Turn in Democratization Studies."

4. Prominent examples of the skepticism regarding the authenticity of these regime anxieties include Chauncey Boucher, "In Re That Aggressive Slaveocracy," *Mississippi Valley Historical Review* 8 (1921): 13–80; and David Brion Davis, *The Slave Power Conspiracy and the Paranoid Style* (Baton Rouge: Louisiana State University Press, 1969).

5. To scholars of European political development, this would likely be read as a fight over national unification, resting along the national dimension rather than the regime dimension. For scholars of American political development, these fights were very much part of the regime contention of the time. In fact, in the United States, one might say that the regime dimension and the national dimension became fused on this issue. For the comparative view, see Lipset and Rokkan, *Party Systems and Voter Alignments*. For the perspective within American political development, see Samuel Beer, *To Make a Nation: The Rediscovery of American Federalism* (Cambridge, MA: Harvard University Press, 1993); McDonald, *States' Rights and the Union*; and John Kincaid, "Democracy versus Federalism in the United States of America," in *Federal Democracies*, 133–55 (London: Routledge, 2010).

6. Some of the foundational works in this vein include V. O. Key Jr., "A Theory of Critical Elections," *Journal of Politics* 17, no. 1 (1955): 3–18; Walter Dean Burnham, "The Changing Shape of the American Political Universe," *American Political Science Review* 59, no. 1 (1965): 7–28; Walter Dean Burnham, *Critical Elections and the Mainsprings of American Politics* (New York: Norton, 1970); Everett Ladd, *American Political Parties: Social Change and Political Response* (New York: Norton, 1970); David Brady, "Congressional Leadership and Party Voting in the McKinley Era: A Comparison to the Modern House," *Midwest Journal of Political Science* 16, no. 3 (1972): 439–59; and Benjamin Ginsberg, "Critical Elections and the Substance of Party Conflict: 1844–1968," *Midwest Journal of Political Science* 16, no. 4 (1972): 603–25.

7. Among scholars who offer causal accounts, most focus on the introduction of new voters as key catalysts. James Sundquist, *Dynamics of the Party System* (Washington, DC: Brookings Institution Press, 1983); John Petrocik, "Realignment: New Party Coalitions and the Nationalization of the South," *Journal of Politics* 49, no. 2 (1987): 347–75.

8. Richard McCormick, "Walter Dean Burnham and 'The System of 1896,'" *Social Science History* 10, no. 3 (1986): 245–62; Karen Orren and Stephen Skowronek, "Institutions and Intercurrence: Theory Building in the Fullness of Time," *Nomos* 38 (1996): 111–46; John Aldrich, *Why Parties? The Origin and Transformation of Political Parties in America* (Chicago: University of Chicago Press, 1995); Larry Bartels, "Electoral Continuity and Change, 1868–1996," *Electoral Studies* 17, no. 3 (1998): 301–26; David Mayhew, *Electoral Realignments: A Critique of an American Genre* (New Haven, CT: Yale University Press, 2002).

9. Orren and Skowronek, "Institutions and Intercurrence," 114–24.

10. In this respect, the focus of the analysis here is even more circumscribed than recent work on party realignment, which narrows the focus but still seeks to understand party realignment across multiple institutional dimensions or levels of governance. See, for example, Edward

Carmines and James Stimson, *Issue Evolution: Race and the Transformation of American Politics* (Princeton, NJ: Princeton University Press, 1989); and David Karol, *Party Position Change in American Politics* (Cambridge: Cambridge University Press, 2012). The analysis here focuses exclusively on parties in Congress. Following the framework developed in chapter 2, I maintain that legislative coalitions will follow their own logic, often independent from the executive.

11. Karen Orren and Stephen Skowronek, *The Search for American Political Development* (Cambridge: Cambridge University Press, 2004).

12. Lipset and Rokkan, "Cleavage Structures, Party Systems."

13. Peter Mair, "Political Parties and Party Systems," in *Europeanization*, ed. P. Graziano and M. P. Vink (London: Palgrave Macmillan, 2008).

14. See Lisbet Hooghe and Gary Marks, "Cleavage Theory Meets Europe's Crises: Lipset, Rokkan, and the Transnational Cleavage," *Journal of European Public Policy* 25, no. 1 (2018): 109–35.

15. Jackson Turner Main, "Government by the People: The American Revolution and the Democratization of the Legislatures," *William and Mary Quarterly* 23, no. 3 (1966): 391–407, https://doi.org/10.2307/1919237.

16. On the influence of the idea of the balanced constitution in the US founding, see R. G. Adams, *Political Ideas of the American Revolution* (Durham, NC: Trinity College Press, 1922); and Gordon Wood, *The Creation of the American Republic, 1776–1787* (Chapel Hill, NC: University of North Carolina Press, 1969), especially chapter 6.

17. Gordon Wood, "Democracy and the American Revolution," in *Democracy, the Unfinished Journey*, ed. John Dunn (Oxford: Oxford University Press, 1992).

18. The doctrines of republicanism in the United States most closely resembled the formulations found in French political discourse. Mark Hulliung, *Citizens and Citoyens: Republicans and Liberals in America and France* (Cambridge, MA: Harvard University Press, 2002).

19. Under the Articles of Confederation, the president was little more than a clerk presiding over Congress. All the powers of the executive were under the direct control of Congress. George Van Cleve, *We Have Not a Government: The Articles of Confederation and the Road to the Constitution* (Chicago: University of Chicago Press, 2019).

20. See Saikrishna Prakash, *Imperial from the Beginning: The Constitution of the Original Executive* (New Haven, CT: Yale University Press, 2015); Louise Dunbar, *A Study in Monarchical Tendencies in the United States from 1776–1801* (1922; Urbana: University of Illinois Press, 1991), 83; Frank Prochaska, *The Eagle and the Crown: Americans and the British Monarchy* (New Haven, CT: Yale University Press, 2008).

21. While most scholars have focused on Alexander Hamilton as the main proponent of the model of the "president as king," it had widespread influence going back to the revolutionary period. See Jeremy Black, *George III: America's Last King* (New Haven, CT: Yale University Press, 2008); Mervyn Davies, *The Influence of George III on the Development of the Constitution* (Oxford: Oxford University Press, 1921); Adams, *Political Ideas of the American Revolution*.

22. Hans Blom, John Christian Laursen, and Luisa Simonutti, eds., *Monarchisms in the Age of Enlightenment: Liberty, Patriotism, and the Common Good* (Toronto: University of Toronto Press, 2007).

23. This was especially true of fiscal capacity and powers related to the conduct of foreign policy, which at this point had been considerably curtailed in European monarchies. See

William Everdell, *The End of Kings: A History of Republics and Republicans* (London: Free Press, 1983).

24. There was in fact a great deal of slippage in the usage and conceptualization of these categories, suggesting there was not such a stark dividing line. For example, one delegate pointed to the government of the state of Massachusetts as a limited monarchy, given the strength of the executive. Another referred to the British prime minister as "King of England, in form if not in substance." Even the manner of election of the president via the Electoral College borrowed heavily from monarchical practices, and for many years, people would refer to the process by which parties nominated candidates as a "kings caucus." See Max Farrand, *The Records of the Federal Convention of 1787* (New Haven, CT: Yale University Press, 1911), 56–57, 165–81. See also Henry D. Gilpin, ed., *The Papers of James Madison*, 9 vols. (New York: Langley, 1840–41), 4:1194.

25. The debate itself was fairly brief and came toward the end of the convention, but a few delegates did vocally oppose the freehold requirement, including George Mason of Virginia, Nathaniel Gorman of Massachusetts, and Benjamin Franklin of Pennsylvania. See Keyssar, *Right to Vote*, 19.

26. Richard Matthews, "James Madison's Political Theory: Hostage to Democratic Fortune," *Review of Politics* 67, no. 1 (2005): 49–67.

27. Madison in Gilpin, *Papers of James Madison*, 3:1253.

28. Historians of the subject largely agree that the issue of suffrage was not a high priority for the founders. In Kirk Porter's 1918 study, he explained that since the issue of suffrage in the colonies was not something that the British had tried to interfere with, it was not a central point of grievance for the revolutionaries, and therefore did not factor heavily in the postrevolutionary period. Many were content to leave the status quo as it was. Keyssar has also noted the conservatism of the founders on the matter, seeing universal suffrage as neither desirable nor necessary for their visions of republican government. This of course begins to change by the 1820s, with extensive agitation in the states. But at the time of the founding, most were satisfied with a limited franchise. See Kirk Porter, *A History of Suffrage in the United States* (Chicago: University of Chicago Press, 1918); and Keyssar, *Right to Vote*.

29. Keyssar, *Right to Vote*, 8–10.

30. Ellsworth in Gilpin, *Papers of James Madison*, 7:1250.

31. Forrest McDonald, *Novus Ordo Seclorum: The Intellectual Origins of the Constitution* (Lawrence: Kansas University Press, 1985). Keyssar puts this figure at about 25 percent in the *Right to Vote*.

32. William Hutchinson, ed., *The Papers of James Madison* (Chicago: University of Chicago Press, 1981), 14. Madison would later offer a defense of slave representation in Federalist 54, which would sidestep these considerations by maintaining that slaves were both persons and property, and that government was instituted to protect both. Madison made explicit, however, that the primary reason to accept the arrangement was political expediency. Alexander Hamilton, James Madison, and John Jay, "Federalist 54: The Apportionment of Members of the House of Representatives among the States," in *The Federalist Papers* (New Haven, CT: Yale University Press, 2009), 279.

33. The disproportionality would be severe. In Virginia, for example, the most populous of the slave states, the free white population was 440,000, the slave population at 300,000. The

inclusion of slaves in the apportionment would increase the representation of the free white population by 75 percent. In South Carolina, the slave population at 97,000 was in fact larger than the free white population of 83,000. The inclusion of the slave population there would more than double the representation of the free white population.

34. Jackson Main notes that the perception that the Constitution favored the few over the many was almost universal among the antifederalists. Jackson Turner Main, *The Antifederalists: Critics of the Constitution, 1781–1788* (Chapel Hill: University of North Carolina Press, 2004). See also David Waldstreicher, *Slavery's Constitution: From Revolution to Ratification* (New York: Farrar, Straus and Giroux, 2010).

35. John Kaminski and Richard Leffler, eds., *A Necessary Evil? Slavery and the Debate over the Constitution* (Madison, WI: Madison House, 1995).

36. "Lycurgus," *Philadelphia (PA) Independent Gazetteer*, October 17, 1787, quoted in Main, *Antifederalists*, 142

37. John Hammond, "'We Are to Be Reduced to the Level of Slaves': Planters, Taxes, Aristocrats, and Massachusetts Antifederalists, 1787–1788," *Historical Journal of Massachusetts* 31, no. 2 (2003): 172–98.

38. Leonard Richards, *The Slave Power: The Free North and Southern Domination, 1780–1860* (Baton Rouge: Louisiana State University Press, 2000).

39. Article 1, Section 2, US Constitution.

40. The first apportionment is specified in Article 1, Section 2, of the Constitution. Some have noted that the ratio first appeared in 1783 in relation to the rate of taxation, but it had not been applied to representation until 1790.

41. Morris in James Madison, *The Constitutional Convention: A Narrative History from the Notes of James Madison*, ed. Edward Larson and Michael Winship (New York: Random House, 2011), 113.

42. Gerry in Madison, *Constitutional Convention*, 109–10.

43. Historian Gerald Sorin has characterized the divide as follows: "Antislavery was a negative force, an attempt to wall in an obnoxious system of labor so that it might die of itself; abolition was a positive force, founded on moral considerations, stoutly denying that slavery could be a good thing for anybody, and perfectly willing to see the social and economic system of the south disrupted"; Gerald Sorin, *Abolitionism: A New Perspective* (New York: Praeger, 1972), 173–74.

44. Sean Wilentz has argued that it was in fact part of the intent of the founders to not only impose limitations on slavery but also strip its core principles of legitimacy. While Wilentz's argument that the founders' intent can be linked directly to the outcome (the end of slavery seven decades later) can certainly be disputed, the work convincingly demonstrates that many antislavery federalists at the time understood themselves to be introducing limitations that would bring an end to slavery. Sean Wilentz, *No Property in Man: Slavery and Antislavery at the Nation's Founding* (Cambridge, MA: Harvard University Press, 2019).

45. Among the antifederalists there were of course strong proponents of slavery as well, whose arguments were the mirror opposite, that the Constitution was insufficient to protect the institution of slavery, which was the cornerstone of southern economies. Similarly, among the federalists there were strong proponents of slavery who adopted a pragmatic position but saw the compromises of the Constitution as sufficient to protect the southern states and their

interests. See Matthew Mason, *Slavery and Politics in the Early American Republic* (Chapel Hill: University of North Carolina Press, 2009), 34–35.

46. Hamilton, Madison, and Jay, "Federalist 54: The Apportionment of Members Among the States," 279.

47. Alexander Hamilton, James Madison, and John Jay, "Federalist 42: The Powers Conferred by the Constitution Further Reconsidered," *Federalist Papers*, 215.

48. Quotes in W.E.B. Du Bois, *Suppression of the African Slave-Trade to the United States of America* (1896; Oxford: Oxford University Press, 2007).

49. W.E.B Du Bois's early work on the slave trade documents these debates both at the convention and beyond, illustrating that a central theme of the debates was whether it was reasonable to expect the southern states to abandon slavery. There was of course disagreement on this, but what is important for the present analysis is that antislavery federalists offered this logic as justification for support of the Constitution. Du Bois, *Suppression of the African Slave-Trade*, especially chapters 6–7.

50. Wilentz, *No Property in Man*, 59.

51. In addition, Du Bois's work demonstrated the inefficacy of the ban itself, the varied ways in which the ban was evaded, and the willingness of the federal government to turn a blind eye to violations. Du Bois, *Suppression of the African Slave-Trade*, especially chapters 6–7.

52. This can also help us understand why the fear of aristocratic encroachment grew in the United States while diminishing in the UK, where similar institutional arrangements seemingly granted significant power to the Lords, an unquestionably aristocratic institution. In the UK, actors' sense of the practical politics of the situation led them to view the threat of the Lords as minimal, even when they launched what by most accounts was a significant regime threat on the eve of WWI. In the United States, actors' perceptions were significantly altered by the fact of western expansion. Simply put, whatever their de jure status, the de facto ability of aristocratic powers to challenge representative institutions in the UK was on the decline throughout the nineteenth century; in the United States, it appeared to be increasing and doing so in unanticipated ways.

53. Robin Einhorn has shown that defenders of slavery also understood the conflict in these terms. Through the lens of taxation, Einhorn shows that slaveholding elites throughout the antebellum period viewed strong democratic government as a threat to the institution of slavery. Robin Einhorn, *American Taxation, American Slavery* (Chicago: University of Chicago Press, 2008).

54. Boucher, "In Re That Aggressive Slaveocracy"; Davis, *Slave Power Conspiracy and the Paranoid Style*.

55. Russel Nye, *Fettered Freedom* (East Lansing: Michigan State University Press, 1963); Larry Gara, "Slavery and the Slave Power: A Crucial Distinction," *Civil War History* 15, no. 1 (1969): 5–18; William Gienapp, "The Republican Party and the Slave Power," in *New Perspectives on Race and Slavery in America*, ed. Robert H. Abzug and Stephen E. Maizlish (Lexington: University Press of Kentucky, 1986), 51, 67.

56. Eric Foner, *Free Soil, Free Labor, Free Men* (New York: Oxford University Press, 1970), 99–102; Richard Sewell, *Ballots for Freedom: Anti-slavery Politics in the United States, 1837–1860* (New York: Oxford University Press, 1976), 200.

57. Fletcher Green, "Democracy in the Old South," *Journal of Southern History* 12, no. 1 (1949): 3–23; Walter Rey Fee, "The Transition from Aristocracy to Democracy in New Jersey,

1789–1829" (PhD diss., Columbia University, 1933). On the influence of feudal structures on labor relations, see Orren's *Belated Feudalism*.

58. Kentucky and Vermont were added even before the First Congress would convene—one slave state and one free state; but as a result of the apportionment clause, this would still disproportionately favor the interest of slave states.

59. Stewart Smith, "Slavery and the Federalist Party, 1789–1808" (PhD diss., University of North Texas, Denton, 1966).

60. Smith, *Slavery and the Federalist Party*, 91, 109; Mason, *Slavery and Politics in the Early American Republic*, 34–35.

61. These party labels were still quite loose at the time, and the place of party in general was an open question. They were most cohesively organized in the first decade of the republic. The Federalist Party began to decline, however, starting in 1800, and by the 1810s it was no longer a strong political force, though candidates continued to use the label. This ultimately gave way to one-party rule during the "era of good feelings" (1816–1824). See Aldrich, *Why Parties?*; John Hoadley, "The Emergence of Political Parties in Congress, 1789–1803," *American Political Science Review* 74, no. 3 (1980): 757–79; and Richard Hofstadter, *The Idea of a Party System: The Rise of Legitimate Opposition in the United States, 1780–1840* (Berkeley: University of California Press, 1970).

62. The end of the transatlantic slave trade in 1808 was a rather feeble gesture given that, at the time, only one state, South Carolina, still engaged in the international trade. It was the domestic market that was of greatest consequence for the preservation and expansion of the institution, and the domestic trade was untouched. Patrick Brady, "The Slave Trade and Sectionalism in South Carolina, 1787–1808," *Journal of Southern History* 38, no. 4 (1972): 601–20.

63. Richards, *Slave Power*, 46.

64. Jan Lewis, "What Happened to the Three-Fifths Clause: The Relationship between Women and Slaves in Constitutional Thought, 1787–1866," *Journal of the Early Republic* 37, no. 1 (2017): 1–46. See also "Resolve for Proposing an Amendment to the Constitution of the United States Respecting an Equal Representation in Congress," in *Acts and Laws of the Commonwealth of Massachusetts* (Boston: Wright and Potter, 1898), 308–10.

65. "Amendments to the Constitution Proposed by the Hartford Convention: 1814," in *The Proceedings of a Convention of Delegates, from the States of Massachusetts, Connecticut, and Rhode-Island . . . Convened at Hartford, in the State of Connecticut, December 15th, 1814* (Boston: Wells and Lilly, 1815).

66. Donald Kennan and Paul Finkelman, eds., *Congress and the Emergence of Sectionalism: From the Missouri Compromise to the Age of Jackson* (Columbus: Ohio University Press, 2008); Mason, *Slavery and Politics in the Early American Republic*, 187.

67. Charles King, ed., *The Life and Correspondence of Rufus King*, 6 vols. (New York: Putnam, 1894–1900).

68. Quoted in Joshua M. Zeitz, "The Missouri Compromise Reconsidered: Antislavery Rhetoric and the Emergence of the Free Labor Synthesis," *Journal of the Early Republic* 20, no. 3 (2000): 447–85, https://doi.org/10.2307/3125065.

69. Quoted in Mason, *Slavery and Politics in the Early American Republic*, 190–91.

70. Quoted in Mason, *Slavery and Politics in the Early American Republic*, 191.

71. For example, historian Alfred Young, in his account of the New York Democratic-Republican Party, consistently places "the Republican interest" in quotes. Jeffrey Pasley refers

to the republican rhetoric as "hyperbolic." John Ashworth refers to Jeffersonian Democrats' desire to oust the "allegedly anti-republican Federalists." Such statements do not take seriously the perspectives of the actors themselves, dismissing such concerns based on our knowledge of the outcomes. To the extent that regime considerations are seriously acknowledged, they are often presented in somewhat technical terms as contrasting views about whether democracy was possible in a large republic or had to be confined to the states to be viable. See Alfred Young, *The Democratic Republicans in New York* (Chapel Hill: University of North Carolina Press, 1967); Jeffrey Pasley, "The Two National 'Gazettes': Newspapers and the Embodiment of American Political Parties," *Early American Literature* 35, no. 1 (2000): 70; and Cecelia Kenyon, "Men of Little Faith: The Anti-Federalists on the Nature of Representative Government," *William and Mary Quarterly* 12, no. 1 (1955): 4–43.

72. Davis, *Slave Power Conspiracy and the Paranoid Style.*

73. Gara, "Slavery and the Slave Power," 5–18.

74. Russel Nye, "The Slave Power Conspiracy: 1830–1860," *Science and Society* 10, no. 3 (1946): 262–74.

75. Richards, *Slave Power.*

76. Finkelman and Kennon, *Congress and the Emergence of Sectionalism.*

77. Edward Pessen, "The Egalitarian Myth and the American Social Reality: Wealth, Mobility, and Equality in the 'Era of the Common Man,'" *American Historical Review* 76, no. 4 (1971): 989–1034; Bruce Laurie, *Working People of Philadelphia, 1800–1850* (Philadelphia, PA: Temple University Press, 1980); Alan Dawley, *Class and Community: The Industrial Revolution in Lynn* (Cambridge, MA: Harvard University Press, 1976); Paul Faler, *Mechanics and Manufacturers in the Early Industrial Revolution: Lynn, Massachusetts, 1780–1860* (Albany: SUNY Press, 1981).

78. Arthur Schlesinger, *The Age of Jackson* (New York: Little, Brown, 1945).

79. Keyssar, *Right to Vote,* 24.

80. As illustrated in the European cases, working-class incorporation often aligned with economic policy coalitions such that the two would not come into conflict. Moreover, conservative forces were more threatened by the fact of contestation than by inclusion. Once parties were reassured that they could compete, new electors represented an opportunity rather than a threat. For an important discussion of conservative parties' orientation toward contestation, see Ziblatt, *Conservative Political Parties.*

81. Note that significant divisions within these economic coalitions existed from the start, with conservative Democrats and liberal Whigs pushing for more centrist policies. These disputes, however, were economic in nature. If anything, they pushed for a different alignment along the economic dimension, not away from it. See Jean Friedman, *The Revolt of the Conservative Democrats: An Essay on American Political Culture and Political Development* (Ann Arbor: University of Michigan Research Press, 1979); Howard Braverman, "The Economic and Political Background of the Conservative Revolt in Virginia," *Virginia Magazine of History and Biography* 60, no. 2 (1952): 266–87; Jeffrey Jenkins and Marc Weidenmier, "Ideology, Economic Interests, and Congressional Roll-Call Voting: Partisan Instability and Bank of the United States Legislation, 1811–1816," *Public Choice* 100 (1999): 225–43.

82. In addition to the structural pressures, Paul Frymer has convincingly argued that a deliberate effort to subdue the sectional divide over slavery was at the heart of the party reorganization during this period. In particular the push to establish national parties was a distinctive

feature of this transformation, aimed to displace local politics, in which the sectional divide was paramount. Paul Frymer, *Uneasy Alliances: Race and Party Competition in America* (Princeton, NJ: Princeton University Press, 1999), 34–39.

83. Schlesinger, *Age of Jackson*.

84. John Ashworth, *"Agrarians" and "Aristocrats": Party Political Ideology in the United States, 1837–1846* (Cambridge: Cambridge University Press, 1987), 31.

85. Robert Remini, *Andrew Jackson and the Bank Wars: A Study in the Growth of Presidential Power* (New York: Norton, 1967).

86. The charter for the Second Bank of the United States was set to expire in 1836, but national Republicans, wanting to force Jackson's hand ahead of the 1832 election, mobilized to renew the charter early. Their calculus was that either Jackson would acquiesce and recharter the bank, or he would veto and suffer backlash in the election, paving the way for a pro-bank figure to take the presidency. Jackson vetoed but suffered little backlash except in his own party, which saw many defections, particularly among conservative Democrats. There are numerous important discussions of the Bank Wars, but a few that highlight the intraparty dynamics include Daniel Walker Howe, *What Hath God Wrought: The Transformation of the American, 1815–1848* (Oxford: Oxford University Press, 2007), 379; and Jean Wilburn, *Biddle's Bank: The Crucial Years* (New York: Columbia University Press, 1967).

87. Leggett's commentary is found in the *New York Evening Post*, November 4, 1834. For a broader discussion of democratic discourse at this time, see Joseph Blau, ed., *Social Theories of Jacksonian Democracy: Representative Writings of the Period 1825–1850* (1954; Indianapolis, IN: Hackett, 2003), 67; and Richard Hofstadter, "William Leggett, Spokesman of Jacksonian Democracy," *Political Science Quarterly* 58, no. 4 (1943): 581–94, https://doi.org/10.2307/2144949.

88. Blau, *Social Theories of Jacksonian Democracy*.

89. Scott James and David Lake, "The Second Face of Hegemony: Britain's Repeal of the Corn Laws and the American Walker Tariff of 1846," *International Organization* 43, no. 1 (1989): 1–29.

90. William Bolt, *The Tariff Wars and the Politics of Jacksonian America* (Nashville, TN: Vanderbilt University Press, 2017); Richard Ellis, *The Union at Risk: Jacksonian Democracy, States' Rights, and the Nullification Crisis* (Oxford: Oxford University Press, 1987).

91. H. W. Brands, *Heirs of the Founders: Henry Clay, John Calhoun and Daniel Webster, the Second Generation of American Giants* (London: Knopf Doubleday, 2019), 143.

92. William Cooper, *The South and the Politics of Slavery, 1828–1852* (Baton Rouge: Louisiana State University Press, 1978); William Belko, "'A Tax on the Many, to Enrich a Few': Jacksonian Democracy vs. the Protective Tariff," *Journal of the History of Economic Thought* 37, no. 2 (2015): 277–89, https://doi.org/10.1017/S1053837215000097.

93. Larry Gara, "Antislavery Congressmen, 1848–1856: Their Contribution to the Debate between the Sections," *Civil War History* 32, no. 3 (1986): 197–207, https://doi.org/10.1353/cwh.1986.0011; William O. Lynch, "Anti-Slavery Tendencies of the Democratic Party in the Northwest, 1848–50," *Mississippi Valley Historical Review* 11, no. 3 (1924): 319–31, https://doi.org/10.2307/1888838.

94. The first apportionment is specified in Article 1, Section 2, of the Constitution. Some have noted that the ratio first appeared in 1783 in relation to the rate of taxation, but it had not been applied to representation. George Van Cleve, *A Slaveholders' Union: Slavery, Politics, and*

the *Constitution in the Early American Republic* (Chicago: University of Chicago Press, 2010), 105–6.

95. B. D. Humes, E. K. Swift, Richard M. Valelly, K. Finegold, and E. C. Fink, "Representation of the Antebellum South in the House of Representatives: Measuring the Impact of the Three-Fifths Clause," in *Party, Process, and Political Change in Congress: New Perspectives on the History of Congress*, vol. 1, ed. David Brady and Matthew McCubbins (Stanford, CA: Stanford University Press, 2002), 456.

96. Historians have also noted that there was some basis to this. Though the conspiratorial claims of the thesis perhaps gave too much credit to southern politicians, analysis supports the claim that the arrangement gave them disproportionate advantage. See Richards, *Slave Power*, 17–19.

97. Seward, *Congressional Globe* (Washington: Blair & Rives, 1834–1873), March 11, 1850.

98. Frequent references could be found in public discourse as well, as with the 1862 publication by Henry O'Reilly, prominent journalist and editor of the *Telegraph*, entitled *Origin and Objects of the Slaveholder Conspiracy against Democratic Principles* (New York: Baker and Godwin, 1862).

99. Michael Holt, *The Fate of Their Country: Politicians, Slavery Extension, and the Coming of the Civil War* (New York: Farrar, Straus and Giroux, 2005); Daniel Walker Howe, *The Political Culture of the American Whigs* (Chicago: University of Chicago Press, 1969); William Brock, *Parties and Political Conscience, 1840–1850* (Millwood, NY: KTO Press, 1979).

100. Michael Holt, *The Political Crisis of the 1850s* (New York: Wiley, 1978), 147–50.

101. Holt, *Political Crisis of the 1850s*, 153–54; Forrest Nabors, *From Oligarchy to Republicanism: The Great Task of Reconstruction* (Columbia: University of Missouri Press, 2017).

102. The first Republican Party platform was approved on July 6 in Jackson, Michigan; quoted in Holt, *Political Crisis of the 1850s*, 149, and in Nabors, *From Oligarchy to Republicanism*, 203.

103. William Gienapp, *The Origin of the Republican Party, 1852–1856* (Oxford: Oxford University Press, 1988), especially chapter 11.

104. William Seward, "The Contest and the Crisis," speech delivered in Buffalo, NY, October 19, 1855, in *Republican Campaign Documents of 1856: A Collection of the Most Important Speeches and Documents Issued by the Republican Association of Washington, During the Presidential Campaign of 1856* (Washington, DC: L. Clephane, 1857).

105. For an account of the historiography, particularly its dismissal of claims of aristocracy and the slave power, see Richards, *Slave Power*, especially 15–20.

106. The foundational thesis comes from Foner, *Free Soil, Free Labor, Free Men*. For other structural accounts, see Mark Summers, "The North and the Coming of the Civil War," in *Why the Civil War Came*, ed. Gabor Boritt (Oxford: Oxford University Press, 1996); and James Huston, *The Panic of 1857 and the Coming of the Civil War* (Baton Rouge: Louisiana State University Press, 1987).

107. Bruce Collins, "The Ideology of the Ante-Bellum Northern Democrats," *Journal of American Studies* 11, no. 1 (1977): 103–21; Jean Baker, *The Political Culture of Northern Democrats in the Mid-Nineteenth Century* (Ithaca, NY: Cornell University Press, 1983).

108. Richard Bensel, *Yankee Leviathan: The Origins of State Central Authority in America, 1859–1877* (Cambridge: Cambridge University Press, 1990).

109. See Holt, *Political Crisis of the 1850s*. In this work, Holt rejects both structural interpretations of party system change and ethno-cultural explanations, which he had offered as an interpretation of the conflict in previous periods. Neither, he maintains, can explain the party system change of the 1850s.

110. Gienapp, *Origins of the Republican Party*. See also William Gienapp, "The Republican Party and the Slave Power," in *New Perspectives on Race and Slavery in America*, ed. Robert Abzug and Stephen E. Maizlish (Louisville: University Press of Kentucky, 1986). James Oakes also offers an important look at Republic Party ideology at the time in *The Scorpion's Sting: Antislavery and the Coming of the Civil War* (New York: Norton, 2014).

111. Tom Scriven, "Slavery and Abolition in Chartist Thought and Culture, 1838–1850," *Historical Journal* 65, no. 5 (2022): 1262–84, https://doi.org/10.1017/S0018246X21000819; Nicholas Hudson, "'Britons Never Will Be Slaves': National Myth, Conservatism, and the Beginnings of British Antislavery," *Eighteenth-Century Studies* 34, no. 4 (2001): 559–76; John Ashworth, David Brion Davis, and Thomas Haskell, *The Antislavery Debate: Capitalism and Abolitionism as a Problem in Historical Interpretation*, ed. Thomas Bender (Berkeley: University of California Press, 1992).

112. Betty Fladeland, *Men and Brothers: Anglo-American Anti-Slavery Cooperation* (Urbana: University of Illinois Press, 1972); Seymour Drescher, *Capitalism and Antislavery: British Mobilization in Comparative Perspective* (London: Macmillan, 1986).

113. Quoted in William Caleb McDaniel, *The Problem of Democracy in the Age of Slavery: Garrisonian Abolitionists and Transatlantic Reform* (Baton Rouge: Louisiana State University Press, 2013), 157.

114. Wendell Phillips, *The Philosophy of the Abolitionist Movement* (New York: American Anti-Slavery Society, 1853).

115. Alexis de Tocqueville, *Democracy in America* (1831; Cambridge, MA: Sever and Francis, 1863), 541. He further asserted that the connections drawn between slavery in the South and European aristocracy were flawed: "In the South, one man, aided by slaves, could cultivate a great extent of country: it was therefore common to see rich landed proprietors. But their influence was not altogether aristocratic as that term is understood in Europe, since they possessed no privileges; and the cultivation of their estates being carried on by slaves, they had no tenants depending on them, and consequently no patronage" (58).

116. Tocqueville's interpretation of US society has also been strongly contested in later scholarship. Many have noted the peculiarity of his liberalism, the fact that most of his interlocutors were northern Whigs, and that he in fact spent little time in the South. See Cushing Strout, "Tocqueville's Duality: Describing America and Thinking of Europe," *American Quarterly* 21, no. 1 (1969): 87–99, https://doi.org/10.2307/2710774; Bartholomew H. Sparrow, "The Other Point of Departure: Tocqueville, the South, Equality, and the Lessons of Democracy," *Studies in American Political Development* 33, no. 2 (2019): 178–208, https://doi.org/10.1017/S0898588X19000099; Howe, *Political Culture of the American Whigs*, 181. See also Roger Boesche, *The Strange Liberalism of Alexis de Tocqueville* (Ithaca, NY: Cornell University Press, 1987); and Guy Aiken, "Educating Tocqueville: Jared Sparks, the Boston Whigs, and Democracy in America," *Tocqueville Review* 34, no. 1 (2013): 169–92.

117. Francis Grund, *Aristocracy in America: From the Sketchbook of a German Nobleman* (London: Richard Bentley, 1839).

118. Peter O'Connor, *American Sectionalism in the British Mind 1832–1866* (Baton Rouge: Louisiana State University Press, 2017); Alan Gallay, *Voices of the Old South: Eyewitness Accounts, 1528–1861* (Athens: University of Georgia Press, 1994).

119. James Stirling, *Letters from the Slave States* (London: Parker and Son, 1857).

120. Carl Wittke, *Refugees of Revolution: The German Forty-Eighters in America* (Philadelphia: University of Pennsylvania Press, 1970).

121. Though Forty-Eighters could be found in both parties, their presence in the Republican Party was much greater. Moreover, it was the political exiles—the Turners—that dominated in the Republican Party. The German immigrants who gravitated to the Democratic Party tended to be Catholics fleeing persecution. See B. C. Levine, *The Spirit of 1848: German Immigrants, Labor Conflict, and the Coming of the Civil War* (Urbana: University of Illinois Press, 1992).

122. Free Soilers frequently referenced the Revolutions of 1848, often likening their position to that of European (especially French) Republicans. Timothy Roberts, *Distant Revolutions: 1848 and the Challenge to American Exceptionalism* (Charlottesville: University of Virginia Press, 2009), 66–67.

123. Quoted in Adolf Zucker, *The Forty-Eighters: Political Refugees of the German Revolution of 1848* (New York: Columbia University Press, 1950), 121.

124. Among the more prominent figures was Carl Schurz, who would serve as a Union general during the Civil War and later in President Rutherford B. Hayes's cabinet. On the role of the Forty-Eighters in the rise of the Republican Party, see Sabine Freitag, "A Republikaner Becomes a Republican: Friedrich Hecker and the Emergence of the Republican Party," *Yearbook of German American Studies* 33 (1998): 1–17; Molly Fischer, "A Passion for Liberty: German Immigrants in the Creation of the Republican Party and the Election of Lincoln," *Saber and Scroll* 6 (2017): 4; and Christian Dippel and Stephan Heblich, "Leadership in Social Movements: Evidence from the 'Forty-Eighters' in the Civil War," *American Economic Review* 111, no. 2 (2021): 472–505.

Chapter 7. The Persistence of Regime Contention in the United States: The Development of Multiple Repertoires

1. Wayne Morgan, *The Gilded Age* (Syracuse, NY: Syracuse University Press, 1970); Robert W. Cherny, *American Politics in the Gilded Age, 1865–1900* (New York: Wiley Blackwell, 1996); Rebecca Edwards, "Politics, Social Movements, and the Periodization of U.S. History," *Journal of the Gilded Age and Progressive Era* 8, no. 4 (2009): 463–73.

2. The system of 1896 has been touted as a major realignment, replacing one set of issues related to the democratic character of the republic with economic concerns as the central vector of politics. Yet critics have argued that this interpretation elides the fact that economic concerns were already very much part of party politics in the 1880s and that the sectional divide resulting from regime concerns continued to shape legislative coalitions well after 1896. The framework offered here casts 1896 as a partial realignment, orienting coalitions more fully toward economic concerns but remaining geographically and therefore politically constrained in ways that continued to impede legislative capacity. Accounts questioning the realignment of 1896 include McCormick, "Walter Dean Burnham"; Bartels, "Electoral Continuity and Change"; Mayhew, *Electoral Realignments*; and Karol, *Party Position Change in American Politics*.

3. William Gillette, *Retreat from Reconstruction, 1869–1879* (Baton Rouge: Louisiana State University Press, 1982), 61–64; Andrew Slap, *The Doom of Reconstruction: The Liberal Republicans in the Civil War Era* (New York: Fordham University Press, 2010).

4. C. Vann Woodward, in an important study of the period, has identified this as an explicit compromise, though other historians have disputed this characterization. The outcome of the election and its significance for Reconstruction are not in dispute, but some historians have expressed doubt that there was an explicit compromise, noting that the political parts were a forgone conclusion and much of the economic parts did not come to fruition. Nonetheless, Woodward offers abundant evidence that whatever the outcomes, actors at the time saw explicit tradeoffs and a quid pro quo in the resolution. C. Vann Woodward, *Reunion and Reaction: The Compromise of 1877 and the End of Reconstruction* (1951; New York: Oxford University Press, 1991); Allan Peskin, "Was There a Compromise of 1877?," *Journal of American History* 60, no. 1 (1973): 63–75, https://doi.org/10.2307/2936329. See also Keith Polakoff, *The Politics of Inertia: The Election of 1876 and the End of Reconstruction* (Baton Rouge: Louisiana State University Press, 1973).

5. Michael Holt, *By One Vote: The Disputed Presidential Election of 1876* (Lawrence: University Press of Kansas, 2008).

6. Woodward, *Reunion and Reaction*, especially chapters 3 and 5.

7. While disputing the explicit nature of the compromise, Polakoff agrees with Woodward's interpretation of the divisions within both parties and the role of interparty factions in bringing about these outcomes. See Polakoff, *Politics of Inertia*, 314.

8. Woodward, *Reunion and Reaction*, 24.

9. Hayes was acutely aware of the rising radicalism within the labor force after the panic of 1873 and ensuing depression, and he saw in it great dangers. He notoriously called in the army to put down the railroad strikes of 1877. Ari Hoogenboom, *The Presidency of Rutherford B. Hayes* (Lawrence: University of Kansas Press, 1988), 89–91.

10. Holt, *By One Vote*.

11. Woodward, *Reunion and Reaction*, 169–70.

12. Allan Peskin, "Who Were the Stalwarts? Who Were Their Rivals? Republican Factions in the Gilded Age," *Political Science Quarterly* 99, no. 4 (1984): 704, https://doi.org/10.2307/2150708; Daniel DiSalvo, *Engines of Change: Party Factions in American Politics, 1868–2010* (Oxford: Oxford University Press, 2012).

13. Peskin, "Who Were the Stalwarts?," 714–16.

14. Charles Calhoun, *From Bloody Shirt to Full Dinner Pail: The Transformation of Politics and Governance in the Gilded Age* (New York: Farrar, Straus and Giroux, 2010).

15. The assassin, Charles Guiteau, who had first sought Garfield's patronage and then sought revenge when it was not provided, exclaimed after shooting the president, "I am a stalwart . . . Arthur is now president of the United States," referring to Garfield's vice president, who was a Stalwart. Allan Peskin, "Charles Guiteau of Illinois: President Garfield's Assassin," *Journal of the Illinois State Historical Society* 70, no. 2 (1977): 130–39.

16. Many Democrats were satisfied with the gridlock, as it was their intent to limit government power. Republicans, however, had an ambitious agenda, including higher tariffs and antitrust legislation, which was consistently thwarted by both the Democrats' obstruction and factions within the Republican Party. Sarah Binder, *Minority Rights, Majority Rule: Partisanship*

and the Development of Congress (Cambridge: Cambridge University Press, 1997), 126–27; Wayne Morgan, "The Republican Party, 1876–1893," in *Arthur Schlesinger, History of US Political Parties 2: 1860–1910* (New York: Chelsea, 1973).

17. James Grant details the convoluted process leading to the ultimate resolution in 1882. James Grant, *Mr. Speaker!: The Life and Times of Thomas Reed, the Man Who Broke the Filibuster* (New York: Simon and Schuster, 2012), 140–49.

18. Elizabeth Sanders, *Roots of Reform: Farmers, Workers, and the American State, 1877–1917* (Chicago: University of Chicago Press, 1999); Richard Bensel, *The Political Economy of American Industrialization, 1877–1900* (New York: Cambridge University Press, 2000).

19. Douglas Irwin, *Clashing over Commerce: A History of US Trade Policy* (Chicago: University of Chicago Press, 2017), chapter 5.

20. The system of 1896 refers to numerous changes having to do with voter turnout, party competition, ideological polarization, and so on. I am interested here specifically in the realignment of 1896, and even more narrowly in the realignment as it pertains to parties in the House. The shifts of voting behavior in the public are of course related and helped consolidate the realignment in successive elections. But the focus here is primarily on legislative behavior. Walter Dean Burnham, "The System of 1896: An Analysis," in *The Evolution of American Electoral Systems*, P. Kleppner, W. D. Burnham, R. P. Formisano, S. P. Hays, R. Jensen, and W. G. Shade, (Westport, CT: Greenwood Press, 1981), 147–202; R. Hal Williams, *Realigning America: McKinley, Bryan, and the Remarkable Election of 1896* (Lawrence: University Press of Kansas, 2010), 1–19; McCormick, "Walter Dean Burnham," 245–62.

21. E. E. Schattschneider, *The Semisovereign People: A Realist's View of Democracy in America* (New York: Holt, Rinehart and Winston, 1960), 9–80.

22. Schattschneider and Caramani both demonstrate that the nationalization of the electorate does not take place in the United States until the 1930s. The lack of national economic coalitions suggests that a full realignment had not yet taken place. See Schattschneider, *Semisovereign People*; and Daniele Caramani, *The Nationalization of Politics: The Formation of National Electorates and Party Systems in Western Europe* (Cambridge: Cambridge University Press, 2004). See also John R. Petrocik, "Realignment: New Party Coalitions and the Nationalization of the South," *Journal of Politics* 49, no. 2 (1987): 347–75, https://doi.org/10.2307/2131305.

23. Eric Schickler notes that among the factors leading to the implementation of the Reed rules, the general legislative incapacity of the preceding decade played an important role. Eric Schickler, *Disjointed Pluralism: Institutional Innovation and the Development of the Reed Rules* (Princeton, NJ: Princeton University Press, 2001).

24. Binder, *Minority Rights, Majority Rule*; Schickler, *Disjointed Pluralism*; Gary W. Cox and Matthew McCubbins, *Setting the Agenda: Responsible Party Government in the US House of Representatives* (Cambridge: Cambridge University Press, 2005); Ronald Peterson, *The American Speakership: The Office in Historical Perspective* (Baltimore, MD: Johns Hopkins University Press, 1997). The common retelling of the introduction of the Reed rules focuses on the specific legislative act that triggered Reed's insistence on recording those present—the certification of a contested election. But the broader policy agenda it was meant to enable must also be understood as part of the dynamics of reform.

25. Quentin R. Skrabec, *William McKinley, Apostle of Protectionism* (New York: Algora, 2008), 26.

26. See Grant, *Mr. Speaker!*, 277. Richard Valelly has also linked the reforms to proposed electoral change and broader strategies of party building. Richard Valelly, "The Reed Rules and Republican Party Building: A New Look," *Studies in American Political Development* 23, no. 2 (2009): 115–42, https://doi.org/10.1017/S0898588X09990022.

27. The connection between obstruction and the tariff issue in particular is discussed at length in Wawro and Schickler, *Filibuster*, especially chapter 6.

28. Schickler, *Disjointed Pluralism*, 35.

29. James L. Huston, "A Political Response to Industrialism: The Republican Embrace of Protectionist Labor Doctrines," *Journal of American History* 70, no. 1 (1983): 35–57, https://doi.org/10.2307/1890520; F. W. Taussig, "The McKinley Tariff Act," *Economic Journal* 1, no. 2 (1891): 326–50, https://doi.org/10.2307/2956253.

30. References to the "old guard" do not necessarily indicate a generational divide, but rather represent an ideological divide. Peskin, "Who Were the Stalwarts?," 711–12.

31. Joanne Reitano, *The Tariff Question in the Gilded Age: The Great Debate of 1888* (University Park: Pennsylvania State University, 1994).

32. Republicans had for some time tried to appeal to southern voters on the matters of economic growth, but the tariff issue remained a significant obstacle. Charles Calhoun, *Conceiving a New Republic: The Republican Party and the Southern Question, 1869–1900* (Lawrence: University of Kansas Press, 2006), especially chapter 8. Reitano also demonstrates that these considerations played a significant role in the elections of 1888. Reitano, *Tariff Question in the Gilded Age*.

33. Of the 164 Republicans elected to the Fifty-First Congress, only 11 came from southern states: 2 from Kentucky, 1 from Louisiana, 3 from North Carolina, 3 from Tennessee, and 2 from Virginia. No Republicans senators came from southern states. Overall, Republicans had struggled and mostly failed since 1877 to establish a presence in the South. Between the Forty-Fifth and Fifty-Sixth Congresses, Republicans gained only 102 out of a possible 1,004 seats in southern states. Boris Heersink and Jeffrey Jenkins, *Republican Party Politics and the American South, 1865–1968* (Cambridge: Cambridge University Press, 2020).

34. Reitano, *Tariff Question in the Gilded Age*.

35. Vincent De Santis, "Benjamin Harrison and the Republican Party in the South, 1889–1893," *Indiana Magazine of History* 51, no. 4 (1955): 279–302.

36. On the party-building objective of the Elections bill, see Valelly, "Reed Rules and Republican Party Building."

37. David Bateman, Ira Katznelson, and John Lapinski, *Southern Nation: Congress and White Supremacy after Reconstruction* (Princeton, NJ: Princeton University Press, 2020); Wendy Hazard, "Thomas Brackett Reed, Civil Rights, and the Fight for Fair Elections," *Maine History* 42 (2004): 1; Stanley P. Hirshson, *Farewell to the Bloody Shirt* (Bloomington: Indiana University Press, 1962).

38. Quoted in Calhoun, *Conceiving a New Republic*, 205.

39. Quoted in Calhoun, *Conceiving a New Republic*, 204.

40. Quoted in Valelly, "Reed Rules and Republican Party Building," 128.

41. Raum's views were highly influential among the old guard. In a book, *The Existing Conflict between Republican Government and Southern Oligarchy*, published in 1884, Raum offered a detailed account of political violence since the end of the war. He dedicated it to "All Lovers of Republican Liberty." Green Raum, *The Existing Conflict between Republican Government and Southern Oligarchy* (New York: Charles M. Green, 1884).

42. Quoted in Calhoun, *Conceiving a New Republic*, 205–6.

43. The machinations behind this outcome are detailed in Bateman, Katznelson and Lapinski, *Southern Nation*, 202–6. See also Hazard, "Thomas Brackett Reed"; and Vallely "Reed Rules and Republican Party Building." On the logrolling aspect of this process, see Wawro and Schickler, *Filibuster*, 147–48.

44. Morgan, "Republican Party, 1876–1893."

45. Taussig, "McKinley Tariff Act."

46. Skrabec, *William McKinley*, 76.

47. Schickler, *Disjointed Pluralism*, 47–49.

48. Schickler, *Disjointed Pluralism*, chapter 3.

49. The term "autocracy" appears during the interwar period, with reference to both the political systems emerging in the Communist world and the organization of labor movements, often juxtaposed in an effort to link the two. James Prickett, "The Ambiguities of Anti-Communism," in *Autocracy and Insurgency in Organized Labor*, ed. Burton Hall (New York: Transaction, 1972), 239–48.

50. Robert Mickey, *Paths out of Dixie: The Democratization of Authoritarian Enclaves in America's Deep South, 1944–1972* (Princeton, NJ: Princeton University Press, 2015).

51. James Sundquist, *The Decline and Resurgence of Congress* (Washington, DC: Brookings Institution Press, 2002), 39; Schickler, *Disjointed Pluralism*, 89–90.

52. The connection between the national budget and responsible government was made explicitly by Arthur Eugene Buck and Frederick Cleveland, two economists and Progressive reformers who led the Commission on Economy and Efficiency appointed by President Taft in 1911. They made their case forcefully in a 1920 book with a foreword from Taft: Arthur E. Buck and Frederick Cleveland, *The Budget and Responsible Government: A Description and Interpretation of the Struggle for Responsible Government in the United States, with Special Reference to Recent Changes in State Constitutions and Statute Laws Providing for Administrative Reorganization and Budget Reform* (New York: Macmillan, 1920).

53. Randall Holcombe, "Government Growth in the Twenty-First Century," *Public Choice* 124, no. 1–2 (2005): 95–114.

54. Ronald Schafer, *America in the Great War: The Rise of the War Welfare State* (Oxford: Oxford University Press, 1991).

55. Tom Hall, "Wilson and the Food Crisis: Agricultural Price Control during World War I," *Agricultural History* 47, no. 1 (1973): 25–46.

56. Donald Horton and E. Fenton Shepard, "Federal Aid to Agriculture since World War I," *Agricultural History* 19, no. 2 (1945): 114–20.

57. Sean Gailmard and John W. Patty, *Learning while Governing: Expertise and Accountability in the Executive Branch* (Chicago: University of Chicago Press, 2013), 167–68; John A. Dearborn, "The 'Proper Organs' for Presidential Representation: A Fresh Look at the Budget and Accounting Act of 1921," *Journal of Policy History* 31, no. 1 (2019): 1–41, 5, https://doi.org/10.1017/S0898030618000325.

58. Dearborn points to several counterfactual scenarios, stressing that handing over power to the executive was by no means the obvious choice. Dearborn, "'Proper Organs' for Presidential Representation."

59. Sundquist, *Decline and Resurgence of Congress*.

60. John A. Dearborn, *Power Shifts: Congress and Presidential Representation* (Chicago: University of Chicago Press, 2021).

61. Schickler identifies deep divisions emerging within the Republican Party coalition at this time and several institutional innovations aimed at remedying it. Schickler, *Disjoined Pluralism*, 85–86.

62. Central Law Journal, "Highlights of the Federal Revenue Act of 1921," 95 Cent. L.J. 106 (1922).

63. In the Senate, the farm bloc was so well established that, for Schickler, it warrants consideration as a form of institutional change. Schickler, *Disjointed Pluralism*, 99.

64. Benjamin Rader, "Federal Taxation in the 1920s: A Re-examination," *Historian* 33, no. 1 (1970): 415–35.

65. Patrick O'Brien, "A Reexamination of the Senate Farm Bloc, 1921–1933," *Agricultural History* 47, no. 3 (1973): 248–63.

66. Robert Murray, *The Politics of Normalcy: Governmental Theory and Practice in the Harding-Coolidge Era* (New York: Norton, 1973), 44–45; Charles Jones, *The Minority Party in Congress* (Boston: Little, Brown, 1970), 70.

67. John Marini, *The Politics of Budget Control: Congress, the Presidency, and Growth of the Administrative State* (New York: Taylor and Francis, 2014).

68. The uneasy liberalism of the New Deal coalition has been the subject of much historical debate, particularly as it pertained to the support of racially discriminatory practices and the accommodation of authoritarian enclaves in the South. The most critical view comes from Ira Katznelson, *When Affirmative Action Was White* (New York: Norton, 2005); and Ira Katznelson, *Fear Itself: The New Deal and the Origins of Our Time* (New York: Liveright, 2013). Some have sought to rehabilitate the image of the New Deal by showing the ways in which national actors worked behind the scenes to advance a progressive agenda: Kevin McMahon, *Reconsidering Roosevelt on Race* (Chicago: University of Chicago Press, 2004). Others have highlighted the peculiar nature of New Deal liberalism as a means of understanding how it accommodated such exclusionary politics: Schickler, *Racial Realignment*. Desmond King and Rogers Smith have argued that New Deal politicians operated within both white supremacist and egalitarian transformative political orders, and this is reflected in the contradictions of the policies they promoted. Desmond King and Rogers Smith, "Racial Orders in American Political Development," *American Political Science Review* 99 (2005): 75–92.

69. Martin Shefter, *Political Parties and the State: The American Historical Experience* (Princeton, NJ: Princeton University Press, 1993); Robert H. Zieger, *Republicans and Labor: 1919–1929* (Lexington: University Press of Kentucky, 2014).

70. Casey Sullivan, "Way before the Storm: California, the Republican Party, and a New Conservatism, 1900–1930," *Journal of Policy History* 26, no. 4 (2014): 568–94.

71. The position of the AFL was to keep labor independent to "reward its friend and punish its enemies." Daniel Schlozman, *When Movements Anchor Parties: Electoral Alignments in American History* (Princeton, NJ: Princeton University Press, 2015), 10.

72. Schlozman, *When Movements Anchor Parties*, chapter 3.

73. Charles Martin, "Negro Leaders, the Republican Party, and the Election of 1932," *Phylon* 32, no. 1 (1971): 85–93.

74. W.E.B. Du Bois, "Address to the Country," speech at Harpers Ferry, West Virginia, August 19, 1906, *Broad Ax* 11, no. 44 (August 25, 1906): 1.

75. In addition to his scholarly writing, Du Bois regularly wrote for prominent magazine and news outlets, particularly *The Nation* and *The Crisis*, which he founded as the official publication of the National Association for the Advancement of Colored People (NAACP). He critiqued both parties for their failures to act on conditions in the South or to advocate for the independence of Black voters. He would for a time join the Socialist Party and briefly the Communist Party, both of which appealed to his transnational sensibilities and desire for solidarity across race and class lines. W.E.B. Du Bois, "The Republicans and the Black Voter," *Nation* 110, no. 2866 (1920): 757–58; W.E.B. Du Bois, "I Won't Vote," *Nation* 183 (1956): 324–25. See also W.E.B. Du Bois, *The Emerging Thought of W.E.B. Du Bois: Essays and Editorials from the Crisis* (New York: Simon and Schuster, 1972).

76. Timothy Thomas Fortune, *Thomas Fortune, the Afro-American Agitator: A Collection of Writings, 1880–1928* (Gainesville: University Press of Florida, 2008); David Oks, "The Election of 1916, 'Negrowumpism,' and the Black Defection from the Republican Party," *Journal of the Gilded Age and Progressive Era* 20, no. 4 (2021): 523–47.

77. Particularly devastating was the inability of the party to act effectively to pass antilynching laws. Megan Francis, *Civil Rights and the Making of the Modern American State* (Cambridge: Cambridge University Press, 2014).

78. Richard Sherman, "The Harding Administration and the Negro: An Opportunity Lost," *Journal of Negro History* 49, no. 3 (1964): 151–68.

79. W.E.B. Du Bois, "Is Al Smith Afraid of the South?," *Nation* 127, no. 3302 (1928): 392–94.

80. Absent any action on Jim Crow, mass migration of Blacks from the South to northern cities became the individualized response to these political failures, and many supported the Democratic Party despite its failure to address the southern question. Keneshia Grant, *The Great Migration and the Democratic Party: Black Voters and the Realignment of American Politics in the 20th Century* (Philadelphia, PA: Temple University Press, 2020).

81. Elliot Rosen, *The Republican Party in the Age of Roosevelt: Sources of Anti-Government Conservatism in the United States* (Charlottesville: University of Virginia Press, 2014).

82. Though the realignment is typically dated at 1932, some identify 1928 as the critical election in which a realignment of the electorate can be detected. V. O. Key noted, "In New England at least, the Roosevelt revolution of 1932 was in large measure an Al Smith revolution of 1928," referring to the shift toward the Democratic Party in a traditional Republican stronghold. Key, "Theory of Critical Elections," 3–18.

83. Nancy Weiss, *Farewell to the Party of Lincoln: Black Politics in the Age of F.D.R.* (Princeton, NJ: Princeton University Press, 2020); Dennis S. Nordin, *The New Deal's Black Congressman: A Life of Arthur Wergs Mitchell* (Columbia: University of Missouri Press, 1997).

84. Mickey, *Paths out of Dixie*.

85. Katznelson, *Fear Itself*, 27–28.

86. This tacit agreement, according to Katznelson, was essential to keeping the New Deal coalition together. Katznelson, *Fear Itself*, 159–61. Schickler also demonstrates that while there were ongoing challenges within the party from early on, Democratic Party leadership remained reluctant to take up these issues. See Schickler, *Racial Realignment*.

87. A realignment within the economic dimension typically involved reshuffling alliances following a new economic calculus. The US realignment of 1932, for example, resembles that which took place in the UK when Labour eclipsed the Liberals as a dominant party. Though

economic interests dominated coalition patterns before and after realignment, the specific combination of interests differed.

88. On the nationalization of the electorate during this period, see Caramani, *Nationalization of Politics*; and Schattschneider, *Semisovereign People*.

89. Julian Zelizer, "The Forgotten Legacy of the New Deal: Fiscal Conservatism and the Roosevelt Administration, 1933–1938," *Presidential Studies Quarterly* 30 (2000): 332–59.

90. Jonathan Alter, *The Defining Moment* (London: Simon and Schuster, 2007), 275.

91. James Sargent, *Roosevelt and the First One Hundred Days: Struggle for the Early New Deal* (New York: Garland, 1981).

92. Kelly Stott, "FDR, Lewis Douglas, and the Raw Deal," *Historian* 63, no. 1 (1990): 105–19.

93. Frank Friedel, *Franklin D. Roosevelt: A Rendezvous with Destiny* (Boston: Little Brown, 1990), 96.

94. Patrick Maney, "The Rise and Fall of the New Deal Congress, 1933–1945," *OAH Magazine of History* 12, no. 4 (1998): 13–19.

95. Historian Basil Rauch termed this the "two New Deals." Basil Rausch, *The History of the New Deal, 1933–1938* (New York: Creative Age Press, 1945).

Conclusion: The Regime Question, Then and Now

1. G. John Ikenberry, *Liberal Leviathan: The Origins, Crisis, and Transformation of the American World Order* (Princeton, NJ: Princeton University Press, 2011); Daniel Deudney and G. John Ikenberry, "The Nature and Sources of Liberal International Order," *Review of International Studies* 25, no. 2 (1999): 179–96; John J. Mearsheimer, "Bound to Fail: The Rise and Fall of the Liberal International Order," *International Security* 43, no. 4 (2019): 7–50, https://doi.org/10.1162/isec_a_00342.

2. Ford and Jennings, "Changing Cleavage Politics of Western Europe," 295–314.

3. Peter Mair and Gordon Smith, eds., *Understanding Party System Change in Western Europe* (London: Routledge, 1990); Geoffrey Pridham, ed., *Securing Democracy: Political Parties and Democratic Consolidation in Southern Europe* (London: Routledge, 1990).

4. Though this campaign was most intense in Germany, similar efforts could be found in other countries as well. The "third force" in France and *democrazia preotetta* in Italy similarly presented themselves as coalitions of democratic defense. See Pepijn Corduwener, *The Problem of Democracy in Postwar Europe: Political Actors and the Formation of the Postwar Model of Democracy in France, West Germany and Italy* (London: Taylor and Francis, 2016); Irwin Wall, *The United States and the Making of Postwar France, 1945–1954* (Cambridge: Cambridge University Press, 1991); and Rosario Forlenza, "The Enemy Within: Catholic Anti-Communism in Cold War Italy," *Past and Present* 235, no. 1 (2017): 207–42, https://doi.org/10.1093/pastj/gtx016.

5. Deborah Kisatsky, *The United States and the European Right, 1945–1955* (Columbus: Ohio State University Press, 2005).

6. Corduwener, *Problem of Democracy in Postwar Europe*; Martin Conway, *Western Europe's Democratic Age: 1945–1968* (Princeton, NJ: Princeton University Press, 2022); Jan-Werner Müller, *Contesting Democracy* (New Haven, CT: Yale University Press, 2011).

7. Germany's mixed electoral system combined seats allocated within single-member districts, with seats allocated through list proportional representation. Originally the two were reconciled to ensure proportionality. The decision in 1953 was to separate the two ballots and

have them operate independently. Without reconciliations, the element of proportionality was lost. Peter James, *The German Electoral System* (London: Taylor and Francis, 2017).

8. The combination of measures reduced the number of effective parties in parliament from ten to six, and the split ballot allowed the CDU, which dominated in the majoritarian portion of the balloting, to sweep to a landslide victory in 1953. See Eckhard Jesse, *Wahlrecht zwischen Kontinuität und Reform: Eine Analyse der Wahlsystemdiskussion und der Wahlrechtsaenderungen in der Bundesrepublik Deutschland, 1949–1983* (Düsseldorf: Droste, 1985), 117–20; Dieter Nohlen, *Wahlrecht und Parteiensystem* (Leverkusen: Leske and Budrich, 1986).

9. Susan Scarrow, "Political Parties and the Changing Framework of German Electoral Competition," in *Stability and Change in German Elections: How Electorates Merge, Converge, or Collide*, ed. Christophe Anderson and Carsten Zelle (London: Praeger, 1998).

10. Carl Cavanagh Hodge, "The Long Fifties: The Politics of Socialist Programmatic Revision in Britain, France and Germany," *Contemporary European History* 2, no. 1 (1993): 17–34, https://doi.org/10.1017/S0960777300000291; Talbot Imlay, "Exploring What Might Have Been: Parallel History, International History, and Post-War Socialist Internationalism," *International History Review* 31, no. 3 (2009): 521–57.

11. Mark Ruff, "Building Bridges between Catholicism and Socialism: Ernst-Wolfgang Böckenförde and the Social Democratic Party of Germany," *Contemporary European History* 29, no. 2 (2020): 155–70, https://doi.org/10.1017/S0960777320000053.

12. Daniel Rogers, "Transforming the German Party System: The United States and the Origins of Political Moderation, 1945–1949," *Journal of Modern History* 65, no. 3 (1993): 512–41.

13. As Eric Schickler has demonstrated, at no point did this system not face serious challenges. Persistent efforts to reform southern politics with the potential to undo the New Deal party system could be found in the states and mid-level party organizations long before the civil rights revolution of the 1960s. Schickler, *Racial Realignment*, 9.

14. Richard Valelly, *The Two Reconstructions: The Struggle for Black Enfranchisement* (Chicago: University of Chicago Press, 2009).

15. This connection was frequently made by the NAACP as it sought to mobilize opposition to Jim Crow policies. See, for example, NAACP, *The Fifteenth Annual Report of the National Association for the Advancement of Colored People* (Washington, DC: National Office, 1925).

16. W.E.B. Du Bois, "The Negro Citizen," in *The Negro in Civilization*, ed. Charles Johnson (New York: Henry Holt, 1930), 461–70.

17. Schickler, *Racial Realignment*, 4.

18. Schickler, *Racial Realignment*.

19. Katznelson, *When Affirmative Action Was White*; Katznelson, *Fear Itself*; King and Smith, "Racial Orders in American Political Development."

20. Mickey, *Paths out of Dixie*, 135–38.

21. Several of the major achievements of the civil rights movement in the 1940s came via the courts. That which most directly affected voting rights was the decision in *Smith v. Allwright*, striking down the all-white primary. Mark Tushnet, *Making Civil Rights Law: Thurgood Marshall and the Supreme Court, 1936–1961* (Oxford: Oxford University Press, 1994).

22. Schickler, *Racial Realignment*; Valelly, *Two Reconstructions*, especially chapter 7.

23. John F. Zipp and Joel Smith, "A Structural Analysis of Class Voting," *Social Forces* 60, no. 3 (1982): 738–59, https://doi.org/10.2307/2578390; Jeff Manza, Michael Hout, and Clem Brooks, "Class Voting in Capitalist Democracies since World War II: Dealignment,

Realignment, or Trendless Fluctuation?," *Annual Review of Sociology* 21 (1995): 137–62; Robert V. Robinson and Jonathan Kelley, "Class as Conceived by Marx and Dahrendorf: Effects on Income Inequality and Politics in the United States and Great Britain," *American Sociological Review* 44, no. 1 (1979): 38–58, https://doi.org/10.2307/2094817.

24. Terry Clark and Seymour Martin Lipset, "Are Social Classes Dying?," *Journal of Social Issues* 6 (1991): 397–410; Geoffrey Evans, *The End of Class Politics? Class Voting in Comparative Context* (Oxford: Oxford University Press, 1999); Giedo Jansen, Geoffrey Evans, and Nan Dirk De Graaf, "Class Voting and Left–Right Party Positions: A Comparative Study of 15 Western Democracies, 1960–2005," *Social Science Research* 42, no. 2 (2013): 376–400.

25. John Aldrich and Richard Niemi, "The Sixth American Party System: Electoral Change, 1952–1992," in *Broken Contract?*, 87–109 (New York: Routledge, 2018); Howard L. Reiter, "Intra-Party Cleavages in the United States Today," *Western Political Quarterly* 34, no. 2 (1981): 287–300, https://doi.org/10.2307/447356.

26. Kriesi, "Restructuration of Partisan Politics"; Herbert Kitschelt, *The Transformation of European Social Democracy* (Cambridge: Cambridge University Press, 1994); Scott Flanagan, "Value Change in Industrial Societies," *American Political Science Review* 81 (1987): 1303–19; Scott Flanagan and Aie-Rie Lee, "The New Politics, Culture Wars, and the Authoritarian-Libertarian Value Change in Advanced Industrial Democracies," *Comparative Political Studies* 36 (2003): 235–70; Simon Bornschier, "The New Cultural Divide and the Two-Dimensional Political Space in Western Europe," *West European Politics* 33, no. 3 (2010): 419–44, https://doi.org/10.1080/01402381003654387.

27. Terry Clark and Seymour Lipset, "Are Social Classes Dying?," *International Sociology* 6, no. 4 (1991): 397–410, 406, https://doi.org/10.1177/026858091006004002.

28. Ronald Inglehart, *Culture Shift in Advanced Industrial Society* (Princeton, NJ: Princeton University Press, 1990); Ronald Inglehart, *Modernization and Postmodernization: Cultural, Economic, and Political Change in 43 Societies* (Princeton, NJ: Princeton University Press, 1997).

29. H. Kriesi, E. Grande, M. Dolezal, S. Bornschier, and T. Frey, "Globalization and the Transformation of the National Political Space: Six European Countries Compared," *European Journal of Political Research* 45, no. 6 (2006): 921–56.

30. L. Hooghe and G. Marks, "A Postfunctionalist Theory of European Integration: From Permissive Consensus to Constraining Dissensus," *British Journal of Political Science* 39, no. 1 (2009): 1–23; L. Hooghe and G. Marks, "Cleavage Theory Meets Europe's Crises: Lipset, Rokkan, and the Transnational Cleavage," *Journal of European Public Policy* 25, no. 1 (2018): 109–35.

31. Rune Stubager, "The Changing Basis of Party Competition: Education, Authoritarian-Libertarian Values and Voting," *Government and Opposition* 48, no. 3 (2013): 372–97, https://doi.org/10.1017/gov.2013.13.

32. It has been demonstrated that the salience of these postmaterial cultural values is higher in more affluent countries. It is noteworthy that these are also the established democracies of the West. See Flanagan, "Value Change in Industrial Societies."

33. Theodor Adorno, *The Authoritarian Personality* (1950; London: Verso, 2019).

34. John Levi Martin, "*The Authoritarian Personality*, 50 Years Later: What Questions Are There for Political Psychology?," *Political Psychology* 22 (2002): 1–26, https://doi.org/10.1111/0162-895X.00223.

35. Roberto Stefan Foa and Yascha Mounk, "The Danger of Deconsolidation: The Democratic Disconnect," *Journal of Democracy* 27, no. 3 (2016): 5–17, https://doi.org/10.1353/jod.2016 .0049; Jack Corbett, "The Deconsolidation of Democracy: Is It New and What Can Be Done about It?," *Political Studies Review* 18, no. 2 (2020): 178–88, https://doi.org/10.1177/147892 9919864785.

36. Jan-Werner Müller, *What Is Populism?* (Philadelphia: University of Pennsylvania Press, 2016); Cas Mudde and Cristóbal Rovira Kaltwasser, *Populism in Europe and the Americas: Threat or Corrective for Democracy?* (Cambridge: Cambridge University Press, 2012).

37. Alexander Bolton and Sharece Thrower, *Checks in the Balance: Legislative Capacity and the Dynamics of Executive Power* (Princeton, NJ: Princeton University Press, 2021).

38. Recent scholarship has shown the two to be interconnected, as staggering levels of inequality have hindered responsiveness of government in both new and established democracies. Larry Bartels, *Unequal Democracy: The Political Economy of the New Gilded Age* (Princeton, NJ: Princeton University Press, 2008); Thomas Piketty, *Capital in the Twenty-First Century* (Cambridge, MA: Harvard University Press, 2017).

39. Kim Scheppele, "Autocratic Legalism," *University of Chicago Law Review* 85, no. 2 (2018): 545–83; Aziz Huq and Tom Ginsburg, "How to Lose a Constitutional Democracy," *UCLA Law Review* 65, no. 78 (2017): 80–169; Robert Kaufman and Stephan Haggard, *Backsliding: Democratic Regress in the Contemporary World* (Cambridge: Cambridge University Press, 2021).

40. Patrick Chamorel, "Macron versus the Yellow Vests," *Journal of Democracy* 30, no. 4 (2019): 48–62, https://doi.org/10.1353/jod.2019.0068.

41. Some have explicitly advanced the idea of constructing a "regime cleavage" to resist Trump. Kenneth Roberts, "Populism, Democracy, and Resistance," in *The Resistance: The Dawn of the Anti-Trump Opposition Movement*, ed. David Meyers and Sidney Tarrow (Oxford: Oxford University Press, 2019), 54–72.

42. Gabriella Ilonszki and Agnieszka Dudzińska, "Opposition Behaviour against the Third Wave of Autocratisation: Hungary and Poland Compared," *European Political Science* 20 (2021): 603–16, https://doi.org/10.1057/s41304-021-00325-x.

43. Sartori, *Parties and Party Systems*, 132–39.

44. Hanna Bäck and Royce Carroll, "Polarization and Gridlock in Parliamentary Regimes," *Legislative Scholar* 3, no. 1 (2018): 2–5; Jennifer McCoy, Tahmina Rahman, and Murat Somer, "Polarization and the Global Crisis of Democracy: Common Patterns, Dynamics, and Pernicious Consequences for Democratic Polities," *American Behavioral Scientist* 62, no. 1 (2018): 16–42, https://doi.org/10.1177/0002764218759576; Alexandre Afonso and Yannis Papadopoulos, "How the Populist Radical Right Transformed Swiss Welfare Politics: From Compromises to Polarization," *Swiss Political Science Review* 21, no. 4 (2015): 617–35; Juan Rodríguez-Teruel, "Polarisation and Electoral Realignment: The Case of the Right-Wing Parties in Spain," *South European Society and Politics* 25, nos. 3–4 (2020): 381–410; Aaron Mentzer, "Polarized Policymaking: The Effect of Ideological Division on Legislative Outcomes in the United States Congress" (PhD diss., West Virginia University, 2021).

45. Max Weber, *The Vocation Lectures*, ed. David Owen and Tracy Strong (1918; New York: Hackett, 2004).

46. Ivan Ascher, "'We Are All Occasional Politicians': For a New Weberian Conception of Politics," *Constellations* 20 (2013): 138–49, https://doi.org/10.1111/cons.12017.

INDEX

Economy Act (1933), US, 227, 235–36

elections, 25, 66, 277n14, 285n58, 294n2; and earlier US, 190, 196–97, 201–2, 210, 213, 303n24, 308n86, 309n86; and France, 146, 151–55, 158, 162–68, 170–71; and Germany, 120–22, 126–31, 133, 142–44; and later US, 218, 221–25, 233, 240, 246, 313n20, 313n24, 314n32, 317n82, 319n8; and UK, 96–102, 107–11

electoral alliances, 160, 163–64, 170

Electoral College, US, 218, 303n24

electorate, the, 33, 88, 100–101, 190, 235, 313n22, 317n82, 318n88. *See also* elections

elite interests, 25–28, 33–37, 86, 147, 150, 234, 248, 282n8, 305n53, 313n24

Emergency Banking Act (1933), US, 235–36

emergency powers, 112–13, 115, 143

Emergency Relief Act (1933), US, 235

Enabling Act, Germany, 141–42, 169

Enabling Act, UK, 111–12

England, 86–88, 111, 212, 269n13. *See also* Frome, England; Leeds, England; United Kingdom; Walsall, England

entrepreneurship, political, 3, 14, 18, 61, 74, 221–22

equilibrium models, 75–76. *See also* punctuated equilibrium models

Erzberger, Matthias, 135–36

Estates General, France, 193

Europeanization, 191, 249, 268n9

exceptionalism, 117–18, 121, 180, 185, 211–12, 300n1

exclusionary politics, 4, 16, 104, 156, 175–76, 241, 245–48, 271n37, 316n68; and US political development, 226–27, 231–34

executive, the, 3, 5, 175, 251, 255, 270n24, 271n28; and France, 147, 153, 169, 172; and Germany, 115, 118, 121–23, 136–42, 290n21; and theoretical framework, 12, 16–17, 23–24, 29, 42–43, 62–65; and UK, 87, 91, 93, 112; and US, 188, 194–96, 214, 216, 227–30, 302n10, 302n19, 303n24, 315n58

Farm Relief Act (1933), US, 235

fascism, 57, 146, 154, 170, 176, 245

Federal Elections bill, US (Lodge bill), 223–24, 240

Federalist 42, 199

Federalist 54, 199, 303n32

Federalist Party, US, 201–2, 305n49, 306n61

federalists, 198–202, 303n32, 304n34, 304n44–45, 305n49, 306n61, 307n71

feudalism, 45, 81–82, 185–87, 194, 201, 300n1

Fifth Republic, France, 152, 175

flexible repertoires, 14–16, 39, 48, 75–78, 134, 272n43, 280n52; and France, 148, 155, 172; and US, 221, 253. *See also* rigid repertoires

Florida, US, 218

Foner, Eric, 200, 210

foreign policy, 109, 136, 164, 167–69, 302n23

Fortune, T. Thomas, 233

Fourth Republic, France, 175

franc, the, 165–66, 168–69

France, 111–13, 140, 271n32, 296n35, 297n42, 298n59, 298n67; background to, 146–49; comparison to, 81, 86, 180, 244, 253, 318n4; episodes, 155–72; and founding of Republic, 149–55; and theoretical framework, 6, 15, 16–17, 31–35, 45, 49, 57–59, 61, 65, 78. *See also* Chamber of Deputies, France; Constitution, France; French Revolution; *individual party names*; July Revolution, France; *names of politicians*; presidents; Second Empire, France; Seize Mai crisis; Third Republic, France

free labor, 210–11

Free Soil Party, US, 209, 213, 239

free states, US, 193, 198, 204, 207–9, 306n58

free trade, 27, 92–97, 99, 102–3, 108–9, 113, 126, 130–34, 207, 284n44

French Revolution, 34–35, 86, 119, 152, 180, 187, 194

Freudian analysis, 250

Frome, England, 89

Gambetta, Léon, 149–53

Garfield, James, 220, 312n15

Gash, Norman, 92, 283n33

Geneva Award, 220

George, Lloyd, 105, 108

Georgia, US, 200

Germany, 81, 84, 99, 318n4, 318n7; background
to, 115–17; and Bismarck, 119–22; comparison to, 104, 111–13, 148, 160–63, 166–75, 183,
194, 214, 281n2; and early party formation, 122–26; episodes, 131–45; and new
alignment, 127–31; and Reconstruction,
244–47; and Sonderweg, 117–18; and
theoretical framework, 6, 15, 17–18, 28,
32–35, 45, 49–52, 55–59, 74, 78. *See also
individual party names; names of politicians;*
Ruhr Valley, Germany; von Bismarck,
Otto; Weimar Republic, Germany

Germany Progressive Party, 120, 123–24

Gerry, Elbridge, 198

Gienapp, William, 211

Gilded Age, US, 217, 226

Gladstone, Herbert, 102

Gladstone, William, 94–98

globalization, 191, 249

Globe Congress (1904), 161

government coalitions, 41, 62–66, 116, 132–35,
146–47, 158, 162–64, 167–68, 277n16

government formation, 23, 29–32, 121, 183

Grand Coalitions, Germany, 138, 140, 142,
144, 246

Grant, Ulysses S., 220

Great Depression, 42, 110, 165, 169, 221, 231, 233

Grund, Francis, 212

Guesde, Jules, 157, 160

Half-Breeds, US, 219–20, 224

Hardie, Keir, 101

Harrison, Benjamin, 223

Hartford Convention (1814), 202

Hayes, Rutherford B., 218–19, 311n124, 312n9

Heidelberg Conference (1884), 130

Herriot, Édouard, 168–69

Hertling, Count, 135

historical institutionalist approaches, 6, 11,
37–40, 46, 48–49, 118, 191; and legislative

coalitions, 60–62, 69–73, 272n38, 272n42,
279n28, 279n36, 280n48

Hitler, Adolph, 115

Holt, Michael, 210, 310n109

Hoover, Herbert, 236

Hours of Work legislation, Germany, 140–42

House of Commons, Prussia, 120

House of Commons, UK, 30, 32, 90–95,
103–4, 112, 275n70, 282n12

House of Lords, UK, 30, 92–93, 103–4,
282n12, 287n81, 305n52

House of Representatives, US, 33, 186, 193,
195–98, 201–2, 208, 222–25, 240

Hungary, 252

ideal types, 45, 49, 180–82, 188–89, 238, 241,
274n64, 275n74

ideologies, 41, 50–56, 63, 65, 272n42; and
France, 146–47, 155, 158, 160, 163–68; and
Germany, 123, 127–28, 137, 144–45; and
UK, 97, 100–103; and US, 195, 210–13,
224–25, 232, 251–53, 310n110, 313n20,
314n30

immigration, 213–14, 240, 311n121

income tax, 94–96, 156, 166, 169, 225–26, 230

increasing returns (feature of path-
dependence), 47, 71–75, 274n58

Independent Labour Party (ILP), Britain,
100–102

industrial interests, 102, 126, 131, 134, 139–40,
169, 174, 205–7, 215–17, 223–27

industrialization, 19, 26, 174, 205, 215, 217–21,
235, 249

Industrial Recovery Act (1933), US, 235

inflation, 42, 59, 115, 140, 164–65

Inglehard, Ronald, 249

institutional change, 24, 69, 71–73, 222, 246,
251, 280n48, 316n63

institutional sequencing, 81–85, 113, 145,
173–175, 269n21, 270n25; and France,
146–147, 150, 172; and Germany, 118–19,
132; and theoretical framework, 12–17,
24–26, 28, 33–37, 39, 43–45, 48, 76; and
US, 179, 183, 193

PRINCETON STUDIES
IN AMERICAN POLITICS

Paul Frymer, Suzanne Mettler, and Eric Schickler, Series Editors

Historical, International, and Comparative Perspectives

Ira Katznelson, Martin Shefter, and Theda Skocpol *Founding Series Editors*

How Americans Think of Taxes: Public Opinion and the American Fiscal State, Andrea Campbell

Attention, Shoppers!: American Retail Capitalism and the Origins of the Amazon Economy, Kathleen Thelen

Divergent Democracy: How Policy Positions Came to Dominate Party Competition, Katherine Krimmel

The Hollow Parties: The Many Pasts and Disordered Present of American Party Politics, Daniel Schlozman and Sam Rosenfeld

How the Heartland Went Red: Why Local Forces Matter in an Age of Nationalized Politics, Stephanie Ternullo

Laboratories against Democracy: How National Parties Transformed State Politics, Jacob M. Grumbach

Rough Draft of History: A Century of US Social Movements in the News, Edwin Amenta and Neal Caren

Checks in the Balance: Legislative Capacity and the Dynamics of Executive Power, Alexander Bolton and Sharece Thrower

Firepower: How the NRA Turned Gun Owners into a Political Force, Matthew J. Lacombe

American Bonds: How Credit Markets Shaped a Nation, Sarah L. Quinn

The Unsolid South: Mass Politics and National Representation in a One-Party Enclave, Devin Caughey

Southern Nation: Congress and White Supremacy after Reconstruction, David A. Bateman, Ira Katznelson, and John S. Lapinsky

California Greenin': How the Golden State Became an Environmental Leader, David Vogel

A NOTE ON THE TYPE

This book has been composed in Arno, an Old-style serif typeface in the classic Venetian tradition, designed by Robert Slimbach at Adobe.

GPSR Authorized Representative: Easy Access System Europe - Mustamäe tee 50, 10621 Tallinn, Estonia, gpsr.requests@easproject.com

www.ingramcontent.com/pod-product-compliance
Lightning Source LLC
Chambersburg PA
CBHW020822270326
41928CB00006B/410